The Times Cookery Book

Katie Stewart was born in Scotland. After taking a domestic science course in Aberdeen, she moved to London to study for a diploma in catering and home management. She took a job with a family in France to perfect her French and then went to the Cordon Bleu school in Paris to take the Cordon Bleu diploma. Back in England she worked as a test supervisor for Nestlé and soon had the opportunity of going to New York, where she learnt about food photography and American foods and methods of cooking, later touring the United States to study regional cookery. On her return to England, Katie Stewart began a career in journalism. She became cookery editor of *Woman's Mirror*, then joined *Woman's Journal*, and for several years now has been food correspondent of *The Times*. Her writing and her television programmes – practical, funny and refreshingly free of gimmickry – provide her with a very busy working life. She lives in Sussex and has a son.

Katie Stewart's *The Times Calendar Cookbook* is also available in Pan.

Other cookery books available in Pan

Mrs Beeton	**All About Cookery**
Ada Boni	**The Talisman Italian Cook Book**
Lousene Rousseau Brunner	**New Casserole Treasury**
Savitri Chowdhary	**Indian Cookery**
Theodora FitzGibbon	**A Taste of Ireland A Taste of London** **A Taste of Scotland A Taste of Wales** **A Taste of the West Country** **A Taste of Paris**
Dorothy Hall	**The Book of Herbs**
Rosemary Hume and Muriel Downes	**The Cordon Bleu Book of Jams, Preserves** **and Pickles**
George Lassalle	**The Adventurous Fish Cook**
Kenneth Lo	**Quick and Easy Chinese Cooking**
Claire Loewenfeld and Philippa Back	**Herbs for Health and Cookery**
edited by R. J. Minney	**The George Bernard Shaw Vegetarian** **Cook Book**
Marguerite Patten	**Learning to Cook World Cookery**
Constance Spry and Rosemary Hume	**The Constance Spry Cookery Book**
Katie Stewart	**The Times Calendar Cookbook**
Marika Hanbury Tenison	**Eat Well and Be Slim** **Deep-Freeze Cookery**

The Times
Cookery Book

Katie Stewart
Illustrated by Pauline Baynes

Pan Books in association with **Collins**

First published 1972 by William Collins Sons & Co Ltd
This edition published 1974 by Pan Books Ltd,
Cavaye Place, London SW10 9PG
in association with William Collins Sons & Co Ltd
6th printing (new format) 1978
© Times Newspaper Ltd 1972
ISBN 0 330 252134 8
Printed in Great Britain by
Cox & Wyman Ltd, London, Reading and Fakenham

Contents

Introduction

This book contains a selection of recipes carefully chosen from those that have been published in *The Times* over the last few years. Some of the recipes will be familiar, others perhaps seen but lost or forgotten, and there are many new ones. The recipes are practical and very varied. They have been chosen to suit both everyday needs and special occasions, and should provide a good source of new ideas.

There are no hard and fast rules about which recipes are right for any particular occasion. The choice of a recipe for a particular meal or menu lies with the cook. The time available for preparation, the equipment and facilities in the kitchen, the time of year and availability of seasonal foods are all important factors to bear in mind. Chapter headings exist to group recipes together in some kind of order and to suggest where they might be particularly suitable, but the cook should feel free to choose and serve recipes as she likes. No amount of advice from an author can take the place of the necessary imagination and initiative on the part of the cook herself.

Timing is an important consideration when planning any menu. Recipes that are to be served cold can be made well ahead, this applies particularly to summer foods. It is as well to remember, however, that the flavour of most cold foods is best when they are at room temperature and not when served chilled from the refrigerator. Such recipes should be removed from the refrigerator ½–1 hour before serving. Most recipes that are served hot, have a stage up to which they can be prepared in advance; any that must be served immediately are clearly indicated in the recipe. Final touches should always be left to the end. Try to have a lemon or two, a few sprigs of fresh parsley, walnuts or glacé cherries in the kitchen, and remember that a simple garnish is always the most effective.

Those who own a freezer will be well aware of the advantages a home freezer has to offer. More than anything else it helps to spread the work load for the cook. Some recipes freeze better than others and those in Chapter 13 are ones that are particularly suitable for freezing. Test and try out other ideas to discover which recipes freeze best, and which are most useful to have on hand. A cook without a freezer should not ignore this section. All recipes, with the exception of the ice creams, can be prepared and served without the long-term storage in the freezer.

Food that has been carefully prepared, deserves to be attractively presented. Plain colours, particularly white china, severely simple in line, show off food most effectively. Bold strong colours and interesting textures can be introduced in the table settings. A vast collection of cookery equipment is not essential for good cooking, but, as in all practical work, there are certain necessary items. Some recipes may require a particular size of tin or mould but after initial purchase these are likely to be used many times over.

Anyone who takes pleasure in cooking and an interest in the food they prepare, enjoys exchanging ideas and finding new recipes. As a cookery writer and author this is what I'm doing all the time. It's always easier to cook the recipes one is familiar with, but it's a wise cook who looks around for new ideas and gradually increases her own collection of well-tried recipes.

International Conversion Tables

The weights and measures used throughout this book are based on metric units and the nearest workable British Imperial standards.

International measures

Measure	*UK*	*Australia*	*New Zealand*	*Canada*
1 pint	20 fl oz	20 fl oz	20 fl oz	20 fl oz
1 cup	10 fl oz	8 fl oz	8 fl oz	8 fl oz
1 tablespoon	⅝ fl oz	½ fl oz	½ fl oz	½ fl oz
1 dessertspoon	⅖ fl oz	no official measure		
1 teaspoon	⅕ fl oz	⅛ fl oz	⅙ fl oz	⅙ fl oz

Conversion of metric to fluid ounces

28·4 millilitres	= 1 fl oz
1 litre (1000 ml or 10 decilitres)	= 35 fl oz (approx 1¾ Imperial pints)
600 ml (6 dl)	= approx 1 Imperial pint (20 fl oz)
300 ml (3 dl)	= ½ Imperial pint (10 fl oz)
150 ml (1·5 dl)	= ¼ Imperial pint (5 fl oz)
70 ml (7 centilitres)	= 4 tablespoons (2½ fl oz)
35 ml (3·5 cl)	= 2 tablespoons (1¼ fl oz)
18 ml (2 cl)	= 1 tablespoon (⅝ fl oz)
12 ml	= 1 dessertspoon (⅔ fl oz)
6 ml	= 1 teaspoon (⅕ fl oz)

(All the above fluid ounce equivalents are approximate)

Equivalents

1 UK (old BSI standard) cup equals 1¼ cups in Commonwealth countries

4 UK tablespoons equal 5 Commonwealth tablespoons

5 UK teaspoons equal 6 New Zealand or 6 Canada or 8 Australia

1 UK dessertspoon equals ⅔ UK tablespoon or 2 UK teaspoons

In British cookery books, a gill is usually 5 fl oz (¼ pint), but in a few localities in the UK it can mean 10 fl oz (½ pint)

Other non-standardized measures include:

Breakfast cup = approx 10 fl oz
Tea cup = 5 fl oz
Coffee cup = 3 fl oz

Oven temperatures

Food type	°C	°F	Gas No	Oven Heat
meringues, keeping food hot	110°C	225°F	¼	very cool
fruit bottling	130°C	250°F	½	very cool
custards, egg dishes, milk puddings	140°C	275°F	1	cool
stews, rich fruit cakes	150°C	300°F	2	slow
slow roasting, plain fruit cakes	170°C	325°F	3	moderately slow
Victoria sponge cakes, biscuits, madeira cake	180°C	350°F	4	moderate
whisked sponges, small cakes	190°C	375°F	5	moderately hot
shortcrust pastry, tarts	200°C	400°F	6	hot
quick roasting, scones, bread	220°C	425°F	7	very hot
flaky and puff pastry, buns, rolls	230°C	450°F	8	very hot

1 Soups

There's a great deal of satisfaction to be had in making your own soups. They have a special 'homemade' flavour which comes from using good ingredients, and from long, slow simmering that extracts all the flavour and goodness from the ingredients.

The use of the electric blender makes it possible to prepare cream soups to perfection. It must be remembered, however, that whereas a liquidizer purées everything, a sieve or Mouli soup mill retains unwanted skin, stalks and pips. Never put into a liquidizer those parts of the raw ingredients not wanted in the recipe afterwards, unless the soup is also to be sieved. Many of these recipes are thickened by the addition of a small quantity of potato. This is a Continental method that is ideal for soups blended in the liquidizer and also excellent for freezing. All soups where potato is used as the thickening agent, freeze better than others.

Stock makes a considerable difference to the flavour of homemade soups. Raw meat bones, poultry carcasses, bacon rinds, flavouring vegetables and a bouquet garni are all used. Stock is not difficult to make, but requires a large pot and long slow simmering to extract all the flavour.

Stock Cubes
The use of stock cubes along with water is a perfectly satisfactory alternative to homemade stock. According to the quantity of water in

the recipe, use the stock cubes as directed on the packet. In most recipes chicken stock cubes should be used, as their milder flavour does not dominate other ingredients.

Light Household Stock
Raw meat bones or the carcasses from poultry or game may be used in this stock.

Rinse the bones, and cut away any surplus fat. Cut off any pieces of meat, and shred them. Place the bones and meat scraps or carcasses in a large saucepan and cover with cold water. For every generous 1 litre (quart) of water, add 1 teaspoon of salt. Add a few flavouring vegetables, a whole onion, 1–2 carrots, a few stalks of celery, a piece of turnip or a leek, but avoid starchy vegetables such as potato. Add a bouquet garni and bring to the boil. Skim, then lower the heat, cover the pan with a lid and simmer gently for 3–4 hours. Strain the liquid and leave overnight to cool. Next day lift the fat off the surface and reboil. The stock is now ready for use.

Use this stock for soups or sauces, and in casseroles.

Meat Stock
Here a brown stock, rich in flavour, is required, as this stock is often cleared and served on its own. You will require a good-sized veal bone, 1 kg (2 lb) shin of beef, and flavouring vegetables as above. Trim away any fat from the bone. Place these in a large saucepan and render down so that the fat runs. Cut the meat into pieces. Remove the scraps of fat from the pan, and add the meat and bone. Fry gently to brown the meat and bone and so give colour to the final stock. Add flavouring vegetables (see above) and 2·25 litres (2 quarts) of water. Add 2 teaspoons salt, and a bouquet garni. Bring slowly to the boil, cover and simmer gently for 4–5 hours. Strain and leave overnight to cool. Next day, lift the fat from the surface and the stock is ready for use.

Use this stock in soups or casseroles, or clear and serve as consommé (see page 14).

Cream of Carrot Soup
Serves 4–6 Time taken 2 hours

450 g (1 lb) carrots	salt
3 large leeks	freshly milled pepper
50 g (2 oz) butter	1·5 dl ($\frac{1}{4}$ pint) single cream
generous 1 litre (2 pints)	
chicken stock	chopped parsley

Scrape and slice the carrots. Trim the tops of the leeks to within
2·5 cm (1 inch) of the white stem, and slice away the roots. Slice
lengthwise through to the centre, and then wash thoroughly in cold
water. Shred the leeks finely.

Melt the butter in a saucepan and add the prepared vegetables.
Sauté gently for 2–3 minutes, or until the vegetables are softened
slightly, but do not allow them to brown. Add the stock, stir well and
bring up to the boil. Cover with a lid and simmer gently for about 1½
hours, or until the vegetables are quite tender.

➤ Draw the pan off the heat. Rub the soup through a sieve or Mouli,
or purée the soup in an electric blender, half at a time. Return the
soup to the pan, check seasoning and reheat. Stir in the cream and
sprinkle with parsley just before serving.

Cream of Chicken Soup

Serves 4–6 Time taken 2 hours

1 chicken carcass	25 g (1 oz) flour
2 carrots	salt
1 onion	freshly milled pepper
3 dl (½ pint) milk	few scraps cooked chicken
1 clove	2–3 tablespoons cream
1 bay leaf	
parsley stalks	chopped parsley
25 g (1 oz) butter	

For the best flavour use a raw chicken carcass left over from jointing
a chicken in another recipe.

Place the chicken carcass in a saucepan with sufficient water to
cover – about 1·5 litres (3 pints) cold water. Add the whole scraped
carrots and half the peeled onion. Bring up to the boil, cover and
simmer gently for about 1 hour. Strain the liquor and return to the
saucepan. Continue to boil until about a generous ·5 litre (1 pint)
reduced chicken stock remains. Draw off the heat and reserve. Remove any scraps of chicken flesh from the carcass and reserve these too.

Place the milk in a saucepan, add the remaining onion half stuck
with the clove, the bay leaf and parsley stalks. Bring up to the boil,
and draw off the heat. Cover and allow to stand for 10 minutes for the
flavours to infuse, then strain.

Melt the butter in the saucepan over low heat. Stir in the flour and
cook gently for a moment. Gradually stir in the warm infused milk
and bring up to the boil, stirring all the time to get a smooth sauce.
Simmer for a few moments, then gradually stir in the reserved

chicken stock. Bring back to the boil, stirring well and check seasoning. Add the pieces of cooked chicken.

Just before serving stir in the cream and parsley.

Onion Soup

Serves 4–6 Time taken 2¼ hours

450 g (1 lb) onions	generous 1 litre (2 pints)
25 g (1 oz) butter	chicken stock
1 (225 g) (½ lb) large potato	salt
freshly milled pepper	grated cheese
few bacon rinds (optional)	

Peel and slice the onions thinly. Melt the butter in a heavy saucepan. Add the onions, cover and cook *very slowly* for 45 minutes–1 hour, shaking the pan occasionally. Remove the pan lid for the last 10–15 minutes to allow the onions to brown; they should be faintly coloured.

Peel and cut the potato into large dice. Add the potato to the pan and stir in the stock. Add a seasoning of salt and pepper and a few bacon rinds tied in a bundle, if you have them. Bring to the boil and then cover and simmer for another hour. Remove the bundle of bacon rinds. Rub the soup through a sieve, or Mouli, or purée in an electric blender. Return the soup to the pan and check seasoning. Reheat and serve.

Pass grated cheese separately.

Hot Leek Soup

Serves 6 Time taken 45 minutes

4 (1 kg) (2 lb) large leeks	salt
1 (225 g) (½ lb) large potato	freshly milled pepper
25 g (1 oz) butter	2–3 tablespoons single cream
scant 1 litre (1½ pints) chicken stock	

Leeks make a delicious winter soup with a pleasant flavour and one that is very popular with children.

Trim the green tops of the leeks to about 2·5 cm (1 inch) of the white part and cut away the base. Cut the leeks lengthwise through to the centre and wash well in cold water. Shred the leeks finely. Peel and cut the potato into large dice.

Melt the butter in a saucepan and add the leeks and potatoes. Cover and cook over low heat for about 5 minutes to allow the vegetables to soften, but not to colour. Stir in the stock and bring up to the boil.

Re-cover and simmer gently for about 30 minutes, or until the vegetables are quite soft. Pass the vegetables and liquid through a sieve, or purée, half at a time, in an electric blender. Return the soup to the pan and season, if necessary, with salt and pepper.

Stir in the cream just before serving.

Artichoke Soup with Fresh Parsley

Serves 6 Time taken 1½ hours

1 kg (2 lb) Jerusalem artichokes	salt
1 medium onion	freshly milled pepper
25 g (1 oz) butter	1·5 dl (¼ pint) single cream
6 dl (1 pint) chicken stock	
3 dl (½ pint) milk	1 tablespoon finely chopped parsley

Peel the artichokes under cold water, which has been acidulated with a little vinegar or lemon juice. This helps to prevent any discolouration of the vegetables after they are peeled. Cut up any large artichokes. Peel and finely chop the onion.

Heat the butter in a saucepan, add the onion and the artichokes Cover, and cook very gently for about 8–10 minutes – do not allow to brown. Add the stock and milk and bring up to the boil. Re-cover, simmer for about 35–40 minutes, or until the vegetables are very soft.

Draw the pan off the heat. Rub the soup through a sieve or Mouli, or purée in an electric blender. Return the purée to the pan, check seasoning and add the cream. Reheat, but do not boil.

Just before serving stir in the chopped parsley.

Homemade Lentil Soup

Serves 4–6 Time taken 1¼ hours
Allow to soak for 24 hours

100 g (4 oz) lentils	15 g (½ oz) butter
generous 1 litre (2 pints) ham or chicken stock	½–1 level teaspoon salt
	25 g (1 oz) flour
2 small carrots	1·5 dl (¼ pint) milk
2 small onions or leeks	

The use of good stock gives the best flavour to lentil soup. Use the cooking liquor from a boiled ham or gammon joint. Chicken stock made from a carcass or stock cubes is also very good.

Soak the lentils overnight in 6 dl (1 pint) of the stock. Next day, scrape and dice the carrots, peel and chop the onions or wash and shred the leeks. Melt the butter in a large saucepan and add the prepared vegetables. Cover with a lid and sauté gently for about 5 minutes, or until the onion or leek is soft but not brown. Stir in the lentils along with the stock in which they were soaked and the remaining stock. Stir and bring up to the boil. Add the salt to taste, cover with a lid and simmer gently for 45 minutes–1 hour, or until the lentils are quite soft.

Draw the pan off the heat, and pass the lentils, vegetables and liquid through a sieve, or purée half at a time in an electric blender. Return the soup to the saucepan. Blend the flour with the cold milk and stir into the soup. Replace the pan over the heat and bring to the boil stirring all the time. Taste and add extra seasoning if required.

Serve hot.

Hot Beetroot Soup

Serves 6   Time taken 1½ hours

450 g (1 lb) raw beetroot	1·25 litres (2½ pints) chicken stock
225 g (½ lb) potatoes	salt
1 small onion	freshly milled pepper
25 g (1 oz) butter	

Always use raw, uncooked beetroot for the best flavour and colour in beetroot soup. For a special occasion, stir a spoonful of unwhipped, double cream into the centre of each serving.

Remove the skins from the beetroot and peel the potatoes. Cut both up into large dice. Peel and finely chop the onion. Melt the butter in a large saucepan. Add the onion, beetroot and potato. Cover with a lid and fry very gently for about 5 minutes, shaking the pan occasionally. Stir in the stock and bring up to the boil, then lower the heat. Recover and simmer for 1 hour.

Draw the pan off the heat, and rub the soup through a sieve, or purée in an electric blender. Return the soup to the pan, season with salt and pepper, and reheat. Serve hot.

Leek and Tomato Soup

Serves 6   Time taken 45 minutes

3 large leeks	freshly milled pepper
25 g (1 oz) butter)	1 teaspoon castor sugar
450 g (1 lb) tomatoes	1 (225 g) (½ lb) large potato
salt	scant 1 litre (1½ pints) chicken stock

Trim base and green tops from the leeks, slit open, wash thoroughly, and shred finely. Melt the butter in a large saucepan. Add the shredded leeks, cover with a lid, and sauté gently for about 5 minutes – the leeks should soften but not brown. Add the washed and halved tomatoes, a good seasoning of salt and pepper, and the sugar. Cover and simmer a further 5 minutes until the tomatoes are quite soft, then add the peeled, diced potato and the stock. Bring up to the boil, cover and simmer gently for 30 minutes, or until the potato is quite soft. Draw off the heat and rub through a sieve, or blend in an electric blender. If a blender has been used, pass the soup quickly through a sieve to remove any small pieces of tomato skin and any pips.

Return soup to the pan, check the seasoning and reheat.

Chestnut Soup

Serves 4–6 Time taken 1½ hours

450 g (1 lb) chestnuts	salt
25 g (1 oz) butter	freshly milled pepper
1 onion	1·5 dl (¼ pint) single cream
1 stalk celery	
generous 1 litre (2 pints) chicken stock	chopped parsley

Serve this soup on a special occasion as it's essentially a party soup. Use fresh chestnuts and buy the best, the larger ones are easier to peel.

Cut a slit on the flat side of each chestnut and place them in a saucepan. Cover with boiling water, reboil and simmer for 10 minutes. Drain and peel away both the outer and inner skins. It is advisable to prepare the chestnuts in two lots; once cool they become difficult to peel.

Melt the butter in a large saucepan. Peel and finely chop the onion. Add to the pan, cover and fry gently for about 5 minutes until tender but not brown. Add the chestnuts and the washed and chopped celery. Add the stock and bring up to the boil. Cover with a lid and simmer gently for 45 minutes–1 hour, or until the vegetables are quite tender.

Draw the pan off the heat and pass the chestnuts, celery and stock through a sieve, or purée the ingredients half at a time in an electric blender. Return the soup to the pan, season with salt and plenty of freshly milled pepper. Stir in the cream and reheat until hot but not boiling.

Sprinkle with chopped parsley and serve very hot.

Celery Soup with Cheese

Serves 4–6 Time taken 1½ hours

450 g (1 lb) potatoes	salt
1 onion	freshly milled pepper
1 head of celery	1·5 dl (¼ pint) single cream
50 g (2 oz) butter	
scant 1 litre (1½ pints) chicken stock	25–50 g (1–2 oz) grated cheese

Select a head of celery that has some leafy parts. These should be chopped and added since they give the soup an excellent flavour.

Peel and slice the potatoes. Peel and finely chop the onion. Separate the head of celery, scrub the stalks well and then shred both the stalks and leaves finely.

Melt the butter in a large saucepan. Add the potatoes, onion and celery. Cover with a lid and sauté gently for about 10 minutes, without allowing the vegetables to take colour. Add the stock and a good seasoning of salt and pepper. Bring up to the boil and simmer gently for 30–40 minutes, or until the vegetables are quite tender.

Draw the pan off the heat and either pass the vegetables and liquid through a sieve or Mouli, or purée in an electric blender. Return the soup to the saucepan, check seasoning and reheat. Stir in the cream before serving.

Serve hot with grated cheese sprinkled over the top.

Watercress Soup

Serves 4–6 Time taken 45 minutes

2 bunches watercress	6 dl (1 pint) chicken stock
1 medium onion	3 dl (½ pint) milk
25 g (1 oz) butter	salt
1 (225 g) (½ lb) large potato	freshly milled pepper

Watercress soup has an attractive green colour and a fresh, almost peppery, taste.

Keeping the bunches of watercress separate, thoroughly wash both in cold water. Set one bunch aside for the garnish. Remove coarse stalks from the remaining bunch and then coarsely chop the leaves and top part of the stalks. Peel and finely chop the onion. Melt the butter in a saucepan, and add the onion. Fry gently for about 5 minutes or until the onion is soft but not brown. Peel the potato and cut into large dice. Add the potato and chopped watercress to the pan and toss in the onion-flavoured butter. Allow to cook for a moment then add the stock and milk. Bring up to the boil, cover and simmer for about 30 minutes.

Draw the pan off the heat. Either pass the soup through a Mouli soup mill, or better still blend to a purée in an electric blender. Return the soup to the pan, season to taste with salt and pepper. Nip off the leafy parts from the bunch of watercress reserved for the garnish. Chop coarsely and add to the soup. Reheat and serve.

Blender Avocado Soup

Serves 4–6 Time taken 15 minutes
Allow several hours to chill

2 ripe avocados
scant 1 litre (1½ pints) chicken stock
1·5 dl (¼ pint) single cream
juice of ½ lemon

salt and freshly milled pepper

chopped chives

Avocado soup has a fresh, delicate flavour, and a pretty pale colour. Serve it well chilled.

Halve the avocados and remove the stones. Scoop out the flesh into the glass container of an electric blender and add the chicken stock. Cover and blend for a few moments until smooth. Pour into a bowl and stir in the cream, lemon juice, and salt and pepper to taste. Chill well, then stir in a few finely chopped chives before serving.

Fish Chowder

Serves 6 Time taken 45 minutes

1 medium-sized (700 g) (1½ lb)
   smoked haddock
1 small bay leaf
few parsley stalks
25 g (1 oz) cornflour
6 dl (1 pint) milk
2–3 tablespoons cooked rice
   (optional)
1 egg yolk

1 slice lemon
6 dl (1 pint) water
40 g (1½ oz) butter
1 onion
2–3 tablespoons cream
lemon juice
freshly milled pepper
pinch ground mace or nutmeg

A very pleasant fish soup, which, if served with crusty bread and butter, would make a meal for four.

Rinse the haddock, remove fins and tail, and cut up into large pieces. Place in a saucepan with the bay leaf, parsley stalks and the slice of lemon. Add the water and bring up to the boil. Lower the heat, cover with a lid and simmer very gently for about 15 minutes, or until the fish is tender. Drain off the liquor but reserve it. When the fish is cool enough to handle, remove the skin and bones and flake the fish but do not mash.

Melt the butter in a large saucepan. Peel and finely chop the onion. Add to the pan and sauté for a few minutes until the onion is soft but not brown. Add the cornflour blended with the milk and stir in the reserved fish liquor. Bring up to the boil, stirring all the time. Reduce the heat and cook very gently for 2–3 minutes. Stir in the flaked fish and the cooked rice. Blend together the egg yolk and cream. Draw the pan off the heat and add the blended mixture. Add the lemon juice, the pepper to taste and a pinch of ground mace or nutmeg.

Serve with croutons of toasted or fried bread.

Cream of Cucumber Soup

Serves 6 Time taken 1 hour

2 large cucumbers	½ onion
25 g (1 oz) butter	1 bay leaf
pinch sugar	15 g (½ oz) butter
salt	1 level teaspoon flour
freshly milled pepper	3 dl (½ pint) chicken stock
·25 litre (1 teacupful) (½ pint) milk	4 tablespoons single cream

This soup can also be served cold, in which case it may need thinning down with a little extra stock. The colour is much improved by the addition of one or two drops of edible green colouring, just sufficient to bring out the palest green colour.

Peel the cucumbers, slice in half lengthways and remove the centre seeds. Slice the cucumber thinly, blanch in boiling water for 2 minutes and drain well. Melt the 25 g (1 oz) butter in a saucepan, add the cucumber, sugar and a seasoning of salt and pepper. Cover with a lid and cook gently for about 15 minutes, or until the cucumber is quite soft.

Meanwhile prepare the white sauce which is used to thicken the soup. Put the milk, onion and bay leaf into a saucepan. Bring to the boil, then draw off the heat and leave to infuse for 10 minutes. Melt the 15 g (½ oz) butter in a small pan, and stir in the flour. Cook for 1 minute, then stir in the strained flavoured milk. Bring to the boil, stirring all the time, and cook gently for 2–3 minutes. Add the chicken stock and the prepared white sauce to the cucumbers. Cover the pan and cook gently for a further 15 minutes. Draw the pan off the heat and pass the soup through a sieve or Mouli, or purée in an electric blender. Return the soup to the saucepan. Check seasoning and reheat. Stir in the cream just before serving.

Vichyssoise

Serves 6 Time taken 1½ hours
Allow several hours to chill

450 g (1 lb) leeks	1 level teaspoon salt
2 onions	freshly milled pepper
50 g (2 oz) butter	1·5 dl (¼ pint) single cream
450 g (1 lb) potatoes	
generous 1 litre (2 pints) chicken stock	1–2 tablespoons finely chopped parsley

Vichyssoise is best made during winter months when leeks are tender and full of flavour. Serve cold for a special celebration, or hot for a family soup.

Trim the tops of the leeks to within 1 inch of the white stem and slice away the roots. Slice lengthwise through to the centre, and then wash thoroughly in cold water. Shred the leeks finely, and peel and chop the onions.

Melt the butter in a large saucepan, add the prepared vegetables and fry gently covered with a lid for about 10 minutes to soften. Stir occasionally and do not allow the vegetables to brown. Add the peeled and diced potatoes and cook for a further 5 minutes, then stir in the hot stock and seasoning. Bring up to the boil, then simmer gently for 30–40 minutes.

Draw the pan off the heat and pass the vegetables and liquid through a sieve or Mouli, or purée the soup in an electric blender. Cool, then stir in the cream.

Check seasoning and chill thoroughly. Stir in the parsley before serving.

Lettuce Soup

Serves 4–6 Time taken 45 minutes
Allow several hours to chill

25 g (1 oz) butter	1 large head lettuce
1 medium-sized onion	salt
1 225 g (½ lb) large potato	freshly milled pepper
scant 1 litre (1½ pints) chicken stock	1–2 tablespoons chopped chives

This lettuce soup served cold with a sprinkling of fresh chives is one of the nicest summer soups. It's a good use for any garden lettuces that are turning to seed.

Melt the butter in a saucepan. Peel and finely chop the onion. Add to the pan. Cover and fry gently for about 5 minutes, or until the onion is soft and tender. Peel and dice the potatoes, and add to the pan. Toss them in the onion-flavoured butter, allow them to cook for a few moments, and then stir in the stock. Bring up to the boil, lower the heat and simmer for about 15 minutes, or until the potato is tender.

Meanwhile, separate the lettuce leaves, wash and coarsely shred them. The lettuce can consist of the coarser outer leaves of several lettuce, the crisp inner leaves of which can then be used for salad. Alternatively use 2–3 smaller lettuce. Either way the amount should be the equivalent of 1 large head. Add the lettuce to the pan, bring back up to the boil and then draw the pan off the heat. Either pass the soup through a Mouli soup mill, or, better still, blend to a purée in an electric blender. Season to taste with salt and pepper. Return to the pan and reheat if serving hot.

Alternatively allow the soup to cool and then chill. It may be necessary to thin the soup down with a little extra stock or single cream. Serve cold sprinkled with finely chopped chives.

Greek Egg and Lemon Soup

Serves 6 Time taken 15 minutes

generous 1 litre (2 pints)
  chicken stock
50 g (2 oz) long grain rice
salt

freshly milled pepper
2 eggs
juice of ½ small lemon

A refreshing, light summer soup and one which should be made using homemade chicken stock.

Bring the chicken stock up to the boil and add the rice. Re-boil and simmer for about 10 minutes, or until the rice is cooked. Season well with salt and pepper.

Beat the eggs and lemon juice together in a basin. Add a little of the hot broth, mix well and add the mixture to the stock and rice. Stirring all the time, heat the soup over a low heat, taking care not to let it boil. Check the seasoning and serve immediately.

Oxtail Soup

Serves 6 Time taken 4–5 hours
Allow stock to stand overnight

1 oxtail	few bacon rinds (optional)
2 carrots	1·5 litres (3 pints) beef stock
2 large onions	25 g (1 oz) flour
2–3 stalks celery	1·5 dl (¼ pint) cold water
25 g (1 oz) dripping	1–2 tablespoons dry sherry
bouquet garni	

Wipe and divide the tail into joints. Blanch the joints: to do this, place them in a saucepan, cover with cold water and bring to the boil; strain and pat dry. The oxtail is now ready for use. Scrape and slice the carrots. Slice the onions and scrub and slice the celery.

Melt the dripping in a large pan and add the oxtail pieces. Fry well on all sides to brown, then drain from the hot fat. Add the prepared vegetables to the hot dripping and fry these until lightly browned. Return the meat to the pan along with the bouquet garni, bacon rinds and the stock or water and salt.

Bring to the boil, cover with a lid and simmer gently for 3–4 hours. Strain the stock off the bones and set aside in a cool place, leaving overnight if possible until the stock is quite cold. Meanwhile remove the meat from the oxtail bones and shred finely.

To finish the soup, remove the layer of fat that has risen to the surface of the oxtail stock and reboil the stock. In a small mixing basin blend the flour and cold water, stir or whisk well to blend thoroughly. Gradually stir into the oxtail soup and bring up to the boil: the soup should thicken slightly. Add the oxtail meat and check the seasoning. If liked, add a few drops of browning to give the soup a rich colour, and stir in the dry sherry.

Chilled Cucumber and Mint Soup

Serves 6 Time taken 45 minutes
Allow several hours to chill

2 medium-sized cucumbers	1·5 dl (¼ pint) single cream
50 g (2 oz) butter	salt
1 small onion	freshly milled pepper
1 small potato	2 tablespoons finely chopped mint
scant 1 litre (1½ pints) chicken stock	

Cut about 5 cms (2 inches) from one of the cucumbers and set aside for the garnish. Peel the remaining cucumbers, cut in half lengthwise, remove the seeds and chop the cucumber flesh coarsely.

Melt the butter in a saucepan. Peel and finely chop the onion. Add to the pan. Cover and cook gently until the onion is soft but not brown. Peel the potato and cut into dice. Add the potato, cucumber and chicken stock to the pan and bring up to the boil. Cover and simmer for 20 minutes, or until the vegetables are tender. Draw off the heat. Rub the soup through a sieve, or purée in an electric blender. Allow to cool. Add the cream, check seasoning, and then chill well.

Before serving stir in the chopped mint and garnish with the thin slices cut from the reserved cucumber.

Iced Carrot and Orange Soup

Serves 4 Time taken 1½ hours

450 g (1 lb) new carrots	1 level teaspoon sugar
1 onion	juice of 4 oranges
25 g (1 oz) butter	1·5 dl (¼ pint) single cream
scant 1 litre (1½ pints) chicken stock	chopped chives
salt	

Scrape the carrots and slice thinly. Peel and thinly slice the onion. Melt the butter in a saucepan, and add the carrots and onion. Fry gently for a few minutes to soften the vegetables but not brown them. Stir in the stock, a seasoning of salt and the sugar. Bring up to the boil, cover with a lid and simmer gently for 1 hour.

Draw the pan off the heat and pass the soup through a sieve, or purée in an electric blender. Add the strained juice of the oranges and the cream. Cool, then chill for several hours.

Sprinkle with chopped chives and serve.

Beef Consommé

Serves 6 Time taken 30 minutes
Allow several hours to chill

generous 1 litre (2 pints) meat stock	salt and pepper
100 g (4 oz) lean steak	2 tablespoons dry sherry
1 egg white and shell	1 lemon

Measure the stock into a large saucepan. Trim away any fat from the steak and cut up into small pieces. Cover the meat with cold water and allow to soak for 10 minutes, then drain. Crack the egg white into a bowl, add the egg shell and crush it.

Add the meat, the egg white and shell to the stock. Bring up to the boil whisking all the time. As the stock comes to the boil, stop whisking and allow the stock to boil right up to the top of the pan. Lower the heat and simmer gently for about 10 minutes, but do not stir or disturb the crust of egg white on the surface.

Draw the pan off the heat and strain through a scalded cloth into a bowl. The consommé should be quite clear. Check the seasoning with salt. To serve hot, add the sherry, or some finely shredded cooked vegetables, and reheat.

To serve cold, check the seasoning and add sherry if liked. Cool, then chill until set. The consommé should be only barely set, certainly never stiff. Stir the consommé up with a fork, and spoon into chilled serving dishes.

Serve with wedges of lemon.

Spanish Summer Soup

Serves 6–8 Time taken 30 minutes
Allow several hours to chill

6–8 spring onions	2 green peppers
½ cucumber	1 small clove garlic
1 thick slice white bread	freshly milled pepper
2 (425 g) (15 oz) tins tomatoes	1 teaspoon castor sugar
4 tablespoons olive oil	3 tablespoons wine vinegar
scant 1 litre (1½ pints) chicken stock	
salt	1 tablespoon chopped parsley

A colourful and most attractive summer soup, this recipe for 'Gazpacho' has a lovely flavour and makes an excellent choice for a summer party.

Trim and chop the spring onions. Peel and chop the cucumber. Halve, deseed and shred the green peppers. Peel the clove of garlic and crush to a purée with a little salt. Trim the crusts from the white bread and soak in a little cold water for a few minutes. Squeeze to remove excess moisture.

Place all the vegetables together in a bowl, add the tinned tomatoes, including the liquid. Add the oil and the bread. Blend these ingredients, half at a time, to a coarse purée in an electric blender. Pour the purée into a large bowl. Stir in the cold stock, a seasoning of salt and pepper to taste, and the sugar and vinegar.

Chill for several hours until ready to serve. Sprinkle with the chopped parsley before serving.

Quick Mushroom Consommé

Serves 6 Time taken 15 minutes

25 g (1 oz) butter	generous 1 litre (2 pints) chicken
1 small onion	stock
225 g (½ lb) button mushrooms	2–3 tablespoons dry sherry

An effective recipe to prepare when there is little time to spare. Use small, closed button mushrooms.

Melt the butter in a saucepan. Peel and chop the onion. Add to the pan and fry gently to soften but not brown. Add the washed, trimmed and thinly sliced mushrooms, cover and fry gently for 2–3 minutes until the juices run out. Stir in the stock and bring almost up to the boil. Draw off the heat and add the sherry before serving.

Cream of Cauliflower Soup

Serves 4–6 Time taken 45 minutes

1 small cauliflower	1 stick celery
salt	1 rounded tablespoon flour
juice of ½ lemon	1·5 dl (¼ pint) milk or cream
scant 1 litre (1½ pints) chicken stock	pinch nutmeg
25 g (1 oz) butter	chopped parsley or chervil
1 medium-sized onion	

Cut the stem off the cauliflower, remove all outer leaves and soak the head in cold, salted water for a few minutes. Half-fill a saucepan with salted water and bring to the boil. Slash deep cuts into the cauliflower stalk and put, head downwards, into the boiling water. Add the lemon juice to keep the cauliflower white and simmer for 10 minutes. Drain and reserve the water; this can be substituted for half the chicken stock in the recipe if liked. Cut the cooked cauliflower in half. Reserve half for garnish and rub the remainder through a sieve to purée.

Melt the butter in a saucepan. Peel and finely chop the onion. Trim and chop the celery. Add to the pan and fry gently for about 10 minutes, or until onion is tender but not brown. Stir in flour and cook gently for a few minutes. Add the chicken stock and cauliflower water if used, stirring all the time. Bring to the boil, then strain. Add the cauliflower purée, check seasoning and reheat. Stir in the cream, reserved cauliflower broken into small florets and a pinch of nutmeg. Sprinkle with a little parsley or chervil and serve.

2 First Courses

Hors d'œuvres are usually very simple, in fact they are not intended
to do anything other than stimulate the appetite. They can be a single
ingredient, a globe artichoke with melted butter, or smoked trout. On
the other hand, they can be a simple presentation of prepared
vegetables, fish, eggs or fruit, in many cases mixed or dressed with
mayonnaise or oil and vinegar dressing. Hors d'œuvres served at home
tend to be carefully prepared single items. The choice of recipe is
important, in that it should contrast the courses to follow. Serve
small quantities and pay a good deal of attention to the garnish.

Aubergine Caviar

Serves 4 Time taken 1½ hours
Allow several hours for mixture to chill

2 large or 3 medium aubergines	salt
2 tablespoons lemon juice	freshly milled pepper
3 tablespoons oil	small piece crushed garlic

Serve this along with taramasalata (see page 266) for an unusual start
to a meal.

Wipe the aubergines and place in a baking or roasting tin. Set in
the centre of a hot oven (200°C, 400°F or Gas No. 6) and bake for
30–40 minutes. Turn occasionally, the aubergines will feel quite soft

when ready. Remove from the oven and cool until warm enough to handle. Cut in half lengthwise and, using a spoon, scoop out the soft flesh into a mixing basin. Mash the pulp with a fork. Season with salt and pepper, and beat in the lemon juice. Gradually beat in the oil, 1 tablespoon at a time. The resulting mixture should be quite thick. Lastly, beat in a small piece of crushed garlic to taste. Spoon into a serving pot and chill until ready to serve.

Serve with hot toast slices.

The mixture may be prepared in an electric blender. After baking, scoop the pulp from the aubergines into the container and add the lemon juice. Cover and blend until smooth. Then, on low speed, blend in the oil and garlic.

Chicken Liver and Mushroom Pâté

Serves 6 Time taken 3–3½ hours
Allow 24 hours for the pâté to mature

450 g (1 lb) chicken livers	freshly milled pepper
100 g (4 oz) streaky bacon rashers	4 tablespoons stock
1 small clove garlic	100 g (¼ lb) button mushrooms
1 small onion, finely chopped	2 eggs
pinch dried thyme	1·5 dl (¼ pint) double cream
1 bay leaf	squeeze of lemon juice
salt	50 g (2 oz) butter

Wash the chicken livers in cold water, then trim and place in a saucepan. Remove the rind and chop the bacon rashers. Remove the papery coating and chop the garlic. Add the bacon, onion, garlic, thyme, bay leaf, a seasoning of salt and pepper and the stock. Bring up to the boil, then lower heat, cover with a lid and simmer gently for 10 minutes. Draw the pan off the heat and remove the bay leaf. Pass the mixture, along with the trimmed mushrooms, through the fine blade of a mincer into a mixing basin; or, alternatively, blend to a purée in a blender. Add the juices from the pan, eggs, cream, lemon juice and an extra seasoning of salt and pepper, and mix well.

Pour into a buttered generous 1-litre (2-pint) pâté or baking dish. Cover with a lid or foil, and stand in a baking tin with cold water to the depth of 1 inch. Bake for 2–2½ hours in the centre of a slow oven (150°C, 300°F or Gas No. 2). Remove from the heat and allow to cool. Melt the butter and pour over the top. Leave in a cold place for at least 24 hours before serving.

Serve with hot toast.

Cucumber and Cream Cheese Mousse

Serves 6 Time taken 1 hour
Allow several hours for mousse to chill

1 large cucumber	½ level teaspoon salt
225 g (½ lb) cream cheese	2 level teaspoons castor sugar
or	15 g (½ oz) powdered gelatine
2 (225 g) (8 oz) cartons	1·5 dl (¼ pint) double cream
cottage cheese	
1·5 dl (¼ pint) mayonnaise	watercress
1·5 dl (¼ pint) cold water	

Peel the cucumber, cut lengthwise and remove the seeds. Chop the cucumber flesh finely. Blend the cream cheese until soft in a mixing basin. If using cottage cheese, pass it through a sieve into the mixing basin. Add the mayonnaise and mix well.

Meanwhile measure the water into a saucepan, add the salt and sugar, and sprinkle in the gelatine. Allow to soak for 5 minutes, then place over low heat and stir until the gelatine has dissolved, but do not boil. Draw off the heat and allow to cool.

Stir the cooled gelatine mixture into the mayonnaise and cheese, add the chopped cucumber and fold in the lightly whipped cream. Mix thoroughly and then pour into a scant 1-litre (1½-pint) ring mould which has been rinsed out with cold water. Chill until set firm. Turn out and garnish with watercress.

Serve with thinly sliced brown bread and butter.

Mussels in Cream and Curry Sauce

Serves 4 Time taken 45 minutes

2·25 litres (2 quarts) fresh mussels	1·5 dl (¼ pint) dry white wine
1 onion, finely chopped	1·5 dl (¼ pint) water

For the Curry Sauce

25 g (1 oz) butter	3–4 tablespoons cream
1 teaspoon curry powder	salt
1 level tablespoon flour	freshly milled pepper

Wash and scrub the mussels in several changes of cold water. Discard any with broken shells or those that do not close tightly. Remove the beard from each one.

Rub the inside of a large saucepan with a buttered paper and sprinkle with the onion. Add the mussels and the white wine and water. Cover the pan and place over a high heat. Shake the pan occasionally and cook for 2–3 minutes or until the mussels have opened up. Lift the mussels out and discard any that remain closed. Strain the reserved cooking liquor. Remove the mussels from the shells and set aside while preparing the curry sauce.

In a saucepan, melt the butter and stir in the curry powder. Cook gently for a few moments and then stir in the flour. Gradually stir in the reserved cooking liquid from the mussels, beating well to get a smooth sauce. Taste and adjust the seasoning.

Arrange the mussels in individual ramekins or soufflé dishes. Add the cream to the sauce and pour over the mussels. Reheat quickly in a hot oven and serve at once.

Mushrooms à la Grecque

Serves 4 Time taken 20 minutes
Leave mushrooms for several hours to marinate

450 g (1 lb) small button mushrooms	freshly milled pepper
3 tomatoes	6 coriander seeds
4 tablespoons olive oil	1 bay leaf
1·5 dl (¼ pint) dry white wine	1 sprig thyme
and water	1 crushed clove garlic
salt	

All kinds of vegetables can be prepared using this method. Courgettes, artichoke hearts, leeks or cauliflower sprigs are among the nicest.

Choose small mushrooms – the tightly closed variety; the larger, open mushrooms are inclined to blacken the juice. Wipe the mushrooms and trim the stalks level with the caps. Nick the skins of the tomatoes, and place the tomatoes in a basin. Cover with boiling water, stand 1 minute, then drain and peel away the skins. Halve, remove centre seeds and chop the tomato flesh coarsely.

Measure the oil, wine and water, a seasoning of salt and pepper, and the coriander seeds, bay leaf, thyme and garlic into a saucepan. Bring them up to the boil and simmer gently for 3 minutes. Then add the trimmed mushrooms and the tomato flesh, and cook gently for 5 minutes, keeping the saucepan covered with a lid. Carefully remove the vegetables to a serving dish. Replace the pan over the heat for 5 minutes and boil rapidly to reduce the wine mixture. Pour the mixture over the mushrooms and leave to cool.

Serve cold as a meal starter with French bread to mop up the marinade.

Cold Curried Prawns

Serves 6 Time taken 1 hour
Allow to stand for several hours

225–350 g (8–12 oz) prepared
    prawns
225 g (8 oz) long grain rice

4 tablespoons prepared oil and
    vinegar dressing

For the Curry Mayonnaise
25 g (1 oz) butter
1 small onion, finely chopped
1 level teaspoon flour
2 level tablespoons curry powder
1 rounded teaspoon concentrated
    tomato purée
4 tablespoons water

¼ tablespoon salt
1 level teaspoon castor sugar
1 tablespoon apricot jam
1·5 dl (¼ pint) mayonnaise
2 tablespoons single cream
juice of ½ lemon

Prepare the prawns; peel fresh and thaw frozen ones. Plain-boil the
rice for 8–10 minutes in salted water or until tender, then drain. Mix
with the oil and vinegar dressing, and allow to cool.

Melt the butter for the curry mayonnaise in a saucepan, add the
onion and sauté very gently for about 5 minutes to soften the onion.
Stir in the flour and curry powder, and fry for a further few minutes
to draw out the oils from the curry powder. Then stir in the tomato
purée which has been diluted with the water, salt, castor sugar and
apricot jam. Bring up to the boil and simmer gently for about 5
minutes. Draw the pan off the heat and strain the mixture into a
basin. Allow to cool, then combine the curry sauce with the mayonnaise, and stir in the cream and lemon juice. At this stage the sauce
may be left several hours or overnight before serving. The flavour is
often improved as a result.
To serve Add the prepared prawns to the curry mayonnaise. Spoon
a little of the rice on to each serving plate, top with the curried
prawns and serve.

Melon, Cucumber and Tomato Salad

Serves 6 Time taken 1 hour
Allow several hours for salad to marinate

1 ripe honeydew melon
1 cucumber
salt
450 g (1 lb) tomatoes

1 tablespoon chopped parsley
1·5 dl (¼ pint) oil and vinegar
    dressing

Cut the melon in half and remove the seeds. Cut each half into quarters and then, using a knife, cut the melon flesh away from the skin. Dice the flesh and place in a mixing basin. Peel and cut the cucumber into 1-cm (½-inch) slices, sprinkle with salt and set aside for 30 minutes. Nick the tomato skins and place the tomatoes together in a mixing basin. Cover with boiling water, allow to stand 1 minute, then drain. Peel the tomatoes, cut in quarters and add to the melon. Drain away the juices that have flowed from the cucumber and add the cucumber. Add the chopped parsley and the oil and vinegar dressing. Toss well to mix and allow to marinate until ready to serve.

This is a colourful combination of ingredients. Spoon into individual plates and serve.

Egg Mousse with Caviar

Serves 6 Time taken 45 minutes
Allow several hours for mousse to chill

6 eggs	salt
1·5 dl (¼ pint) double cream	freshly milled pepper
3 dl (½ pint) chicken stock	1 small jar caviar-style
15 g (½ oz) powdered gelatine	lumpfish roe
1 teaspoon Worcestershire	
sauce	watercress

Place the eggs in a saucepan, cover with cold water and bring to the boil. Simmer for 6–8 minutes to hard boil. Drain, cool the eggs in cold water immediately to prevent further cooking, then remove the shells. Leave submerged in water until quite cold.

Sieve the egg yolks into a basin. Chop the egg whites and add to the yolks. Lightly whip the cream. Measure 3 tablespoons of the stock into a teacup and sprinkle in the gelatine. Allow to soak for 5 minutes. Pour the remaining stock into a saucepan. Add the soaked gelatine and stir over low heat until the gelatine has dissolved. Remove from the heat and allow the stock to cool. If liked, stir over iced water to speed up the process. When the stock is beginning to thicken and set, pour at once into the egg mixture along with the cream. Blend quickly and evenly. Add the Worcestershire sauce and a seasoning of salt and pepper to taste. Pour into a china soufflé serving dish and spread level. Cover with a square of foil and chill until set firm.

Either spoon the caviar over the egg mousse and serve from the dish; or, turn the egg mousse out on to a serving plate, surround with a garnish or watercress and spoon the caviar over the top of the mousse.

Serve with thinly sliced brown bread and butter.

Cauliflower Vinaigrette

Serves 4 Time taken 20 minutes
Allow to stand until quite cold

1 large cauliflower	1 tablespoon finely chopped
2 tablespoons chopped onion	parsley
or spring onion	

For the Dressing

salt	$\frac{1}{4}$ teaspoon French mustard
freshly milled pepper	3 tablespoons wine vinegar
1 level teaspoon castor sugar	4–5 tablespoons salad oil

Break the cauliflower head into sprigs of even size and wash well. Using a small sharp knife, pare away as much of the skin from the stalks as possible. Add the cauliflower sprigs to boiling salted water with a little lemon juice added and cook for about 10 minutes or until just tender. Drain well and place them in a salad bowl. Add the chopped onion and parsley. Set aside while preparing the dressing.

Place a good seasoning of salt and freshly milled pepper in a small mixing basin. Add the sugar and mustard. French mustard gives a pleasant bite to the salad dressing. Stir in the vinegar and mix well to dissolve the seasonings. Add the oil and taste for flavour. Pour the dressing over the warm cauliflower sprigs.

Toss gently and leave until cold before serving.

Eggs en Cocotte with Cream

Serves 2 Time taken 15 minutes

4 eggs	freshly milled pepper
salt	4 tablespoons cream

Warm four small ramekin dishes and very thoroughly butter each one. Carefully crack an egg into each. Season well with salt and pepper and spoon a tablespoon of cream over each egg.

Place the ramekin dishes in a large roasting or baking tin and fill with boiling water to within 1 cm ($\frac{1}{2}$ inch) of the rims of the dishes.

Cover and place in the centre of a preheated moderate oven (180°C, 350°F or Gas No. 4). Poach the eggs for 10–12 minutes; the whites should be set but the yolks still runny.

Serve at once in the dishes.

Scallops in Cream Sauce

Serves 6 Time taken 15 minutes

8 fresh scallops	salt and pepper
40 g (1½ oz) butter	1·5 dl (¼ pint) single cream

Have the scallops removed from the shells. Rinse and slice into two or three pieces according to size. Heat the butter in a pan and, when frothing, add the scallops. Fry gently, turning occasionally for about 5 minutes.

Season to taste, add the cream and reheat gently without boiling. Serve at once.

Globe Artichokes with Whipped Butter

Serves 4 Time taken 1 hour

4 globe artichokes	lemon juice or vinegar

For the Whipped Butter

100 g (4 oz) butter	salt
2–3 tablespoons hot water	freshly milled pepper
lemon juice	

The whipped butter for this recipe is best made using an electric hand mixer. Beating liquid into butter by hand is hard work.

Trim the long stalks and soak the artichokes in cold salted water for 1 hour to remove all the dust. Rinse and prepare each one in turn. Using a sharp knife, cut about 1 cm (½ inch) off the top of each one. Then, using scissors, snip off the tips of all the leaves around the sides. Trim the stalk level with the base of the artichoke and remove any tough or discoloured leaves around the base. Trim the bases neatly with a knife, and plunge the prepared artichokes into a bowl of cold water with lemon juice or vinegar added to keep the bases white.

Bring a large pan of cold salted water up to the boil. Add a little lemon juice or vinegar and the prepared artichokes. Simmer gently until tender – takes about 25–30 minutes. Take care not to overcook;

when ready, a leaf will pull away quite easily. Lift the artichokes from the pan with a perforated spoon and drain them upside down for a moment. When the artichokes are cool enough to handle, gently part the centre leaves and pull out the tender cone of leaves in the centre called the 'choke'.

Meanwhile cream the butter to soften and then beat in the hot water. Beat well so that the butter becomes light and creamy. Beat in lemon juice to taste, and a seasoning of salt and pepper.

Arrange each of the artichokes on a serving plate. Pass the whipped butter separately so that it may be spooned into the centre of the warm artichoke. The butter will melt and as the leaves are pulled away they should be dipped in the butter.

Smoked Salmon Pâté

Serves 4 Time taken 15 minutes
Allow several hours for pâté to chill

225 g (½ lb) inexpensive
   smoked salmon or smoked
   salmon trimmings
50 g (2 oz) butter

1 tablespoon olive oil
1–2 tablespoons lemon juice
4 tablespoons double cream
pinch cayenne pepper

If using smoked salmon trimmings, cut away any pieces of skin or small bones. Mince the smoked salmon flesh or chop it finely. Place the butter and oil in a mixing basin and cream together very thoroughly. Gradually beat in the smoked salmon until the mixture becomes a thick paste. Beat in the lemon juice, the cream and cayenne pepper.

Pile into a small serving pot and chill for a few hours. Serve with hot toast.

Melon Balls with Orange

Serves 4–6 Time taken 15 minutes
Allow several hours for mixture to chill

1 large ripe honeydew melon
100 g (4 oz) castor sugar
finely grated rind and juice of
   1 large orange

juice of ½ lemon

fresh mint leaves

Serve this fruit cocktail in chilled glasses with sugared rims. Dip the rim of each glass first in a little lightly mixed egg white, then in castor sugar. Leave them to stand for several hours so that they dry frosty and white.

Slice the melon in half, scoop out the seeds and cut the melon into quarters. Using a round vegetable baller, scoop out the flesh. Press the cutter into the melon flesh and twist round sharply. Work along each section of melon to scoop out as many as possible. Place the melon balls in a basin. Sprinkle with sugar. Add the finely grated rind of the orange, and the strained orange and lemon juice. Toss the mixture to blend all the ingredients and then set aside in a cool place for several hours or overnight. Juices will run from the melon to form a delicious orange-flavoured syrup.

Chill for an hour or so before serving, then carefully spoon the melon and juices into individual glasses. Garnish with a sprig of fresh mint and serve.

Devilled Whitebait

Serves 4 Time taken 15 minutes

450 g (1 lb) whitebait	cayenne pepper
seasoned flour	1 lemon
oil for deep-frying	

Rinse the whitebait carefully, drain well and pat dry in a kitchen cloth. Roll a few at a time in the seasoned flour. Fry the whitebait and turn on to crumpled paper. Continue flouring and frying the fish until all are fried.

Reheat the oil and add all the whitebait together. Fry for just 1 minute to crispen. Drain well and turn on to a hot serving dish. Sprinkle with extra salt and cayenne pepper.

Serve with quarters of lemon and slices of brown bread and butter.

Hot Baked Grapefruit

Serves 4 Time taken 30 minutes

2 grapefruit	Demerara sugar
4 dessertspoons medium dry or sweet sherry	15 g (½ oz) butter

Cut the grapefruit in half horizontally, and, using a grapefruit knife, loosen the segments. Discard the pips and cut the centre core from each half. Arrange the grapefruit close together in a baking or roasting tin. Spoon the sherry into each grapefruit, sprinkle liberally with

Demerara sugar and place a small nut of butter on top of each half.

Place in the centre of a hot oven (200° C, 400°F or Gas No. 6) and bake for 15 minutes. Spoon over any juices that may remain in the baking tin and serve at once while hot.

Shellfish Cocktail

Serves 6 Time taken 30 minutes
Allow to stand for several hours

225–350 g (8–12 oz) prepared prawns, crabmeat or lobster flesh	6 crisp lettuce leaves 6 cucumber slices

For the Cocktail Sauce

3 rounded tablespoons mayonnaise	squeeze of lemon juice
3 tablespoons tomato ketchup	dash Tabasco sauce (optional)
2–3 tablespoons cream	
1 teaspoon Worcestershire sauce	paprika pepper

Thaw shellfish if necessary. Wash the lettuce leaves, choosing six large crisp leaves, and shred finely – easiest way is to roll up the leaves together then shred across. Put the shredded lettuce along with a sprinkling of water in a polythene bag and place in the refrigerator. Combine all the ingredients together for the cocktail sauce, making sure enough lemon juice is added to sharpen the flavour. All this may be done well in advance.

When ready to serve, place a little of the shredded lettuce in the base of each of six individual glasses. Combine the shellfish and sauce together and spoon into each one. Garnish the rim of the glass with a slice of cucumber cut into the centre of the slice so that it can be slotted on to the edge, and sprinkle with paprika pepper.

Egg and Prawn Mayonnaise

Serves 4 Time taken 30 minutes
Allow mixture to stand for 1 hour

4 eggs	4 crisp lettuce leaves
4 rounded tablespoons mayonnaise	100 g (4 oz) prepared prawns
1 carton soured cream	
1 level teaspoon curry powder	paprika pepper

Hard-boil the eggs, drain and plunge in cold water. Then remove the shells and leave the eggs submerged in water until cold.

Combine together the mayonnaise, soured cream and curry powder, and chill for 1 hour for flavour to develop and sauce to thicken a little. Slice the cooled hard-boiled eggs in half and arrange, rounded side upwards, in pairs on crisp lettuce leaves. Fold the prawns into the mayonnaise dressing and spoon over the eggs.

Sprinkle with paprika pepper and serve with thinly sliced brown bread and butter.

Grapefruit with Crème de Menthe

Serves 6 Time taken 15 minutes
Allow several hours to chill

4–5 large grapefruit
50 g (2 oz) castor sugar

1 miniature bottle of crème de menthe

Grapefruit prepared this way has a delicate green colour and a delicious fresh peppermint flavour. Ideal to serve before a rich meal.

Cut the grapefruit in two and, using a grapefruit knife, loosen the segments in each half. Squeeze the flesh and juice into a basin.

Add the castor sugar and crème de menthe. Stir so that the green colour blends evenly and the sugar dissolves. Chill to emphasize the refreshing peppermint flavour.

Spoon into six individual glasses and serve.

Eggs Stuffed with Sardine

Serves 4 Time taken 30 minutes

4 eggs
1 tin sardines
salt and pepper
squeeze of lemon juice

1 tablespoon cream or mayonnaise
chopped parsley
4 crisp lettuce leaves

Hard-boil the eggs, remove the shells and slice the eggs in half lengthways. With the tip of a knife blade push the yolks out of the whites into a mixing basin. Add the sardines (tails removed) and mash the ingredients with a fork. Season with salt and pepper to taste and beat in the lemon juice and cream or mayonnaise.

Spoon or pipe the filling back into the egg white halves, dividing it equally between each one. Sprinkle with chopped parsley. Arrange the stuffed eggs in pairs on each of four crisp lettuce leaves.

Serve with thinly sliced brown bread and butter.

Eggs in Curry Mayonnaise

Serves 4 Time taken 45 minutes

4 eggs

4 crisp lettuce leaves

For the Curry Sauce
15 g (½ oz) butter
½ small onion, finely chopped
1 level dessertspoon curry powder

4 tablespoons tomato juice
dash Worcestershire sauce
1·5 dl (¼ pint) mayonnaise

Hard-boil the eggs, drain and plunge into cold water. Shell and leave submerged in cold water until required.

Melt the butter in a saucepan. Add the onion and fry gently for about 5 minutes or until the onion is tender but not brown. Add the curry powder, stir to blend and fry gently for a further few minutes. Draw the pan off the heat and stir in the tomato juice and the Worcestershire sauce. Allow to cool.

Measure the mayonnaise into a bowl, strain in the curry-flavoured liquid and blend well. Drain the eggs and cut each one in half lengthwise with a wet knife. Arrange in pairs on crisp lettuce leaves. Spoon over the curry sauce and serve.

Avocado Mousse

Serves 6 Time taken 1 hour
Allow several hours for mousse to chill

1·5 dl (¼ pint) cold water
15 g (½ oz) powdered gelatine
1·5 dl (¼ pint) chicken stock
3 small or 2 large avocado pears
salt

freshly milled pepper
½ large onion
2 teaspoons Worcestershire sauce
1·5 dl (¼ pint) mayonnaise
1·5 dl (¼ pint) double cream

Unmould this avocado mousse when ready to serve. Avocado mixtures tend to discolour on the surface if allowed to stand for any length of time before serving.

Measure the water into a small saucepan, sprinkle over the gelatine and set aside for 5 minutes. Then warm gently over a low heat until the gelatine is dissolved and the mixture clear, but do not allow to boil. Draw the pan off the heat, stir in the stock and set aside to cool for a few minutes.

Halve the avocado pears and remove the stones, then scoop out the flesh with a dessertspoon into a mixing basin and mash down the flesh with a fork until smooth. Grate the onion finely on to a saucer and measure out 1 teaspoon of onion juice. Add the onion juice to the avocado flesh. Season with salt and freshly milled pepper, and add the Worcestershire sauce. Slowly pour in the gelatine mixture and stir until just beginning to thicken. Then gently fold in the mayonnaise and the lightly whipped cream. Pour into a wetted scant 1-litre (1½-pint) mould and chill until set firm. Unmould on to a serving dish.

For a pretty colour contrast garnish in the centre with a few prawns tossed in oil and vinegar dressing.

Marinated Kipper Fillets with Onion

Serves 4 Time taken 15 minutes

1 packet boned kipper fillets
1 small onion sliced into rings

1 bay leaf

For the Marinade
1 level teaspoon castor sugar
salt and freshly milled pepper

3 tablespoons wine vinegar
4 tablespoons olive oil

Remove skin from each fillet, then arrange the kipper fillets in a shallow serving plate along with the onion rings and bay leaf. Combine ingredients for the marinade, check flavour and pour over the kippers. Leave for several hours.

Serve with slices of buttered brown bread.

Moules Frites

Serves 4 Time taken 25–30 minutes

2·25 litres (2 quarts) mussels
1 egg
toasted breadcrumbs
oil for deep frying

4 wedges of lemon
sprigs of parsley
tartare sauce

Discard any mussels with broken shells and any that remain open. Scrub the mussels and, using a knife, pull away the beards. Clean them thoroughly in several changes of cold water.

Butter the inside of a large saucepan, add 2–3 tablespoons of water and all the mussels. Cover with a lid and place over a high heat. Shake the pan over the heat for 3–5 minutes until the mussels have steamed open. Draw off the heat and remove the mussels from the pan. Discard any mussels that have remained closed. Take the mussels out of the shells.

Coat the mussels in the lightly mixed egg and then roll in the toasted breadcrumbs. Deep-fry, half at a time, in hot oil for 2–3 minutes until golden brown.

Drain well and serve hot with a garnish of lemon wedges and parsley sprigs. Pass the tartare sauce separately.

Snails with Garlic Butter

Serves 4 Time taken 20–30 minutes
Serve at once

1 (215 g) (7½ oz) tin
    Escargots au naturel containing 24 snails, with shells

For the Garlic Butter

175 g (6 oz) butter	salt
3 cloves garlic	freshly milled pepper
3 tablespoons finely chopped parsley	

Wipe the snail shells and drain the snails from the tin. Set aside while preparing the garlic butter.

Cream the butter until soft. Lightly crush the garlic cloves and peel away the skins. Add a little salt and, with the tip of a knife, mash the garlic to a purée, and add to the butter. Add the parsley and a seasoning of pepper. Mix well.

Take each shell in turn and, using a knife, push a little of the garlic butter into the shell. Then push a snail right into the shell and finally seal the entrance of the shell with more garlic butter.

Place the prepared snails on fireproof snail plates – allow six shells per person. When ready to serve, place them in a hot oven (200°C, 400°F or Gas No. 6) and heat through until the snails are hot and the butter is bubbling and beginning to brown. Serve at once with hot French bread, which can be broken off and used to mop up the melted butter on each plate.

3 Lunch & Supper

Cheese, pasta, eggs and rice form the basis for many easily made and appetizing recipes; so also do some of the less expensive cuts of offal. Care in the preparation of these recipes is essential; flavour is important and a simple but attractive garnish results in many tasty meals made at a fairly low cost. Many are almost a meal in themselves and can be served with a salad, hot crisp rolls or French bread. They help to give the variety necessary in everyday menus.

Cauliflower and Bacon Savoury

Serves 4 Time taken 30 minutes

1 large cauliflower	1 onion
15 g (½ oz) vegetable fat	6 bacon rashers

For the Cheese Sauce

50 g (2 oz) butter	40 g (1½ oz) flour
4·5 dl (¾ pint) liquid	salt
100 g (4 oz) grated Cheddar cheese	freshly milled pepper

Trim the cauliflower, and break into medium-sized sprigs. Cook in boiling salted water, just to cover, until tender – takes 8–10 minutes. Drain and reserve 1·5 dl (¼ pint) of the cooking water for the sauce. Arrange the cauliflower sprigs in a buttered serving dish and keep warm. Peel and finely chop the onion. Trim and chop the bacon rashers. Melt the fat in a frying pan. Add the onion and bacon and fry until the onion is soft – takes about 5 minutes. Sprinkle over the cauliflower and keep warm.

Melt the butter for the sauce in a small pan and stir in the flour. Cook gently for 1 minute. Make the reserved cauliflower-water up to 4 dl (¾ pint) with milk. Gradually stir into the saucepan, beating well all the time to get a really smooth sauce. Bring to the boil and allow to cook for 2–3 minutes. Add all but 1 tablespoon of the cheese, and season well with salt and pepper. Stir over a low heat until the cheese has melted, then pour over the cauliflower sprigs. Sprinkle with the remaining cheese and pass under a hot grill until the top is crisp and brown.

Croque Monsieur

Serves 4 Time taken 45 minutes

8 slices white bread	4 slices cooked ham
8 slices Gruyère cheese	50–75 g (2–3 oz) butter for frying

The slices of ham and cheese should be approximately the same size as the slices of bread, so that they can be trimmed neatly. Ideally the cheese should be fairly thinly sliced, whereas the ham can be cut a little more generously.

On four of the bread slices arrange first a slice of cheese, then ham and finally another slice of cheese. Top with a second slice of bread, press gently together and trim the sides evenly.

Fry the sandwiches gently, two at a time, in plenty of hot butter. When beginning to brown, turn and fry the second side. Turn several times, adding more butter if necessary, so that the pan does not become dry. Cook until golden brown and crisp, then remove from the pan and keep hot in the oven while frying the remaining two. Cut each one in half diagonally and serve hot.

Risotto Milanese

Serves 4 Time taken 30–40 minutes

225 g (8 oz) long grain rice	6 dl (1 pint) chicken stock
3–4 lean bacon rashers	100 g (¼ lb) button mushrooms
1 small onion	100 g (¼ lb) grated cheese
40 g (1½ oz) butter	

A light and easily made lunch or supper dish that does not require any special ingredients.

Wash the rice in cold water and drain thoroughly. Trim and chop the bacon rashers. Peel and finely chop the onion. Melt 25 g (1 oz) of the butter in a saucepan and add the bacon and onion. Fry for a few minutes until the onion is soft but not brown, then stir in the rice. Mix well to coat the rice with the butter and onions, then stir in the hot stock. Bring up to the boil, stirring all the time, then lower the heat, cover with a lid and simmer gently for 20–30 minutes. Stir occasionally. The rice will become quite tender and absorb all the liquid.

Meanwhile trim and slice the mushrooms. When the risotto is almost ready, quickly fry the mushrooms in the remaining butter. Using a fork, fold these into the rice together with half the grated cheese. Turn the risotto into a hot serving dish and sprinkle with remaining cheese.

Serve at once with salad.

Eggs Mornay

Serves 4 Time taken 45 minutes

700 g (1½ lb) potatoes	15 g (½ oz) butter
salt	1–2 tablespoons creamy milk
freshly milled pepper	4 hard-boiled eggs

For the Sauce

25 g (1 oz) butter	salt and pepper
25 g (1 oz) flour	100 g (4 oz) grated Cheddar cheese
3 dl (½ pint) milk	

Peel and boil the potatoes. When cooked, mash with plenty of seasoning and the butter. Add a little milk and beat well until smooth and creamy. Spoon the mashed potato into a buttered 1-litre (1½- or 2-pint) baking or pie dish and spread over the base and around the sides to make a nest shape. Set aside and keep warm while preparing the sauce.

Melt the butter in a small pan and stir in the flour. Cook over low heat for 1 minute. Gradually add the milk and bring to the boil, stirring well all the time to get a smooth sauce. Season well and add half the grated cheese. Leave over low heat to cook for 2–3 minutes. Draw the pan off the heat and add the sliced hard-boiled eggs.

Pour the sauce mixture into the centre of the potato nest. Top with remaining grated cheese. Place in the centre of a hot oven (200°C, 400°F or Gas No. 6) and bake for 15–20 minutes, or until bubbling hot and browned.

Serve with a salad or sliced tomato and cucumber, tossed in oil and vinegar dressing.

Welsh Rarebit

Serves 4 Time taken 15 minutes

25 g (1 oz) butter	salt
175 g (6 oz) grated Cheddar cheese	freshly milled pepper
1 tablespoon milk, beer or whisky	1 egg yolk (optional)
dash of made mustard	4 slices of hot toast

Melt the butter in a saucepan. Add the cheese, and the milk or beer, both of which are traditional, or the whisky which is not traditional but gives the rarebit a delicious flavour. Add the mustard and a seasoning of salt and pepper and stir over low heat, until the cheese has melted and the mixture is smooth. Draw off the heat and beat in the egg yolk. The addition of the egg makes the mixture rather more firm and lighter in texture.

Have the hot toast ready and arrange the slices on the grill pan. It is a good idea to place them on a sheet of kitchen foil, to catch any mixture that runs off the sides of the toast. Spoon the mixture on to each slice of toast. Place under a high heat to brown quickly and then serve at once.

Pancakes with Spinach and Cheese

Serves 4–6 Time taken 45 minutes
12 prepared pancakes (see page 188)

For the Filling

450 g (1 lb) fresh spinach	40 g (1½ oz) flour
or	4·5 dl (¾ pint) milk
1 (350 g) (12 oz) packet frozen	salt
spinach	freshly milled pepper
40 g (1½ oz) butter	100 g (4 oz) grated Gruyère cheese

Have the pancakes prepared and hot. If using fresh spinach, wash well in cold water and remove centre rib from the leaves. Cook in a covered pan over moderate heat (no water required) for about 10–15 minutes, or until juice flows and the spinach is tender. Drain well and chop finely. If using frozen spinach, cook according to the packet instructions.

Melt the butter in a saucepan over low heat and stir in the flour. Cook gently for a moment, then gradually stir in 3 dl (½ pint) of the milk, beating well all the time to make a thick white sauce. Bring up to the boil and cook gently for 2–3 minutes, then season with salt and pepper and stir in all but 25 g (1 oz) of the cheese. Stir about half this sauce into the spinach purée. Fill the pancakes with the mixture, roll up and place in a buttered baking or serving dish.

Thin down the sauce that remains with the rest of the milk to make a coating consistency. Check seasoning again and then pour over the pancakes. Sprinkle with the remaining cheese and brown well in a hot oven (200°C, 400°F or Gas No. 6) for about 10 minutes.

Serve hot.

Pancakes can be made in advance. Cook, then reheat them in a foil parcel in the centre of a hot oven (200°C, 400°F or Gas No. 6) for 15 minutes.

Chicken Liver Risotto

Serves 4 Time taken 45 minutes–1 hour

1 onion	salt
1 green pepper	freshly milled pepper
4 rashers bacon	175–225 g (6–8 oz) chicken livers
65 g (2½ oz) butter	seasoned flour
225 g (8 oz) long grain rice	
6 dl (1 pint) chicken stock	grated cheese
100 g (4 oz) small mushrooms	

Peel and finely chop the onion. Halve, deseed and shred the green pepper. Trim and chop the bacon rashers. Melt 25 g (1 oz) of the butter in a heavy saucepan or flameproof casserole. Add the bacon, onion and green pepper. Cover with a lid and sauté gently for about 5 minutes until the onion and green pepper are soft but not brown. Add the rice and stir to mix with the butter and onions. Stir in the hot chicken stock and bring up to the boil, stirring all the time. Lower the heat, cover with a tight-fitting lid and simmer gently for about 20–30 minutes on top of the cooker, or cook in a moderate oven (180°C, 350°F or Gas No. 4) for 30–40 minutes. Either way cook until the rice is tender and all the liquid has been absorbed.

Meanwhile wash, trim and slice the mushrooms. Place in a saucepan with 1·5 dl (¼ pint) of water, 15 g (½ oz) of the remaining butter and a seasoning of salt and pepper. Bring up to the boil, then simmer for about 5 minutes until tender. Drain and reserve the mushrooms. Trim the chicken livers with scissors, dip in seasoned flour and then fry gently in the remaining 25 g (1 oz) of butter. Drain and cut the livers into slices.

When the rice is cooked, fold the mushrooms and chicken livers gently into the risotto using a fork. Pile the risotto on a hot serving dish and scatter plenty of grated cheese over the top. Serve at once.

Tagliatelle with Crispy Bacon

Serves 2 Time taken 15–20 minutes

100–175 g (4–6 oz) tagliatelle	1 egg yolk
4 rashers bacon	4 tablespoons cream
freshly milled black pepper	
4 tablespoons dry white wine	grated Parmesan cheese

Tagliatelle, also called fettuccine, are ribbon noodles. They can be green in colour, in which case spinach has been added to the dough, or they can be plain.

Add the tagliatelle to a large pan of boiling salted water. Boil without a lid until tender – about 12 minutes – then drain at once.

Meanwhile trim, chop and lightly fry the bacon. When just beginning to crispen, sprinkle the bacon with freshly ground black pepper and stir in the wine. Add the cooked tagliatelle and heat gently. Draw the pan off the heat and add the egg yolk mixed with the cream. Turn the tagliatelle over in the cream mixture. Taste and season if necessary.

Turn into a hot serving dish and sprinkle with grated Parmesan cheese.

Cheese Aigrettes

Serves 2–3 Time taken 30 minutes

50 g (2 oz) plain flour	40 g (1½ oz) grated Parmesan cheese
15 g (½ oz) butter	pinch cayenne pepper
1·5 dl (¼ pint) water	pinch dry mustard
1 egg	½ level teaspoon salt
1 egg yolk	oil for deep frying

Sift the flour on to a square of greaseproof paper and set aside. Measure the butter into a small saucepan, add the water and bring up to the boil. Draw off the heat and immediately tip in the sieved flour. Stir well with a wooden spoon and then beat to get a smooth mixture that leaves the side of the pan clean. Allow to cool until the hand can be held comfortably against the sides of the pan.

Lightly mix the whole egg and egg yolk together in a small bowl. Add, a little at a time, to the mixture in the pan, beating well between each addition. Stir in the cheese, cayenne pepper, mustard and salt. Drop the mixture in heaped teaspoonfuls into hot deep fat. Fry gently until golden brown, turning them once. Cook as many at a time as the pan will comfortably hold, and keep prepared ones hot while frying remaining batches. Altogether the mixture should make about 1 dozen.

Serve at once, sprinkled with extra grated cheese and a green salad or hot buttered toast.

Spaghetti with Bolognese Sauce

Serves 4 Time taken 1 hour

225–350 g (8–12 oz) spaghetti	25 g (1 oz) butter

For the Bolognese Sauce

1 medium onion	freshly milled pepper
1 clove garlic	1–2 tablespoons tomato purée
2 tablespoons oil	pinch mixed herbs
450 g (1 lb) minced beef	3 dl ($\frac{1}{2}$ pint) stock
225 g ($\frac{1}{2}$ lb) fresh tomatoes	1 wine glass red wine
2 level tablespoons flour	
1 level teaspoon salt	grated Parmesan cheese

Start with the preparation of the Bolognese sauce. Peel and finely chop the onion and garlic. Heat the oil in a medium-sized saucepan and add the onion. Cover and cook gently for about 5 minutes until the onion is soft but not brown. Stir in the garlic and minced beef and brown quickly. Meanwhile, scald and peel the tomatoes and cut them in half.

Stir the flour, salt, a seasoning of pepper, peeled tomatoes, tomato purée and mixed herbs into the meat mixture. Add the stock and red wine, and bring up to the boil. Lower the heat, cover with a lid and simmer gently for 40–45 minutes. Stir occasionally to prevent the sauce sticking and add a little extra stock if necessary – the final sauce should not be too thick.

About 15 minutes before serving, add the spaghetti to a large pan of boiling salted water. Boil without a lid until tender – about 10 minutes – then drain at once. Warm the butter in the saucepan, add the spaghetti and toss, or turn using two spoons, until the spaghetti is nicely glazed. Turn into a hot dish. Pour the Bolognees sauce over and sprinkle grated cheese generously on top.

Scrambled Egg with Mushroom

Serves 4 Time taken 10 minutes

1 (275 g) (10½ oz) tin cream of mushroom soup	freshly milled pepper
	25 g (1 oz) butter
8 eggs	
salt	chopped parsley

This may sound a little unusual but in fact is very nice. On other occasions cream of chicken, vegetable or celery soup may be used. Take care to use the cream soups. Concentrated soups would be too strong in flavour when used undiluted.

Empty the contents of the tin of mushroom soup into a mixing basin and stir until smooth. Crack the eggs into the basin and add a seasoning of salt and pepper. Whisk well until blended.

Melt the butter in a large frying pan over low heat. Pour in the mushroom mixture and cook gently, stirring occasionally until the mixture has thickened and is beginning to set.

Sprinkle with parsley and serve with hot toast.

Spaghetti Milanese

Serves 4 Time taken 45 minutes

100 g (¼ lb) sliced cooked ham	100 g (¼ lb) small mushrooms
50 g (2 oz) butter	225–350 g (8–12 oz) spaghetti

For the Tomato Sauce

1 rasher of bacon	freshly milled pepper
1 small onion	1 teaspoon castor sugar
1 carrot	squeeze lemon juice
25 g (1 oz) butter	1 rounded tablespoon cornflour
350–450 g (¾–1 lb) tomatoes	4 tablespoons water
3 dl (½ pint) stock	
salt	grated Parmesan cheese

Start with the preparation of the tomato sauce. Trim and chop the bacon rasher. Peel and finely chop the onion and carrot. Melt the butter in a saucepan and add the bacon rasher. When the fat begins to run from the bacon, add the onion and carrot, and fry gently for about 5 minutes. Wash and quarter the tomatoes, and add to the ingredients in the pan. Cover and cook gently for about 5 minutes, or until the tomatoes are soft and the juices have been drawn out.

Stir in the stock, a seasoning of salt and pepper, the sugar and lemon juice. Cover with a lid and simmer gently for about 30 minutes. Draw off the heat and rub the sauce through a sieve. Discard the skin and pips and pieces of bacon and return the sauce to the pan. Blend the cornflour and water and stir into the sauce. Bring up to the boil stirring all the time. Simmer for a few moments to get the right consistency and then check the flavour.

Meanwhile cut the ham into thin strips and slice the mushrooms. Sauté the mushrooms lightly in half the butter. About 15 minutes before serving, add the spaghetti to a large pan of boiling salted water. Boil without a lid until tender – about 10 minutes – then drain. Heat the remaining butter in the saucepan, add the spaghetti and toss until glazed. Fold in the ham and mushrooms, and turn into a hot dish. Pour the tomato sauce over and sprinkle generously with grated cheese.

Canneloni with Tomato Sauce

Serves 4 Time taken 45 minutes

8 squares canneloni pasta	tomato sauce (see page 171)

For the Stuffing

1 small onion	1 tablespoon finely chopped parsley
25 g (1 oz) butter	1 lightly beaten egg
225 g (8 oz) cooked meat	
salt	50–75 g (2–3 oz) grated Parmesan
freshly milled pepper	cheese
1 level tablespoon flour	

When cooking large pieces of pasta such as canneloni or lasagne, it is advisable to add 1 tablespoon of oil to the cooking water. This helps prevent the pieces from sticking together. Tomato sauce for recipes like this can be kept ready-made in the home freezer.

Prepare the stuffing for the canneloni. Peel and finely chop the onion. Melt the butter in a saucepan, add the onion and fry gently, covered with a lid, until the onion is soft. Meanwhile mince the cooked meat finely. Add the onion and any butter in the pan to the meat (a little finely chopped garlic may be added at this stage if liked). Season well with salt and pepper, and stir in the flour and parsley. Add sufficient lightly beaten egg to bind the mixture together, set aside until ready to use.

Add the canneloni to a pan of boiling salted water. Reboil and simmer gently for 15 minutes. When cooked, drain immediately in a colander and separate the pieces. Cool until they can be handled easily. Using lightly floured hands, shape spoonfuls of the meat mixture into eight sausage shapes. Roll up each one in a square of cooked canneloni.

Spoon a little of the prepared tomato sauce into a fireproof serving dish. Place the canneloni in the dish in rows and top with remaining sauce. Sprinkle with grated cheese and place above centre in a hot oven (200°C, 400°F or Gas No. 6) and heat through until bubbling hot and brown.

Serve with a little extra cheese.

Spanish Omelette

Serves 4 Time taken 30 minutes

8 eggs	3 medium-sized onions
salt	2–3 green peppers
freshly milled pepper	2 tablespoons oil
4 tomatoes	50 g (2 oz) butter

Crack the eggs into a basin and whisk thoroughly with a fork. Add a seasoning of salt and freshly milled pepper and set aside while preparing the vegetables.

Nick the skins of the tomatoes and place in a basin. Cover with boiling water, allow to stand for 1 minute, then drain and peel away the skins. Slice the tomatoes evenly. Peel and slice the onions. Halve, deseed and shred the green peppers.

Heat the oil in a frying pan and add the onions and peppers, fry gently for about 8–10 minutes until both are soft but not brown. Draw the pan off the heat and add the pepper and onion mixture to the beaten eggs. Leave behind as much of the oil in the pan as possible. Add the tomatoes to the mixture.

Melt a quarter of the butter in a small frying pan or omelette pan over moderate heat and, when bubbling hot, ladle in a quarter of the egg and vegetable mixture. Fry gently over the heat, and, as the egg sets at the edge of the pan, draw the mixture back gently with the prongs of a fork to allow some of the mixture on the surface to run underneath. Repeat this several times until the omelette is set but still moist. Repeat the procedure until all four omelettes are made.

Serve at once, with a salad, and fried potatoes or hot toast.

Devilled Scrambled Egg

Serves 4 Time taken 15–20 minutes

8 eggs	1 level teaspoon dry mustard
1·5 dl (¼ pint) single cream	½ teaspoon Worcestershire sauce
1 level teaspoon salt	75 g (3 oz) butter
freshly milled pepper	225 g (8 oz) button mushrooms

Scrambled eggs with added seasoning and flavouring can become a speciality. Crack the eggs into a mixing basin, add the cream, salt, pepper, mustard and Worcestershire sauce. Beat well to mix and set aside.

Heat half the butter in a frying pan over a low heat. Strain in the egg mixture and stir over a moderate heat. Stir occasionally but not constantly, drawing the mixture away from the base of the pan as it thickens. Continue until the mixture is set but still a little moist and then draw off the heat.

Meanwhile, fry the mushrooms separately in the remaining butter. Draw the pan off the heat and serve the scrambled egg with the mushrooms.

Cheese Soufflé

Serves 4 Time taken 1 hour

25 g (1 oz) butter	100 g (4 oz) grated Cheddar cheese
25 g (1 oz) flour	½ level teaspoon made mustard
1·5 dl (¼ pint) milk	6 large eggs
salt	
freshly milled pepper	paprika pepper

Melt the butter in a large saucepan over a low heat. Stir the flour into the hot butter and cook over low heat for 1 minute but do not allow to brown. Gradually stir in the milk, beat well to make a smooth sauce. Bring up to the boil, stirring all the time. At this stage the mixture will be very thick. Cook gently for 1–2 minutes, then draw off the heat and add salt and pepper to taste. Add the grated cheese and mustard. Replace over low heat and stir until the cheese has melted and the mixture is smooth, draw off the heat and check the seasoning. Allow the mixture to cool until the hand can be held comfortably against the side of the pan.

Crack the eggs one at a time, placing the whites together in a large basin and beating the yolks thoroughly into the cheese mixture. Finally add a pinch of salt to the whites and whisk until stiff. Using a metal tablespoon, first fold 2 tablespoons of the beaten whites into the cheese sauce to lighten the mixture, then, using a gentle cutting movement, fold in the remaining beaten whites.

Pour into an ungreased generous 1-litre (2-pint) soufflé dish. The mixture should fill the dish. Scrape a palette knife over the top of the mixture, smoothing the surface level and sealing the edges against the sides of the dish. This gives a level top to the soufflé. Wipe the sides of the soufflé dish clean and place it at once in the centre of a pre-heated moderate oven (180°C, 350°F or Gas No. 4) and bake for 45 minutes. The soufflé should be well-risen and firm but still slightly soft in the centre. Remove from the heat, dust with paprika pepper and serve at once.

Spinach with Eggs and Cheese

Serves 4 Time taken 30 minutes

4 eggs	1 (350 g) (12 oz) packet frozen
450 g (1 lb) fresh spinach	spinach
or	

For the Cheese Sauce

25 g (1 oz) butter	salt and pepper
25 g (1 oz) flour	100 g (4 oz) grated Cheddar cheese
3 dl ($\frac{1}{2}$ pint) milk	

Soft-boil the eggs, then plunge them into cold water and remove the shells. If using fresh spinach, wash well in cold water and remove centre rib from the leaves. Place in a large saucepan, add no water, there will be sufficient clinging to the leaves. Cover with a lid and bring up to the boil. Cook for 10–15 minutes. Drain well, then chop coarsely. Alternatively prepare frozen spinach according to packet directions and leave to heat through while preparing sauce.

Melt the butter over low heat and stir in the flour. Cook gently for 1 minute. Gradually stir in milk and bring to the boil, stirring until thick and smooth. Simmer gently for 2–3 minutes, then season to taste with salt and pepper. Stir in half the grated cheese, and remove the pan from the heat.

Spoon the spinach into base of a heatproof serving dish. Make four hollows in it with the back of a spoon and place a soft boiled egg in each hollow. Pour the cheese sauce over the top. Sprinkle with remaining cheese and grill until bubbling hot and brown.

Chicory with Ham in Cheese Sauce

Serves 4 Time taken 1¼ hours

6–8 heads chicory	6–8 slices cooked ham

For the Cheese Sauce

25 g (1 oz) butter	freshly milled pepper
25 g (1 oz) flour	100 g (4 oz) grated Cheddar cheese
3 dl (½ pint) milk	¼ teaspoon made mustard
salt	

Remove any bruised outer leaves from the chicory. Wash quickly, then, with a pointed knife, remove the hard core at the base of each stalk. Add to boiling salted water and cook for 15–20 minutes, or until just tender. Drain thoroughly and wrap each head of chicory in a slice of cooked ham. Place close together in a well-buttered baking dish and set aside while preparing the sauce.

Melt the butter in a saucepan. Stir in the flour and cook gently for a few moments. Gradually stir in the milk. Bring up to the boil, stirring all the time, until the sauce is thick and smooth. Season to taste with salt and pepper, then, reserving 1 tablespoon of the cheese, stir the remainder into the sauce. Add the mustard to give a spicy flavour. Stir the sauce over the heat, until the cheese has melted and the mixture is smooth. Pour over the chicory and sprinkle with reserved cheese. Place in the centre of a moderately hot oven (190°C, 375°F or Gas No. 5) and bake for about 20 minutes, or until thoroughly heated. Serve hot.

Soufflé au Parfait

Serves 4 Time taken 1 hour

50 g (2 oz) butter	pinch nutmeg
50 g (2 oz) flour	4 eggs
1·5 dl (¼ pint) milk	1 (225 g) (8 oz) tin Swiss pâté
salt	Le Parfait
freshly milled pepper	

Melt the butter in a medium to large saucepan over a low heat. Stir in the flour and cook gently for 1 minute. Gradually beat in the milk, stirring all the time to make a thick sauce. Bring up to the boil, then draw the pan off the heat, add a good seasoning of salt and pepper, and a pinch of nutmeg. Remove the pâté from the tin and cut into chunks. Add to the sauce and stir until melted and blended into the mixture.

Separate the eggs and beat the egg yolks into the soufflé mixture. Whisk the whites in a mixing basin until stiff and, using a metal spoon, fold into the mixture. Pour into a buttered 1-litre (1½-pint) soufflé dish and set in the centre of a moderate oven (180°C, 350°F or Gas No. 4) and bake for 40 minutes.

Serve at once with a tossed salad.

Lasagne

Serves 6 Time taken 3 hours

225 g (½ lb) lasagne	1 egg
225 g (½ lb) fresh ricotta cheese	75–100 g (3–4 oz) grated Parmesan cheese

For the Meat Sauce

1 large onion	freshly milled pepper
1 clove garlic	1 (425 g) (15 oz) tin tomatoes
2 tablespoons oil	1–2 tablespoons tomato purée
450 g (1 lb) lean minced beef	1·5 dl (¼ pint) stock
salt	

Made up dishes like lasagne with layers of meat sauce, and stuffed canneloni, are more effort to prepare. They make excellent party dishes, however, because they are assembled in advance and then reheated for serving.

Start the recipe by preparing the meat sauce. Peel and finely chop the onion. Peel and chop the garlic. Heat the oil in a large saucepan and add the onion. Cover and cook gently for about 5 minutes until the onion is soft. Add the garlic and beef, and fry for a further few minutes, stirring to brown the meat well. Season with salt and pepper. Stir in the contents of the tin of tomatoes, the tomato purée and the stock. Bring up to the boil, then lower the heat, cover and simmer gently for about 1½ hours. The sauce should be fairly thick. When ready, draw the pan off the heat and check the seasoning.

Add the lasagne to a pan of boiling salted water. Boil without a lid until tender – about 15–20 minutes – then drain in a colander and separate the pieces. Meanwhile mix together the ricotta cheese and egg. If preferred sieved cottage cheese may be used instead of ricotta cheese. Have Parmesan cheese handy.

Spoon a little of the meat sauce into the base of a large shallow baking dish. Top with a layer of lasagne. Next, spoon on a layer of ricotta cheese and sprinkle with Parmesan cheese. Repeat, ending with a layer of sauce and sprinkle with the remaining Parmesan cheese. Heat through in a moderate oven (180°C, 350°F or Gas No. 4) for 30–40 minutes, or until bubbling hot and browned. Allow to stand for 5 minutes before serving.

Serve with a tossed salad.

Sautéed Liver with Mushrooms

Serves 4 Time taken: 15–20 minutes

450 g (1 lb) lambs' liver
milk
seasoned flour
50 g (2 oz) butter
225 g (½ lb) button mushrooms

1–2 tablespoons finely chopped
    mixed parsley and chives
juice of ½ lemon

Trim the thinly sliced liver and place in a shallow dish. Add milk to cover and leave to soak for 1 hour. Lift the liver from the milk, drain well and then dip both sides in the seasoned flour. Melt the butter in a frying pan, add the liver and brown quickly on both sides. Lower the heat, add the sliced mushrooms, and the chopped parsley and chives. Cover with a lid and cook gently for 4–5 minutes, shaking the pan occasionally.

When ready, squeeze over the lemon juice and serve.

Stuffed Liver with Bacon

Serves 4 Time taken 1 hour

4 slices lambs' liver
seasoned flour

25 g (1 oz) vegetable fat
4 lean bacon rashers

For the Stuffing
1 small onion
65 g (2½ oz) fresh white
    breadcrumbs
25 g (1 oz) shredded beef suet

½ level teaspoon salt
pinch mixed herbs
1 tablespoon chopped parsley
1 small egg

Trim and wash the liver, pat dry and dip both sides in seasoned flour. Trim the bacon rashers, set them in a cool place while preparing the stuffing.

Peel and finely chop the onion. Mix together the breadcrumbs, onion, suet, salt, mixed herbs, parsley and lightly beaten egg. Stir with a fork to make a moist crumbly consistency. Spoon a quarter of the stuffing on each piece of liver, press on firmly and cover with a bacon rasher.

Melt the fat in a small roasting tin. When hot add the slices of liver and cover with a buttered paper. Place the tin in the centre of a moderate oven (180°C, 350°F or Gas No. 4) and bake for 30 minutes or until the liver is tender.

Serve with a rich brown sauce.

Omelette Fines Herbes

Serves 4 Time taken 15 minutes

8 eggs	salt
1 tablespoon water	freshly milled pepper
4 tablespoons chopped fresh herbs	60 g (2 oz) butter

'Fines herbes' consist of chopped fresh parsley, chervil and tarragon. They add a particularly good flavour to an omelette.

Crack the eggs into a basin and add the water. Whisk with a fork to break up the eggs, and then add the herbs and a seasoning of salt and pepper. Cut the butter into 15-g (½-oz) pieces.

For each omelette, place one piece of the butter in an omelette or small frying pan, and heat until melted and frothy. Add a quarter of the egg mixture and stir for a moment over a moderate heat. Then stop stirring and start just drawing the edge of the omelette into the centre of the pan with a fork so that the liquid egg runs underneath. Do this two or three times at separate places, then, when the egg is set but still a little soft in the middle, draw off the heat. Loosen the edges and fold both opposite sides into the centre. Tap the pan to loosen the omelette and shake so that the omelette slides over to the edge of the pan opposite the handle, Fold both edges of the omelette into the centre. Push the omelette to the far side of the pan ready to turn out. Quickly turn the pan over on to a plate so that the omelette falls out with folded edges underneath. Serve at once.

Start immediately preparing the next omelette.

Kidneys in Sherry Sauce

Serves 4 Time taken 30 minutes

8 lamb kidneys	salt
50 g (2 oz) butter	freshly milled pepper
1 medium-sized onion	2 tablespoons dry sherry
1 rounded tablespoon flour	
3 dl (½ pint) chicken stock	chopped parsley

Using scissors, snip out the core from each kidney. Remove any skin and cut the kidneys in half. Melt half the butter in a frying pan; when hot, add the kidneys and fry gently for 2–3 minutes. Remove the kidneys from the pan and keep hot. Peel and chop the onion. Add the remaining butter to the pan together with the onion. Fry gently until the onion is tender and a little brown. Replace the kidneys in the pan and sprinkle with the flour. Stir to blend the flour with the butter, and then stir in the hot stock. Mix well and bring up to the boil stirring all the time. Still stirring, simmer for about 5 minutes. When no red juices flow from the kidneys they are cooked through; by this time too the sauce will be a rich brown. Check the seasoning and stir in the sherry. Pour into a hot serving dish and sprinkle with chopped parsley.

Serve with plain boiled rice.

Fried Lambs' Sweetbreads

Serves 4 Time taken 1½ hours

450 g (1 lb) lambs' sweetbreads	brown breadcrumbs
salt	50 g (2 oz) butter
chicken stock (see recipe)	4–8 rashers bacon
1 egg	

Soak the sweetbreads for several hours in cold water, changing the water once or twice. This soaking extracts the blood and helps to keep the sweetbreads white. Rinse and place the sweetbreads in a saucepan. Cover with fresh cold salted water and bring up to the boil. Draw off the heat and drain the sweetbreads. When cool enough to handle, remove all fat, loose tissue and skin. Replace the sweetbreads in the pan and add chicken stock to cover. Bring up to the boil, lower the heat and simmer for 45 minutes, or until sweetbreads are tender. Drain and press the sweetbreads between two plates. Leave until cold.

Cut large sweetbreads in half at an angle. Dip first in beaten egg and then roll in brown breadcrumbs to coat. This may be done in advance. Melt the butter in a frying pan, add the sweetbreads and fry gently for about 5 minutes, turning to brown them evenly. Meanwhile arrange the trimmed bacon rashers under a preheated grill to cook.

Serve the sweetbreads and bacon together.

4 Casseroles

Stewing or casseroling implies long slow moist cooking with a measured quantity of liquid in a pan or casserole with a tight-fitting lid. Cooking can be done either on top of the cooker or in the oven. Either way the liquid should simmer gently and never boil, since this toughens the meat. The amount of liquid used should be such that the flavours and nutrients extracted from the meat and any added vegetables are retained and served in a gravy with no waste. A small quantity of liquid can be used, provided the pan has a tight-fitting lid. There will be only a small amount of evaporation and little risk of scorching, if the cooking is gentle.

In a brown stew the meat is tossed in seasoned flour; this should not be thrown away but retained for thickening the gravy at a later stage. The meat pieces are browned in hot fat; this seals the outside of the meat, helping to retain the juices and moisture during cooking, and gives the finished casserole a more appetizing appearance. After this, some of the seasoned flour should be added to the hot fat in the pan and cooked gently until quite brown before the liquid is stirred in. This again gives the liquid a good colour but, if not sufficient, gravy browning may be added.

A 'blanquette' is usually prepared with veal, chicken or rabbit. In this case the meat, with the exception of chicken, is blanched in boilding water to keep the flesh white. Then the meat is simmered in a light stock. Often it is thickened at a later stage with egg yolks or cream, which are added to enrich the recipe.

Flavouring can be added in the form of a bouquet garni; this is simply a bay leaf, some parsley stalks and a spring of thyme tied together in a bundle with a long thread which should be attached to the pan handle for easy removal afterwards. Garlic can be added if the outer papery coating is removed from the clove and then the clove well crushed with salt. Shredded green peppers, small whole blanched onions, sliced mushrooms and even a little sweetness in the form of soaked prunes are nice.

Use a light flavoured stock made by using a chicken cube, or a mixture of wine and stock, sometimes with tomatoes added. Cider is pleasant used in pork recipes, and in some recipes meat or game is marinated in wine beforehand and then the marinade is added at a later stage, as part of the liquid in the recipe. With vegetables added, single stews and casseroles make complete meals in one dish.

When meat is braised it should be cooked first by browning and then in the oven with a bed of flavouring vegetables under the meat, and just enough stock to keep the meat moist. In this case the bed of vegetables is only for flavouring the liquid and not part of the final recipe. The gravy is nearly always thickened separately at a later stage with more expensive vegetables, such as mushrooms or courgettes, added before serving.

Cast-iron casseroles are excellent for stews, casseroles or braising. The meat can be browned in the pan over direct heat and then later cooked in the oven. Cooking stains can be removed from the outside of the casserole before serving by using a damp corner of a teacloth and a little salt as an abrasive.

All casseroles like these can be cooked in advance. When reheated they should be brought up to simmering. Where a recipe is enriched with egg or cream, or extra ingredients are added for garnish, leave this final stage until ready to serve.

Braised Pheasant in Wine

Serves 4 Time taken 1½–2 hours

1 plump pheasant	25 g (1 oz) flour
75 g (3 oz) butter	salt
2 medium onions	freshly milled pepper
2 carrots	100 g (¼ lb) buttum mushrooms
3 dl (½ pint) white wine	
bouquet garni	chopped parsley
stock	

Although generally accepted that tender young game birds are best roasted, pheasant which tends to have a fairly dry flesh can be braised or casseroled with very good results.

Wipe the pheasant and truss into a neat shape. Cut the legs short so that the bird will fit into a casserole dish. Heat 25 g (1 oz) of the butter in a large, fireproof casserole, add the pheasant and brown well on all sides. Peel and slice the onions and carrots. Lift the pheasant from the pan and add the prepared onions and carrots to the hot fat. Fry gently until the vegetables are slightly softened and the onion a little brown. Replace the pheasant in the casserole, add the white wine and the bouquet garni. Cover with a lid and place in the centre of a moderately hot oven (190°C, 375°F or Gas No. 5) and cook for 1 hour.

When the pheasant is cooked, lift from the pan, cool slightly and then divide into serving portions. Strain the cooking liquid from the pan and discard the vegetables. Make the liquid up to 4·5 dl (¾ pint) with hot stock made from water and a chicken stock cube. Return the liquid to the casserole. Blend 25 g (1 oz) of the remaining butter with the flour to make a *beurre manié*. Add in small pieces to the hot liquid and stir until melted. Replace over the heat and bring up to the boil, stirring until thickened and smooth. Check the seasoning and then replace the pheasant pieces in the casserole. Trim and slice the mushrooms, and add to the remaining butter melted in a frying pan. Fry for a few moments, then add to the contents of the casserole. Reheat thoroughly, then sprinkle with chopped parsley and serve.

Chicken with Lemon

Serves 4 Time taken 1½–2 hours

1 (1·5 kg) (3 lb) chicken	1 tablespoon oil
salt	2 carrots
freshly milled pepper	few parsley stalks
1 medium onion	pinch saffron
25 g (1 oz) butter	6 dl (1 pint) boiling water

For the Sauce

25 g (1 oz) butter	1·5 dl (¼ pint) double cream
25 g (1 oz) flour	2 egg yolks
3 dl (½ pint) stock	juice of ½ lemon
salt	
freshly milled pepper	few slices of lemon

Joint the chicken into eight pieces. Trim neatly and season well with salt and pepper. Peel and slice the onion. Heat the butter and oil in a large frying pan, add the onion and fry gently until softened but not brown. Peel and slice the carrots. Add to the pan and arrange the chicken pieces on top. Add the water to almost cover the chicken pieces, the parsley stalks and the saffron. Bring up to the boil, then lower the heat until just simmering. Cover with a lid and leave to cook for 1 hour.

When the chicken is cooked, lift the pieces from the pan, place in a hot serving dish and keep warm. Strain the liquid from the pan into a bowl. Skim away as much fat from the surface of the stock as possible, and then measure out 3 dl (½ pint) of the stock.

Melt the butter for the sauce in a saucepan and stir in the flour. Cook for a few moments then gradually stir in the measured stock. Bring up to the boil, stirring well all the time to get a smooth sauce. Check the seasoning and allow to cook gently for 1–2 minutes. Meanwhile blend the cream and egg yolks in a basin. Draw the saucepan off the heat, stir in the blended eggs and cream, and the lemon juice. Strain the sauce over the chicken pieces.

Garnish the dish with a few slices of fresh lemon and serve.

Chicken with Barbecue Sauce

Serves 4 Time taken 1½ hours

1 (1·5 kg) (3 lb) chicken	1 green pepper
salt	4 tablespoons tomato ketchup
freshly milled pepper	2 tablespoons wine vinegar
50 g (2 oz) butter	50 g (2 oz) soft brown sugar
1 tablespoon oil	1 teaspoon made mustard
2 onions	1 tablespoon Worcestershire sauce

Joint the chicken into eight pieces. Trim neatly and season with salt and pepper. Turn on the oven heat to hot (200°C, 400°F or Gas No. 6) and heat half the butter in a large roasting pan. When hot add the chicken pieces. Turn each piece of chicken in the hot butter and baste well. Replace in the oven and allow the chicken to roast for about 30 minutes. Turn the pieces occasionally to encourage them to brown.

Meanwhile melt the remaining butter and the oil in a large saucepan. Peel and thinly slice the onions. Halve, deseed and shred the green pepper. Add to the pan, stir to mix with the butter and then cover with a lid. Fry over gentle heat for about 10 minutes, or until the vegetables are soft. Mix together the tomato ketchup, wine vinegar, soft brown sugar, mustard and Worcestershire sauce in a basin. When the vegetables are soft, add the contents of the basin to the pan. Stir well to mix, bring up to the boil and then draw off the heat.

Remove the chicken pieces from the oven and pour away the hot fat in the pan. Pour over the barbecue sauce. Lower the oven heat to moderate (180°C, 350°F or Gas No. 4). Replace the chicken joints in the oven and continue roasting at the lower temperature, basting frequently, for a further 30 minutes.

Serve hot with rice pilaff and salad.

Coq au Vin

Serves 4 Time taken 1½–2 hours

1 (1·5 kg) (3 lb) chicken
seasoned flour
75 g (3 oz) butter
100 g (¼ lb) lean bacon rashers
450 g (1 lb) small onions
1 shallot
1 clove garlic
1–2 tablespoons brandy
3 dl (½ pint) red wine

3 dl (½ pint) chicken stock
225 g (½ lb) button mushrooms
1 teaspoon tomato purée
bouquet garni
salt
freshly milled pepper
25 g (1 oz) plain flour

chopped parsley

Joint the chicken into eight pieces. Trim neatly and roll in seasoned flour. Melt 50 g (2 oz) of the butter in a large frying pan. Trim and chop the bacon, add the bacon pieces and fry gently until the bacon fat runs. Add the chicken pieces and fry to seal and brown on all sides. Remove the chicken pieces from the pan and reserve. Add the peeled, whole onions and fry gently to brown, then add the finely chopped shallot and finely chopped garlic. Replace the chicken pieces in the pan, add the brandy and flame. Shake the pan to spread the flames. When they subside, add the red wine. Turn the contents of the pan into a casserole. Add the stock, mushrooms, tomato purée and bouquet garni. Season with salt and pepper, and cover with a lid. Place in the centre of a moderate oven (180°C, 350°F or Gas No. 4) and cook for 1 hour.

Lift the cooked chicken pieces, the onions, mushrooms and the pieces of bacon from the pan to a hot serving dish. Remove the bouquet garni. Pour the liquid into a saucepan. Blend the remaining butter and flour together to make a *beurre manié* and add to the liquid in small pieces. Stir until melted, then place the pan over the heat and bring up to the boil, stirring until the sauce has thickened. Check seasoning and strain over the chicken. Sprinkle with chopped parsley and serve.

Chicken Paprika

Serves 4 Time taken 1–1½ hours

1 (1·5 kg) (3 lb) chicken
salt
freshly milled pepper
1 onion
25 g (1 oz) butter
1 level teaspoon paprika

4·5 dl (¾ pint) chicken stock
1 tablespoon tomato purée
1·5 dl (¼ pint) single cream
1 rounded tablespoon flour
juice of ½ lemon

Joint the chicken into eight pieces. Trim neatly and season with salt and pepper. Peel and finely chop the onion. Melt the butter in a large frying pan and add the onion. Fry gently for about 5 minutes, until the onion is soft but not brown. Stir in the paprika and 1·5 dl (¼ pint) of the stock. Add the chicken pieces to the pan, allow the mixture to come to the boil, then lower the heat, cover with a lid and simmer gently for about 45 minutes. Turn the chicken pieces occasionally.

Lift the pieces of cooked chicken from the pan into a hot serving dish. Add the remaining stock and tomato purée to the pan and reheat. Pour the cream into a small basin and sift the flour over the surface. Whisk to blend the cream and flour; there should be no lumps. Stir this into the hot liquid in the pan. Cook over moderate heat, stirring all the time, until the mixture has thickened and comes to the boil. Add the lemon juice and simmer gently for 5 minutes. Pour over the chicken pieces. Serve with plain boiled rice.

Beef Goulash

Serves 4–6 Time taken 3–3½ hours

700 g–1 kg (1½–2 lb) lean stewing
  steak
450 g (1 lb) onions
25 g (1 oz) dripping
1 clove garlic
1 level teaspoon caraway seeds
1 rounded tablespoon paprika

1 level tablespoon flour
1 (425 g) (15 oz) tin tomatoes
salt
freshly milled pepper
3 dl (½ pint) stock
2–3 tablespoons soured cream

Wipe the meat, trim and cut away the fat. Cut the meat into neat pieces. Peel and slice the onions. Melt the dripping in a saucepan, and when hot add the meat. Fry quickly to seal the meat on all sides, and then remove the meat from the pan. Add the onions to the hot fat and fry gently to soften them. Stir occasionally and then allow them to brown.

Peel the clove of garlic and pound with the caraway seeds, then add to the onions in the pan, along with the paprika and the flour. Stir well to mix, and then add the tinned tomatoes, a seasoning of salt and pepper, and the stock. Stir well and bring up to the boil. Replace the meat in the pan. Lower the heat and cover with a lid. Simmer very gently for 2½ hours, or until the meat is quite tender. If preferred, the ingredients can be turned into a casserole and cooked in a slow oven (150°C, 300°F or Gas No. 2) for 2½–3 hours. Stir in the soured cream at the last minute. Serve with plain boiled noodles tossed in butter.

Casserole of Beef with Prunes

Serves 4 Time taken 2½–3 hours

700 g (1½ lb) lean stewing steak	salt
seasoned flour	freshly milled pepper
50 g (2 oz) dripping	1 tablespoon tomato purée
2 medium onions	8 soaked prunes
225 g (½ lb) new carrots	
6 dl (1 pint) stock	chopped fresh parsley

Trim away any fat or gristle and cut the meat into neat pieces. Roll in seasoned flour. Heat the dripping in a frying pan, add the meat and brown evenly on all sides. Lift the meat from the pan and place in a casserole dish. Peel and finely chop the onions. Peel and slice the carrots. Add these to the casserole.

Stir 1 tablespoon of the seasoned flour into the hot fat remaining in the frying pan. If necessary, add a little extra fat to absorb the flour. Cook, stirring all the time, over moderate heat, until the mixture is well browned. Gradually stir in the hot stock and bring up to the boil. Check seasoning and stir in the tomato purée. Draw the pan off the heat and strain the gravy over the contents of the casserole dish.

Cover the casserole with a tight-fitting lid and place in the centre of a slow oven (150°C, 300°F or Gas No. 2), and cook for 2½ hours. About 1 hour before the end of the cooking time add the drained prunes. (If tenderized prunes are used, add about 30 minutes before the end of the cooking time since they cook more quickly.) Re-cover the casserole and continue to cook until meat, vegetables and prunes are tender.

Sprinkle with chopped parsley and serve.

Sweet and Sour Pork

Serves 4 Time taken 1½–2 hours

1 (1 kg) (2½ lb) piece pork sparerib	4 tablespoons vinegar
50 g (2 oz) vegetable fat	75 g (3 oz) soft brown sugar
2 medium onions	1 tablespoon soy sauce
1 large green pepper	¼ level teaspoon salt
1 (350 g) (12 oz) tin pineapple chunks	2 level tablespoons cornflour

Pork sparerib or pork tenderloin are the best cuts to buy for this kind of recipe. The meat requires to be fairly lean.

Strip away the pork rind, and, removing any bone, cut the meat into small, neat chunks. Discard any fat and sinew. Heat half the fat in a frying pan, add the pieces of meat and fry gently to seal on all sides. Meanwhile peel and slice the onions and halve, deseed and shred the green pepper. Melt the remaining fat in a large saucepan and add the prepared vegetables. Cover, and cook gently to soften but not brown the onion. Drain all the fat away from the pork and add the pieces of meat to the softened vegetables.

Drain the pineapple chunks from the tin, reserving the juice. Make the juice up to 3 dl (½ pint) with water. Add the juice to the pork and vegetables, together with the pineapple pieces. Add the vinegar, sugar, soy sauce and salt to the pan. Stir to mix and bring up to the boil. Cover and simmer gently for about 1 hour, or until the pork is tender.

Blend the cornflour with a little water to make a thin paste. Add a little of the hot liquid from the pan. Stir and then pour into the saucepan. Bring back to the boil, stirring gently until the sauce has thickened and is clear.

Serve with plain boiled rice.

Blanquette of Veal

Serves 4 Time taken 2 hours

700 g (1½ lb) boneless stewing veal	4 dl (¾ pint) chicken stock
1 onion	salt and pepper
1–2 carrots	1 small bay leaf

For the Sauce

50 g (2 oz) butter

25 g (1 oz) plain flour

3 dl (½ pint) cooking liquor

100 g (¼ lb) button mushrooms

2 egg yolks

2 tablespoons cream

Discard any skin or fat and cut the meat into neat chunks. Blanch by adding to boiling water, simmer for 2 minutes, then drain – this preserves the light colour of the meat. Peel and thinly slice the onion and carrots. Place these in the base of a large saucepan, add the meat, stock, a seasoning of salt and pepper, and the bay leaf. Bring up to the boil, skim if necessary, then lower the heat, cover with a lid and simmer gently for 1½ hours until the meat is tender. Draw off the heat, remove the bay leaf and strain the liquor, reserving it for the sauce. Keep the meat and vegetables hot.

Melt 25 g (1 oz) of the butter for the sauce in a saucepan and stir in the flour. Cook gently for 1 minute, then gradually stir in 3 dl (½ pint) of the hot cooking liquor. Bring up to the boil, stirring all the time – add a little more stock if necessary to make a fairly thin sauce. Check seasoning and add the meat and vegetables. Draw the pan off the heat. Trim the mushrooms and fry for 2–3 minutes in the remaining 25 g (1 oz) of butter. Add to the meat then stir in the blended egg yolks and cream. Reheat but do not boil.

Serve with plain boiled rice.

Casserole of Chicken

Serves 4 Time taken 1½–2 hours

1 (1·5 kg) (3 lb) chicken

seasoned flour

50 g (2 oz) butter

3 onions

2–3 green peppers

225 g (½ lb) tomatoes

salt

freshly milled pepper

1 teaspoon castor sugar

1·5 dl (¼ pint) chicken stock

Joint the chicken into eight pieces. Trim neatly and roll in seasoned flour. Add to the hot butter melted in a frying pan. Brown on both sides, then lift the pieces of chicken into a casserole.

Peel and slice the onions. Halve, deseed and shred the green peppers. Add these to the hot fat in the pan. Cover and fry gently for about 10 minutes to soften them. Meanwhile nick the skins of the tomatoes and place in a basin. Cover with boiling water, allow to stand for 1 minute, then drain and peel away the skins. Slice the tomatoes and add to the chicken joints in the casserole together with the softened onions and peppers. Season with salt and pepper and add the sugar. A little added sugar gives a slight sweetness to the vegetables which is nice. Add the stock to the casserole. Cover with a lid, place in the centre of a moderate oven (180°C, 350°F or Gas No. 4) and cook for 1 hour.

Serve the chicken joints with the cooked vegetables and juice from the casserole.

Oxtail with Whole Onions

Serves 4   Time taken 5–6 hours

1 jointed oxtail	6 dl (1 pint) stock
salt	salt
freshly milled pepper	freshly milled pepper
1 bay leaf	1 (65 g) (2½ oz) tin tomato purée
450 g (1 lb) small onions	juice of ½ lemon
450 g (1 lb) carrots	
25 g (1 oz) dripping	chopped parsley
2 level tablespoons flour	

Oxtail needs long, slow cooking to make it really tender and it is ready when the meat falls away from the bones.

Wipe the oxtail and place in a large saucepan. Cover with cold water, add a good seasoning of salt and pepper, and the bay leaf. Bring up to the boil, skim away any froth that appears on the top of the water, cover with a lid and then simmer gently for 2 hours.

Peel the onions, leaving them whole. Place in a saucepan with cold water to cover and bring up to the boil. Simmer for 5 minutes then drain. Peel and thickly slice the carrots. Reserve these vegetables until the oxtail is ready. Lift the oxtail from the pan and strain and reserve the stock. Allow the stock to stand for 5 minutes. (The partly cooked oxtail and stock can be left to stand overnight if it is more convenient.)

Using a ladle or spoon, skim off the surface layer of fat and measure off 6 dl (1 pint) of the stock. Place the onions, carrots and oxtail in a large casserole.

Melt the dripping in a saucepan and add flour, continue frying gently to brown the flour. Gradually stir in the measured pint of stock and bring up to the boil. Season with salt and pepper, stir in the tomato purée and lemon juice. Strain over the oxtail and vegetables in the casserole, cover with a lid and place in the centre of a slow oven (170°C, 325°F or Gas No. 3) and cook for a further 2½–3 hours.

Sprinkle with chopped parsley and serve.

Navarin of Lamb

Serves 4 Time taken 2–2½ hours

1 kg (2–2½ lb) neck of lamb	bouquet garni
seasoned flour	4·5 dl (¾ pint) stock
50 g (2 oz) butter	1 (65 g) (2½ oz) tin tomato purée
1 medium onion	salt
450 g (1 lb) new carrots	freshly milled pepper

For the Garnish

6 button onions	225 g (½ lb) green peas, shelled
12 new potatoes	chopped parsley

A casserole of sweet young lamb with new spring vegetables makes a perfect combination.

Trim the meat into neat pieces. Dip each piece in seasoned flour and then fry in the hot butter to brown on all sides. Fry the pieces, a few at a time, and then lift the meat from the pan and place in a casserole dish. Peel and slice the onion. Scrape and slice the carrots. Add to the casserole along with the bouquet garni. Sprinkle about 1 tablespoon of the seasoned flour into the hot fat remaining in the frying pan and cook gently until beginning to brown. Gradually stir in the hot stock and the tomato purée, and mix well until boiling. Strain over the ingredients in the casserole dish. Add a good seasoning of salt and pepper. Cover with a lid, place in the centre of a slow oven (170°C, 325°F or Gas No. 3) and cook for 1½ hours.

Meanwhile peel the button onions leaving them whole, place in a saucepan and cover with cold water. Bring up to the boil, simmer for 2 minutes, then drain. About 40 minutes before serving remove the bouquet garni from the casserole. Add the scraped new potatoes, the blanched small onions and the shelled green peas. Re-cover and finish cooking time.

Sprinkle with chopped parsley before serving.

Lamb Cutlets Shrewsbury

Serves 4 Time taken 2 hours

8 lamb cutlets	4 tablespoons redcurrant jelly
15 g (½ oz) vegetable fat	2 tablespoons Worcestershire sauce
100 g (¼ lb) button mushrooms	freshly milled pepper
juice of 1 lemon	pinch ground nutmeg
1 level tablespoon flour	
1·5–3 dl (¼–½ pint) stock	chopped parsley
salt	

Trim the excess fat from the cutlets. Heat the fat in a frying pan, then brown the cutlets on both sides in the hot fat. Trim and slice the mushrooms. Remove the cutlets from the pan and place in a casserole dish with the mushrooms. Measure the redcurrant jelly, Worcestershire sauce and lemon juice into a saucepan. Stir over low heat until the jelly has melted and the ingredients blended. Stirring with a whisk often helps the redcurrant jelly to soften. Draw off the heat.

Add the flour to the hot fat remaining in the frying pan, if necessary add an extra nut of fat to help absorb the flour. Stir over low heat for about 10 minutes, until the mixture has turned a golden brown. Stir in first the jelly mixture, and then sufficient stock to make a thick gravy. Bring up to the boil stirring all the time to get the mixture smooth. Taste and season with salt, pepper and nutmeg. Strain the gravy over the cutlets. Cover and place in a moderately slow oven (170°C, 325°F or Gas No. 3) and cook for 1½ hours.

Sprinkle with parsley and serve the cutlets in the spicy rich gravy.

Meat Balls in Gravy

Serves 4 Time taken 1½–2 hours

450 g (1 lb) minced beef	seasoned flour
1 onion, finely chopped	4·5 dl (¾ pint) stock
salt	2 teaspoons tomato purée
freshly milled pepper	1 level tablespoon cornflour
2 thin slices of white bread	1 teaspoon vinegar
1–2 tablespoons milk	
1 egg	chopped parsley
50 g (2 oz) butter	

Place the minced beef and finely chopped onion together in a bowl, and add a good seasoning of salt and pepper. Trim the crust from the break and place the bread slices in a small basin. Add the milk and allow the bread to soak for a few minutes, then squeeze away excess moisture. Add the squeezed bread to the meat along with the egg. Mix the ingredients, preferably with the hands, to make a soft well-blended mixture. With slightly oiled fingers shape the mixture into twelve small meat balls.

Melt the butter in a frying pan. Roll the meat balls in seasoned flour and add to the hot fat. Fry to brown them on all sides, shaking the pan gently so that they keep a neat round shape. Lift the meat balls from the pan and place in a fireproof casserole. Pour away the fat from the frying pan and add the stock and tomato purée to the hot pan. Stir to mix well and bring up to the boil. Pour over the meat balls. Cover the casserole and either simmer the meat balls over very low heat, or place in a slow oven (150°C, 300°F or Gas No. 2), and cook gently for 1 hour.

When ready to serve, blend the cornflour with a little water to make a smooth paste. Place the casserole over direct heat and stir in the blended cornflour. Stir gently to blend the ingredients, then bring up to the boil. Check seasoning and then add the vinegar to sharpen the flavour.

Sprinkle with chopped parsley and serve.

Carbonnade of Beef

Serves 6 Time taken 3 hours

6 large onions	freshly milled pepper
50 g (2 oz) butter	6 dl (1 pint) light ale
1 kg 200 g (2½ lb) lean stewing steak	1 tablespoon brown sugar
	1 teaspoon vinegar
1 rounded tablespoon flour	slices of French bread
salt	French mustard

Peel and slice the onions. Melt half the butter in a saucepan, add the onions and fry gently for about 15 minutes, or until soft and golden brown. Trim the meat and cut into pieces. Melt the remaining butter in a large frying pan and add the meat. Fry gently, turning the meat to brown on all sides. Sprinkle with the flour, stir to blend and season with salt and pepper. Gradually add half the ale and bring to the boil stirring well. Draw off the heat. Spoon half the fried onions into the base of a large casserole dish. Add the meat and the liquid from the frying pan. Top with the remaining onions and add the remaining ale to just cover the meat. Add the sugar, cover with a lid and place in the centre of a slow oven (170°C, 325°F or Gas No. 3) and cook for 2½ hours.

About 45 minutes before the cooking time is complete, bring the casserole out of the oven. Stir in the vinegar and place a few slices of French bread spread with French mustard on top of the meat. Put in as many slices, mustard-side up, as the casserole will allow. Push the bread down into the meat gravy; the pieces will rise again to the surface. Replace the casserole in the oven without the lid; this allows the layer of bread to become crisp and golden brown. Complete the cooking time and serve.

Chicken with Pineapple

Serves 4 Time taken 1½ hours

1 (1·5 kg) (3 lb) chicken
seasoned flour
50 g (2 oz) butter
1 onion
1 green pepper

1 (450 g) (1 lb) tin pineapple chunks
2 tablespoons brown sugar
2 tablespoons vinegar
4 tablespoons tomato ketchup
juice of ½ lemon

Joint the chicken into eight pieces. Trim and roll in seasoned flour. Melt the butter in a frying pan, add the chicken pieces and fry gently, turning to brown on all sides. Lift the chicken pieces from the pan and place in a casserole. Peel and finely slice the onion. Halve, deseed and shred the green pepper. Add these to the hot fat in the frying pan, cover and fry gently for about 10 minutes, or until the onion and peppers are soft but not brown. Add these to the chicken in the casserole.

Drain the syrup from the pineapple chunks. Measure the syrup and make up to 3 dl (½ pint) with water. Reserve the pineapple for adding later. Pour the syrup into a saucepan, add the sugar, vinegar and tomato ketchup. Stir to blend and bring to the boil. Pour over the chicken in the casserole and cover with a lid. Place in the centre of a moderate oven (180°C, 350°F or Gas No. 4) and bake for 1 hour. About 15 minutes before cooking time is complete, add the pieces of pineapple, and lemon juice to taste. Return to the oven and complete cooking time.

Serve with plain boiled rice.

Beef Curry

Serves 4 Time taken 2½ hours

1 kg (2 lb) lean stewing steak
25 g (1 oz) butter
2 medium onions
1 clove garlic
3–4 level tablespoons curry
    powder
1 level tablespoon flour

4·5 dl (¾ pint) stock
1 rounded tablespoon mango
    chutney
1 rounded tablespoon brown sugar
juice of ½ lemon
salt
freshly milled pepper

In this recipe for beef curry, the raw meat is cooked in the curry sauce and has a very good flavour. It can be prepared in advance and reheated.

Trim the meat, cut into neat pieces and place in a casserole dish. Heat the butter in a saucepan. Slice the onion and add to the pan. Fry gently for a few moments to soften, then stir in the finely chopped garlic and the curry powder. Sauté very gently for a further 5 minutes to draw out the oils and flavour from the curry powder. Stir in the flour and then the stock. Bring to the boil, add the chutney, sugar, lemon juice and seasoning of salt and pepper.

Draw off the heat and pour the curry sauce over the meat, cover the casserole, place in a slow oven (170°C, 325°F or Gas No. 3), and cook for 2 hours, or until the meat is tender.

Serve with plain boiled rice.

Chilli con Carne

Serves 4 Time taken 3½ hours

700 g (1½ lb) lean stewing steak	3 dl (½ pint) stock
2 tablespoons oil	1 (425 g) (15 oz) tin peeled tomatoes
1 medium onion	½ teaspoon salt
1 clove garlic	1 teaspoon castor sugar
1 level tablespoon chilli powder	1 (425 g) (15 oz) tin red kidney
2 level tablespoons flour	beans

This is a variation of a chilli con carne recipe that has been adapted for cooking in the oven.

Trim the meat, discarding any fat, and cut into neat pieces. Heat the oil in a large frying pan. Peel and slice the onion and add to the pan. Fry gently for about 5 minutes until the onion is soft. Crush the garlic clove, remove the outer papery coating and chop the garlic finely. Add the garlic to the onions along with the meat. Fry for a further few minutes to brown the pieces of meat. Mix together the chilli powder (use less if a milder flavour is preferred) and the flour. Sprinkle over the meat and onions, and stir to blend. Gradually stir in the hot stock. Blend well and bring up to the boil.

Draw the pan off the heat, and tip the contents into a casserole dish. Add the contents of the tin of tomatoes, the salt and sugar. Cover with a lid and place in the centre of a slow oven (170°C, 325°F or Gas No. 3) and cook for 3 hours, or until the meat is tender. About 15 minutes before the end of the cooking time, add the drained kidney beans.

Serve with plain boiled rice.

Beef Stroganoff

Serves 4 Time taken 20–30 minutes

450 g (1 lb) fillet or sirloin steak
1 onion
225 g (½ lb) button mushrooms
50 g (2 oz) butter
salt

freshly milled pepper
1 carton (1·5 dl) (¼ pint) sour cream

chopped parsley

For the beef stroganoff use top quality meat that is suitable for quick frying. Cook the vegetables in the butter first to avoid overcooking the meat. Then add the meat, finish the recipe quickly.

Trim the steak and cut into thin strips about 5 cm (2 inches) by 1 cm (½ inch). Peel and finely chop the onion. Trim and slice the mushrooms. Melt 25 g (1 oz) of the butter in a large frying pan and add the onion. Fry gently for a few minutes until the onion is softened, then add the mushrooms and fry for 2–3 minutes to cook them. Drain these vegetables from the pan and keep warm.

Add the remaining butter to the pan and add the steak. Fry quickly, stirring with a spoon, to seal and cook the meat on all sides – about 3–4 minutes, or to your own taste. Replace the onion and mushrooms in the pan, and season well with salt and pepper. Lower the heat and stir in the sour cream. Reheat thoroughly but do not boil, then sprinkle with chopped parsley.

Serve at once with plain boiled rice, and perhaps ratatouille which goes very well with the stroganoff, and a salad.

Casserole of Pigeons

Serves 4 Time taken 2½ hours

4 pigeons, cleaned and drawn
75 g (3 oz) butter
225 g (½ lb) new carrots
2 medium onions
225 g (½ lb) button mushrooms
bouquet garni

2 pieces finely pared lemon rind
6 dl (1 pint) chicken stock
25 g (1 oz) flour
salt
freshly milled pepper
juice of ½ lemon

Remove any feathers and stubbly bits from the pigeons and put the birds into 25 g (1 oz) melted butter in a large casserole. Fry for 5–10 minutes, turning to brown on all sides. Remove the casserole from the heat and pour off the hot butter. Scrape and slice the carrots, and peel and slice one onion, and add to the casserole. Trim the mushroom stalks (reserving caps) and put the mushroom stalks in the casserole with the bouquet garni and lemon rind. Pour in the stock and cover with a lid. Cook in the centre of a very moderate oven (170°C, 325°F or Gas No. 3) for 1½ hours, or until the birds are tender.

When cooked, lift the pigeons from the casserole and strain the cooking liquor. Reserve both the liquor and vegetables. Using a sharp knife, cut down each side of the breatbone of each pigeon, and gently lift away the breast flesh. Replace these in the casserole. Remove the bouquet garni and lemon rind, and return the vegetables to the casserole.

Melt half the remaining butter in a saucepan. Peel and finely chop the remaining onion. Add to the pan, cover and cook gently for 5 minutes to soften. Stir in the flour and continue to cook uncovered, until the mixture becomes a nutty brown colour; this takes about 15 minutes. Stir occasionally to prevent scorching. Gradually stir in the reserved cooking liquor, beating well all the time to get a smooth, thin sauce. Bring to the boil, and simmer for about 5 minutes, stirring occasionally. Melt the rest of the butter and quickly fry the sliced mushroom caps. Add these to the casserole.

Check the seasoning in the sauce and add lemon juice. Strain the sauce over the contents of the casserole. Replace in the oven to heat through, and serve.

Casserole of Kidneys in Red Wine

Serves 6 Time taken 2 hours

6–8 lambs' kidneys	1·5 dl (¼ pint) red wine
225 g (½ lb) chipolata sausages	1 (65 g) (2½ oz) tin tomato purée
2 medium onions	salt
50 g (2 oz) butter	freshly milled pepper
1 level tablespoon flour	225 g (½ lb) mushrooms
4·5 dl (¾ pint) stock	1 small packet frozen peas

Remove any fat from around the kidneys and remove the skin. Snip out the core from each using scissors and then cut the kidneys in half. Separate the sausages. Peel and slice the onions. Melt the butter in a frying pan and add the onions. Fry gently for about 5 minutes, or until onions are soft and a little brown. Add the kidneys and sausages, and fry for a further few moments to brown. Remove from the heat and transfer the contents of the pan to a casserole.

Stir the flour into the hot fat remaining in the frying pan and cook gently for a few moments to brown the flour. Stir in the stock, red

wine and tomato purée. Season well with salt and pepper and bring
to the boil. Draw off the heat and strain over the contents of the
casserole. Cover with a lid and place in the centre of a moderate oven
(180°C, 350°F or Gas No. 4) and cook for 1½ hours. Trim and slice
the mushrooms. About 15 minutes before the end of the cooking
time, add the mushrooms and peas. Replace in the oven and complete
cooking time.

Beef Olives

Serves 4 Time taken 2½–3 hours

4 thin slices of rump steak	1·5 dl (¼ pint) stock
seasoned flour	1 tablespoon sherry
25 g (1 oz) dripping	1 level tablespoon cornflour
2 carrots	salt
2 onions	freshly milled pepper
bouquet garni	

For the Stuffing

25 g (1 oz) butter	little grated lemon rind
100 g (4 oz) mushrooms	salt
50 g (2 oz) fresh breadcrumbs	freshly milled pepper
1 tablespoon chopped parsley	

Trim the meat, then place each piece in turn between wetted squares
of greaseproof paper and beat out flat with a rolling pin. The wetted
paper helps prevent the meat sticking to the rolling pin. Set aside and
prepare the stuffing.

Melt the butter in a saucepan. Trim and coarsely chop the mushrooms. Add to the pan and fry gently for 2–3 minutes. In a small
basin, mix together the breadcrumbs, parsley and lemon rind. Add
the mushrooms and butter from the pan, then, using a fork, blend in
the ingredients and season well with salt and pepper.

Divide the stuffing into four portions and place one portion on each
piece of meat. Roll each piece of meat neatly, enclosing the stuffing
inside. Tie neatly like a parcel with fine string and roll each one in
seasoned flour.

Melt the dripping in a large saucepan, add the beef olives and fry
to brown on all sides. Lift the meat from the pan. Peel and slice the
carrots and onions. Add to the hot fat and fry for a few moments until
the onion softens. Replace the beef olives on top of the vegetables.
Add the bouquet garni and the stock, which should just cover the

vegetables. Cover with a lid and simmer gently for 1½–2 hours.

When cooked, lift out the beef olives, remove the string and keep warm. Strain the cooking liquid and discard the vegetables. Measure about 3 dl (½ pint) of the liquid and return to the pan. Stir in the sherry and the cornflour which has been blended with a little cold water, to make a thin paste. Bring back up to the boil, stirring all the time. Check the seasoning, pour over the meat and serve.

Lamb Chops with Pineapple

Serves 4 Time taken 1¼ hours

4 chump chops of lamb	freshly milled pepper
salt	1 (225 g) (8 oz) tin pineapple rings

Trim the chops neatly and season both sides with salt and pepper. Arrange in a casserole dish and top each one with a ring of pineapple. Spoon over a little of the juice from the tin, and cover the casserole with a lid.

Place in the centre of a moderate oven (180°C, 350°F or Gas No. 4) and cook for 1 hour. To serve top each chop with a pineapple ring and then spoon a little juice from the casserole over it.

Moussaka

Serves 4 Time taken 1 hour

1 large onion	2 teaspoons tomato purée
5–6 tablespoons olive oil	1·5 dl (¼ pint) stock
450 g (1 lb) minced lean beef	4 aubergines
1 level teaspoon salt	175 g (6 oz) grated hard cheese
freshly milled pepper	

For the Sauce

25 g (1 oz) butter	salt
25 g (1 oz) flour	freshly milled pepper
3 dl (½ pint) milk	1 egg

Peel and finely chop the onion. Heat 1 tablespoon of the oil in a saucepan. Add the onion, cover and fry gently to soften for 5 minutes. Add the minced beef and fry gently to brown, then stir in the seasoning, tomato purée and stock. Bring up to the boil, cover with a lid and simmer gently for 30 minutes.

Meanwhile peel and slice the aubergines, and fry lightly in the remaining oil. Aubergines soak up a fair amount of oil, and extra may need to be added to the pan as they cook.

Arrange a layer of cooked aubergines in the base of a large fireproof casserole and sprinkle with a little of the cheese. Cover with a second layer of aubergines and more cheese, reserving a little for the top. Top with the meat mixture and a final layer of aubergines.

Melt the butter for the sauce over low heat and stir in the flour. Cook gently for 1 minute, then gradually stir in the milk beating well all the time. Bring up to the boil, season with salt and pepper, and simmer for 1–2 minutes. Draw off the heat and beat in the egg. The addition of egg helps the sauce to form a topping that remains on the surface of the Moussaka. Pour the sauce over the Moussaka. Sprinkle with the remaining cheese. Place the casserole in the centre of a moderate oven (180°C, 350°F or Gas No. 4) and bake for 30–35 minutes, or until bubbling hot and browned.

Serve with a tossed green salad.

Pork Chops with Tomato and Green Pepper Sauce

Serves 4 Time taken 1½ hours

4 sparerib pork chops	salt
seasoned flour	freshly milled pepper
15 g (½ oz) dripping or vegetable fat	1 tablespoon Worcestershire sauce
1 onion	juice of ½ lemon
1 green pepper	1 level desertspoon castor sugar
1 (425 g) (15 oz) tin tomatoes	1·5 dl (¼ pint) stock

Trim any fat that is extra, from the chops and dip both sides of the meat in seasoned flour. Add to the hot fat in a frying pan, brown quickly on both sides, then lift the chops from the pan and place in a casserole dish.

Peel and slice the onion. Deseed and shred the green pepper. Add the onion and green pepper to the hot fat in the pan, and fry gently for about 5 minutes, stirring occasionally until the onions are softened. Stir in the contents of the tin of tomatoes and a good seasoning of salt and freshly milled pepper. Stir in the Worcestershire sauce, lemon juice, sugar and the stock. Bring up to the boil, then draw the pan off the heat and pour the contents over the pork chops.

Cover with a lid and place the casserole in the centre of a moderate oven (180°C, 350°F or Gas No. 4) and bake for 1 hour. Serve the pork chops with the vegetables and sauce spooned from the casserole.

5 Roasts

Roasting is one of the most traditional methods used for cooking meat, poultry and game. Originally the term implied spit-roasting in front of an open fire, but this has been superseded by cooking in a tin in the oven.

Meat chosen for roasting should be of good quality and well hung. Less tender cuts, or very small joints, can be pot roasted. In this case the meat is cooked in a covered container, with liquid added and simmered gently over direct heat or in the oven. The longer, more moist, cooking keeps the meat juicy and makes it tender.

The presence of a certain amount of fat in the meat gives flavour and keeps it moist during roasting. Joints should be lightly greased with a little dripping, lard or vegetable fat before going into the oven. The traditional method is to 'sear' or cook the meat at a higher temperature (230°C, 450°F or Gas No. 8) for a short time – usually about 15 minutes – then reduce the heat to moderately hot (190°C, 375°F or Gas No. 5) for the remainder of the cooking time. A hot oven seals the surface, browning it and closing in the natural juices. Basting is the accepted procedure for protecting the outside of the meat while it cooks through. The melted fat from the tin, spooned over the joint from time to time, forms a screen, filtering the heat so that the joint cooks under the best conditions. Where possible the joint should be placed on a stand in the roasting tin or on a bed of vegetables so that it cooks above the level of any juices or gravy which might drain from the meat. A few scraped carrots and a peeled onion, cut in thick slices and placed in the roasting tin, allow the heat to reach all surfaces of the joint evenly. Low temperature roasting at 170°C, 325°F or Gas No. 3 is excellent for small and stuffed joints and for cheaper cuts of meat, and is very good for turkey or any joint over 2 kg 250 g (5 lb) in weight, where the long cooking time required makes a 'seared' outside thick and hard. Low temperature roasting is not suitable for pork since the meat requires to be thoroughly cooked, nor for small chickens. Both of these produce better results when roasted at a higher temperature.

After taking the roast out of the oven (with the exception of venison) allow it to stand for 10–15 minutes. The flesh carves more easily and retains more juices this way, and, so long as the skin is not broken (this applies to chicken or turkey in particular) or the meat carved, the joint will not lose its heat.

Beef is nicest slightly underdone; lamb is also nice underdone but is more often well done – never overcook or it becomes dry. Veal, pork and venison should all be well done. Chicken and turkey should be well cooked but not overcooked; juices coming from the birds still tinged with pink indicate that more cooking is needed.

How to Make Good Gravy

Gravy is an important accompaniment for any roast meat, poultry or game. Stock is required for all gravies and should be made from poultry giblets or a stock cube or vegetable cooking water.

For a thin gravy to serve with roast meat or game, strain off all the fat from the roasting tin, but tip back into the tin any flavouring vegetables or crispy brown bits. Add 6 dl (1 pint) of stock or vegetable water. Stir and bring to the boil, and boil briskly until reduced by half. Taste and correct the seasoning. Strain into a hot sauce-boat; skim away any fat that rises to the surface. Makes 3 dl (½ pint).

For a thick gravy to serve with roast meat or poultry strain off all but 1 tablespoon of the fat from the roasting tin and stir in 1 tablespoon flour – sufficient to absorb all the fat in the pan. Stir over the heat until the flour has absorbed all the fat, and browned. Stir in 6 dl (1 pint) stock or vegetable cooking water. Bring up to the boil stirring well all the time to get a smooth gravy. Cook for 2–3 minutes after boiling. Taste and correct seasoning, and strain into a hot gravy boat. Makes 6 dl (1 pint).

There is an interesting variation on the method of making gravy for a roast. Before the meat is put to roast, place 1 tablespoon of flour in the centre of the roasting pan. Place the joint of meat (or chicken) on top and put the dripping in the tin. Roast in the usual manner basting the joint. During the cooking the flour absorbs juices from the meat and combines with the dripping in the pan to become a dark brown colour. When the meat is done, lift out of the tin. Pour off excess fat and, stirring or whisking well, add 6 dl (1 pint) of stock or vegetable cooking water to the pan. Bring to the boil, stirring well, simmer for 2–3 minutes. Strain into a hot gravy-boat and serve. Makes 6 dl (1 pint).

ROAST MEAT
Roast Best End of Lamb

Serves 3 Time taken 1½ hours

1 piece best end of lamb with 6–7 cutlets	bed of roasting vegetables
1 clove garlic	15–25 g (½–1 oz) vegetable fat or dripping
seasoned flour	

A roast best end of lamb makes an excellent small mid-week joint.

The butcher will skin and chine the joint for you to make it easier to carve. Wipe the joint with a clean damp cloth, then rub the surface all over with a cut clove of garlic. Dredge a little seasoned flour over the fatty part of the meat, and rub it well in to get a crisper, golden finish.

Place the joint of meat in a roasting tin on a bed of roasting vegetables. Add a little vegetable fat or dripping, place the meat in the centre of a moderate oven (180°C, 350°F or Gas No. 4) and roast for about 1¼ hours. Lamb is better roasted slowly, it gives a more juicy and succulent joint. Baste occasionally after 30 minutes' cooking time.

When the joint is ready, lift on to a heated plate and keep hot. To make a thin gravy, pour away the fat from the roasting tin, leaving only the dark pan drippings and the flavouring vegetables. Place the tin over direct heat and allow to become very hot. Add about ·25 litre (1 teacupful) of cold water. The mixture will boil furiously, the purpose of this being to let the water evaporate and reduce slightly. Swirl the mixture round the tin and stir so that all the bits are mixed in. Boil for a moment, then draw off the heat and check the seasoning. Strain into a hot gravy boat. Carve the lamb into cutlets.

Serve with the gravy, French beans and new potatoes.

Roast Loin of Lamb Persillé

Serves 6 Time taken 2–2½ hours

1 (1·5–2 kg) (3½–4 lb) loin of lamb
salt
1 clove garlic
100 g (4 oz) butter

8 rounded tablespoons fresh white
   breadcrumbs
4 tablespoons finely chopped parsley
grated rind and juice of ½ lemon

Wipe the joint with a clean damp cloth, then season with salt ready for roasting. Using the tip of a knife, make small incisions under the skin of the joint at intervals over the surface. Remove the outer papery coating from the clove of garlic and cut the garlic into thin slivers. Insert these into the small cuts, pushing them under the skin. Place the meat in a roasting tin and spread half the butter over the skin. Place in the centre of a moderate oven (180°C, 350°F or Gas No. 4) and roast for 1½ hours, basting occasionally.

In the meantime, melt the remaining butter and mix it with the white breadcrumbs, parsley and grated lemon rind in a small basin. When the roasting time is complete, remove the pieces of garlic from the joint and squeeze the lemon juice over the surface of the joint. Press the breadcrumb mixture over the surface of the joint to form a crust. Turn the oven heat up to hot (200°C, 400°F or Gas No. 6) and replace the joint in the oven for a further 20 minutes, or until the covering is golden brown and crisp.

Serve roast lamb prepared this way with a gravy made using the pan drippings.

To carve, cut down between each chop.

Roast Beef with Yorkshire Pudding

Serves 4–6 Time taken 2–2½ hours

1 (1–1·5 kg) (2–3 lb) piece of top
   rump or topside

dripping or lard
bed of roasting begetables

For the Yorkshire Pudding
100 g (4 oz) plain flour
pinch salt
1–2 eggs

3 dl (½ pint) mixed milk and water
25 g (1 oz) dripping or lard

Sirloin and wing rib on the bone, or boned and rolled, can be used for this recipe. Top rump and topside are the choice pieces of beef for roasting.

Wipe the meat and spread lightly with a little dripping or lard. Place extra fat in the roasting tin. Set the joint on a bed of roasting vegetables, place in the centre of a very hot oven (220°C, 425°F or Gas No. 7) and roast for 15 minutes. Lower the heat to moderately hot (190°C, 375°F or Gas No. 5) and roast for the remaining cooking time, allowing 15 minutes per 450 g (1 lb) plus 15 minutes for a rare roast, and 20 minutes per 450 g (1 lb) plus 15 minutes for a well-done joint. Baste frequently. Any roast vegetables, such as potatoes or parsnips, should be blanched in boiling water for 5 minutes, then well-drained and placed around the joint. Give them at least 1 hour of cooking time in the oven and baste frequently.

While the roast is cooking, prepare the batter for the Yorkshire pudding. Sieve together the flour and salt into a basin. Make a well in the centre, add the egg and about half the liquid. (Use liquid in the proportion of two-thirds milk and one-third water.) Using a wooden spoon, mix from the centre, gradually drawing in the flour from the edges of the basin. Mix to a smooth batter, then gradually stir in the remaining milk. Pour into a jug and leave until ready to cook.

About 40 minutes before the end of the cooking time raise the oven heat to very hot (220°C, 425°F or Gas No. 7). Place the joint lower down in the oven. Put the lard or dripping in an ovenproof dish or small roasting tin and heat on the top shelf in the oven until smoking hot. Quickly pour in the batter all at once. Replace in the oven and cook for about 40 minutes, or until risen and crisp.

Rolled Stuffed Breast of Lamb

Serves 4 Time taken 2–2½ hours

1 (1 kg) (2 lb) piece of breast of lamb
lemon juice
freshly milled pepper

seasoned flour
bed of roasting vegetables

For the Stuffing
1 small onion
½ cooking apple
15 g (½ oz) butter
225 g (½ lb) pork sausage meat
2 heaped tablespoons fresh white
  breadcrumbs

1 heaped teaspoon finely chopped
  parsley
pinch powdered rosemary
2 tablespoons lightly mixed egg

For the Gravy
3 dl (½ pint) cider
1 tablespoon honey

1 rounded teaspoon cornflour

When pennies have to be counted, it is useful to know how to make the most of the cheaper cuts of meat. Rolled, stuffed breast of lamb makes a good meal for four.

Skin and slice through the centre of the meat and cut away the small bones. Trim away lean meat adhering to the bones, chop and reserve for adding to the stuffing. Sprinkle the inside of the meat with a little lemon juice and freshly milled pepper. Set aside while preparing the stuffing.

Peel and chop the onion and apple. Melt the butter in a saucepan and add the onion and apple. Sauté gently for a few moments, until the onion is softened but not brown. Add the sausage meat and stir over gentle heat for 4–5 minutes. Draw the pan off the heat, and stir in the breadcrumbs, parsley, rosemary and beaten egg to bind. Mix well. Spread the stuffing evenly over the meat. Roll the meat up neatly, but not tightly, and secure with string. Rub in a little seasoned flour over the surface. Put the prepared meat into a roasting tin on a bed of roasting vegetables. Slow roast in a very moderate oven (170°C, 325°F or Gas No. 3) for 1½ hours.

Lift out the meat and pour away the fat from the roasting pan. Bring the cider to the boil and stir in the honey. Replace the meat in the tin and pour the cider over. Return to a moderately hot oven (190°C, 375°F or Gas No. 5) and roast for a further 20 minutes, basting occasionally with the cider and honey mixture. Lift the meat from the pan on to a hot serving dish. Strain off the liquor into a saucepan. Blend the cornflour with a little water and stir into the pan. Bring to the boil, check the seasoning and serve as a gravy.

Roast Lamb en Croute

Serves 6–8 Time taken 3–4 hours

1 boned shoulder of lamb	salt
100 g (¼ lb) small mushrooms	freshly milled pepper
25 g (1 oz) butter	225 g (½ lb) homemade puff pastry
2 tablespoons finely chopped parsley	egg and milk for glazing

Ask the butcher to bone the shoulder of lamb. Wipe the meat and set aside while preparing the stuffing.

Trim and finely chop the mushrooms and add to the hot butter in a frying pan along with the chopped parsley. Fry quickly for a few moments just to cook the mushrooms lightly. Draw off the heat and season with salt and pepper. Spoon the mushroom mixture (leaving any juices behind in the pan) into the pocket in the joint where the bone has been removed. Pack the mixture evenly, then roll the joint to close it, and tie securely with string. Place in a roasting tin with a little extra dripping or cooking fat, and roast in a moderate oven (180°C, 350°F or Gas No. 4) for 1½ hours. Remove from the oven and set the joint aside until quite cold. Then remove the string and cut away any excess fat from around the joint.

Roll the pastry out to an oblong a little longer than, and four times the width of, the joint. Trim the edges of the pastry with a sharp knife, and then cut across into two pieces of one-third and two-thirds. Place the joint, with any open edges downwards, on the larger piece of pastry. Fold the pastry upwards to cover the sides of the meat, and fold up any ends. The joint should now be covered with pastry except for the top. Roll the remaining strip of pastry a little longer so that it is long enough to cover the top and overlap the ends of the meat. Damp the edges of the pastry around the joint with a little beaten egg and milk. Place on the second piece of pastry to cover the top of the joint and the ends. Press all edges well together to seal and completely cover the meat. Use any pastry trimmings to decorate the top. Brush the whole joint with beaten egg and milk, and set aside until ready to cook. Then place above centre in a very hot oven (220°C, 425°F or Gas No. 7) and bake for 30 minutes, or until the pastry is golden brown.

Serve sliced. Any that is left over can be used cold.

Roast Fillet of Beef with Mustard Butter

Serves 8 Time taken 2–2½ hours

1 (1 kg) (2½ lb) piece beef fillet	25–50 g (1–2 oz) butter

For the Mustard Butter

100 g (4 oz) butter	squeeze of lemon juice
1 teaspoon made mustard	
1 tablespoon finely chopped parsley	watercress

This is a joint to prepare for a dinner party. It is easy to carve and there is very little waste.

Ask your butcher to cut the piece of meat from the thick end of the fillet if possible. Then ask him to trim away all excess fat and tie the meat into a neat shape. Since all the fat has been removed from the joint, the meat must be protected during roasting with extra fat, otherwise the meat will dry in the oven heat and spoil. For this reason ask for a little of the trimmed fat for roasting the meat, or, on the other hand, the butcher may lard the joint for you. This means that he will tie a thin strip of fat over the joint, which you leave on during roasting, but remove before serving.

Place the prepared joint in a roasting tin with the butter. If not larded, cover with the extra pieces of beef fat. Place in the centre of a preheated slow oven (170°C, 325°F or Gas No. 3) and roast for 1 hour for a rare joint or 1½ hours for a medium rare. Baste often to keep the meat moist. This is a very tender cut of meat and is nicest rare or undercooked.

Meanwhile prepare the mustard butter. Cream the butter in a mixing basin until soft. Add the mustard – use English mustard for the best flavour – parsley and a squeeze of lemon juice. Spoon the butter on to a square of kitchen foil, shape into a fat roll and then twist the ends up like a cracker. Chill until firm.

Remove the string and the added pieces of fat from the joint. Place the meat on a heated serving platter, garnish with watercress at each end. Unwrap and slice the chilled mustard butter. To serve, simply cut the meat into thick slices and top each portion with a pat of mustard butter.

Beef Pot Roast

Serves 4–6 Time taken 2½–3 hours

1 kg (2–2½ lb) rolled brisket of beef	bouquet garni
seasoned flour	1·5 dl (¼ pint) stock
25 g (1 oz) dripping	25 g (1 oz) butter
2 onions	1 tablespoon finely chopped parsley
2 large carrots	1 level tablespoon cornflour
salt and pepper	2 tablespoons cold water

The best cuts to use for pot roasting are rolled brisket, topside or silverside.

Wipe the meat and roll in the seasoned flour. Melt the dripping in a large saucepan, add the meat and brown on all sides. Lift the meat from the pan and set aside. Peel and slice the onions and peel and slice the carrots. Add the onions and carrots to the hot fat, and fry for a few moments to brown lightly. Season with salt and pepper, then replace the meat in the pan on top of the vegetables. Add the stock – there should be sufficient to just cover the vegetables. Add the bouquet garni, cover with a lid and simmer gently, allowing 30–40 minutes per 450 g (1 lb) and 30 minutes extra. Add a little extra stock during cooking time if necessary.

When cooked, lift the meat from the pan on to a hot serving dish. Strain the cooking liquor from the vegetables, make up to 4·5 dl (¾ pint) with extra stock, and pour into a saucepan. Blend the cornflour with the water. Stir in a little of the hot cooking liquor from the saucepan, blend well and return all to the saucepan. Bring up to the boil, stirring all the time. Check the seasoning. Pour into a gravy boat and serve with the pot roast.

Baked Gammon with Cherry Sauce

Serves 4 Time taken 1½ hours
Soak gammon for 24 hours

1 (1 kg) (2½ lb) piece of gammon corner	Demerara sugar

For the Flour and Water Paste

450 g (1 lb) plain flour	3 dl (½ pint) water

For the Cherry Sauce

1 (450 g) (1 lb) tin cherries	1 level tablespoon cornflour
25 g (1 oz) sugar	1 tablespoon water
1 tablespoon vinegar	

One of the traditional methods of cooking gammon is to bake it in a flour and water paste. Using this method, all the gammon juices are retained.

Soak the gammon for 24 hours in cold water to cover, changing the water several times during soaking – this removes excess salt, necessary when gammon is to be baked. Drain and wipe dry, and set aside while preparing a flour and water paste.

Sieve the flour into a mixing basin and make a well in the centre. Add the water all at once and mix to a rough dough. Turn out on to a floured board and knead lightly. Roll the dough out evenly to a circle large enough to enclose the joint of gammon. Place the gammon with the rind downwards in the centre of the dough, then wrap the dough firmly around to enclose the gammon completely. Moisten the edges with water and press firmly together to seal. Place in a greased roasting tin with sealed edges underneath and bake in the centre of a moderate oven (180°C, 350°F or Gas No. 4), allowing the usual baking time for gammon, that is 20 minutes per 450 g (1 lb) plus

20 minutes extra, and an additional 15 minutes for the heat to penetrate the flour and water crust.

Meanwhile prepare the cherry sauce, using black cherries or stoned
morello cherries. Strain the cherries, stone them if necessary, and
place in a saucepan. Measure the juice and make up to 3 dl ($\frac{1}{2}$ pint)
with water. Add the juice, sugar and vinegar to the cherries. Place
the pan over moderate heat and stir until the sugar has dissolved.
Blend the cornflour and water in a small bowl, stir in a little of the hot
cherry juice, blend well, and return it all to the saucepan. Stir over
low heat until the mixture thickens and comes to the boil. Draw off
the heat.

When the gammon is baked, crack the flour and water crust open
and lift out the gammon joint. Using a sharp knife, strip away the
rind and mark the fat in a criss-cross pattern. Coat the surface of the
fat with Demerara sugar and replace the gammon in a hot oven for
about 15 minutes to glaze the surface.

Serve the gammon with the cherry sauce.

Crown Roast of Lamb

Serves 6 Time taken 2–2$\frac{1}{2}$ hours

1 crown roast of lamb	25–50 g (1–2 oz) dripping
salt	1 small tin apricot halves
freshly milled pepper	mint jelly

For the Stuffing

25 g (1 oz) soaked dried apricots	1 tablespoon chopped walnuts
$\frac{1}{2}$ cooking apple	rind of $\frac{1}{2}$ lemon
65 g (2$\frac{1}{2}$ oz) fresh white breadcrumbs	25 g (1 oz) melted butter

A crown roast of lamb consists of two pieces of best end of lamb
chined and then tied or sewn together in the shape of a crown. A
space in the centre is left for the stuffing. The butcher will prepare
this for you.

Place the joint in a large roasting tin. Season with the salt and
pepper, and wrap a small piece of foil round the top of each rib to
prevent it from scorching during cooking. Place in the roasting tin
and set aside while preparing the stuffing.

Using a pair of scissors, snip the apricots up fairly small. Peel,
core and chop the apple. Combine together the apricots, breadcrumbs, apple, nuts and finely grated lemon rind. Then, using a fork,
mix in the melted butter.

Pack the stuffing into the middle of the crown roast. Place with a little dripping in the roasting pan. Put in the centre of a moderate oven (180°C, 350°F or Gas No. 4) and roast for 1½ hours.

When cooked, remove the pieces of foil and top each rib with a cutlet frill, and garnish the dish with drained apricot halves filled with mint jelly.

To carve, cut down between the rib bones and allow two chops per person.

Roast Veal with Orange

Serves 6–8 Time taken 3½–4 hours

1·5 kg (3½ lb) shoulder or best end
  of veal
salt and freshly milled pepper
75 g (3 oz) butter

bed of roasting vegetables
1 small bay leaf
3 dl (½ pint) dry cider
1 level dessertspoon cornflour

For the Stuffing
50–75 g (2–3 oz) streaky bacon
25 g (1 oz) butter
pinch thyme
1 rounded teaspoon finely chopped
  parsley
50 g (2 oz) seedless raisins
1 small egg
grated rind and juice of ½ orange

1 small onion
50 g (2 oz) fresh white breadcrumbs
½ level teaspoon salt
¼ level teaspoon pepper
pinch ground mace or nutmeg
bunch watercress

Ask the butcher to bone the joint. Sprinkle the inside with seasoning and set aside while preparing the stuffing.

Trim and chop the bacon finely, and cook gently in the butter for a few moments. Peel and chop the onion. Add to the pan and cook for another few minutes until the onion is soft but not browned. Draw off the heat and, using a fork, stir in the breadcrumbs, thyme, parsley and raisins. Lightly mix the egg with the grated orange rind, orange juice and seasoning. Add to the stuffing and mix to make a moist mixture.

Pack the stuffing over the inside of the meat and roll up neatly. Tie with string and spread half the softened butter over the joint. Place the joint on a bed of roasting vegetables. Add the bay leaf, the remaining butter and half the cider. Cover with foil, place in the centre of a moderately hot oven (190°C, 375°F or Gas No. 5) and roast for 30 minutes per 450 g (1 lb) and 30 minutes extra. After 1 hour, turn the joint and baste well. Re-cover and return to the oven. Half an hour before serving remove the foil, turn the joint again, pour in the remaining cider and baste well. Return to the oven for the remaining cooking time.

When cooked, lift the veal from the pan and place on a hot serving dish. Keep warm while preparing the gravy. Blend the cornflour with 2–3 tablespoons of water and pour into the roasting tin with the vegetables and juices from the meat. Bring to the boil stirring all the time. Season with salt and pepper, and strain into a hot sauce boat.

Garnish with watercress, and serve with the gravy.

Roast Pork with Baked Apples

Serves 4–6 Time taken 2–2½ hours

1 (1–1·5 kg) (2¼–3 lb) piece pork sparerib	4–6 cooking apples sugar
salt	butter
25–50 g (1–2 oz) lard or white vegetable fat	

Check the weight of the joint to calculate the cooking time, and make sure that the rind is well scored. Wipe the joint and rub the skin over with salt. Set in a roasting tin with the lard. Place in the centre of a hot oven (220°C, 425°F or Gas No. 7) to seal the joint. Baste with the hot fat and, when the fat begins to spit, lower the heat to moderate (180°C, 350°F or Gas No. 4). Roast, allowing a total time of 35 minutes per 450 g (1 lb) plus 35 minutes extra.

Select even-sized apples and allow 1 apple per person. Wash and core the apples keeping them whole. Run round the centre of each apple with the tip of a sharp knife just cutting the skin. This allows the apples to bake without bursting. Set them close together in a baking or roasting tin. Place 2 teaspoons of sugar in each one and a nut of butter on top. Add 1 tablespoon of water to the pan. Place in the hot oven along with the roast for the last hour of cooking time. When ready, the apples should be quite soft. Raise the oven temperature for the last 10 minutes or so to get a crisp crackling on the pork. Dish up the meat and then prepare a thickened gravy with the pork drippings.

Serve the pork with the gravy and baked apples.

Roast Gammon with Crackling

Serves 6–8 Time taken 1½ hours

1 (2 kg) (4 lb) piece Danish
  unsmoked gammon corner

This is one of the easiest roast joints to prepare. If a mild cured, unsmoked gammon joint is used there is no need to soak it.

Wash and dry the gammon. Using a sharp knife, score the rind in a criss-cross diagonal pattern. Wrap the joint tightly in kitchen foil and place in a roasting tin. The foil should remain round the joint for the first 20 minutes of cooking time to help keep the shape of the joint. Where a strung bacon or gammon joint is being roasted, the foil will not be necessary. Place the gammon in the centre of a moderate oven (180°C, 350°F or Gas No. 4) and roast, allowing 20 minutes per 450 g (1 lb) plus 20 minutes extra. After the first 20 minutes cut the foil open, using a knife, and pull the foil back so that it does not cover the gammon. There is no need to remove the foil from the pan.

Replace the gammon in the oven for the remaining cooking time, basting once or twice with the drippings and juices in the pan. Increase the oven to hot (220°C, 425°F or Gas No. 7) for the last 15 minutes to brown the fat. When the cooking time is complete, remove the joint from the tin; the crackling should be brown and crisp.

Serve the gammon hot, with fresh green vegetables and new potatoes. Any that is left over is delicious cold with a salad.

ROAST POULTRY
Butter Roast Chicken with Herbs

Serves 4 Time taken 1¼ hours

1 (1·5 kg) (3 lb) oven-ready chicken   freshly milled pepper
75 g (3 oz) butter   fresh parsley and chives
salt   1 clove garlic

Wipe the chicken and remove the giblets from the inside. Cream 50 g (2 oz) of the butter with a seasoning of salt and freshly milled pepper, plenty of fresh chopped parsley and chives and a little piece of crushed, chopped garlic. Spoon inside the bird and close the tail-end of the bird with a skewer.

Place the chicken on its side in a roasting tin, spreading the exposed surface with the remaining butter. Place in the centre of a hot oven

(200°C, 400°F or Gas No. 6). After 20 minutes baste the bird, turn over on to the other side and baste again. After a further 20 minutes turn the bird breast upwards, baste again and roast for a last 20 minutes – 1 hour in all.

Carve and serve with the herb-flavoured butter spooned from inside over each portion.

Chicken Pot Roast
Serves 6 Time taken 2–2½ hours

1 (2 kg) (4 lb) oven-ready chicken	1 tablespoon vegetable oil
salt	100 g (¼ lb) lean bacon rashers
freshly milled pepper	12 button onions
50 g (2 oz) butter	1 kg (2 lb) potatoes

For the Stuffing

chicken liver	100 g (4 oz) sausage meat
1 tablespoon fresh white breadcrumbs	chopped parsley
1 tablespoon chopped parsley	

Remove the giblets from the chicken and reserve the chicken liver. Season the inside and outside of the chicken with salt and pepper. Set aside while preparing the stuffing.

Mash the chicken liver with a fork and mix with the sausage meat, breadcrumbs and chopped parsley. Place the stuffing inside the bird, pull the neck skin over and under the chicken, securing it with the wing tips under the bird.

Heat the butter and oil in the casserole and lightly brown the chicken on all sides. Meanwhile, trim away the rind and cut the bacon into small dice. Peel the onions leaving them whole. Place them together in a saucepan, cover with cold water and bring up to the boil. Drain and then add to the chicken with the bacon. Cover with a lid and cook over a gentle heat for about 15 minutes. Peel and dice the potatoes. Add to the pan, turning the potatoes in the fat. Re-cover with the lid and place the casserole in a moderate oven (180°C, 350°F or Gas No. 4) and cook for 1 hour.

Lift the chicken from the casserole and carve into slices. Gently toss the cooked potatoes, onions and bacon in the juices in the casserole. Sprinkle with salt and chopped parsley, and serve with the chicken.

Roast Capon with Lemon and Parsley Stuffing

Serves 6 Time taken 2½–3 hours

1 (2 kg) (4 lb) oven-ready capon	50 g (2 oz) butter

For the Stuffing

100 g (4 oz) butter	finely grated rind of 1 lemon
100 g (4 oz) fresh white breadcrumbs	4 tablespoons finely chopped parsley
pinch thyme or marjoram	freshly milled pepper
salt	

Wipe the bird and remove any giblets from inside. Set aside while preparing the stuffing.

Melt the butter for the stuffing in a saucepan over low heat. Measure the breadcrumbs, lemon rind, and herbs into a basin. Season with salt and pepper. Using a fork, stir in the melted butter and mix to a moist crumbly consistency. Spoon a little into the neck of the capon, and the remainder into the body cavity. Pull the neck skin under the front of the bird, twist the wings so that they lie under the bird, then secure the neck skin and wings underneath with a skewer. Skewer the tail-end closed and tie the legs firmly in position.

Put the bird in a roasting tin. Smear with a little of the butter and put the remainder in the tin. Cover with a buttered paper and roast in the centre of a moderately hot oven (190°C, 375°F or Gas No. 5) for 20 minutes per 450 g (1 lb) plus 20 minutes extra. Remove the buttered paper and baste well towards the end of the cooking time to allow the bird to brown.

When ready, lift the roast capon from the tin on to a hot serving dish. Remove any skewers and string, and serve with a thin gravy made from the drippings in the pan.

Roast Duckling with Pineapple

Serves 4 Time taken 2 hours

1 (2 kg) (4 lb) oven-ready duckling	2 tablespoons clear honey
salt	1 tablespoon hot water

For the Pineapple Sauce

1 (400 g) (14½ oz) tin pineapple rings	1·5 dl (¼ pint) giblet stock
15 g (½ oz) butter	juice of ½ lemon
1 small onion	1 level tablespoon cornflour

Wipe the duckling, rub a little salt into the skin and prick the surface all over with the prongs of a fork. Place the duckling in a roasting tin, add 2 tablespoons cold water – no fat – and place the tin in the centre of a moderate oven (180°C, 350°F or Gas No. 4). Roast, allowing 20 minutes per 450 g (1 lb). Place the duckling giblets in a saucepan, cover with cold water and bring up to the boil. Simmer for 30 minutes, then strain the giblets and reserve the stock.

After 1 hour of the roasting time for the duckling, pour away the fat from the roasting tin. Blend the honey with the hot water and brush some of the mixture generously over the surface of the duckling, then return to the oven to complete the roasting time. Brush the duckling once or twice with the honey mixture, until the skin is glazed and golden brown.

When the duckling is cooked, remove from the roasting tin and keep hot. Pour away any further duck fat, leaving only the dark pan drippings behind. Drain the tin of pineapple, reserving the pine-apple rings and make the juice up to 1·5 dl (¼ pint) with water. Add the pineapple juice, stock and lemon juice to the roasting pan. Bring up to the boil in the pan, stirring to blend in the dark pan drippings and then strain into a basin. Melt the butter in a saucepan. Finely chop the onion and add to the butter. Fry gently for about 5 minutes until soft. Stir in the pineapple gravy. Blend the cornflour with a little extra water and stir in. Bring the mixture up to the boil, stirring all the time until the sauce has thickened. Cut the pineapple rings into pieces and add to the sauce. Heat through and serve with the roast duckling.

Normandy Roast Duckling

Serves 4 Time taken 2 hours

1 (2 kg) (4 lb) oven-ready duckling	1 small (75 ml) (⅛ pint) carton
salt	double cream
1 small bottle dry cider	

For the Stuffing

75 g (3 oz) butter	salt and pepper
100 g (4 oz) fresh white breadcrumbs	1 level dessertspoon castor sugar
450 g (1 lb) cooking apples	pinch ground cinnamon

This is a delicious way to serve roast duckling. Add 2 tablespoons of brandy to the gravy along with the cream for a special occasion.

Wipe the duckling and rub the skin over with salt. Set aside while preparing the stuffing.

Melt the butter in a heavy frying pan, add the breadcrumbs and stir over moderate heat until the butter is absorbed and the crumbs are golden brown. Peel, core and dice the apples. Add to the pan, cover with a lid and cook very gently until the apples have softened – takes about 15 minutes. Remove the lid, stir gently to mix, add a good seasoning of salt and pepper, and the sugar and cinnamon.

Draw the pan off the heat and spoon the stuffing inside the duckling. Close the tail-end with a skewer and place in a roasting tin with 2 tablespoons water. Place in the centre of a moderate oven (180°C, 350°F or Gas No. 4) and cook for 20 minutes per 450 g (1 lb). After 15 minutes, prick the skin with a fork to let the fat run off, and then, 15 minutes before the end of the cooking time, remove the duckling from the oven. Pour off all the fat and pour the cider over the duckling. Replace the bird in the oven and cook for the remaining time, basting from time to time.

When the cooking time is complete, lift the duckling from the tin on to a carving board. Place the roasting tin over moderate heat and simmer until cider is reduced by about half.

Meanwhile cut the duckling into four separate portions and arrange in a serving dish.

Spoon the stuffing from the carcass into a small basin. Stir the cream into the duck gravy, reheat and then strain over the duckling. Serve with the stuffing.

Roast Chicken with Oatmeal Stuffing

Serves 4–6 Time taken 1½ hours

1 (2 kg) (4 lb) oven-ready chicken	butter or white vegetable fat

For the Stuffing

1 large onion	salt
175 g (6 oz) medium oatmeal	freshly milled pepper
75 g (3 oz) shredded suet	

The stuffing for this particular recipe is Scottish; it has a delicious flavour and is very easy to prepare.

Wipe the chicken and set aside while preparing the stuffing. Peel and finely chop the onion. Add to the oatmeal and suet and season well. (If preferred, 75 g (3 oz) of vegetable fat can be rubbed into the oatmeal and the suet omitted.) At this stage the stuffing mixture is quite dry and loose and, if liked, a tablespoon of water can be stirred in to bind the mixture. Spoon most of the stuffing into the body cavity of the chicken and a little into the neck. Skewer or tie the bird into shape and place in a roasting tin. Add the butter or vegetable fat and cover the breast of the chicken with a buttered paper.

Place in the centre of a moderate oven (190°C, 375°F or Gas No. 5) and roast, allowing 20 minutes per 450 g (1 lb) plus 20 minutes extra. Towards the end of the cooking time, remove the paper to allow the chicken to brown. When cooking time is completed, test by piercing the chicken with the point of a sharp knife in the thick part of the leg. Juices coming out should be colourless; if at all pink, return for further cooking.

Lift the chicken on to a hot serving dish. Serve with bread sauce (see page 177) and a thin gravy made from the drippings in the pan.

ROAST GAME
Roast Goose with Potato Stuffing

Serves 8 Time taken 4–5 hours
1 (4·5 kg) (10 lb) oven-ready goose   little flour

For the Potato Stuffing
1 kg (2 lb) hot mashed potato   pinch mixed herbs
1 large onion, finely chopped   freshly milled pepper
liver from the goose   1 egg
75 g (3 oz) butter
1–2 tablespoons finely chopped
    parsley

If a frozen oven-ready goose is used, allow to thaw slowly over a period of at least 12 hours.

Wipe the goose, remove the giblets from the inside and reserve the liver for the stuffing. Set the goose aside while preparing the stuffing.

Mix together the hot potato, onion, chopped goose liver, butter cut in pieces, parsley and mixed herbs. Season to taste with salt and pepper, and bind the mixture together with the lightly beaten egg. Pack the stuffing into the tail-end of the bird and skewer closed.

Rub the skin of the goose over with flour and then, using the prongs of a fork, prick the breast of the goose well. Place in a roasting tin and cover with a sheet of buttered greaseproof paper or foil. Set the bird in the centre of a hot oven (200°C, 400°F or Gas No. 6) and roast for

30 minutes, then lower the heat to 190°C, 375°F or Gas No. 5 and roast for the remaining time, allowing 20 minutes per 450 g (1 lb) plus 20 minutes extra. Remove the paper or foil after 45 minutes' cooking time to allow the bird to brown. During the roasting time, ladle some of the fat out of the tin, if it becomes rather full. When the goose is ready, lift from the tin and remove any skewers.

Serve with apple sauce and a thin gravy.

Roast Venison with Cranberry Sauce

Serves 6–8 Time taken 2 hours

1 (2 kg) (4 lb) piece saddle of venison 225 g (½ lb) streaky bacon rashers or
salt   mutton flank

cranberry sauce

Cuts for roasting can be taken from the fore-quarter or saddle, which is very sweet, or from the hind-quarter, which is considered more tender. Venison is a very lean meat and should be well-protected during roasting.

Rub the piece of venison with salt and cover with the trimmed streaky bacon rashers, or wrap a boned piece of mutton flank round the joint.

Place the joint in a covered roasting tin, or cover the joint in an open roasting tin with kitchen foil. Place in a very hot oven (220°C, 425°F or Gas No. 8) for about the first 15 minutes. Then lower the heat to moderately hot (190°C, 375°F or Gas No. 5) for the remaining cooking time. Allow 20 minutes per 450 g (1 lb) plus 20 minutes extra.

When ready, serve the venison on very hot plates. Venison congeals and sets very quickly, and the roast should not be taken out of the oven more than 3–5 minutes before serving.

Serve with gravy made using the pan drippings, and cranberry sauce (see page 176).

Roast Pheasant

Serves 6–8 Time taken 1½ hours

1 brace of pheasant   50 g (2 oz) butter
6–8 streaky bacon rashers   flour
1 large carrot
1 medium onion   watercress

The butcher sells pheasants plucked and ready for roasting. For a small fee, he will usually prepare any birds taken to the shop.

Wipe the pheasants and cover the breasts with bacon rashers. Peel and thickly slice the carrot and onion, and place in the roasting tin to form a bed of vegetables. Place the pheasants on top. Add half the butter to the tin and spread the remainder over the birds. Place in the centre of a very hot oven (220°C, 425°F or Gas No. 7) for 10 minutes. Then lower the heat to hot (200°C, 400°F or Gas No. 6) and continue to roast, younger birds for 30–40 minutes and older birds for up to 1 hour. Baste fairly often and about 10 minutes before the end of the cooking time remove the bacon rashers. Baste the birds again and then dredge lightly with flour. Return to the oven to complete cooking time and brown the birds.

Lift on to a hot serving dish and garnish with watercress. Serve with a thin gravy made from the drippings in the pan, and a purée of chestnuts (see page 178).

Roast Wild Duck

Serves 4 Time taken 45 minutes

2 wild duck	watercress
salt	
softened butter	

To get rid of any fishy flavours in wild duck, place the birds in the roasting pan with boiling water, salt and sliced onion. Baste the birds with this for some minutes. Then pour away the liquid and roast as usual.

Wipe the birds and rub the skin all over with salt. Smear with butter and place together in a roasting tin. Set in the centre of a very hot oven (220°C, 425°F or Gas No. 7) and roast for 25–30 minutes. Baste fairly frequently and do not overcook.

Serve with a thin gravy, a garnish of watercress and a green, or chicory and orange, salad.

Roast Grouse with Bacon Rolls

Serves 4 Time taken 1 hour

2 grouse	2 rounds of toast
25 g (1 oz) butter	4 rashers back bacon
4 rashers streaky bacon	
flour	
	watercress

Place a nut of butter inside each trussed bird. Reserve the grouse livers and place the remaining butter in the roasting tin. Cover the breasts of the birds with the streaky bacon rashers and place in a roasting tin, breast-sides up. Place in the centre of a hot oven (200°C, 400°F or Gas No. 6) and roast for $\frac{1}{2}$–$\frac{3}{4}$ hour. About 10 minutes before the cooking time is complete, remove the bacon rashers and dust the birds with flour. Baste again and replace in the oven to complete the cooking time.

Cut two rounds of toasted bread using a large pastry cutter, and arrange on a serving dish. Spread with the lightly fried and mashed livers from the birds. Remove the string from the grouse and arrange on the toast. Trim and flatten the back rashers with a knife. Cut each rasher in half and roll up. Skewer and then grill quickly for a few moments.

Garnish the cooked grouse with the bacon rashers and watercress. Serve with game chips and a thin gravy, made using stock and the drippings in the roasting tin.

Roast Partridge with Wild Rice

Serves 4 Time taken 1$\frac{1}{2}$–2 hours

4 small partridge	flour
50 g (2 oz) butter	

For the Wild Rice

6 dl (1 pint) stock	225 g ($\frac{1}{2}$ lb) button mushrooms
freshly milled pepper	1$\frac{1}{2}$ level teaspoons salt
100 g (4 oz) wild rice	2 tablespoons finely chopped parsley
2 medium onions	
175 g (6 oz) long grain rice	few green grapes
40 g (1$\frac{1}{2}$ oz) butter	

Buy the partridge trussed ready for roasting. If the birds are small allow one per person; larger birds could serve two.

Measure the stock into a saucepan and add the salt and pepper. Stir in the washed and drained wild rice. Peel and finely chop the onions. Add to the pan and soak the ingredients for 30 minutes. Bring to the boil, stirring occasionally, then reduce the heat, cover the pan with a lid and simmer gently for 20 minutes. Add the washed, long grain rice and continue to simmer very gently for a further 20 minutes. Stir occasionally and make sure that the heat is low, otherwise the rice will dry out too quickly. Trim and slice the mushrooms. Melt the butter in a frying pan and add the mushrooms. Fry for a few moments then add to the rice, together with the chopped parsley. Toss well to mix, then draw off the heat and keep warm.

Meanwhile place the partridge in the centre of a hot oven (200°C, 400°F or Gas No. 6) and roast for 30 minutes. Remove the protective strips of fat covering the partridge towards the end of the cooking time. Dredge the birds with a little flour, baste and replace in the oven to finish cooking.

When ready to serve, remove all strings and skewers from the birds and lift on to a serving dish. Pile the wild rice on one side of the dish, garnish with the grapes and serve.

6 Fish

With a few exceptions, the seasons for fresh fish are less dramatic than those for fruit and vegetables. With the approach of spring, most white fish are plump and plentiful, and quantities of fresh roe appear on the market.

White fish in particular have a delicate flavour and they must be cooked carefully to preserve this. Cod, haddock and plaice are excellent all-purpose fish, whereas halibut and turbot are highly prized for their excellent flavour and texture, and for this reason are expensive. Dover and lemon sole are universally praised for their firm, white, delicate flesh. Skate is a firm-textured white fish with a delicious flavour, and is also excellent cold.

During summer months shellfish such as crab, lobster, prawns and scampi, and fish such as salmon, salmon trout and turbot, come into their own. Unlike many other fish these are delicious served cold. All are excellent for meals during warm weather, when appetites tend to sink a little.

Of all fish, salmon is one of the most highly prized and the most controversial. There are many theories and much conflicting advice about cooking it. The salmon with the finest flavour are those caught early in the season. These are expensive but as the season passes the price comes down. The following methods of cooking show that there is quite a distinct difference in the method used, according to whether the salmon is to be served hot or cold.

To Poach Salmon for Serving Hot

A piece of salmon which is to be cooked and served hot should be poached in a *court bouillon*. For this, measure into a large pan sufficient water to cover the piece of fish. For each generous 1 litre (quart) of water add 2 level teaspoons of salt, 1 small onion, thinly sliced, 1 bay leaf, 6 white peppercorns, juice of 1 lemon and a few washed parsley stalks. Bring to the boil and simmer for 15 minutes. Add the piece of salmon, bring back up to the boil, then lower the heat and allow to poach very gently. The time taken depends on the thickness of the fish rather than the weight; allow 10 minutes per 450 g (1 lb) when cooking a thick piece and 7 minutes per 450 g (1 lb) for a thinner piece. Drain well, lift away the skin and serve with Hollandaise sauce, hot cucumber, shrimp or anchovy sauce.

To Cook Salmon for Serving Cold

Here is a fool-proof method used by many Scottish cooks and ideal to use when the salmon is to be served cold. The method remains the same for any sized piece of salmon.

Fill a pan with sufficient lightly salted cold water to cover the piece of fish. If necessary place the piece of salmon in the pan to measure this, but remove it before bringing the water up to the boil. Add the salmon, bring back to the boil, and then boil hard for *exactly 2 minutes*. Draw the pan off the heat, particularly if it is over an electric hot-plate. Cover with a tight-fitting lid and leave for 12 hours, or until quite cold. Some cooks like to add vinegar to the water. The bigger the piece of salmon the more water and the larger the pan, the longer it takes to cool. In this way the method adapts itself to any size of salmon or salmon-cut, and the slow cooling keeps the flesh moist.

To Grill Salmon Cutlets

Salmon cutlets can be cut up to 2·5 cm (1 inch) thick. Brush the cutlets liberally on both sides with melted butter. Arrange on a grill pan and place at least 7·5 cm (3 inches) away from the heat under a hot grill. Grill for up to 12 minutes, depending on the thickness of the pieces, turning once to cook both sides. Baste with melted butter when turning. To test whether cooked, press the salmon in the centre near the bone – the flesh should feel firm and come away from the bone easily.

Serve with hot melted butter or parsley butter.

Smoked Haddock Kedgeree

Serves 4 Time taken 1 hour

700 g–1 kg (1½–2 lb) smoked haddock on the bone	50 g (2 oz) butter
	225 g (8 oz) long grain rice
few sprigs of parsley	1 small onion
1 small bay leaf	6 dl (1 pint) boiling fish liquor
1 lemon	2–3 eggs
few peppercorns	freshly milled pepper

Cooking the rice in the fish poaching liquor gives this kedgeree an excellent flavour.

Rinse and cut the haddock into large pieces. Place in a saucepan and add scant 1 litre (1½ pints) of water to cover. Add the washed stalks from the parsley (reserve curly tops for garnish), the bay leaf, half the lemon cut in slices and a few peppercorns. Bring up to the boil, then lower the heat and simmer very gently until the fish is tender – about 10–15 minutes. Strain off the cooking liquor and reserve 6 dl (1 pint) for the cooking of the rice.

Melt 25 g (1 oz) of the butter in a saucepan over low heat. Peel and finely chop the onion. Add to the pan, cover with a lid and cook very gently for about 5 minutes to soften but not brown the onion. Stir in the rice and mix well with the butter and onion. Check seasoning in the reserved fish liquor, add salt if necessary, then stir into rice and bring to the boil. Cover and simmer until the rice is tender and the liquid absorbed – takes about 20–30 minutes.

Meanwhile remove the bones and skin from the cooked fish, break into flakes. Hard-boil the eggs, then shell and cut into quarters. Using a fork, fold these into the cooked rice together with a seasoning of freshly milled pepper, the remaining butter cut in pieces and a little juice from the remaining lemon half. Serve hot.

Marinated Herrings

Serves 4 Time taken 1 hour
Allow herring to cool for several hours

4 fresh herrings	few parsley stalks
½ onion	1 bay leaf
salt	few peppercorns
freshly milled pepper	1 small onion
1·5 dl (¼ pint) wine vinegar	½ level teaspoon salt
1·5 dl (¼ pint) water	1 teaspoon brown sugar

Marinated herrings make an ideal summer meal with potato salad. They can also be served as a meal starter, garnished with a lemon slice and served with brown bread and butter.

Scale and wash the herrings. Cut away the heads and tails, and slit each fish open down the belly. Clean out the inside, open out the herring and turn over on to the working surface. Press firmly down the backbone to loosen it, then gently pull the bone away. Peel and finely chop the half onion. Sprinkle over the flesh side of each herring fillet. Season with salt and pepper. Roll up each herring from head to tail, and pack together in a baking dish so that the herrings remain tightly closed.

Place the vinegar and water in a saucepan and add the parsley stalks, bay leaf, peppercorns, peeled onion, salt and sugar. Bring to the boil and simmer for 3 minutes, then strain over the herrings. Cover with a lid or a buttered paper and place in the centre of a moderately hot oven (190°C, 375°F or Gas No. 5) and cook for 30 minutes. Remove from the heat and allow to cool in the liquor. Lift the herrings from the liquor and serve.

Lobster Newburg

Serves 4 Time taken 45 minutes

2 (450–700 g) (1–1½ lb) cooked
  lobsters

For the Sauce

100 g (4 oz) butter	1 level tablespoon flour
2–3 tablespoons medium dry sherry	3 dl (½ pint) single cream
freshly milled pepper	squeeze of lemon juice
salt	paprika pepper
2 egg yolks	

Split each lobster down the backbone and remove the flesh from both the body and the claws. Cut any large pieces of flesh, but keep the pieces chunky, and place in a mixing basin.

When ready to serve, melt the butter in a large frying pan, add the lobster pieces and fry for 2–3 minutes. This initial frying will make the pink parts in the lobster flesh go an attractive red colour, and also warms through the meat. Lift flesh from the pan into a heated serving dish, add the sherry to the hot butter and simmer until the liquid is reduced a little.

In a small mixing basin whisk together the egg yolks and flour, then gradually whisk in the cream. Pour the mixture quickly into the frying pan and stir with the whisk until the sauce is thickened and just simmering. Because of the small amount of flour added there is no risk of the sauce separating. Lower the heat and simmer gently for about 1 minute. Season with plenty of fresh pepper from the mill, salt to taste and a squeeze of lemon juice to sharpen the flavour. Draw the pan off the heat and strain the sauce over the hot lobster. Sprinkle with paprika pepper. Serve with plain boiled rice.

Pickled Herrings

Serves 6 Time taken 2¼ hours
Allow 5–6 days for herring to pickle

| 6 herrings | 1 onion |

For the Brine

| 50 g (2 oz) salt | 6 dl (1 pint) water |

For the Spiced Vinegar

| 6 dl (1 pint) white vinegar | 1 dried chilli |
| 1 tablespoon mixed pickling spice | 1 bay leaf |

Herrings prepared like this will keep in a refrigerator for up to four weeks. They are very good to eat simply with a salad and brown bread and butter, or served as an hors d'œuvre.

Scale and wash the herrings, cut away the heads and tails. Slit each herring down the belly and clean the inside. Turn each herring open-side downwards on a working surface. Press firmly down the back bone to loosen it. Turn the herring over and pull away the back bone and remove any smaller bones.

Mix the salt and water, and soak the herring fillets in the brine for 2 hours.

Meanwhile prepare the spiced vinegar. Put the vinegar and pickling spices in a saucepan, and bring slowly to the boil. Remove from the heat and leave to infuse for 30 minutes. Strain and allow to cool. Drain the herring fillets from the brine. Peel and finely slice the onion. Roll up each herring fillet with a little sliced onion inside. Secure each fillet with a cocktail stick and pack into a wide-necked jar. Add the chilli and the bay leaf, and finally add the spiced vinegar. Cover and leave for 5–6 days before using.

Smoked Haddock Mousse

Serves 6 Time taken 1 hour
Allow several hours for mousse to chill

1 kg (2 lb) smoked haddock on
  the bone
1 carrot
1 onion
few parsley stalks
1 bay leaf
salt

few peppercorns
1 level tablespoon powdered gelatine
freshly milled pepper
pinch cayenne pepper
juice of $\frac{1}{2}$ lemon
3 dl ($\frac{1}{2}$ pint) double cream

Cut the haddock into pieces and place in a saucepan. To estimate
amount required, add water to cover. Remove the fish and add the
peeled and sliced carrot and onion, the parsley stalks, bay leaf, salt
and peppercorns to the pan. Bring to the boil and simmer gently for
10–15 minutes. Replace the smoked haddock in the pan and poach
gently for about 10–15 minutes, or until the fish is cooked. Remove
the fish from the pan, skin, bone and flake the flesh.

Boil the liquid in the pan for a further 10 minutes to reduce. Draw
off the heat, strain and measure off 1·5 dl ($\frac{1}{4}$ pint) of this fish stock.
Return the fish stock to the pan and add the gelatine. Allow to soak
for a few moments then stir over low heat until dissolved. Remove
from the heat and allow to cool.

Add the cooled gelatine to the fish and blend well. Season with
freshly milled pepper, a pinch of cayenne and lemon juice to taste.
Lightly whip the cream and fold into the mixture. Pour into a soufflé
dish and chill for several hours before serving.

Fish in Yeast Batter

Serves 4 Time taken 1½ hours

700 g (1½ lb) cod or haddock fillet

seasoned flour

For the Yeast Batter
15 g ($\frac{1}{2}$ oz) fresh yeast
pinch castor sugar
1·5 dl ($\frac{1}{4}$ pint) tepid mixed milk and
  water

75 g (3 oz) plain flour
pinch salt

Using a yeast batter means that the coating on the fish will keep
crisp after frying. It has a nice flavour too.

Rinse the fish fillets and pat dry. Using a sharp knife cut away the dark skin underneath. If you salt your fingers, you will be able to grip the fish tail firmly while doing this. Cut the fillets into suitably sized pieces removing any obvious bones. Sift seasoned flour on to a plate – simply add salt and pepper to plain flour. Set both aside until the batter is ready.

Stir the yeast and sugar into the warmed mixed milk and water. Sift the flour and salt over the surface and, using a whisk, beat until the batter is smooth. Cover with a cloth and stand in a warm place for 30–40 minutes until frothy. Stir before using.

Dip fish pieces first in the seasoned flour, shake off surplus, and then dip pieces in batter. The flour removes any moisture on the fish surface and helps the batter coat the pieces better. Allow excess batter to drain away then add to the hot deep fat and fry for about 5 minutes until crisp and brown.

Serve at once with lemon or with tomato sauce.

Trout with Almonds

Serves 4 Time taken 45 minutes

50 g (2 oz) unblanched almonds	75 g (3 oz) butter
4 trout	juice of ½ lemon
seasoned flour	

Whole almonds, freshly blanched and cut into thin slivers give the best results. Flaked almonds could be used instead.

Cover the whole, unblanched almonds with boiling water and allow to stand for a few minutes. Drain and pop the almonds out of the skins, then, with a sharp knife, cut the nuts into thin slivers. Almonds are easier to cut thinly when they are warm and newly blanched.

Gut the trout, leaving on the heads. Rinse under cold water and pat dry. Roll each one in seasoned flour. Melt 50 g (2 oz) of the butter in a large frying pan and, when frothy, add the trout. Fry the trout for about 6–8 minutes, or until browned and cooked, turning them over once. Lift from the pan on to a hot serving dish and keep hot.

Add the remaining butter and the almonds to the pan. Fry the almonds in the hot butter until they become golden brown, then draw the pan off the heat and add the lemon juice. Stir to blend well, then spoon the almonds, butter and juices from the pan over the trout, and serve.

Lobster Thermidor

Serves 4 Time taken 1 hour

2 (450–700 g) (1–1½ lb) cooked
   lobsters
1·5 dl (¼ pint) white wine
1 shallot finely chopped
1 teaspoon made mustard
25 g (1 oz) butter
25 g (1 oz) flour

3 dl (½ pint) milk
salt
freshly milled pepper
2–3 tablespoons cream

25 g (1 oz) Parmesan cheese

Split each lobster open down the backbone and remove the flesh
from both the body and the claws. Cut up the flesh coarsely and set
aside ready for use. Wipe the shells clean and reserve.

Measure the wine, chopped shallots and mustard into a saucepan.
Bring to the boil and simmer for about 5 minutes to reduce. Meanwhile melt the butter in a second saucepan and stir in the flour. Cook
gently for a few moments over low heat, then gradually stir in the
milk. Bring to the boil stirring all the time to get a smooth sauce.
Season with salt and pepper, and then strain in the reduced wine
mixture and add the cream. Stir together carefully, check the seasoning and add the lobster pieces. Reheat gently for a few moments, then
draw off the heat.

Dividing the mixture equally, spoon the lobster meat and sauce
into the reserved shells. Sprinkle with the cheese and place under a
hot grill to brown. Serve at once.

Moules Marinière

Serves 4 Time taken 30 minutes

2·25 litres (2 quarts) fresh mussels
1 small onion
4–6 tablespoons dry white
   wine

25 g (1 oz) butter
1 level teaspoon flour

chopped parsley

Discard any mussels with broken shells. If some are open, tap sharply
with another mussel; they will close up if still alive; discard any that
remain open. Scrub the mussels and, using a knife, pull away the
beard, shake them vigorously in cold water. Pour away and re-cover
with fresh water. Repeat until the water remains clear. It is important
to clean mussels well, as any sand or grit in the sauce spoils the taste.

Using a buttered paper, thoroughly butter the inside of a saucepan
large enough to take all the mussels. Sprinkle with the chopped onion

and add the wine. Simmer for 3–5 minutes to cook the onion, then place all the mussels in the pan at once. Cover with a lid and set over a high heat to cook, shaking the pan, for about 3–5 minutes until the mussels have fully opened. Draw the pan off the heat, remove the mussels from the pan. Discard any that have remained closed. Remove the open shells from each and place the mussels in hot soup plates or a bowl. Keep hot.

Cream the butter and flour together and add to the liquid remaining in the pan. Stir over low heat, until thickened and boiling – the sauce should be fairly thin. Pour over the mussels. Sprinkle with chopped parsley and serve.

Smoked Fish en Coquilles

Serves 4 Time taken 1¼ hours

450–700 g (1–1½ lb) smoked haddock or smoked cod fillet	½ bay leaf
	few parsley stalks
3 dl (½ pint) milk	few peppercorns
slice of lemon	40 g (1½ oz) butter
1 teaspoon lemon juice	25 g (1 oz) flour
50 g (2 oz) grated cheese	fresh breadcrumbs
small pinch cayenne pepper	
450 g (1 lb) well-seasoned creamed potatoes	slices of lemon or sprigs of parsley

These attractive and individual fish dishes are ideal for lunch or supper. They can be prepared in advance and reheated when ready to serve.

Rinse the fish and cut into convenient pieces. Put into a saucepan with the milk, slice of lemon, bay leaf, parsley stalks and peppercorns. If necessary, add a little water to almost cover the fish. Simmer for 15 minutes, then strain off the liquor and reserve 3 dl (½ pint) for the sauce. Leave the fish to cool for a few minutes, then carefully remove the skin and any small bones and break the fish into flakes.

Melt the butter over low heat and stir in the flour. Gradually mix in the reserved fish cooking liquor. Stir all the time until the sauce is smooth. Bring to the boil and cook gently for 2 minutes. Add the lemon juice, half the cheese and the cayenne pepper, and mix well. Then fold in the flaked fish.

Have ready four deep scallop shells, well-greased. Pipe a border of creamed potatoes around the edges, or, if you have no piping bag and tube, arrange a border of creamed potatoes and rough it up with the prongs of a fork. Pile the fish mixture in the centre. Sprinkle the remaining grated cheese on top and a light sprinkling of breadcrumbs. Add a nut of butter and brown near the top of a moderately hot oven (190°C, 375°F or Gas No. 5) for about 15 minutes.

Garnish with a slice of lemon or a sprig of parsley and serve.

Smoked Haddock and Bacon

Serves 4 Time taken 45 minutes

700 g (1½ lb) smoked haddock fillet	3 dl (½ pint) milk
1–2 slices lemon	salt
4 rashers bacon	freshly milled pepper
1 onion	squeeze lemon juice
40 g (1½ oz) butter	4 rounds hot buttered toast
25 g (1 oz) flour	

Rinse the fish and cut into four pieces. Place in a saucepan, add water to cover and a few slices of lemon. Poach gently until tender – about 15 minutes. Drain and cool for a few minutes, then remove the skin and break up the fish into flakes. Meanwhile trim and chop the bacon and peel and finely chop the onion. Fry both the bacon and onion gently in 15 g (½ oz) of the butter until the onion is softened but not brown. Draw off the heat.

Melt the remaining 25 g (1 oz) of butter in a saucepan and stir in the flour. Cook for a moment over the heat and then gradually stir in the milk. Bring to the boil, stirring all the time to get a smooth sauce. Season with salt and pepper to taste. Stir in the bacon, onion and flaked fish, and add the lemon juice to taste. Reheat and pile on to rounds of hot buttered toast and serve.

Sole Bonne Femme

Serves 4 Time taken 1¼ hours

2 sole	½ wine glass dry white wine
1 shallot	little chopped parsley
salt and pepper	25 g (1 oz) butter
100 g (¼ lb) button mushrooms	1 slightly rounded tablespoon flour
juice of ½ lemon	4 tablespoons single cream

Ask the fishmonger to skin and fillet the sole for you; take home the bones and skin for making fish stock.

Well-butter a large saucepan or frying pan. Sprinkle with the finely chopped shallot, then add the fillets of fish folded in half, and season with salt and pepper. Separate the mushroom stalks and caps. Reserve the stalks and slice the caps, add these, the lemon juice, wine and chopped parsley to the fish. Cover with a buttered paper and a lid, and poach gently for about 10 minutes until the fish is tender. Meanwhile place the fish bones and trimmed mushroom stalks in a saucepan, cover with cold water and bring up to the boil. Simmer for 20 minutes then strain and reserve 3 dl ($\frac{1}{2}$ pint) of the fish liquor.

When cooked, lift the fish and mushrooms from the pan, place in a hot serving dish and keep warm. Reduce the liquid in the pan by boiling rapidly to about 2 tablespoons. Add the reserved fish liquor. Cream the butter and flour together to make a *beurre manié*. Add in pieces to the fish stock. Stir until boiling, then draw the pan off the heat. Stir in the cream, check seasoning and strain over the fillets of sole. Place under a pre-heated hot grill and brown before serving.

Sole en Goujons

Serves 4 Time taken 45 minutes
Can be prepared in advance

4 good-sized fillets of sole	1 dessertspoon oil
seasoned flour	brown breadcrumbs
1 large egg	salt

For the Tartare Sauce

2 heaped tablespoons mayonnaise	1 tablespoon thick cream
1 teaspoon finely chopped capers	$\frac{1}{2}$ teaspoon very finely chopped onion
1 teaspoon finely chopped gherkins	
1 teaspoon finely chopped parsley	lemon wedges

Ask the fishmonger to skin and prepare the sole fillets for you. Rinse and pat them dry. Cut each fillet in half making a slantwise cut right across – the same angle as you would slice a French loaf. Then cut each half lengthways into 3–4 narrow strips or *goujons*. Toss these in seasoned flour, then shake in a sieve to get rid of the surplus flour. Lightly mix the egg and oil in a shallow plate – the addition of oil makes the egg go further, otherwise two eggs will be required to coat all the fish pieces. Dip the *goujons* first in the beaten egg mixture, drain and then roll in the brown crumbs. Shake away any loose crumbs and pat coating on firmly. Up to this stage the *goujons* can be prepared in advance and pieces of fish kept to fry at a later stage.

Combine together the mayonnaise, cream, capers, gherkins, parsley and onion for the tartare sauce.

When ready to serve, fry the fish in hot deep fat until crisp and golden, about 2–3 minutes. Drain thoroughly on absorbent kitchen paper. Sprinkle with salt, garnish with lemon wedges.

Serve with the tartare sauce.

Prawn Pilaff

Serves 4 Time taken 1 hour

scant 1 litre (1½ pints) fresh prawns	1 small onion
	225 g (½ lb) long grain rice
1 slice of lemon	freshly milled black pepper
few parsley stalks	juice of ½ lemon
75 g (3 oz) butter	2 hard-boiled eggs

Rinse and shell the prawns. Place the shells in a pan with scant 1 litre (1½ pints) water, the slice of lemon and a few parsley stalks. Simmer for 15 minutes. Remove pan from the heat, strain and reserve 6 dl (1 pint) of the stock.

Melt 50 g (2 oz) of the butter in a saucepan. Peel and finely chop the onion. Add to the pan and sauté for a few minutes to soften. Add the rice and mix well, then stir in the reserved stock. Cover the pan and simmer for 20–30 minutes, or until the rice is cooked and the water absorbed.

Meanwhile melt the remaining butter and add the prawns. Heat through gently and season with pepper. Fold into the cooked rice with lemon juice to taste, and chopped hard-boiled eggs. Pile the pilaff in a hot dish and serve.

Baked Salmon Trout

Serves 6 Time taken 1–1¼ hours
Can be served hot or cold

1 (1–1·5 kg) (2½–3 lb) salmon trout	½ sliced lemon
salt	few parsley stalks
25–50 g (1–2 oz) butter	

One of the easiest and most effective ways of cooking salmon trout is to wrap the whole fish in foil and bake in the oven. Using this method the flesh remains moist and all juices are preserved.

A 900 g–1 kg (2–2¼ lb) salmon trout will serve four, a 1–1·5 kg

(2½–3 lb) fish will serve six and a 1·5–2 kg (3½–4 lb) fish will serve eight.

Have the fish cleaned but left whole. Place in the centre of a large square of well-buttered foil. Season with salt. Cut the butter in pieces. Place the butter, lemon slices and parsley stalks over the fish. Fold the foil over the top and turn up the ends to wrap up the salmon trout completely, and to keep in the butter while baking. Place in a large roasting tin, or on a baking tray, and set in the centre of a moderate oven (180°C, 350°F or Gas No. 4). Bake for 20 minutes per 450 g (1 lb).

To serve Open the foil and pour the butter and juices from the package into a small saucepan. Discard the lemon and parsley, and lift the skin away from the fish. Separate the flesh down the centre following the line of the bone. Serve the flesh in pieces, lifting the centre bone away. Heat the butter and juices in the saucepan and spoon a little over each portion of fish. Decorate with an extra slice of lemon and serve.

Scallops au Gratin

Serves 4 Time taken 1 hour

Can be prepared in advance

4 large scallops	1 lemon slice
3 dl (½ pint) milk	salt and pepper
1 bay leaf	

For the Sauce

25 g (1 oz) butter	salt and pepper
1 level tablespoon flour	50 g (2 oz) grated Cheddar cheese
2 dl (⅓ pint) cooking liquor	¼ teaspoon made mustard

For the Topping

25 g (1 oz) butter	4 lemon slices
2 heaped tablespoons fresh white breadcrumbs	

When purchasing fresh scallops from the fishmonger ask for the *deep* half shell. It is useful as a serving dish for the cooked fish.

Cut the prepared scallops into six or eight pieces, and place in a saucepan along with the milk, bay leaf, lemon and salt and pepper. Bring to the boil, then lower the heat and poach for 15–20 minutes. Drain from the cooking liquor and reserve 2 dl (⅓ pint or 1 teacupful) for the sauce. Discard the bay leaf and lemon slice.

Melt the butter in a saucepan over low heat, stir in the flour and cook for 1 minute. Gradually beat in the cooking liquor, beating well to get a smooth sauce. Bring to the boil, and simmer for 2–3 minutes. Season well and add the cheese and mustard, and the cooked scallops. Spoon the mixture into four buttered scallop shells or individual gratin dishes and keep warm while preparing the topping.

Melt the butter over a low heat. Draw the pan off the heat and, using a fork, stir in the breadcrumbs until the butter is absorbed. Sprinkle over the scallops, then place on a baking tray above centre in a moderate oven (180°C, 350°F or Gas No. 4) and bake for 15 minutes, until lightly browned and bubbling hot. Garnish with lemon and serve.

Baked Halibut with Cheese and Parsley Sauce

Serves 4 Time taken 1¼ hours

700 g–1 kg (1½–2 lb) halibut steak	2 tablespoons mlik
salt	15 g (½ oz) butter
juice of ½ lemon	

For the Sauce

25 g (1 oz) butter	freshly milled pepper
25 g (1 oz) flour	50 g (2 oz) grated Cheddar cheese
3 dl (½ pint) milk	2 tablespoons single cream
salt	finely chopped parsley

Rinse the fish and place the steaks in a large, well-buttered baking dish. Season with salt and squeeze over the lemon juice. Add the milk and place a small nut of butter on each steak. Cover the dish with buttered paper, place in the centre of a moderate oven (180°C, 350°F or Gas No. 4) and bake for 45 minutes, until fish is white and flakes easily from the bone.

Meanwhile melt the butter for the sauce in a pan over low heat. Stir in the flour and cook gently for 1 minute. Gradually stir in the milk, beating in each addition well, before adding the next. Bring up to the boil and simmer for 1–2 minutes. Season with salt and freshly milled pepper, and add the cheese. Stir until cheese has melted, and then leave over very low heat until ready to serve.

Drain the liquid from the cooked fish into the sauce, then gently lift the skin away from the steaks and remove the centre bone. Lift the fish out on to hot serving plates, stir the cream and parsley into the sauce, pour over and serve.

Scallop Kebabs

Serves 4 Time taken 30 minutes

4–6 scallops
juice of ½ lemon
freshly milled black pepper

8 streaky bacon rashers
1 (225 g) (8 oz) tin pineapple cubes
oil or butter

Ask the fishmonger to clean the scallops and remove from shell. Rinse and cut each scallop into quarters, then sprinkle with the lemon juice and pepper. Trim the bacon rashers and stretch each one, using the blade of a knife and flattening them out along a clean working surface. Cut the rashers in half and wrap each half round a piece of scallop.

Thread on four long skewers alternately with pineapple cubes. Brush skewers with oil or melted butter and place under a preheated hot grill. Grill for about 10 minutes, turning for even cooking. Serve at once with salad.

Salmon Mousse

Serves 4–6 Time taken 2 hours
Allow several hours for mousse to chill

450 g (1 lb) fresh salmon
3 dl (½ pint) milk
1 bay leaf
1 small onion
25 g (1 oz) butter

25 g (1 oz) plain flour
salt
freshly milled pepper
1·5 dl (¼ pint) mayonnaise
1·5 dl (¼ pint) double cream

For the Lemon Aspic
1·5 dl (¼ pint) cold water
15 g (½ oz) powdered gelatine
1 tablespoon lemon juice

1 tablespoon wine vinegar

½ small cucumber

Place the salmon in a square of buttered kitchen foil, fold up the edges to wrap the fish in a parcel. Place in a large saucepan, cover with cold water and bring slowly to the boil. Simmer gently for 10 minutes, then drain and allow to cool. When cold, unwrap the salmon carefully. Remove the skin and all bones from the salmon and set the flesh aside until needed.

Measure the milk into a small saucepan, add the bay leaf and peeled onion and bring slowly to the boil. Draw off the heat and leave to infuse for 10 minutes. Strain the milk and reserve. Melt the butter in a saucepan and stir in the flour. Cook gently for 1 minute, then gradually stir in the infused milk, beating well to get a smooth sauce. Bring the sauce up to the boil and cook very gently for 2–3 minutes. Season with salt and pepper, and strain into a basin. Cover the surface of the sauce with a piece of buttered paper to prevent a skin forming on the surface and leave until cold.

Pound or work the salmon until smooth, then beat in the cold sauce and mayonnaise. Measure the cold water for the lemon aspic into a saucepan and sprinkle over the gelatine. Leave to soak for 5 minutes, then stir over low heat until dissolved. Draw off the heat and add the lemon juice and vinegar. Set aside 2 tablespoons of the mixture for the decoration and stir the remainder into the salmon mousse. Lightly whip the cream and fold into the mixture. Pour into a 1-litre (1½–2-pint) soufflé dish.

Garnish with thin slices cut from the cucumber. Add 2 tablespoons of water to the reserved lemon aspic (if this has set in the meantime, stir over warm water to soften) and spoon over the surface of the mousse to cover the cucumber. Chill until ready to serve.

Crab Mousse

Serves 6 Time taken 30 minutes
Allow to chill for several hours

450 g (1 lb) prepared crab meat   1·5 dl (¼ pint) mayonnaise
175 g (6 oz) fresh cream cheese   salt and freshly milled pepper

For the Lemon Aspic
1·5 dl (¼ pint) cold water   1 tablespoon wine vinegar
15 g (½ oz) powdered gelatine
1 tablespoon lemon juice

Mix the brown and white crab meat together, discarding any small pieces of bone or sinews. Mix the cream cheese and mayonnaise together thoroughly in a basin, and stir in the crab meat. Season with salt and pepper, and set aside while preparing the lemon aspic jelly.

Measure the cold water into a saucepan and sprinkle over the gelatine. Leave to soak for 5 minutes, then stir over low heat until dissolved but do not allow to boil. Draw off the heat and add the lemon juice and vinegar. Reserve about 2 tablespoons of the mixture for the final glaze and stir the remainder into the crab meat mixture. Blend well and pour the mousse into a 1-litre (1½–2-pint) soufflé or serving dish. Chill until set firm.

Warm the reserved aspic jelly to soften and add 2 extra tablespoons of water to dilute it slightly. Decorate the top of the crab mousse with thin slices of cucumber, then spoon over the remaining jelly to cover the surface. This final glaze of aspic is important, to prevent the surface of the mousse from going dark in colour. Chill again until ready to serve.

Serve with salad.

Deep-fried Scampi

Serves 4 Time taken 30 minutes

350–450 g (¾–1 lb) prepared scampi   oil for deep frying

For the Batter

50 g (2 oz) plain flour	4 tablespoons water
pinch salt	1 egg white
1 dessertspoon olive oil	

Rinse the scampi, pat dry and set aside while preparing the batter.

Sieve the flour and salt into a small basin and hollow out the centre. Add the oil and water and, using a wooden spoon, mix from the centre outwards, gradually drawing in the flour from around the sides of the bowl. Beat well to get a smooth batter. Whisk the egg white until stiff and, using a metal spoon, fold into the batter.

Heat the oil until hot. When ready to fry, dip the scampi, one at a time, in the batter. Use a fork for dipping, so that all excess batter drips away leaving the scampi with just a thin coating. Place, a few at a time, in the hot oil and fry until golden brown – takes about 2–3 minutes. Turn them once to get even browning. Drain for a moment on absorbent kitchen paper. Keep the fried scampi hot in the oven, uncovered so that the batter remains crisp, while frying the rest.

Serve the fried scampi at once with wedges of lemon and tartare sauce.

Fried Herring in Oatmeal

Serves 4 Time taken 15–20 minutes

4 herrings	medium oatmeal for coating
milk	15 g (½ oz) butter for frying
salt and pepper	

Scale and wash the herrings. Cut away the heads and tails from the fish. Slit each herring down the belly, and clean out the inside. Place the herrings on a clean working surface with the inside spread open against the board. Press down the back to loosen the bone, turn over and pull away the bone from each one. Do this in advance, rinse the herring fillets and place in the refrigerator, covered until ready to cook.

Dip both sides of the herrings into milk, seasoned with salt and pepper, and then into oatmeal. Coat thoroughly and then shake away any loose oatmeal. Melt the butter in a frying pan; only a small amount is required as herrings need very little extra fat. Place the fish flesh-side down in the hot butter and cook gently for about 4 minutes. Turn carefully to avoid breaking the fish, and cook on the second side until lightly browned.

Serve hot with grilled lean bacon.

Grilled Red Mullet

Serves 4 Time taken 30–45 minutes

4 red mullet	olive oil
salt	
freshly milled pepper	parsley

Scrape the scales from the red mullet, cut off the fins but leave on the head and tail. Gut the fish and keep the liver. Wash well.

Sprinkle the inside of each fish with a little salt and pepper, and put the liver back. Brush each one with olive oil and put a little oil in the grill pan before putting in the fish. Grill quickly for 3 minutes, then turn the fish over and baste well. Reduce the heat and continue grilling until the mullet are cooked, about a further 15 minutes.

Serve on a hot dish and garnish with parsley.

Red Mullet Baked en Papillote

Serves 4 Time taken 45 minutes

4 red mullet	1 tablespoon lemon juice
salt	
freshly milled pepper	parsley and lemon
olive oil	

Scrape the scales from the red mullet, cut off the fins but leave on the head and tail. Gut the fish and keep the livers. Wash well, sprinkle the inside of each fish with a little salt and pepper and put the livers back. Wrap the fish carefully in well-oiled greaseproof paper, twisting the ends securely. Arrange on a baking sheet and place in a moderately hot oven (190°C, 375°F or Gas No. 5) and bake for about 15–20 minutes.

When cooked, loosen the paper and carefully arrange the fish on a hot plate. Add the lemon juice to the liquid which will have collected in the paper, and pour this over the fish.

Garnish with parsley and a slice of lemon and serve.

7 Cold Table

Pâtés, terrines and cold meats make ideal summer meals. Serve a pâté or terrine for a light lunch or supper, accompanied by hot toast and a tossed salad. Galantines and cold meats are more versatile and can be served with hot new vegetables or with a salad and warm crisp rolls, whichever is preferred. Pickles, chutneys, mustard or horse-radish sauce make tangy extras. Recipes that are served cold have many advantages; they can be prepared well in advance making meal times more relaxed and flexible, and they are ideal for entertaining.

Aspic Jelly

Makes 2 pints Time taken 30 minutes
Make in advance

1 litre (1¾ pints) good beef or
    chicken stock
50 g (2 oz) powdered gelatine

1·5 dl (¼ pint) dry white wine
2 egg whites and shells

Use aspic jelly to glaze galantines, pâtés, chicken joints and cold meats. The surface of jelly protects the food and keeps it moist.

Measure all but 1·5 dl (¼ pint) of the stock into a large saucepan. Pour the 1·5dl (¼ pint) stock into a small basin and sprinkle in the gelatine. Allow to soak for 5 minutes. Then add to the saucepan. Whisk the wine with the egg whites and shells, and add to the pan.

Whisk continuously over gentle heat until the mixture becomes milky. Stop at once, raise the heat and bring up to the boil. Lower the heat and allow to simmer for 10 minutes. Do not stir or break the crust that forms on the surface.

Draw the pan off the heat and pour through a scalded cloth or jelly bag into a basin. Allow to cool.

To use the aspic jelly The aspic jelly should be allowed to cool and then chilled or stirred over ice until almost on setting point. At this stage it will coat foods and give them an attractive finish. It is advisable to chill small amounts of the jelly each time, since food usually needs more than one coating to give an even, attractive finish.

Where a decoration of small cut vegetables is to be placed on the food, one coating is required to fix the decoration and a second coat for a final glaze.

Place the food to be glazed on a wire cooling-tray set over a plate. Spoon the chilled, almost setting, jelly over the food evenly and quickly. As the aspic runs off into the plate it can be collected and re-used. Any left-over aspic should be allowed to set and then chopped with a wet knife and arranged round the food as decoration.

Raised Veal and Ham Pie

Serves 6 Time taken 3–3½ hours
Make in advance

350 g (12 oz) plain flour	2·25 dl (1½ gills) mixed milk and
1 level teaspoon salt	water
100 g (4 oz) lard	

For the Filling

700 g (1½ lb) lean veal	2 hard-boiled eggs
225 g (½ lb) gammon	
1 level teaspoon salt	beaten egg and milk
freshly milled pepper	1 teaspoon gelatine
grated rind of ¼ lemon	1·5 dl (¼ pint) stock
1 tablespoon chopped parsley	

First prepare the filling. Trim the veal and gammon, and cut both into small neat pieces. Add the salt and a seasoning of pepper, the finely grated lemon rind and the chopped parsley. Set aside while preparing the pastry.

Sift together the flour and salt, and set in a warm place. Measure the lard and mixed milk and water (about 12 tablespoons) into a small saucepan. Place over moderate heat and bring gradually to the boil so that the fat melts in the liquid. When boiling rapidly, pour immediately into the centre of the sifted flour. Beat well with a wooden spoon, until the mixture clings together in a ball leaving the sides of the basin clean. Turn on to a board and knead lightly to make a smooth dough.

This pastry should be moulded while it is still warm. Set aside a small piece for the lid. Flatten the remaining pastry to about 1 cm (½ inch) thick and place in the base of either a well-greased, 23 × 13 × 5-cm (9 × 5 × 2-inch) large loaf tin or a 15-cm (6-inch) round deep cake tin. Using the knuckles, press the pastry from the centre to the sides. When the base is covered, press the pastry up the sides of the tin. Make sure that there is no layer of thick pastry between the base and the sides of the tin, and that the pastry has not been pressed too thinly, particularly on the sides. Bring the pastry up to overlap the rim.

Pack in half of the filling, then place the shelled, hard-boiled eggs down the centre. Cover these with the remaining filling. Roll out the reserved piece of pastry for the lid. Damp the edges of the pie and cover with the lid. Make a hole in the centre and decorate the pie with any pastry trimmings. Brush with beaten egg and milk to glaze.

Place the pie in the centre of a hot oven (200°C, 400°F or Gas No. 6) and bake for 20 minutes. Lower the heat to moderate (180°C, 350°F or Gas No. 4) and bake for a further 2–2½ hours. Brush occasionally with beaten egg and milk to make the pastry shiny and brown. Allow the baked pie to cool, then remove from the tin.

Dissolve the gelatine in the hot stock. Allow to cool until beginning to thicken and set. Pour through the hole in the centre of the pie. The jelly will fill any spaces inside the pie between the filling and the pie crust. Leave for several hours for the jelly to set firm. Serve sliced with salad.

Boned Stuffed Chicken

Serves 6 Time taken 3–4 hours
Make in advance

1 (1·5 kg) (3 lb) oven-ready chicken	1 bay leaf
lemon juice	25 g (1 oz) butter
2 carrots	few rashers streaky bacon
1 onion	

For the Stuffing

225 g (½ lb) lean veal
1 gammon rasher cut 2·5 cm
    (1 inch) thick
225 g (½ lb) sausage meat
1 small egg
1 tablespoon lemon juice

50 g (2 oz) fresh white breadcrumbs
rind of ½ small lemon
pinch ground ginger, mace and
    nutmeg
freshly milled pepper

A boned and stuffed chicken looks most attractive when sliced. Easy to serve and economical, it makes a good choice for a buffet supper.

Prepare the stuffing before starting on the bird. Trim any skin or fat from the veal. Remove the rind and fat from the gammon. Cut the gammon fat into three or four long strips, then cut three or four long strips of lean meat from the gammon. Mince the remaining gammon twice, together with the veal. Lightly mix the egg and lemon juice. Reserve the strips of gammon fat and lean. Place the minced gammon and veal, sausage meat, breadcrumbs, finely grated lemon rind, seasoning and egg mixture in a bowl. Mix thoroughly.

Turn the chicken on to its breast and slit right down the back. Cut off the tail. With a fairly short-bladed, sharp knife, carefully work the flesh away from the carcass until the leg joint is reached. Locate the thigh bone and scrape the meat away from it. Cut neatly through the cartilage of the ball and socket joint at each end. Remove the thigh bone but leave the drumstick in position. Continue until the wing joint is reached. Sever the cartilage where the wing joins the body but leave the bone in. Carry on to the ridge of the breast bone. Starting at the centre back, repeat for the other side. Cut very carefully along the ridge of breast bone to free the carcass. Take care at all times not to cut through the skin.

Place the boned bird, skin-side down, on the board. Sprinkle with a little lemon juice to help keep the breast white. Pack half the stuffing down the centre of the bird. Arrange alternating strips of the fat and lean gammon on top. Cover with the remaining stuffing and then shape into a neat mound, approximately the size of the carcass, which has been removed. Fold the sides up and over the stuffing. Thread a large needle with twine, dip the fingers in salt so that they do not slip, and stitch, making sure that the thread can be easily withdrawn. At the neck end, fold the neck skin over and under towards the back of the bird, tuck in neatly and stitch across. Turn the bird over and mould the breast into a good, plump shape. Tuck the wings close to the body underneath and run a skewer through.

Press the drumsticks against the sides of the bird. Taking about a yard of string, wrap the centre of it twice around the drumsticks. Cross the string over the back and take it around the wings. Tie in a bow for easy removal before carving. Cover the finished bird and store in the refrigerator or cool larder until ready to cook.

Prepare and thickly slice the carrots and onion, and arrange them in a roasting tin with the bay leaf and the butter. Place the bird on top, cover with a few rashers of streaky bacon and then cover completely with foil. Place in a hot oven (200°C, 400°F or Gas No. 6) and cook for 30 minutes. Lower the heat to moderate (180°C, 350°F or Gas No. 4) and cook for a further hour. Remove the bacon rashers, baste the bird well and return to the oven without covering for a final 20 minutes to brown. When cooked, remove the skewer and string, and leave the chicken until quite cold.

Carve the chicken across the breast in slices. Serve with salad.

Terrine of Chicken

Serves 6 Time taken 2½–3 hours
Make in advance

1 (2 kg) (4 lb) oven-ready chicken	freshly ground black pepper
1 small onion	1 tablespoon finely chopped parsley
350 g (¾ lb) pork sausage meat	1 egg
1 level teaspoon salt	4–6 rashers streaky bacon

Reserve the chicken liver from the giblets. Then, with a very sharp knife, carefully remove the chicken breast from the bone, cutting as close as possible to the bone. Remove the skin and cut the flesh into strips and set aside.

Joint the chicken and remove the remainder of the flesh in pieces, scraping off as much as possible. Discard any chicken skin. Peel the onion and cut into quarters. Pass the chicken flesh, chicken liver and onion through the mincer. Place in a mixing basin, add the sausage meat, salt and pepper, chopped parsley and egg. Mix and then beat the ingredients to blend them thoroughly.

Trim and stretch the bacon rashers with the back of a knife. Cut each rasher in half, and arrange two or three pieces of bacon in the base of a 1-litre (1½–2-pint) terrine or pâté dish. Put in two or three tablespoons of the minced mixture and press down firmly. Arrange some of the strips of chicken flesh across on top of this and repeat the layers until the dish is full. Top with two or three pieces of bacon. Cover the dish with a lid or with a square of kitchen foil. Place in a large shallow roasting tin with water to come 2·5 cm (1 inch) up the sides of the dish. Place in the centre of a moderately slow oven (170°C, 325°F or Gas No. 3) for 2 hours. Remove from the oven and set aside under a weight until cold. Serve, cut in slices, with salad.

Duck Pâté

Serves 6 Time taken 4–4½ hours
Make in advance

1 (1·5–2 kg) (3½–4 lb) oven-ready
  duckling
50 g (2 oz) butter
450 g (1 lb) lean pork tenderloin
225 g (½ lb) pork fat or belly of pork
pinch sage
1 tablespoon chopped parsley

salt
freshly milled pepper
pinch nutmeg
1 egg
2 tablespoons orange liqueur
225 g (½ lb) unsmoked streaky
  bacon rashers

For the Decoration
few slices fresh orange

aspic jelly

Wipe the duck and reserve the duck liver. Rub the duck over with butter and place in a roasting tin. Set in a hot oven (200°C, 400°F or Gas No. 6) and roast for 30 minutes. Remove from the heat and cool for a few moments, then lift the partly roasted flesh from the bones. Cut the breast pieces into thick strips and reserve. Remove any pieces of skin from the remainder of the duck flesh. Trim the pork fillet and cut into pieces. Trim away any rind from the pork fat. Mince the duck flesh, duck liver, pork tenderloin and pork fat together twice. Mix in the sage, parsley, a seasoning of salt and pepper, the nutmeg and the egg to bind. Mix well.

Line a 1-litre (1½–2-pint) terrine or pâté dish with half the trimmed bacon rashers and put in half the duck mixture. Arrange the pieces of duck breast on top and spoon over the orange liqueur. Top with the remaining mixture. Cover with the rest of the bacon rashers, a buttered paper and a lid.

Place the terrine in a larger roasting tin with cold water to the depth of 2·5 cm (1 inch). Place in the centre of a slow oven (110°C, 225°F or Gas No. ¼) and cook for 3 hours.

When cooked, remove the lid and leave the pâté to cool overnight under a weight. Remove the pâté from the terrine. Wash the terrine clean and replace the pâté. Top with thin slices of fresh orange and then glaze with the melted aspic jelly to cover the pâté and fill any spaces at the side of the dish. Chill until the aspic has set firm.

Serve sliced with salad.

Vitello Tonnato

Serves 6 Time taken 8–10 hours
Make in advance

1 kg (2½ lb) boned and rolled loin
  of veal
1 onion
1 carrot

1 teaspoon salt
rind and juice of ½ lemon
1·5 dl (¼ pint) dry white wine

For the Tuna Mayonnaise
1 (90 g) (3½ oz) tin tuna fish
1 tablespoon lemon juice
3 anchovy fillets
1·5 dl (¼ pint) mayonnaise
freshly milled pepper

capers
lemon slices
gherkins

Place the meat, along with the meat bones, in a saucepan. The butcher should give you the bones after having prepared the pieces of meat for you. Peel and slice the onion, and scrape and slice the carrot. Add to the pan along with the salt, thinly pared lemon rind and the lemon juice. Add the wine and sufficient cold water to cover the meat. Bring up to the boil, then lower the heat. Cover with a lid and cook gently for 1½ hours. Draw off the heat and allow the meat to cool in the liquor.

Meanwhile prepare the tuna mayonnaise. Drain the tuna fish from the tin. Using a wooden spoon, mash the tuna fish with the lemon juice and anchovy fillets. Rub the mixture through a sieve and beat again to make a smooth purée. Add the mayonnaise and blend together. Season well with freshly milled pepper.

Thinly carve the cold meat and arrange the slices on a serving dish. Spoon over the tuna mayonnaise to cover the meat completely. Leave to chill for several hours.

Serve garnished with capers, lemon slices and gherkins.

Bacon with Mustard Glaze

Serves 8 Time taken 2½–3 hours
Allow for overnight soaking   Prepare in advance

1 (2 kg) (4 lb) middle gammon joint
10 peppercorns

1 bay leaf
1 tablespoon Demerara sugar

For the Mustard Glaze
175 g (6 oz) Demerara sugar
juice of ½ lemon

3 tablespoons water
2 tablespoons made mustard

Soak the gammon overnight in cold water, then rinse under running water the next day. Weigh the joint and calculate the cooking time; 20 minutes to every 450 g (1 lb) plus 20 minutes over.

Put the gammon into a large saucepan with the peppercorns, bay leaf and 1 tablespoon of the Demerara sugar. Cover with water and bring up to the boil slowly – this should take about 30 minutes. Turn the heat down and simmer gently for half the calculated cooking time.

Meanwhile prepare the glaze. Combine together in a saucepan the sugar, lemon juice, water and mustard. Cook over a low heat until the sugar has dissolved, then bring to the boil and cook rapidly to a thin syrup.

When the bacon is half-cooked, remove the joint from the water. Using a sharp knife, strip off the rind. Score the fat into diamonds and place in a roasting tin. Baste with the glaze. Place in the centre of a preheated moderate oven (180°C, 350°F or Gas No. 4) and baste frequently with the glaze for the remainder of the cooking time. The joint should be a rich golden colour. Allow to cool. Serve sliced with salad.

Chicken Mousse

Serves 6 Time taken 5–6 hours
Make in advance

1 (1·5 kg) (3 lb) oven-ready chicken
1 onion peeled and stuck with a
  clove
1 tablespoon salt
25 g (1 oz) butter
25 g (1 oz) flour
3 dl (½ pint) chicken stock
15 g (½ oz) powdered gelatine

3 tablespoons cold water
salt
freshly milled pepper
1 small tin anchovy fillets
dash tarragon vinegar
3 dl (½ pint) double cream
1 tablespoon chopped fresh parsley
  or chives

For the Decoration
cucumber slices
1 level teaspoon powdered gelatine

1·5 dl (¼ pint) chicken stock

Place the chicken in a large pan. Add the onion, sufficient cold water to cover, and the salt. Bring up to the boil and simmer for 1 hour. Draw off the heat and allow the chicken to cool in the stock. Skim off the fat and measure out 4·5 dl (¾ pint) of the stock. Lift the chicken flesh from the bones. Remove any skin, mince the flesh finely and place in a bowl.

Melt the 25 g (1 oz) butter in a pan and stir in the flour. Cook for a moment, then gradually stir in the 3 dl ($\frac{1}{2}$ pint) of reserved chicken stock. Bring up to the boil stirring well, then lower the heat and allow to simmer gently for about 5 minutes. Meanwhile measure the cold water into a cup and sprinkle in the gelatine. Allow to soak for about 5 minutes.

When the sauce is ready, check the seasoning and draw off the heat. Add the soaked gelatine and stir long enough for the gelatine to melt. Add to the cooked, minced chicken and beat thoroughly to make a smooth mixture. Drain and mash the anchovies. Add the anchovies and vinegar to taste. Fold in the lightly whipped cream and herbs. Pour into a white china soufflé dish for serving.

Garnish with cucumber slices. Dissolve the gelatine in the remaining reserved chicken stock to make a little aspic to glaze the surface. Stir the jelly over the ice cubes until almost setting. Spoon quickly over the surface of the chicken mousse. Chill until ready to serve.

Beef Galantine

Serves 6 Time taken 4$\frac{1}{2}$–5 hours
Make in advance

450 g (1 lb) lean beef steak	65 g (2$\frac{1}{2}$ oz) fresh white breadcrumbs
225 g ($\frac{1}{2}$ lb) cooked ham, cut in	2 large eggs
one piece	1 level teaspoon salt
1 onion	freshly milled pepper
4 tomatoes	

An old fashioned beef galantine, steamed in a pudding basin, is a very easy recipe to prepare and an excellent one for the weekend. It can be made in advance and should be left under a weight overnight.

Trim away any fat from the steak and ham, and cut both into pieces. Peel the onion and cut into quarters. Mince together the steak, ham and onion, passing them through the mincer two or three times. Peel the tomatoes, cut them in half and rub through a sieve into a basin to extract all the juice and flesh. Add this to the meat mixture along with the breadcrumbs, eggs and seasoning. Beat the mixture thoroughly together. Spoon into a buttered generous 1-litre (2-pint) pudding basin. Cover with double thickness of greased greaseproof paper and tie tightly with string. Steam gently for 4 hours. Use either a proper steamer, or place the pudding basin on an upturned saucer in a saucepan with boiling water one-third up the sides of the basin. Keep the pan topped up with boiling water during the cooking time so that it does not boil dry.

When cooked remove the paper and string. Re-cover the galantine with fresh greaseproof paper, lightly greased. Place a saucer on top and a heavy weight to press the galantine down. Leave overnight until quite cold. Turn out.

Serve sliced with salad and sour-cream horseradish sauce (see page 180).

Danish Meat Balls

Serves 4 Time taken 30 minutes
Make in advance

225 g (½ lb) lean steak
225 g (½ lb) pork tenderloin
1 medium-sized onion
25 g (1 oz) plain flour
1 egg

1 level teaspoon salt
freshly milled pepper
milk
50 g (2 oz) butter

Although often served hot, these meat balls are delicious cold with a salad. They make an excellent lunch dish.

Trim away any fat or gristle from the steak and cut the steak in pieces. Peel the onion and cut in quarters. Mince the steak, pork and onion two or three times. Place in a mixing basin, mix well and then stir in the flour. Add the egg, salt and a seasoning of pepper. Blend well, adding sufficient milk to make a fairly soft mixture.

Melt the butter in a frying pan. Drop the mixture by tablespoons into the hot butter. From this amount of mixture you should get about eight portions. Fry over moderate heat on both sides until well browned – takes about 20 minutes. Once the meat balls brown on the underside, turn over with a palette knife and brown on the second side. Drain well and allow to cool.

Serve cold with salad and a sweet pickle or chutney.

Pressed Ox Tongue

Serves 6–8 Time taken 4–4½ hours
Allow 24 hours for soaking   Make in advance

1 (2 kg) (4 lb) salted or pickled
    ox tongue
1 onion

2 cloves
2 carrots
1 bay leaf

Wash the tongue and soak for 24 hours in cold water. Change the water once or twice. Place the tongue in a large pan, cover with fresh, cold water and bring to the boil. Drain off the water and re-cover with fresh cold water. Peel the onion and stick with the cloves. Scrape the carrots, leaving them whole. Add the onion, carrots and bay leaf to the pan. Bring to the boil and simmer gently for 3–3½ hours until tender. Remove any scum from the water when it rises and add extra boiling water, if necessary, to keep the tongue covered. To test when the tongue is ready, run a sharp skewer point into the tip of the tongue. If this feels tender, the tongue is cooked.

Drain from the pan and plunge the tongue into cold water. Immediately remove the skin, the duct, gristle and any bones from the back of the tongue. Curl the tongue round and fit it *tightly* into a deep cake tin, or baking dish, approximately 15 cm (6 inches) in diameter. Cover with a plate and press down with a heavy weight. Leave for 24 hours, then turn out of the dish. There should be sufficient jelly set around the tongue and extra aspic jelly should not be needed.

Serve with Cumberland sauce (see page 176) and salad.

Mutton Pies

Serves 4 Time taken 3–3½ hours
Make in advance

225–350 g (½–¾ lb) lean mutton
seasoned flour
1 onion

pinch mixed herbs
salt
freshly milled pepper

For the Pastry
350 g (12 oz) plain flour
½ level teaspoon salt

100 g (4 oz) dripping
225 ml (1½ gills) water

Scottish mutton pies are delicious eaten hot and newly baked, or cold with salad. They are excellent for a picnic.

Cut the mutton in small pieces, discard any fat and roll the meat in seasoned flour. Peel and finely chop the onion. Place the meat in a casserole with the onion, herbs and a seasoning of salt and pepper. Add sufficient hot water to cover the meat. Cover the casserole, place in a slow oven (170°C, 325°F or Gas No. 3) and cook for about 1½ hours or until tender.

When the meat is ready, prepare the pastry. Sieve the flour and salt into a mixing basin. Place the dripping and water (about 12 tablespoons) in a saucepan. Bring up to the boil and add all at once to the flour. Mix with a wooden spoon to a rough dough, then turn out on to a board and knead until smooth. Set aside a quarter of the pastry for the pie tops and keep warm.

Divide the remaining dough into 4 equal pieces. Roll each piece out to a circle large enough to line 7·5-10-cm (3-4-inch) pie rings, or use large scone cutters. Line the rings with the pastry. Fill the pies with the meat mixture and add a little of the stock to moisten. Damp the edges of the pie with water, and cover with the reserved pastry rolled out to make the lids. Press edges together and trim. Make a hole in the centre of each and brush the pies with a little milk. Place in the centre of a moderately hot oven (190°C, 375°F or Gas No. 5) and bake for 40 minutes. Remove the rings after 30 minutes. Allow to cool.

Serve with salad.

Glazed Salt Beef

Serves 6 Time taken 2 hours
Allow 24 hours for soaking   Make in advance

1 kg (2 lb) boned and rolled salt brisket of beef	few crushed peppercorns bouquet garni
3 onions	

For the Meat Glaze

½ beef stock cube	1 rounded teaspoon powdered gelatine
1·5 dl (¼ pint) water	
gravy browning	1 tablespoon water

Wipe the meat and soak for 24 hours in cold water. Change the water several times. Drain and place in a large saucepan. Peel and slice the onions, and add to the pan with the peppercorns. Cover with fresh cold water and a lid, and bring slowly to the boil. Skim well and add the bouquet garni.

Cover with a lid and simmer gently, allowing 25 minutes per 450 g (1 lb) plus 25 minutes extra. When cooked, draw the pan off the heat and leave the meat in the cooking liquor until cool enough to handle. Then take the meat out, cover with a plate and a weight, and press until cold.

Prepare the meat glaze. Dissolve the beef cube in the water, add a drop of gravy browning and bring to the boil. Meanwhile, soak the gelatine in the water for 2-3 minutes. Add this to the boiling liquor, draw the pan off the heat and stir until the gelatine has dissolved. Cool until beginning to thicken, and then use to glaze the meat. Leave until the glaze has set.

Serve the salt beef sliced with sweet and sour cucumber pickles.

Potted Hough

Serves 4 Time taken 4½–5 hours
Make in advance

450 g (1 lb) hough (shin of beef)	1 teaspoon salt
1 (1 kg) (2 lb) nap bone or beef shin bone	freshly milled pepper

Place the meat and the bone in a saucepan and cover with cold water – the quantity should be approximately 1·75 litres (3 pints). Bring to the boil, cover with a lid and simmer gently for 4 hours. Add a little extra boiling water when necessary, but, by the time the meat has cooked, the liquid should have reduced by about half. Remove the bone and meat from the pan, and strain the liquid and reserve.

Cut the meat into small pieces or pass through the mincer. If the meat is minced it gives the hough a smoother texture, but on the other hand, some cooks prefer to see the meat cut in small pieces. Skim the fat from the reserved stock and return the stock to the pan – there should be about a scant 1 litre (1½ pints). Add the meat and season to taste with the salt and freshly milled pepper. Bring to the boil, then draw off the heat and pour into two or three small or one large mould. Cool, then chill until set firm.

To serve Loosen the jelly around the edge of the mould and turn out; the hough should unmould quite easily. Serve with salad.

Cold Lamb with Apricot Stuffing

Serves 6 Time taken 2–2½ hours
Make in advance

2 boned breasts of lamb	3 onions
25 g (1 oz) butter	2–3 carrots

For the Apricot Stuffing

100 g (4 oz) dried apricots	1 level teaspoon salt
100 g (4 oz) seedless raisins	75 g (3 oz) butter
1 large green pepper	
275 g (10 oz) fresh white breadcrumbs	

Wipe the meat and trim away any surplus fat. Season and lay flat, skin-side down, on a clean working surface.

Meanwhile prepare the stuffing. Put the apricots and raisins into a saucepan, cover with cold water, bring up to the boil and then strain.

Snip the apricots into small pieces and place in a bowl. Halve, deseed and chop the green pepper. Add the raisins, breadcrumbs, salt and green pepper. Melt the butter, pour on the ingredients and mix with a fork until blended. Divide the stuffing equally between the breasts of lamb and spread evenly to within about 1 cm ($\frac{1}{2}$ inch) of the edges. Roll up from one end and tie securely with string.

Melt the butter in a saucepan, add the meat and brown. Lift it from the pan. Peel and quarter the onions, and scrape and slice the carrots. Add the prepared vegetables to the pan. Place the meat on top and add sufficient water just to cover the vegetables. Cover the pan with a lid and bring slowly to the boil. Lower the heat and simmer gently for 1$\frac{1}{2}$ hours.

Remove the meat from the pan and place under a heavy weight. Leave overnight in a cool place. Next day remove the string and trim the ends evenly.

Serve sliced with salad.

Cold Roast Chicken with Pâté Stuffing

Serves 6 Time taken 2–2$\frac{1}{2}$ hours
Make in advance

1 (1·5 kg) (3 lb) oven-ready chicken   50 g (2 oz) butter
salt   4–6 streaky bacon rashers
$\frac{1}{2}$ lemon

For the Stuffing
225 g (8 oz) liver pâté   salt
225 g (8 oz) fresh white   freshly milled pepper
   breadcrumbs   1 small egg
$\frac{1}{2}$ onion
1 tablespoon finely chopped parsley   watercress

Wipe the chicken and rub the inside with a little salt and the outside with the cut lemon. Set aside while preparing the stuffing.

Using a fork, mix the pâté with the breadcrumbs. Peel and finely chop the onion. Add onion, parsley and seasoning, and mix in sufficient lightly beaten egg to make a moist but not soft mixture. Fill the neck cavity with a little of the stuffing. Pull the neck skin down over the stuffing and underneath the bird. Twist the wings forward and under, and secure both with a skewer. Place the remaining stuffing in the body cavity of the bird and skewer the tail-end closed.

Place the chicken in a roasting tin, smear with a little of the butter and place the remainder in the pan. Cover the breast with the trimmed bacon rashers and a piece of kitchen foil. Place in the centre of a moderately hot oven (190°C, 375°F or Gas No. 5) and roast for 20 minutes per 450 g (1 lb) plus 20 minutes. Baste frequently. About 15 minutes before cooking time is complete remove the bacon rashers and foil. Return chicken to the oven to brown. Then remove from the heat and allow to cool.

Serve garnished with freshly washed watercress and a tossed salad.

Potted Hare

Serves 4–6 Time taken 5–6 hours
Make in advance

450 g (1 lb) hare pieces	6 dl (1 pint) water
1 tablespoon vinegar	grated lemon rind
150 g (6 oz) butter	salt
1 medium onion	freshly milled pepper
2 carrots	pinch ground nutmeg
1 small clove garlic	1 tablespoon sherry
1 bay leaf	

Wipe the pieces of hare with a damp cloth and place in a bowl. Cover with cold water and add the vinegar. Leave to stand for 2–3 hours then drain and pat dry.

Melt 25 g (1 oz) of the butter in a frying pan, add the pieces of hare and fry over moderate heat, turning to brown the pieces evenly. Remove from the pan and place the hare in a saucepan. Peel and finely chop the onion. Add onion to the hot butter remaining in the frying pan and fry gently for a few moments to soften. Scrape the carrots and cut in half. Add the softened onions and the carrots to the hare. Add the peeled clove of garlic, the bay leaf and the water. Bring up to the boil, cover with a lid and simmer gently for about 2½ hours or until the hare is tender.

Lift the hare pieces from the pan. Remove the flesh from the bones and mince the flesh into a basin. Melt 100 g (4 oz) of the butter with a little finely grated lemon rind. Add to the hare and beat well with a wooden spoon to mix. Season with salt, freshly milled pepper and add the nutmeg. Beat in the sherry. Spoon the mixture into a pot and spread level. Melt the remaining 25 g (1 oz) of butter and pour over the surface. Leave to chill for several hours.

Serve with hot toast or crisp French bread.

Raised Pork Pies

Serves 4 Time taken 2½–3 hours
Make in advance

225 g (½ lb) pork sausage meat
salt and pepper
pinch powdered sage

2 hard-boiled eggs
egg and milk for glazing

For the Pastry
225 g (8 oz) plain flour
1 level teaspoon salt
75 g (3 oz) white fat or lard

5 full tablespoons mixed milk and
and water

Small raised pork pies are easier to make than large ones. These pies make a pleasant lunch or supper dish. Cut each pie in half and serve with salad.

Season the pork sausage meat and add a pinch of sage. With lightly floured hands, shape half the meat round each of the hard-boiled eggs, then set aside while preparing the pastry.

Sieve the flour and salt into a warm mixing basin. Measure the fat and liquid into a small saucepan and bring to the boil. Pour immediately into the centre of the sieved flour and mix to a smooth ball with a wooden spoon. Turn on to a board and knead lightly.

Divide the pastry in half and reserve a little from each portion for the lid and decoration. Shape each portion of pastry into a pie as follows. Mould the pastry into a round, flatten out the centre to make the base, and pinch the edges of the pastry up to make the sides. Place the pork filling in the centre and gradually work the pastry up round the pork filling to form an edge. Roll the reserved piece of pastry out to form a lid. Dampen the edge of the pie with a little mixed egg and milk, and place the lid over the top. Pinch the edges to seal and snip round with a pair of scissors to make a turret border. Make a hole in the centre and decorate with leaves made from any remaining pastry. Prepare the second pie in the same manner.

Fix a greased band of paper round each pie and brush the tops with mixed egg and milk. Set the pies on a baking try and place in the centre of a hot oven (200°C, 400°F or Gas No. 6) and bake for 20 minutes. Lower the heat to moderate (180°C, 350°F or Gas No. 4) and bake for a further 40 minutes. Remove the band of paper from around the sides after 30 minutes' cooking time and brush the whole pie with mixed egg and milk to glaze. When baked, allow the pies to cool.

Cut each pie in half and serve with salad.

Cold Curried Chicken

Serves 6 Time taken 2–3 hours
Make in advance

1 (1·5 kg) (3 lb) oven-ready chicken	50 g (2 oz) butter

For the Curry Mayonnaise

1 tablespoon olive oil	juice of ½ lemon
1 small onion	2 rounded tablespoons sweet
1 level tablespoon curry powder	chutney
1·5 dl (¼ pint) stock	3 dl (½ pint) mayonnaise
1 rounded teaspoon tomato purée	3 tablespoons single cream

Wipe the chicken and place a little of the butter inside. Spread the bird with the remaining butter, cover with a buttered paper and place in a roasting tin. Set in the centre of a hot oven (200°C, 400°F or Gas No. 6) and roast for 1–1½ hours. Remove from the heat and allow to cool.

Meanwhile prepare the sauce. Heat the oil in a saucepan. Peel and finely chop the onion. Add to the pan, cover and fry very gently for 5 minutes, or until the onion is soft. Stir in the curry powder and cook a further few minutes to bring out the flavour. Stir in the stock, tomato purée, strained lemon juice and chutney. Stir until boiling, then simmer for 5 minutes. Draw off the heat and strain the sauce into a basin. Allow to cool, then stir in the mayonnaise and cream.

Remove the flesh from the chicken carcass and arrange in a serving dish in chunky pieces. Spoon over the curry mayonnaise. Serve with rice and pineapple salad (see page 162).

Pressed Spiced Beef

Serves 6–8 Time taken 3 hours
Allow 24 hours for marinating   Make in advance

1 (1 kg) (2 lb) piece fresh rolled brisket of beef	12 peppercorns
cooking salt	blade of mace
3–4 cloves	4 tablespoons vinegar

Rub the meat over with cooking salt. Place in a deep bowl with the cloves, peppercorns, mace, vinegar, and just enough water to cover. Leave to marinate for 24 hours, turning several times.

Drain and place the meat in a large casserole, cover with enough of the marinade to come about halfway up the joint, then add the peppercorns but discard the cloves and mace. Cover with a lid and place in the centre of a slow oven (170°C, 325°F or Gas No. 3) and cook for 2½–3 hours.

Leave the meat in the liquor until cool enough to handle. Drain, place under a heavy weight and leave until quite cold.

Serve sliced with salad.

Spiced Peaches

Serves 6 Time taken 10–15 minutes
Make in advance

1 (850 g) (1 lb 14 oz) tin peach halves
4 tablespoons white malt vinegar
2·5 cm piece (1 inch) of cinnamon stick

75 g (3 oz) soft brown sugar
1 rounded teaspoon whole cloves
1 rounded teaspoon whole allspice

Drain the syrup from the tin of peaches into a saucepan and stir in the sugar, vinegar and spices. Bring up to the boil slowly, stirring to dissolve the sugar. Simmer quickly for 5 minutes. Add the peach halves, bring up to the boil again and simmer for a further 5 minutes.

Draw the pan off the heat. Put the peaches and the spiced syrup into a dish and leave until cold. Put in the refrigerator and chill for a few hours, or overnight, before serving.

Serve the chilled peach halves with cold gammon or pork.

Honey Glazed Gammon

Serves 6–8 Time taken 8 hours
Allow to soak overnight Make in advance

1 (1 kg 600 g) (3½ lb) piece gammon corner

For the Honey Glaze
2 tablespoons clear honey
50 g (2 oz) soft brown sugar

1 teaspoon prepared English mustard

Soak the gammon for several hours or overnight, covered in cold water. Drain, then place skin-side down in a large saucepan and cover with fresh, cold water. Bring up to the boil, then lower the heat and simmer gently for 1½ hours. Top up with extra boiling water when required to keep the gammon covered. Draw the pan off the heat and leave the gammon to cool in the liquid.

When cold, lift the gammon from the pan, and strip away the rind, using a sharp knife. Score the fat in a criss-cross pattern and place the gammon in a roasting tin. In a small bowl, blend together the honey, sugar and mustard to a stiff paste. Spread this over the surface of the gammon. Place in the centre of a hot oven (200°C, 400°F or Gas No. 6) and bake for about 15–20 minutes, or until the gammon is golden brown. Baste often with the glaze, as it melts and runs into the tin. Leave until cold.

Serve sliced with salad.

Pheasant Pâté

Serves 6 Time taken 3¼–4 hours
Make in advance

450 g (1 lb) lean veal	450 g (1 lb) pork fat
1–2 tablespoons brandy	1 egg
2 tablespoons dry white wine	pinch dried thyme
1 plump pheasant	1 tablespoon chopped parsley
25 g (1 oz) butter	

Trim the veal and cut into pieces. Place in a basin and add the brandy and white wine. Leave to marinate for 1 hour. Meanwhile wipe the pheasant, rub the surface of the bird with the butter and place in a roasting tin. Set in a hot oven (200°C, 400°F or Gas No. 6) and roast for about 15–20 minutes. Remove from the heat, cool slightly and then lift the partly roasted flesh from the bones. Mince the pheasant flesh with the veal and half the pork fat. Season with salt and pepper, add any marinade remaining in the basin from the veal, beat in the egg, thyme and chopped parsley.

Line a 1-litre (1½–2-pint) terrine or pâté dish with some of the remaining pork fat cut in thin strips. Pack the pâté mixture into the dish. Cover with the remaining strips of pork fat. Cover the terrine with a lid or buttered kitchen foil. Stand the dish in a roasting tin with water 2·5 cm (1 inch) up the sides of the dish. Place in the centre of a slow oven (110°C, 225°F or Gas No. ¼) and cook for 2½ hours. Remove from the oven and allow to cool under a weight. Allow to stand for 24 hours before serving.

Serve sliced with salad.

Cold Roast Duck with Rice Pilaff

Serves 4 Time taken 2–3 hours
Make in advance

1 (2 kg) (4 lb) oven-ready duckling   salt

For the Rice Pilaff

6 soaked prunes	225 g (8 oz) long grain rice
1 medium onion	6 dl (1 pint) duck stock
1 green pepper	1 level teaspoon salt
25 g (1 oz) butter	1 small tin red pimentos

Remove the giblets from inside the duckling. Wipe the bird and rub the skin with salt. Prick well all over with a fork, put in a roasting tin and add 2 tablespoons of water. Roast in the centre of a moderate oven (180°C, 350°F or Gas No. 4) for 20 minutes per 450 g (1 lb). Remove from the pan and set aside until cold.

Cover the duck giblets generously with cold, salted water, bring up to the boil and simmer for 30 minutes to make a stock. Strain, skim, check the seasoning and reserve 6 dl (1 pint).

Put the soaked prunes, and the water in which they were soaked, into a pan and bring to the boil. Simmer gently until just tender. Draw off the heat and leave to cool. Peel and finely chop the onion. Halve, deseed and shred the green pepper. Melt the butter in a saucepan and add the onion and green pepper. Cover and fry gently for about 10 minutes until the onion is soft but not browned. Add the rice and toss with the butter and vegetables. Stir in the duck stock and salt, and bring to the boil. Cover with a lid and leave to simmer gently for about 20 minutes, or until the rice is tender and the liquid absorbed. Draw off the heat, turn the mixture into a bowl and set aside until quite cold.

When ready to serve, cut the duckling into four portions and arrange on a serving platter. Drain the prunes and remove the stones. Coarsely chop the prune flesh and the drained red pimentos. Fold both into the rice with a fork and spoon the rice pilaff on to the serving dish around the duck.

Serve with a tossed salad.

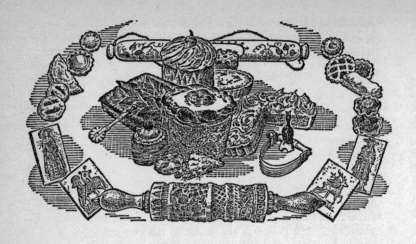

8 Pastries & Pies

A light hand with pastry is a gift some cooks are born with and others acquire with practice. Pastry is basically a mixture of flour, fat and water. It is the method of incorporating these three that determines the type of pastry, and the handling on the part of the cook, that determines the quality of the final result.

For shortcrust pastry butter, margarine, vegetable fat or lard may be used. Butter gives a good flavour and a crisp pastry. Vegetable fat gives pastry a pleasant 'short' texture but lacks flavour. Lard, being a pure fat, gives a very short texture, and, being soft, it tends to melt while being rubbed in and, if not used carefully, can make the pastry tough. A mixture of fats gives the best results, the favourite choice being a mixture of butter and vegetable fat. Fats should be used cool but never straight from the refrigerator. To rub in very cold fat would require heavy handling and result in over-mixing. If the fat is hard, especially where a mixture of two fats is being used, allow them to stand at room temperature until soft. Beat them together on a plate with a knife until blended, then rub in lightly and evenly. Always use plain flour; if self-raising flour is substituted it should be remembered that the raising agent will make a rather cake-like pastry instead of a crisp, short pastry, and is acceptable only where a sweet moist filling is being used.

Once prepared, always allow the pastry to rest, either in a cool corner of the kitchen or in a polythene bag in the refrigerator. (The polythene protects the pastry from the drying effect of the refrigerator. When unprotected a skin forms on the outside of the dough which is inclined to crack when rolled out afterwards.) This resting period allows the gluten in the flour which has been stretched during preparation to loosen its elasticity. If not allowed for, the pastry will be difficult to roll out and will shrink badly during baking.

Rough puff, flaky and puff pastry are the most delicious and most versatile of all pastries. In each case the high proportion of fat used in the recipe means that they have to be prepared more carefully than shortcrust. They are not difficult to make, but there are certain points which need watching to ensure success. In most recipes the pastry is interchangeable, the choice depending on the type of result required. Rough puff is the easiest of all to make and gives a light, crisp pastry. Flaky pastry is a little more complicated to prepare but a more versatile pastry, giving a rise as well as crispness. Puff pastry is the most difficult to make but the most versatile of all. It gives the best rise and looks the most attractive.

In all cases where these rich pastries are used, the recipes themselves are usually quite simple – only the pastry needs careful preparation. Since the nature of the pastry is such that it is better well rested before baking, the ideal way to work is to make the pastry well in advance when there is more time and the kitchen is cool.

The object of rolling and folding the pastry is two-fold. First to get many wafer-thin layers of pastry and butter, giving a flaky texture. Secondly to enclose air which makes the pastry light and gives a good rise. These pastries should be rolled and folded at least six times, but care should be taken not to over-roll, otherwise the fat simply mixes with the dough instead of remaining in layers.

Resting the pastry as it's made is one of the most important rules. When dough is worked it becomes elastic, making it difficult to roll out because it tends to shrink back. If baked without resting, the pastry would shrink badly. Resting allows the fat to firm up slightly and the dough to relax, making it easier to handle. The dough should be protected by placing in a polythene bag or wrapped in a piece of greaseproof paper and a damp teacloth. If the pastry has been left in a refrigerator for as long as 12–14 hours, it should be allowed to come up to kitchen temperature. Otherwise the fat, which will have hardened more than the dough, will break through the pastry on rolling out.

Once rolled to the shape required in a recipe, it is important that the edges of the pastry are cut cleanly to free the pastry layers and allow the pastry to rise. Straight edges should be cut with a very sharp, floured knife. Circles of pastry should be cut with a round cutter dipped in flour, and stamped out without twisting the cutter. All rich pastries such as these should be baked on trays that are wet with cold water. They are baked in a hot oven to ensure a good rise and the moisture on the tray helps to prevent the pastry from scorching too quickly on the underside.

Preparing Pastry for a Recipe

When a recipe lists 100 g ($\frac{1}{4}$ lb) or 225 g ($\frac{1}{2}$ lb) of pastry in the ingredients, this does not mean the total weight of the pastry but means the weight of the flour only. It should be regarded as a guide for the amount of pastry to make up.

Note: All tins used for baking are standard sizes. Metric measures and equivalent sizes can be found on page viii.

Plain Shortcrust Pastry

Makes 100 g ($\frac{1}{4}$ lb) pastry Time taken 10 minutes

100 g (4 oz) plain flour	25 g (1 oz) vegetable fat
pinch of salt	2 tablespoons water
25 g (1 oz) butter or margarine	

Sift together flour and salt. Measure the fat on to a plate. Using a knife blade, beat down the fats and mix until soft and blended. Add to the flour and rub in evenly. To 'rub in' means to pick up small handfuls of fat and flour and rub very lightly with the thumbs and fingertips so that the mixture falls back through the fingers into the mixing basin. This action not only blends together the fat and flour but also incorporates air which helps to make a light pastry. It is important not to over-mix the pastry at any stage, and rubbing in should stop when the mixture looks crumbly.

Add the water all at once into the centre of the mixture. Blend, using a fork, until the mixture clings together in a ball, leaving the basin sides clean. Turn the dough on to a lightly floured surface, and knead lightly to make a smooth, fairly stiff dough. Set the pastry to rest for 10 minutes before using.

Rich Shortcrust Pastry

Makes 225 g ($\frac{1}{2}$ lb) pastry Time taken 10 minutes

225 g (8 oz) plain flour
100 g (4 oz) butter
50 g (2 oz) icing sugar

2 egg yolks
2 tablespoons water

This recipe makes particularly nice, crisp pastry that is very suitable for dessert or cake recipes. The prepared pastry can be kept for several days ready made in the refrigerator.

Sift the flour into a basin. Add the butter cut in pieces and rub into the mixture. Add the sifted icing sugar and make a well in the centre. Place the egg yolks and water in the centre of the ingredients, then, using a fork, mix to a rough dough in the basin. Turn out on to a lightly floured working surface and knead for a few moments until smooth. Shape into a ball, then place in a polythene bag or wrap in greaseproof paper and chill in the refrigerator for about 30 minutes before using.

Shortcrust Pastry Mix

Time taken 10 minutes

900 g (2 lb) plain flour
2 level teaspoons salt

225 g (8 oz) white vegetable fat
225 g (8 oz) margarine

A home-made pastry mix, kept at hand in the refrigerator can save a lot of kitchen time. The pastry mix keeps cool in the refrigerator, making it easy to handle, and pastry required in a recipe can be made in minutes by simply stirring water into a measured amount of the mix.

Sift the flour and salt into a large mixing basin. Place the vegetable fat and margarine together on a large plate. If they are hard from the refrigerator, allow them to stand at room temperature just long enough to soften so that they can be blended together with a palette knife. Add the blended fats to the flour and, using the fingertips, rub the fat into the flour until the mixture is evenly mixed. Cut through the mixture two or three times with a sharp knife to remove any lumps of fat that might remain, then spoon the mixture into a large polythene bag. Close tightly and place in the refrigerator. This mix can be used at intervals over a period of 2–3 months.

To use the mix If your recipe calls for 100 g (4 oz) *shortcrust pastry*

measure out 175 g (6 oz) of the mix into a basin. For 175 g (6 oz) *shortcrust pastry*, measure out 250 g (9 oz) of the mix and for 225 g (8 oz) *shortcrust pastry* measure out 350 g (12 oz) of the mix. Using a fork, stir in sufficient cold water (anything from 1–3 tablespoons) according to the amount of mix and stir to a rough dough in the basin. Turn out on to a lightly floured board, knead lightly and the pastry is ready for use.

Rough Puff Pastry

Makes 225 g ($\frac{1}{2}$ lb) pastry Time taken 1 hour

225 g (8 oz) plain flour	75 g (3 oz) vegetable fat
$\frac{1}{2}$ level teaspoon salt	1·5 dl ($\frac{1}{4}$ pint) cold water to mix
75 g (3 oz) butter or margarine	1 teaspoon lemon juice

Sieve flour and salt into a mixing basin. Blend together the butter or margarine and vegetable fat, then form in lumps about the size of walnuts. If the fat is very soft, cool for a while until it becomes a little firmer.

Add the lumps of fat to the sieved flour, then stir in the mixed water and lemon juice. Mix with a palette or table knife until the mixture begins to cling together in a rough dough. Draw the mixture together gently with the fingers and turn out on to a lightly floured board and with your fingers lightly shape into a ball of dough but do not knead.

Shape into a rectangle, then roll into an oblong strip about three times as long as it is wide. Mark the pastry into thirds, fold one end up and the other down over it – envelope style. Give the pastry a half-turn clockwise, so that the folded edges are top and bottom. Seal edges and repeat the rolling, folding and turning four times more. Leave the pastry to rest for 15 minutes between each alternate rolling. Set the finished pastry aside to rest for 30 minutes before using.

Flaky Pastry

Makes 225 g ($\frac{1}{2}$ lb) pastry Time taken 1 hour

225 g (8 oz) plain flour	75 g (3 oz) vegetable fat
$\frac{1}{2}$ level teaspoon salt	1·5 dl ($\frac{1}{4}$ pint) water
75 g (3 oz) butter	1 teaspoon lemon juice

Sift together the flour and salt into a mixing basin. With a knife mix the fats together on a plate until softened and blended. Spread evenly over a plate and mark into four equal portions. Rub one portion into the sieved flour. Add the mixed water and lemon juice, and mix to a rough dough in the mixing basin. Turn out on to a lightly floured working surface and knead to a smooth dough. Place in a polythene bag and leave to rest for 10 minutes before rolling out.

Roll out the dough to an oblong shape, about three times as long as it is wide. Mark into thirds and over the top two-thirds of the dough, place one-third of the remaining fat in small pieces. Do this with the tip of a table knife, leaving the fat in small lumps. Distribute the fat evenly, allowing spaces between lumps of fat so that plenty of air may be trapped during folding. Fold the lower uncovered section of pastry up over the centre, and the top down over both. Give a half turn clockwise so that the folded sides are now top and bottom. Seal edges with the rolling pin and roll out again. Repeat and rest the dough 15–20 minutes between each turn until all the fat has been added. Roll and fold once more, then leave in a cool place for 30 minutes before using.

Puff Pastry

Makes 225 g ($\frac{1}{2}$ lb) pastry Time taken 1$\frac{1}{2}$–2 hours

225 g (8 oz) plain flour
$\frac{1}{2}$ level teaspoon salt
25 g (1 oz) vegetable fat

1·5 dl (scant $\frac{1}{4}$ pint) cold water
200 g (7 oz) butter

Sieve the flour and salt into a mixing basin. Beat down the vegetable fat on a small plate, then add to the flour mixture and rub in. Make a well in the centre and add the liquid all at once. Using a fork, mix quickly to a rough dough. Turn out on to a lightly floured working surface and knead lightly. Place the dough in a polythene bag and put in a cool place to rest for at least 30 minutes.

Cut the butter into pieces on to a large plate and then, using a palette knife, work until pliable to make shaping easier. With lightly floured hands, quickly make the butter into a flat shape about 15 cm (6 inches) wide by 10 cm (4 inches) deep.

Roll the rested dough out to an oblong, about 1 cm ($\frac{1}{2}$ inch) wider each side than the butter shape, and long enough for the ends to fold into the centre and slightly overlap. Place the butter in the centre of the dough and fold both ends in to the centre to enclose the butter completely. Press sides and centre edge to seal. Give the dough a half-turn clockwise so that the sealed edges now face top and bottom. Roll the pastry out to an oblong about three times as long as it is wide. Roll with short sharp strokes – never roll the length of the pastry otherwise air bubbles may be forced to break the surface. Avoid rolling the dough too thinly and keep the corners square. Mark the pastry in three, then fold the bottom third up and over the centre and the top down over both. Seal the edges and give a half-turn clockwise again. The pastry has now had one roll and fold. Repeat this, and then place the pastry to rest for 30 minutes. Give the pastry two more rolls and folds, then wrap and rest as before; finally, another two rolls and folds – a total of six – then wrap and store in a cool place until ready for use. Baking instructions should be followed according to the recipe being used, but remember the richer the pastry the hotter the oven. Puff pastry is usually baked in a very hot oven (220°C, 425°F or Gas No. 7) for the initial part of the baking, to get a good rise.

SAVOURY PASTRY RECIPES

Steak and Kidney Pie

Serves 4–6 Time taken 3–3½ hours

700 g (1½ lb) stewing steak	pinch mixed herbs
225 g (½ lb) ox kidney	salt
seasoned flour	freshly milled pepper
15 g (½ oz) dripping or vegetable fat	6 dl (1 pint) stock
1 onion	225 g (½ lb) flaky pastry
	egg and milk

Wipe the steak, trim away the fat and cut steak into neat cubes. Snip away any core from the kidney and cut into pieces. Roll the meat in seasoned flour, then fry quickly in the hot fat until browned on all sides. Lift the meat into a saucepan. Peel and slice the onion and add to the pan along with the mixed herbs, a seasoning of salt and pepper, and the stock. Bring up to the boil, cover with a lid and simmer gently for 1½ hours to partly cook the meat. When cooking time is complete, strain off all but about 1·5 dl (¼ pint) of the gravy and set aside while preparing the pie top.

On a lightly floured surface roll the pastry out about 2·5 cm (1 inch) larger all round than a scant 1-litre (1½-pint) pie dish. Using the pie dish as a guide, cut out a cover for the pie from the centre of the pastry. Using the pastry trimming, cover the greased rim of the dish. Spoon the meat and gravy from the saucepan into the pie dish. Damp the pastry rim with cold water and then cover the whole pie with the pastry top. Press edges together to seal and trim away any excess pastry. With a knife, flute the edges together to seal. Make a hole in the centre of the pie and decorate with leaves of pastry cut from any remaining pieces. Brush the pie surface with egg and milk before sticking the decoration in place. Place the pie above centre in a very hot oven (220°C, 425°F or Gas No. 7) and bake for 30 minutes. Lower the heat to moderate (180°C, 350°F or Gas No. 4) and bake for a further 40 minutes to 1 hour.

Serve hot with any reserved gravy or stock from the initial cooking.

Cornish Pasties

Makes 4 small pasties Time taken 45 minutes–1 hour

225 g (½ lb) shortcrust pastry   egg and milk

For the Filling
225 g (8 oz) lean beef steak   1 tablespoon finely chopped parsley
2 medium-sized potatoes   1 level teaspoon salt
1 medium onion   freshly milled pepper
½ level teaspoon dried mixed herbs   1–2 tablespoons stock

Make the pastry and set aside while preparing the filling. Trim away any fat from the meat and shred the meat finely. Peel the potatoes and cut into small dice, and peel and chop the onion. Mix all these together in a basin along with the mixed herbs, parsley, salt, pepper and enough stock just to moisten.

Divide the pastry into four portions. Roll each portion out on a lightly floured working surface to a circle 13–15 cm (5–6 inches) in diameter. Trim to a neat circle, if necessary using a saucer as a guide. Divide the filling equally and place in the centre of each pastry circle. Damp the edges of the pastry and draw the two opposite sides together over the filling. Press the edges together firmly over the top of the pastry. Crimp the sealed edge on each pasty neatly. Brush with a little beaten egg and milk, and place the pasties on a baking tray. Place in the centre of a hot oven (200°C, 400°F or Gas No. 6) and bake for 15 minutes. Then lower the heat to moderately hot (190°C, 375°F or Gas No. 5) and bake for a further 20–25 minutes.

Serve hot with a savoury brown gravy or serve cold with a salad.

Quiche Lorraine

Serves 4–6 Time taken 1 hour

100 g (¼ lb) shortcrust pastry

For the Filling

2 eggs	4 lean rashers unsmoked bacon
1·5 dl (¼ pint) single cream	15 g (½ oz) butter
salt	50 g (2 oz) Gruyère cheese
freshly milled pepper	

Roll the pastry out on a lightly floured working surface slightly larger all round than a 20-cm (8-inch) flan ring or quiche tin. Line the tin with the pastry and trim the edges neatly. Set aside while preparing the filling.

Whisk together the eggs and cream, and season with salt and pepper. Trim the bacon rashers and cut into thin strips. Fry quickly in the butter, then drain and sprinkle over the base of the pastry case. Thinly slice the Gruyère cheese and place on top, then pour over the egg mixture. Place in the centre of a moderately hot oven (190°C, 375°F or Gas No. 5) and bake for 40–45 minutes. The filling should be set firm and the top a golden brown.

Serve warm with a salad.

Bacon and Mushroom Flan

Serves 4 Time taken 45 minutes

100 g (¼ lb) shortcrust pastry

For the Filling

2–3 rashers lean bacon	100 g (4 oz) button mushrooms
1 small onion	8 g (¼ oz) butter

For the Sauce

25 g (1 oz) butter	freshly milled pepper
25 g (1 oz) flour	2 tablespoons cream
3 dl (½ pint) milk	50 g (2 oz) grated Cheddar cheese
salt	

Roll out the pastry on a lightly floured surface to a circle slightly larger than a greased 18-cm (7-inch) flan ring or shallow cake tin. Line the ring or tin with pastry and trim the edges. Fill the centre of the flan with a piece of crumpled kitchen foil to keep the shape while baking. Bake in the centre of a hot oven (200°C, 400°F or Gas No. 6) for 10–12 minutes. Remove the foil a few moments before the end of the cooking time. Set the pastry case aside while preparing the filling.

Trim the bacon rashers and chop into small pieces. Finely chop the onion. Heat the bacon in a frying pan until the fat runs, then add the chopped onion. Fry gently until the onion is tender but not brown. Remove from the heat and sprinkle the onion and bacon over the base of the pastry case. Trim and wipe the mushrooms, put them in a saucepan with cold water to cover and add the butter. Bring to the boil and simmer gently for 5 minutes. Drain and reserve the mushrooms.

Prepare a sauce by melting the butter in a small saucepan. Stir in the flour, then gradually beat in the milk. Cook gently, stirring all the time, until the sauce is thick and boiling. Continue to cook gently for a few moments, then draw off the heat, season well with salt and pepper, and stir in the cream and reserved mushrooms. Pour over the contents of the pastry case. Sprinkle generously with grated cheese and brown under a hot grill.

Serve warm, cut in wedges, with a salad.

French Onion Tart

Serves 4–6 Time taken 1¼ hours

100 g (¼ lb) shortcrust pastry

For the Filling

450 g (1 lb) onions	freshly milled pepper
50 g (2 oz) butter	2 eggs
salt	1·5 dl (¼ pint) fresh or soured cream

Roll the pastry out on a lightly floured working surface slightly larger all round than a 20-cm (8-inch) flan ring, or quiche tin with a loose base. Line the tin with the pastry and trim the edges neatly. Set aside in a cool place while preparing the filling.

Peel and slice the onions. Add to the melted butter in a pan. Cover and sauté gently for about 10 minutes until the onions are quite soft, then remove the lid and continue to fry until the onions are lightly browned. Draw the pan off the heat and allow to cool for a few moments. Lightly mix the eggs and fresh or soured cream, and stir into the onions. Season well with salt and pepper and pour the mixture into the pastry case.

Place in the centre of a moderately hot oven (190°C, 375°F or Gas No. 5) and bake for 40–45 minutes.

Serve warm with a salad.

Chicken and Mushroom Vol au Vents

Makes 6   Time taken 1½ hours

225 g (½ lb) puff pastry   egg and milk

For the Filling
75 g (3 oz) butter   350 g (12 oz) cooked chicken meat
50 g (2 oz) flour   100 g (¼ lb) button mushrooms
6 dl (1 pint) milk
salt and pepper   chopped parsley
2–3 cooked chicken joints
   or

Vol au vent cases can quite easily be prepared and baked early in the
day or the day before they are required, then heated through and
served with a hot filling.

Roll the prepared pastry out to about ·5 cm (¼ inch) in thickness,
take care to roll no thinner. Using a floured plain 7·5-cm (3-inch)
round cutter, stamp out twelve circles of pastry. Transfer half of
these to a wetted baking tray and arrange not too close together.
Brush with a little beaten egg and milk.

Using a smaller 5-cm (2-inch) plain round cutter stamp out the
centres of the remaining six. Lift up the pastry rings, taking care not
to pull them out of shape, and *turn them over* on to the plain bases.
Press gently to seal the rings on to the pastry bases and brush the
tops with a little beaten egg and milk. Place the circles cut from the
centre on a separate baking tray – these will make the lids. Leave in a
cool place or refrigerator to rest for 15–20 minutes.

Place just above centre in a preheated, very hot oven (220°C,
425°F or Gas No. 7) and bake for 15–20 minutes, until well risen and
beginning to brown. Lower the heat to hot (200°C, 400°F or Gas
No. 6) and bake for a further 10 minutes or until the pastry cases are
quite crisp. Bake the small pastry tops separately in a very hot oven
(220°C, 425°F or Gas No. 7) for about 10 minutes. While still warm
scoop a little of the softer inside pastry from each vol au vent with a
teaspoon – this allows for a more generous portion of filling.

To reheat before use, arrange on a baking try, place in the centre
of a moderate oven (180°C, 350°F or Gas No. 4) and heat through
for 15–20 minutes.

To prepare the filling, melt 50 g (2 oz) of the butter in a pan over a
low heat and stir in the flour. Cook gently for 1 minute, then gradually
stir in the milk a little at a time. Beat each addition of milk in well

before adding the next, and bring up to the boil. Add salt and freshly milled pepper to taste, then simmer the sauce for about 5 minutes.

Meanwhile cut the cooked chicken meat into pieces, slice and lightly fry the mushrooms in the remaining butter. Drain the mushrooms from the butter and add the mushrooms to the sauce along with the chicken.

Spoon the filling generously into the hot pastry cases. Top with the baked lids and sprinkle with a little chopped parsley before serving.

Cheese Tartlets

Makes 12 Time taken 30 minutes

100 g ($\frac{1}{4}$ lb) shortcrust pastry

For the Filling

2 eggs	salt
2 tablespoons milk	freshly milled pepper
75 g (3 oz) grated Cheddar or Gruyère cheese	pinch cayenne

These cheese tartlets look pretty when they are hot, but are also nice cold for a picnic or packed lunch. Bake them in small tartlet moulds or barquette shapes for a cocktail party.

On a lightly floured surface, roll out the pastry thinly. Using a round 6-cm (2½-inch) floured cutter, stamp out twelve circles of pastry. Line twelve tartlet tins with the pastry and set aside in a cool place while preparing the filling.

In a basin mix together the eggs, milk and grated cheese. Add salt and pepper to taste, and a pinch of cayenne pepper. Lightly mix the ingredients with a fork. Place a teaspoon of the mixture in each lined pastry case. Place in the centre of a hot oven (200°C, 400°F or Gas No. 6) for 5–10 minutes. Then lower the heat to moderately hot (190°C, 375°F or Gas No. 5) and bake for a further 5 minutes.

Serve as soon as they come out of the oven.

SWEET PASTRY RECIPES

Strawberry and Cream Cheese Tarts

Makes 12 tartlets Time taken 30 minutes

100 g (¼ lb) rich shortcrust pastry

For the Filling

15 g (½ oz) butter	2 tablespoons strawberry jam
1 level tablespoon castor sugar	or
100 g (4 oz) cream cheese	redcurrant jelly
225 g (½ lb) fresh strawberries	juice of ½ lemon

Roll out the prepared pastry thinly and, using a 6-cm (2½-inch) round, floured cutter, stamp out twelve circles of pastry. Line twelve tartlet tins with the pastry. Prick each base well with a fork and set aside to chill for 15 minutes. Place in the centre of a hot oven (200°C, 400°F or Gas No. 6) and bake for 10 minutes. Allow to cool while preparing the filling.

Cream the butter and sugar until light. Add the cream cheese and beat until smooth. Place a teaspoon of the mixture in each baked pastry case. Top each tart with three strawberries. Sieve the jam or jelly into a saucepan, add the lemon juice and stir over low heat until melted and blended. Use to glaze each strawberry tart.

Lemon Meringue Pie

Serves 6 Time taken 1 hour
Can be made in advance

100 g (¼ lb) shortcrust pastry

For the Filling

50 g (2 oz) cornflour	rind and juice of 2 lemons
225 g (8 oz) castor sugar	2 egg yolks
3 dl (½ pint) water	

For the Meringue

2 egg whites	100 g (4 oz) castor sugar

Roll the pastry out to a circle large enough to line a 20-cm (8-inch) flan ring or tart tin. Line the tin with the pastry and fill the centre with a piece of crumpled kitchen foil to keep the shape while baking. Place above centre of a hot oven (200°C, 400°F or Gas No. 6) and bake for 12 minutes, removing the foil a few minutes before the end of cooking time.

Meanwhile, measure the cornflour and sugar into a small saucepan. Gradually stir in the water and mix well to blend the cornflour. Add the finely grated lemon rind and bring up to the boil over a moderate heat. Stir all the time until thickened and boiling. Cook for 1 minute, then draw the pan off the heat. Stir in first the strained lemon juice, then the egg yolks and mix well. Pour the mixture into the baked pastry case.

Whisk the egg whites until stiff, add half the sugar and whisk again. Then gently fold in the remaining sugar and spoon over the pie. Replace in a slow oven (140–150°C, 275–300°F or Gas Nos. 1–2) and bake for 30 minutes or until crisp.

Serve cold with cream.

Apricot Amber

Serves 6 Time taken 1½ hours
Can be made in advance

100 g (¼ lb) shortcrust pastry

For the Filling

450 g (1 lb) apricots	100 g (4 oz) castor sugar
50 g (2 oz) butter	2 egg yolks
rind and juice of 1 lemon	

For the Meringue

2 egg whites	100 g (4 oz) castor sugar

Roll the pastry out on to a lightly floured working surface and line a 20-cm (8-inch) flan ring or tart tin. Set aside in a cool place while preparing the filling.

Wipe and remove the stalks from the apricots. Melt the butter in a saucepan, add the apricots, finely grated lemon rind and strained juice, and the sugar. Stir over low heat until sugar has dissolved, then cover with a lid and simmer gently for about 20 minutes until the apricots are quite soft and cooked to a pulp. Press the apricots occasionally while cooking to soften them more quickly. Draw the pan off the heat and pass the fruit and juices from the pan through a sieve into a basin to make a purée. Rub the apricots hard to get through all the flesh, then discard all skin and stones remaining in the sieve. Add the yolks of egg to the apricot mixture and mix well.

Pour the purée into the pastry case. Place in the centre of a moderate oven (180°C, 350°F or Gas No. 4) and bake for 30–35 minutes.

When cooking time is almost completed prepare the meringue. Stiffly beat the egg whites, add half the sugar and beat again until thick. Fold in the remaining sugar, using a metal spoon, then pile into the centre of the baked apricot filling. Spread over the surface of the pie, roughing up the surface for an attractive appearance and replace in the centre of the oven. Bake for about 10 minutes to brown the meringue.

Serve cold with cream.

Apricot Tart

Serves 6 Time taken 1 hour
Can be made in advance

100 g (¼ lb) shortcrust pastry

For the Filling

450 g (1 lb) ripe apricots	1 egg yolk
50 g (2 oz) sponge cake crumbs	1·5 dl (¼ pint) double cream
50 g (2 oz) castor sugar	

For the Glaze

2 good tablespoons apricot jam   juice of ½ lemon

Sponge cake crumbs are sprinkled over the base of fresh fruit flans to absorb the fruit juices. Crumbled, trifle sponge cakes are ideal for this purpose.

Roll out pastry thinly and use to line a 20-cm (8-inch) round flan ring or tart tin. Prick the base with fork prongs and fill the centre with a piece of crumpled kitchen foil to keep the shape while baking. Bake above centre in a hot oven (200°C, 400°F or Gas No. 6) for 12 minutes until the pastry case has set and is lightly browned. Remove foil a few minutes before the end of cooking time.

Halve and stone the apricots. Sprinkle the cake crumbs over the base of the pastry case. Arrange the apricot halves, rounded side upwards, to fill the tart, and sprinkle with sugar. Mix together the egg yolk and cream, and spoon over the fruit. Replace in the centre of the oven and bake for a further 15 minutes, or until the filling has set.

Meanwhile, spoon the apricot jam into a saucepan and add the strained lemon juice. Stir constantly over moderate heat until the mixture is boiling. When the apricot tart is baked, spoon the hot glaze over the entire surface. Take care to glaze each apricot-half, otherwise they darken in colour on cooling. Allow the tart to cool.

Serve cold with cream.

Plum Flan with Almonds

Serves 4 Time taken 45 minutes

100 g (¼ lb) shortcrust pastry

For the Filling
450 g (1 lb) purple plums
50 g (2 oz) sponge cake crumbs
50 g (2 oz) castor sugar

1 level teaspoon ground cinnamon
50 g (2 oz) unblanched whole almonds

Roll out the prepared pastry to a circle slightly larger than a 20-cm (8-inch) tart tin or flan ring. Set tin on a baking tray. Line with the pastry. Prick the pastry base and set aside while preparing the filling.

Halve the plums and remove the stones. Sprinkle the sponge cake crumbs (use trifle sponge cakes) over the base of the pastry case. Arrange the plum halves on top to fill the tart. Sprinkle with the mixed sugar and cinnamon. Coarsely shred the almonds and sprinkle over the fruit.

Place the tart in the centre of a hot oven (200°C, 400°F or Gas No. 6) and bake for 20 minutes. Then lower the heat to moderate (180°C, 350°F or Gas No. 4) and bake for a further 10–15 minutes.

Serve warm or cold with cream.

Mille Feuilles

Makes 12–16 slices Time taken 2 hours
Bake pastry layers in advance for filling

225 g (½ lb) puff pastry
For the Filling
raspberry jam
6 dl (1 pint) double cream
25–50 g (1–2 oz) castor sugar

1 teaspoon vanilla essence

icing sugar

These are ideal for a buffet supper party. Do not fill with cream too long in advance of serving.

Cut the prepared puff pastry into three equal portions, so that each pastry layer can be rolled and baked separately. On a lightly floured working surface roll one piece of the pastry out fairly thinly to a shape large enough to cover a baking tray of approximately 32 by 23 cm (13 by 9 inches). The shape of the tray does not matter too much, as long as you use the same one each time. Wet the baking tray with cold water and line with pastry. Trim away any overlapping edges with a sharp knife. Prick the surface all over with the prongs of a fork – this helps even rising – and put to rest in a cool place for 10 minutes before baking. Place above centre in a pre-heated, very hot oven (220°C, 425°F or Gas No. 7) and bake for 10–15 minutes, according to pastry thickness. When crisp and golden brown, remove from the oven and allow to cool on a wire cooling tray while preparing and baking the next layer. Repeat until all layers are baked and leave the pastry until quite cold.

To assemble the slices Set aside the best layer for the top, the second for the base and the other one for the middle. It is best to assemble the slices on a firm flat surface such as a pastry board. Place the base layer flat side down on the board, and spread lightly with raspberry jam. Cover with the centre layer rough side downwards and flat base facing up. Half-whip the double cream, add the sugar and vanilla essence, and whisk until light and fluffy. Spoon the whipped cream on to the flat surface of the pastry layer and spread evenly. Top with the remaining layer, rough side downwards and flat base facing upwards to give the finished slices a level top. Sift with icing sugar all over the surface and set in a cool place or refrigerator to chill for 30 minutes.

Using a very sharp knife, first trim the sides evenly, then cut lengthwise down the centre, so that you have two long strips. These are now cut across into six or eight slices according to the size required.

Apple and Blackberry Pie

Serves 4 Time taken 1½ hours

225 g (½ lb) shortcrust pastry   milk

For the Filling

225 g (½ lb) blackberries   2 tablespoons water
100 g (4 oz) castor sugar   450 g (1 lb) cooking apples

Prepare the shortcrust pastry and set aside to rest while preparing the filling.

Wash the blackberries and place in a saucepan. Add the sugar and water, and place over low heat. Cover and simmer gently for about 5–10 minutes until the blackberries are tender. Draw the pan off the heat, strain the blackberries and reserve the juice. Set the blackberries aside until cool. Peel, core and slice the apples.

Divide the pastry in two and roll out one piece slightly larger than a buttered 20–23-cm (8–9-inch) shallow pie plate. Line the plate with the pastry. Fill the pie with layers of the apple slices and the blackberries, then add 4–5 tablespoons of the reserved blackberry juice to moisten.

Roll out the remaining pastry to a circle large enough to cover the pie. Cut slits in the centre to make vents for the pie. Dampen the pastry rim and cover the whole pie with the pastry top. Press round the edges to seal and trim away excess pastry. Flute the edges of the pie and press round the rim with the floured prongs of a fork.

Brush the pie with milk and place in the centre of a hot oven (200°C, 400°F or Gas No. 6) and bake for 20 minutes to cook the pastry. Then lower the heat to slow (170°C, 325°F or Gas No. 3) and bake for a further 20 minutes to cook the filling.

Serve hot with cream.

Apple and Cranberry Pie

Serves 6 Time taken 1½ hours

225 g (½ lb) shortcrust pastry   milk

For the Filling
225 g (½ lb) fresh cranberries   1·5 dl (¼ pint) water
450 g (1 lb) cooking apples   225 g (8 oz) castor sugar
3 level tablespoons cornflour

Prepare the shortcrust pastry and set aside to rest while preparing the filling.

Wash the cranberries, removing the soft berries and stalks. Peel, core and thinly slice the apples. In a small basin, blend the cornflour with a little of the measured water to make a smooth blend. Pour the remaining water into a large saucepan and add the cranberries and apples, and stir in the cornflour blend. Stir over moderate heat until the mixture thickens and comes up to the boil. By this time the cranberries will have softened. Simmer for 1 minute, then draw off heat and leave until cold.

Divide the pastry in two and roll out one piece slightly larger than a buttered 20–23-cm (8–9-inch) shallow pie plate. Line the plate with the pastry. Spoon the cranberry and apple filling into the centre of the pie.

Roll out the remaining pastry to a circle large enough to cover the pie. Cut slits in the centre to make vents for the pie. Dampen the pastry rim and cover the whole pie with the pastry top. Press round the edges to seal and trim away excess pastry. Flute the edges of the pie and press round the rim with the floured prongs of a fork. Brush the pie with a little milk and place above centre in a hot oven (200°C, 400°F or Gas No. 6) and bake for 25–30 minutes.

Serve warm cut in wedges with cream.

Eccles Cake

Makes 16 Time taken 45 minutes

225 g (½ lb) rough puff pastry or
   pastry trimmings

For the Filling

25 g (1 oz) butter	100 g (4 oz) cleaned currants
25 g (1 oz) soft brown sugar	1 level teaspoon mixed spice
25 g (1 oz) chopped peel	

If using pastry trimmings, collect them up carefully. Place them flat piece over flat piece so as not to destroy the 'layering' of fat and dough. Roll out the pastry very thinly to a thickness of about ·25 cm (⅛ inch) and leave to rest while preparing the filling.

Melt the butter in a saucepan and stir in the sugar, peel, currants and spice. Mix well and set aside ready for use.

Cut the pastry into sixteen rounds, using an 8–10-cm (3½–4-inch) cutter, or cut round the edge of a saucer with a knife. Place a spoonful of filling in the centre of each round. Damp the pastry edges with water, then draw up the pastry edges and seal together.

Turn over and roll out into circles about 8 cm (about 3–3½ inches) across. The dried fruit will begin to show through the pastry. Make three slits with a sharp knife across the top of each one. Brush with milk and sprinkle with extra sugar. Arrange the Eccles cakes on a wetted baking tray and place above centre in a very hot oven (220°C, 425°F or Gas No. 7) and bake for 15–20 minutes, or until brown. Allow to cool before serving.

Rhubarb and Orange Pie

Serves 4 'Time taken 1½ hours

225 g (½ lb) shortcrust pastry castor sugar
milk

For the Filling
700 g (1½ lb) rhubarb rind of 1 small orange
100–175 g (4–6 oz) brown sugar

Prepare shortcrust pastry and set aside to rest for 10 minutes. Wash, trim and cut rhubarb into pieces about 2·5 cm (1 inch) long.

Divide the pastry in two. Roll out one piece to a circle slightly larger than a buttered 20–23-cm (8–9-inch) shallow pie plate. Line the plate with the pastry. Fill the pie with layers of rhubarb, the brown sugar and finely grated orange rind.

Roll out the remaining pastry to a circle large enough to cover the pie. Cut slits in the centre to make vents for the pie. Dampen the pastry rim and cover the whole pie with the pastry top. Press round the edges to seal and trim away excess pastry. Flute the edges of the pie and press round the rim with the floured prongs of a fork. Brush over the pie with a little milk. Place above centre in a moderately hot oven (190°C, 375°F or Gas No. 5) and bake for about 40 minutes. Remove the pie from the oven, brush again with milk and sprinkle with castor sugar. Return the pie to the oven for a further 10 minutes to crispen.

Serve hot or cold cut in wedges with cream.

Fresh Lemon Tart

Serves 6 Time taken 1 hour
Can be made in advance

100 g (¼ lb) shortcrust pastry

For the Filling
3 large eggs rind and juice of 2 large lemons
175 g (6 oz) castor sugar 50 g (2 oz) butter

On a floured working surface roll the pastry out to a circle slightly larger than a 20-cm (8-inch) flan ring or tart tin. Line the tin with the pastry and fill the centre with a piece of crumpled kitchen foil to keep the shape while baking. Place above centre in a hot oven (200°C,

400°F or Gas No. 6) and bake for 12 minutes. Remove the foil during the last few minutes of baking time.

Meanwhile, crack the eggs into a medium-sized mixing basin, add the sugar, finely grated lemon rind and the butter cut in pieces. Set the basin over a pan of boiling water – it's best to bring the water in the pan up to the boil and then draw the pan off the heat before setting the basin over the top. Using a wooden spoon, stir the ingredients until the sugar has dissolved, the butter melted and all the ingredients are blended. Remove the basin from the heat and strain in the lemon juice. Stir well to mix, then pour the filling into the baked pastry case.

Replace in the centre of the oven, this time at moderate (180°C, 350°F or Gas No. 4) and bake for 20–25 minutes, or until the filling has set.

Serve cold with cream.

9 Vegetables & Salads

Root vegetables, green vegetables and salad vegetables form an important part of our daily diet. They require just as much attention as any other section of the menu. Interesting combinations of ingredients, correct use of seasonings and careful cooking, give vegetables the importance they deserve.

Cook and serve them simply, in order to preserve their distinctive, delicate flavour. Where possible prepare, select and cook fresh vegetables that are in season.

VEGETABLES

Duchesse Potatoes

Serves 4 Time taken 45 minutes

700 g (1½ lb) potatoes	25 g (1 oz) butter
salt	2 eggs
freshly milled pepper	15 g (½ oz) melted butter

Potatoes prepared in this way can be made in advance and browned when ready to serve.

Scrub and peel the potatoes and cut up any large ones. Place in cold salted water, bring to the boil and cook until tender – about 15–20 minutes. Drain at once, then return the potatoes to the pan and set over the heat for a minute to dry off excess moisture. Press the potatoes through a sieve into a mixing basin. Beat in a good seasoning of salt and pepper, the butter, and enough beaten egg to give a smooth piping consistency.

Spoon the mixture into a large nylon or cotton piping bag fitted with a rosette piping tube. Pipe out whorls of potato on a buttered baking tray. Brush each one with melted butter. Place the potatoes above centre in a hot oven (200°C, 400°F or Gas No. 6) for about 10 minutes, or until heated through and golden brown.

Celeriac and Potato Purée

Serves 4–6 Time taken 45 minutes

700 g (1½ lb) celeriac	freshly milled pepper
225 g (½ lb) potatoes	15 g (½ oz) butter
salt	cream

A purée of celeriac, with a little potato added, is a vegetable that goes very well with game.

Peel and cut up both the celeriac and the potatoes. Place in a saucepan and cover with cold salted water. Celeriac tends to discolour and should be placed in acidulated water as it is prepared, if not to be used immediately. Bring the vegetables to the boil and simmer for 20–30 minutes, or until tender.

Drain well, return the vegetables to the hot pan and dry for a moment over the heat. Mash well, adding plenty of salt and pepper. Beat in a little butter and cream to make a smooth purée. Serve hot with game.

Purée of Brussels Sprouts

Serves 4–6 Time taken 30 minutes

700 g (1½ lb) Brussels sprouts	freshly milled pepper
salt	1·5 dl (¼ pint) double cream
25 g (1 oz) butter	

Trim the sprouts and add to a pan of boiling, salted water. Cook for 10–15 minutes, or until just tender. Drain thoroughly. Melt the butter in the hot pan and add the cooked sprouts. Season well with freshly milled pepper and sauté gently for a few minutes.

Draw the pan off the heat and pass the sprouts through a Mouli to make a purée. Return to the saucepan and reheat, gradually beating in the cream. Serve hot.

Vegetable Marrow with Tomato

Serves 4 Time taken 1¼ hours

4 tomatoes
1 small marrow
1 large onion
2–3 stalks celery
1 level teaspoon salt

1 level teaspoon sugar
freshly milled pepper
25 g (1 oz) butter

chopped parsley

In this recipe the vegetables cook in their own juices and the result is a delicious blend of flavours.

Skin and slice the tomatoes. Wipe and peel the marrow, then halve and scoop out the seeds. Cut the marrow into small cubes. Peel and chop the onion. Scrub the celery, trim and slice thinly.

Well-butter a casserole dish and put in alternate layers of marrow, tomato, onion and celery, Sprinkle each layer with a little of the salt and sugar, and a seasoning of pepper. Finish with a layer of marrow and dot with the butter. Cover with a tight-fitting lid, place in the centre of a moderate oven (180°C, 350°F or Gas No. 4) and bake for 40–50 minutes, or until the vegetables are tender.

Sprinkle with chopped parsley and serve.

Courgettes with Mint

Serves 4 Time taken 30 minutes

450 g (1 lb) courgettes
50 g (2 oz) butter

freshly milled pepper
1 tablespoon chopped fresh mint

Trim the ends off the courgettes and slice thickly. Add to a saucepan of boiling salted water. Reboil and simmer for 2 minutes, then drain.

Melt the butter in a large frying pan. Add the courgettes, cover and fry gently for about 15 minutes until soft. Draw off the heat and season with freshly milled pepper.

Sprinkle with the chopped mint and serve.

French Beans and Onions

Serves 4 Time taken 20 minutes

450 g (1 lb) French beans
1 onion
25 g (1 oz) butter

salt
freshly milled pepper
½ teaspoon wine vinegar

Snap off stems and tips of the beans but leave the beans whole. Cook in plenty of boiling salted water for 15 minutes, or until tender but still firm.

Peel and chop the onion. Melt the butter in a saucepan. Add the onion, cover with a lid and cook gently for about 5 minutes, until the onion is soft but not brown. Drain the beans and add to the onion, tossing well to coat the beans with onion and butter. Reheat over a low heat for a few minutes. Draw off heat, season with salt and freshly milled pepper, add vinegar, toss and serve.

Braised Celery

Serves 4 Time taken 1½ hours

2 medium heads celery	few bacon rinds
1 carrot	3 dl (½ pint) beef stock
1 onion	
small piece of swede	chopped parsley
½ bay leaf	

Trim off root and leafy tops from celery. Remove coarse, outer stalks, scrub well and chop finely. Put in a shallow pan together with the peeled and finely chopped carrot, onion and swede. Add the bay leaf and bacon rinds and the stock, barely to cover.

Wash the celery hearts thoroughly and cut each heart downwards into two. Place on top of the bed of vegetables, cover with a butter paper and a close fitting lid. Cook gently until tender – about 40 minutes.

Carefully lift out the celery hearts and place them in a greased entrée dish. Strain off the liquor from the pan and reduce it by rapid boiling without a lid, until there is about ½ teacup left. Pour over the celery. Cover with a buttered paper and cook in a moderate oven (180°C, 350°F or Gas No. 4) for about 15 minutes.

Sprinkle with chopped parsley and serve.

Plain Boiled Rice

Serves 4 Time taken 15 minutes

225 g (8 oz) long grain rice	1–2 level teaspoons salt
1–1·5 litres (2–3 pints) boiling water	

Place the rice in a sieve or colander, wash well under cold running water and remove any dark or discoloured grains. Drain and sprinkle into the boiling salted water. Add slowly, so that the water never comes off the boil. Boil rapidly for 8 minutes, stirring occasionally to make sure no grains stick to the base of the pan.

To test when cooked, pinch a grain of rice between the thumb and forefinger – there should be no hard core. Draw the pan off the heat, strain the rice into a colander and hold under running *hot water* for a few seconds, just enough to rinse the grains free from any starchy cooking water. (Some cooks like to return the rice to the hot saucepan, cover with a lid and allow to steam dry in the base of the pan for a few minutes.)

Fluff the rice with a fork and serve.

Ratatouille

Serves 6 Time taken 1½ hours

2 medium onions	450 g (1 lb) tomatoes
2 green peppers	1 teaspoon sugar
1 clove garlic	freshly milled pepper
4 teaspoons olive oil	salt
2–3 medium aubergines	
450 g (1 lb) courgettes	chopped parsley

Peel and slice the onions. Halve, deseed and shred the green peppers. Peel and chop the garlic. Heat the oil in a large, heavy frying pan, add the onions, green peppers and garlic. Cover with a lid and cook gently for about 15 minutes, until tender. Shake or stir the contents of the pan occasionally, taking care not to allow the onions or peppers to brown. Meanwhile, peel and cut the aubergines into cubes. Leave the courgettes unpeeled, cut into thick slices and then blanch by adding to a pan of boiling water. Allow the water to reboil and then simmer the courgettes for 2 minutes. Drain and refresh under cold water. This helps preserve the colour and removes any bitterness from the skins.

Add the prepared aubergines and courgettes to the pan, cover and cook gently for a further 30 minutes. Nick the skins on the tomatoes, place in a mixing basin, cover with boiling water and allow to stand 1 minute. Then drain and peel away the skins. Slice the tomatoes coarsely, add to the pan with the sugar. (The sugar is not traditional but the slight sweetness improves the finished flavour.) Season with freshly milled pepper, re-cover and continue cooking for a further 15 minutes – the total cooking time for ratatouille should not exceed 1 hour. When ready to serve adjust seasoning with salt and freshly milled pepper.

Sprinkle with chopped parsley and serve.

Hot Cucumber with Cream Sauce

Serves 4 Time taken 40 minutes

1 large cucumber	15 g (½ oz) butter
1 level teaspoon castor sugar	salt

For the Sauce

25 g (1 oz) butter	salt
25 g (1 oz) flour	freshly milled pepper
1·5 dl (¼ pint) cooking liquid	1 egg yolk
1·5 dl (¼ pint) milk	2 tablespoons single cream

Trim the ends and peel the cucumber. Slice across into 1-cm (½-inch) slices. Place in a saucepan and just cover with water. Add the sugar, 15 g (½ oz) of the butter and a seasoning of salt. Bring up to the boil, then lower the heat, cover with a lid and simmer gently for 20 minutes. Cucumber slices will feel quite tender when cooked. Drain, reserving 1·5 dl (¼ pint) of the cooking liquid. Place the cucumber in a buttered serving dish and keep hot while preparing the sauce.

Melt the 25 g (1 oz) of butter in the hot saucepan. Stir in the flour and cook gently for 1 minute. Make the reserved cucumber cooking liquid up to 3 dl (½ pint) with the cold milk. Gradually stir this mixture into the saucepan, stirring all the time. Bring up to the boil, stirring until the sauce has thickened and is boiling. Season with salt and freshly milled pepper, and allow to simmer for 4–5 minutes. Blend together the egg yolk and cream and stir into the sauce just before drawing off the heat. Pour over the hot cucumber and serve.

Mustard Glazed Onions

Serves 4 Time taken 20 minutes

450 g (1 lb) small onions	2 level tablespoons prepared
50 g (2 oz) butter	English mustard

These onions are delicious served with steak or roast beef.

Peel the onions leaving them whole. Place in a saucepan and cover with cold water. Add salt and bring up to the boil. Simmer gently for about 15 minutes, or until the onions are tender. Test with the tip of a sharp knife blade. When ready drain from the water and keep the onions hot.

Add the butter to the hot saucepan and allow to melt. Stir in the mustard, then add the onions. Toss well to coat the onions in the butter and mustard glaze. Serve at once.

Rice Pilaff

Serves 4 Time taken 30 minutes

25 g (1 oz) butter
1 onion

225 g (8 oz) long grain rice
6 dl (1 pint) chicken stock

Melt the butter in a saucepan. Add the onion, cover with a lid, and cook gently for about 5 minutes, or until soft and golden brown. Add the washed rice, toss to coat with butter, then stir in the hot stock. Stir until reboiling, then cover with a lid and cook very gently, until stock is absorbed and rice is tender – about 20 minutes.

Serve with steaks, grilled sausages, braised beef or chicken casserole dishes.

Red Cabbage with Orange

Serves 6 Time taken 2 hours
Allow to marinate overnight

700 g (1½ lb) red cabbage
2 oranges
1 small onion
1 small clove garlic
50 g (2 oz) castor sugar

3 tablespoons wine vinegar
salt
freshly milled pepper
25 g (1 oz) butter

Red cabbage goes particularly well with roast pork, duck or game. This recipe has a very nice flavour emphasized by allowing the ingredients to marinate overnight.

Remove coarse outer leaves from the red cabbage. Quarter the cabbage, cut away any core and then shred the cabbage finely. Wash in cold salted water, then drain and place in a large basin. Add the grated rind and strained juice from both the oranges. Peel and finely chop the onion. Peel and chop the garlic. Add the onion, garlic, sugar, vinegar, and a good seasoning of salt and pepper. Set aside overnight to marinate, tossing the ingredients occasionally.

Melt the butter in a large saucepan or fireproof casserole. Add the red cabbage and all the other ingredients. Bring just to simmering, then cover with a lid and cook gently for 1½ hours. Stir occasionally. When cooked all the liquid should have evaporated.

SALADS

Old Fashioned Egg Salad

Serves 4 Time taken 45 minutes

6 eggs
1 round or Webb lettuce

1 large onion

For the Dressing
salt
freshly milled pepper
2 tablespoons vinegar
4 tablespoons olive oil
1 teaspoon Worcestershire sauce

1 tablespoon finely chopped parsley
2 tablespoons grated Cheddar
cheese

Cover the eggs with cold water and bring up to the boil. Simmer for 8 minutes to hard-boil, then drain and cover immediately with cold water to prevent further cooking. Drain, peel away the shells and leave the eggs submerged in water until cold.

Separate the lettuce into leaves and wash thoroughly. Tear away any coarse stems and tear large leaves in two. Arrange the leaves in the base of a salad bowl. Peel and finely chop the onion. Slice the eggs and arrange over the lettuce in layers with the onion. Set aside while preparing the dressing.

Place a seasoning of salt and pepper in a mixing basin. Add the vinegar and stir to dissolve the salt, then add the oil and Worcestershire sauce. Mix well and pour over the salad.

Sprinkle with chopped parsley and cheese, and serve.

Chicory and Orange Salad

Serves 4 Time taken 15 minutes

3 heads of chicory
2–3 tablespoons oil and vinegar
dressing

1 large orange

Cut away the base and remove any damaged outer leaves from the chicory. Wipe the heads of chicory and then cut across into chunks. Toss the chicory in the oil and vinegar dressing, and place in a salad bowl. Cut away the outer skin and white pith from the orange, using a sharp knife. Then cut out the sections of orange flesh, leaving the white skin in between the sections behind. Add these to the salad, toss and serve.

Pear and Grape Salad

Serves 4 Time taken 20 minutes

4 ripe dessert pears
75–100 g (3–4 oz) fresh cream cheese
1–2 tablespoons prepared oil and
   vinegar dressing

225 g (½ lb) black grapes
4 crisp lettuce leaves

This is a very easy recipe that tastes delicious. It looks unusual and rather pretty; the idea originated in America, where it is a very popular salad.

Peel the pears, keeping them whole, then cut in half and, using a teaspoon, scoop out the cores. In a basin, blend the cream cheese with sufficient dressing to make a soft mixture that will spread fairly easily.

Using a knife, spread the cream cheese mixture over the rounded side of each pear-half to cover it completely. Halve and deseed the grapes, and then press the grape halves close together over the surface of the pears, so that each pear-half resembles a small bunch of grapes. Arrange the pear-halves on each of the four lettuce leaves.

Serve with cold ham or gammon.

Potato and Cucumber Salad

Serves 4 Time taken 30–40 minutes

450 g (1 lb) new potatoes
½ cucumber
1·5 dl (¼ pint) mayonnaise
2–3 tablespoons single cream

salt
freshly milled pepper
finely chopped chives or parsley

Scrub or scrape the potatoes and add to plenty of boiling salted water. Cook until just tender – about 10 minutes – then drain. Meanwhile, peel the cucumber and cut lengthwise; remove the seeds and then dice the cucumber flesh. Add to a pan of boiling water, and reboil, then drain. This blanches the cucumber and preserves the nice green colour.

When the potatoes are cool enough to handle, cut into small dice and combine with the cucumber. Thin down the mayonnaise with the cream. Add to the potatoes and fold in to blend the ingredients. Season with salt and pepper, pour into a salad bowl and sprinkle with finely chopped chives or parsley.

California Salad

Serves 4 Time taken 15 minutes

1 small lettuce
2 stalks celery
½ cucumber
2 tomatoes

1 dessert apple
1 banana
juice of ½ lemon
2–3 tablespoons salad cream

Wash and drain the lettuce and separate into leaves. Tear the leaves into smaller pieces if large, and set aside.

Shred the stalks of celery, peel and dice the cucumber, peel and slice the tomatoes and the apple, and slice the banana. Squeeze the lemon juice over the apple and banana to keep them white. Place the prepared ingredients together in a bowl and toss with the salad cream.

Arrange the reserved lettuce in the base of a salad bowl and spoon the tossed ingredients on top.

Serve with cold chicken, ham, cold gammon or pork.

Coleslaw

Serves 6 Time taken 30 minutes

½ white cabbage heart
2–3 new young carrots
2 dessert apples
1–2 sticks celery

4–5 tablespoons oil and vinegar
  dressing
3 rounded tablespoons mayonnaise
4 tablespoons single cream

Rinse the cabbage leaves under cold water and remove any outer damaged leaves. Cut in half, cut away the core, and then shred the cabbage finely. Place in a large mixing basin and add the scrubbed and coarsely grated carrots, the apples, peeled, quartered and coarsely grated, and the scrubbed and finely shredded celery. Toss the salad with 4–5 tablespoons oil and vinegar dressing. Leave to chill for 15–20 minutes.

Meanwhile, in a small basin, thin down the mayonnaise with the cream. Pour over the salad and toss well to mix before serving.

Rice and Pineapple Salad

Serves 6 Time taken 30 minutes

100 g (4 oz) long grain rice
4–5 tablespoons oil and vinegar
  dressing
2 rings tinned pineapple

1 small green pepper
few spring onions
2 tablespoons seedless raisins

Wash the rice well, then cook in boiling salted water for 8–10 minutes until tender. Drain well and place in a salad bowl. Add about 3 tablespoons of the oil and vinegar dressing to the hot rice, toss to glaze all the rice grains and set aside until cold.

Finely chop the pineapple rings. Halve, deseed and finely chop the green pepper. Wash, trim and shred the spring onions. Add all these together with the raisins and another 2 tablespoons of dressing to the rice. Toss well to mix.

Serve with cold meat or poultry, and in particular with any cold dish, with curry mayonnaise.

SALAD DRESSINGS

Mayonnaise is a sauce that many use but few bother to make for themselves. It is an emulsion of eggs and oil and its simplicity makes it enormously versatile. Many flavours can be added to make different variations.

Points to Watch
1   Always use oil and egg yolks that are at room temperature. Eggs straight from the refrigerator are too cold. Oil that is too warm will not thicken, and oil that has congealed in cold weather should be brought up to room temperature slowly.
2   Use tarragon or white wine vinegar or lemon juice. Malt vinegar may be used but its harsh taste will spoil the delicate flavour of the mayonnaise. Olive oil is, of course, traditionally used, but, for those who do not care for the strong flavour, corn oil should be used instead.
3   Use a hand whisk, spoon or fork for mixing, and pour the oil directly on to the part where you are mixing, so that the oil is immediately drawn into the mixture.
4   Mayonnaise should not curdle if carefully prepared but, if it does, simply start again and beat the curdled mixture slowly into another egg yolk.

Mayonnaise
Makes 1·5 dl (¼ pint) Time taken 15–20 minutes

1 egg yolk	1 dessertspoon wine vinegar or
pinch dry mustard	lemon juice
salt	1·5 dl (¼ pint) salad oil
freshly milled pepper	1 dessertspoon boiling water

Place the egg yolk in a deep mixing basin. Add the mustard, seasonings and a little of the vinegar or lemon juice. Place the basin on a damp cloth or sponge square; this helps to steady the basin while mixing. Have the oil measured into a jug for easy pouring.

Whisk the ingredients to blend, then add the oil very slowly drop by drop, whisking all the time until the mayonnaise begins to thicken; this will happen when about half the oil has been added. Add the rest of the vinegar or lemon juice, then hold the jug of oil well above the basin and trickle in the oil, in a thin steady stream. Whisk all the time and allow the oil to fall directly on to the whisk so that the oil is quickly drawn into the mayonnaise. By the time all the oil is added, the mayonnaise will be very thick. Whisk in the boiling water. This addition of boiling water makes the mayonnaise lighter in colour and slightly softer in consistency.

Blender Mayonnaise

Makes 3 dl ($\frac{1}{2}$ pint) Time taken 10 minutes

2 egg yolks	2 tablespoons wine vinegar or
salt	lemon juice
freshly milled pepper	3 dl ($\frac{1}{2}$ pint) olive oil
pinch mustard	1 tablespoon boiling water

Never attempt to make less than half a pint of mayonnaise in a blender, unless it is a very small one. A small quantity of mixture will not blend properly in a large machine.

Put the egg yolks and seasonings in a clean, dry blender. Add the vinegar or lemon juice, then, using the lowest speed, blend them together.

Remove the centre cap in the blender top and begin pouring the oil from a jug very slowly on to the egg yolks, still on the lowest speed. Add the oil very gradually at first, almost drop by drop from the lip of the jug. The mayonnaise will not begin to thicken until the blades are about half covered by the mixture, but still continue adding the oil slowly. When the mayonnaise begins to thicken, add the oil more quickly in a steady stream until it is all added. Lastly add the boiling water and switch the blender off.

Mayonnaise Variations

Aspic mayonnaise Make up a coating mayonnaise by mixing together 2 rounded tablespoons mayonnaise with 2 tablespoons cream. Sprinkle $\frac{1}{2}$ level teaspoon powdered gelatine into 1 dessert-spoon cold water. Leave to stand for 5 minutes, then add 1 tablespoon boiling water and stir to dissolve the gelatine. Strain this into the mayonnaise, stir and leave until just beginning to set. Use to coat cold lightly poached or boiled eggs or curlets of cold cooked fish such as turbot or salmon.

Coating mayonnaise When mayonnaise is used for dressing an hors d'œuvre, it should be thinned down with the addition of cream. To the basic recipe stir in 2–3 tablespoons cream or, for a sharper, very pleasant dressing, add 1 carton soured cream and use as required.

Tartare sauce To the basic recipe add 1 rounded dessertspoon each chopped gherkin, capers and parsley. Serve with fish, particularly hot fried fish.

Curry mayonnaise Add $\frac{1}{2}$ level teaspoon curry powder to the egg yolk when preparing the basic recipe and, if liked, rub the bowl with a crushed garlic clove before starting on the recipe. Use as a dressing for hard-boiled eggs.

Garlic mayonnaise Add garlic cloves according to taste. Lightly crush the clove, peel away the outer papery coating and chop finely; add this to the egg yolk when preparing the basic recipe.

Herb mayonnaise Add 2 tablespoons cream, 1 tablespoon finely chopped parsley and 2 tablespoons finely chopped chives to the basic recipe. Serve with fish or meat salads.

Oil and Vinegar Dressing

Serves 4 Time taken 10 minutes

salt
freshly milled pepper
1 teaspoon castor sugar

pinch dry mustard
2 tablespoons wine vinegar
4–6 tablespoons salad oil

Put the seasoning of salt and pepper, the sugar and the mustard into a wide-necked, screw-topped jar. Add the vinegar, cover and shake for a moment to dissolve the seasonings. Add the oil, re-cover and shake vigorously until a smooth emulsion has been formed.

The dressing will keep for several days in a cool place, but should be shaken up before use. Larger quantities can be kept at hand in the refrigerator, especially during summer months.

Oil and Vinegar Variations

Fines Herbes Add 2 teaspoons chopped parsley, or half parsley and half chervil, and a teaspoon chopped chives. Serve with simple green salad and vegetable salad.

Piquante dressing Add 1 rounded teaspoon finely chopped shallot and the same of chopped capers and gherkins. Serve with potato salad or flaked cooked fish.

Garlic dressing Add ½ clove garlic very finely chopped and 1 teaspoon chopped parsley. Serve with crisp chicory or endive.

Mint dressing Add 1 teaspoon finely chopped fresh mint. Serve with potato salad or salad of fresh pears.

Tomato cream dressing Stir in 1 tablespoon tomato ketchup and 2 tablespoons thick cream. Serve with fish salads or hard-boiled eggs.

Blue cheese dressing Add 25 g (1 oz) crumbled Roquefort cheese. Use over green salad to be served with steak.

10 Sauces

Saucemaking is one of the most important and most rewarding branches of cookery. In general, always check and re-check seasoning or flavour in a sauce before serving. Consistency is important: a coating sauce should just coat the back of a wooden spoon but level out as it runs back into the saucepan. A pouring sauce should be thinner and flow easily from a sauce-boat; simply increase the liquid in the recipe by half again. A binding sauce is a thick sauce, used in many made-up dishes to bind food, or as the base of a hot savoury soufflé – in this case only half the normal amount of liquid should be used.

SAVOURY SAUCES

White Sauce

Makes 3 dl (½ pint) sauce for savoury recipes Time taken 25 minutes

3 dl (½ pint) milk
½ onion, stuck with a clove
1 bay leaf
25 g (1 oz) butter or margarine

25 g (1 oz) plain flour
salt
freshly milled pepper

Measure the milk into a saucepan and add the onion and bay leaf. Bring almost to the boil, then draw off the heat, cover with a lid and leave to infuse for 5–10 minutes.

Melt the butter or margarine in a saucepan over low heat and stir in the flour. This is called a 'roux'. Cook the roux gently for a further minutes or so, until it lightens in colour and takes on a grainy texture. Do not allow the roux for a white sauce to brown at this stage or the colour of the final sauce will be affected. Gradually stir in the warm flavoured milk a little at a time. Cold milk may be used if time is short, but the warm infused milk not only adds to the flavour of the sauce but makes blending easier, and there is less risk of the sauce becoming lumpy. Each addition of milk should be thoroughly beaten in before the next is added. Bring the sauce to the boil and allow to simmer for 3–5 minutes to ensure thorough cooking of the flour. Season with salt and pepper, then add any further ingredients.

Quick methods of preparing white sauce

Blending method Time taken 10 minutes

Using the blending method, omit the initial stage of infusing the milk and, therefore, the onion and bay leaf, but use the other ingredients as given above. Measure the milk into a mixing basin and sift the flour on to it. Using a whisk, mix the two together quickly and thoroughly. Melt the fat in a saucepan over low heat, then pour in the blend and cook, stirring all the time until the sauce is boiling. Continue to simmer gently for a further 2–3 minutes, then season and add any further ingredients.

Roux mix method Time taken 10 minutes

Another method is to make a roux mix and store this in the refrigerator to be used in small quantities when a white sauce is required. For this melt 225 g (8 oz) butter or margarine in a heavy saucepan and stir in 225 g (8 oz) plain flour. Cook over low heat, stirring occasionally to prevent the mix from browning at all on the base of the pan. When it becomes light in colour, and sandy and crumbly in texture – takes about 15 minutes – draw the pan off the heat and allow to cool. Stir occasionally to break up the roux. Spoon into a screw-topped jar, cover and keep in the refrigerator. It will keep up to 1 month. To use this roux, heat 3 dl ($\frac{1}{2}$ pint) milk in a saucepan until almost boiling. Draw the pan off the heat and add 2 tablespoons of the mix. Stir until the roux has melted, then replace over moderate heat and stir until the sauce has thickened and is boiling. Cook gently for 2–3 minutes, then season and use as required.

White Sauce Variations

To the basic well-seasoned white sauce add any of the following.
Cheese Stir in ½ level teaspoon made mustard and 75 g (3 oz) grated Cheddar cheese. Serve with fish, egg or vegetable recipes.
Parsley Add 1 tablespoon freshly chopped parsley. Stir in a squeeze of lemon juice, if the sauce is to be served with fish. Serve with fish, vegetable or chicken recipes, or with boiled ham.
Egg Gently fold in 1–2 coarsely chopped hard-boiled eggs. Serve with fish and vegetable recipes.
Mustard Stir in 1 level teaspoon made mustard blended with 1 tablespoon vinegar. Serve with grilled herring or mackerel.
Shrimp Add 100 g (4 oz) prepared shrimps, a squeeze of lemon juice and ¼ level teaspoon anchovy essence or 1 tablespoon tomato ketchup. Serve with fish recipes.

Preparing white sauce for fish recipes
In a recipe where fish is poached in the oven, it is advisable to cook the fish in milk with seasoning and a nut of butter; then, when the fish is cooked, strain the milk. Use this, made up to 3 dl (½ pint) with fresh milk, for making a sauce. This gives the sauce a good flavour along with a squeeze of lemon juice, which should be added after the seasoning.

Checking errors
However carefully recipes are followed, there is always the possibility that something can go wrong and often in the case of sauces the consistency is not quite as expected.
If the sauce is too thin, mix flour and cold water to form a smooth paste, using 1 level tablespoon flour to 1½ tablespoons cold water. Add gradually to the sauce, and then stir over the heat until thickened.
If the sauce is too thick, stir in a little more of the liquid used in the sauce – and remember to re-check the seasoning.
If the sauce is lumpy, beat thoroughly with a whisk, and then strain into a second saucepan. Alternatively blend for a few seconds in an electric liquidizer.
To keep a white sauce hot, do not stir in all the liquid stated in the recipe – leave about 2–3 tablespoons. Allow the sauce to thicken, then add the remaining liquid and run this over the surface of the sauce

without stirring. The liquid on the surface will prevent a skin forming. When ready to serve, stir in the liquid and use the sauce. Never leave the sauce over even the lowest heat, but stand the base of the pan in a larger roasting tin of simmering water. This way it will keep hot without scorching.

Brown Sauce

Makes 3 dl (½ pint) Time taken 1 hour

1 small onion	4·5 dl (¾ pint) hot stock
1 carrot	1 teaspoon concentrated tomato
25 g (1 oz) dripping or	purée
white vegetable fat	salt
2 bacon rashers	freshly milled pepper
25 g (1 oz) plain flour	

Peel the onion, scrape the carrot and cut both into small dice. Melt the fat in a saucepan, and add the vegetables and the trimmed, chopped bacon rashers. Sauté gently until the onion is soft and the vegetables become golden brown. Stir in the flour and continue to cook gently, until the flour is a rich nutty brown colour – takes about 15–20 minutes. Gradually stir in the hot stock, beating well after each addition to get a smooth sauce. Add the tomato purée and bring to the boil. Season lightly with salt and pepper, then cover and simmer gently for about 30 minutes. Draw off the heat and strain through a fine sieve. Check the seasoning, reheat if required and use.

Brown Sauce Variations

Mushroom Add 50–75 g (2–3 oz) small sliced mushrooms which have first been sautéed in butter. Serve with fried liver, savoury pasties, such as Cornish pasties, or steak.

Madeira Add 3 tablespoons Madeira wine to the finished sauce. Serve with grilled or fried steaks, chops or ham.

Piquante Add 1 dessertspoon Worcestershire sauce and 1 tablespoon vinegar to the finished sauce. Serve with meat patties, croquettes and cutlets made from cooked meat.

Fresh Tomato Sauce

Makes 3 dl (½ pint) Time taken 45 minutes

25 g (1 oz) butter
1 rasher bacon
1 small onion
1 small carrot
450 g (1 lb) ripe tomatoes
3 dl (½ pint) chicken stock

1 rounded tablespoon flour
salt
freshly milled pepper
1 teaspoon castor sugar
squeeze of lemon juice

Melt the butter in a saucepan, trim and chop the bacon rasher. Peel and slice the onion and carrot. Fry the bacon for a few moments in the hot fat. Add the sliced onion and carrot and fry gently for a further 5 minutes. Wash and quarter the tomatoes and add to the ingredients in the saucepan. Cover and allow to cook gently for about 5 minutes, or until the tomatoes are soft and the juices have been drawn out.

Stir in the stock. Blend the flour with about 3 tablespoons of cold water. Stir into the pan along with a seasoning of salt and pepper, the sugar and lemon juice. Cover with a lid and simmer for 30 minutes. Draw off the heat and rub the sauce through a sieve. Discard the skin and pips and reheat the sauce. Check the seasoning and use as required.

Serve with fried fish, with veal or chicken, and in any recipe that calls for 3 dl (½ pint) tomato sauce.

Velouté Sauce

Makes 3 dl (½ pint) Time taken 15 minutes

25 g (1 oz) butter
25 g (1 oz) flour
3 dl (½ pint) hot stock
salt

freshly milled pepper
squeeze of lemon juice
1 egg yolk
4 tablespoons cream

A velouté sauce is one made using the same method as a basic white sauce, but using hot stock instead of milk, and it is enriched afterwards with egg yolk and cream. It can be used for coating cooked fish, chicken or veal and in each case the appropriate stock must be used in the initial preparation.

Melt the butter in a saucepan over low heat. Stir in the flour and cook gently for a few moments until the mixture lightens in colour, but do not allow to brown. Gradually stir in the hot stock, beating well all the time to get a smooth sauce. Bring to the boil and simmer gently for about 5 minutes. Season to taste with salt and pepper and add a squeeze of lemon juice.

Blend the egg yolk and cream in a basin and strain the sauce into the egg mixture. Stir well all the time to blend the sauce evenly. Return the sauce to the saucepan and reheat sufficiently to cook the egg, but do not allow the sauce to boil. Check the seasoning again and use as required.

The sauce can be poured over fish, chicken or veal and, if liked, additional ingredients can be added, such as sautéed mushrooms, cooked asparagus tips, shrimps or prawns.

Curry Sauce

Makes scant ·5 litre (¾ pint) Time taken 1¼ hours

1 medium-sized onion	2–4 level tablespoons curry powder
1 small apple	25 g (1 oz) flour
25 g (1 oz) butter or margarine	½ small bay leaf
1 small clove garlic	generous ·5 litre (1 pint) beef stock
½ level teaspoon caraway seeds	1 teaspoon black treacle
1 teaspoon curry paste (optional)	1 tablespoon sweet chutney
½ level teaspoon salt	squeeze of lemon juice
1 tablespoon desiccated coconut	

A good curry sauce is a very useful recipe to have. Make it mild or hot, sharp or slightly sweet, to suit individual taste. This sauce is better made a day in advance, giving the flavours time to mellow and mature before using.

It can be used as a sauce for serving with cooked meat, fish or eggs, or it can be poured over fresh meat or chicken before cooking.

Peel and chop the onion, peel and core and finely dice the apple. Melt the butter in a saucepan, add the onion and apple and fry gently for about 5 minutes to soften. Stir in the curry powder, and cook for a few minutes to draw out the flavour, then stir in the flour. Pound together the bay leaf, garlic and caraway seeds. Add the curry paste, salt, coconut and pounded garlic mixture to the pan. Stir in the stock and bring to the boil. Cover and simmer gently, stirring occasionally, for about 1 hour. Stir in the treacle, chutney and a squeeze of lemon juice to taste. Strain and use as required.

Mushroom Sauce

Serves 4 Time taken 15 minutes

50 g (2 oz) butter	225 g (½ lb) fresh small mushrooms
1 small onion	salt

freshly milled pepper
pinch dried mixed herbs

1 rounded teaspoon flour
1·5 dl (¼ pint) single cream

Very small tightly closed mushrooms must be used for this recipe, as mushrooms that are open will discolour the sauce, making it dark.

Melt half the butter in a frying pan over low heat. Peel and finely chop the onion. Add to the pan and fry very gently for about 5 minutes, until the onion is soft but not browned. Meanwhile trim and wash the mushrooms in cold water, then drain and slice.

Add the remaining butter and the sliced mushrooms to the pan and cook them gently for about 2–3 minutes, shaking the pan occasionally. When the mushroom juices begin to run season well with salt and pepper, add the herbs and stir in the flour. Stir in the cream and bring to the boil, stirring gently until the sauce has thickened. Simmer for a moment.

Serve with steaks, lamb or veal chops, grilled or fried chicken, or with omelettes.

Orange Sauce

Makes 3 dl (½ pint) Time taken 45 minutes
Can be made in advance

4 tablespoons granulated sugar
2 tablespoons water
2 tablespoons wine vinegar
3 dl (½ pint) giblet stock

1 tablespoon thick orange marmalade
2 large oranges
1 level tablespoon cornflour
1 tablespoon water

This recipe has a particularly good flavour. A rich colour and sweetness comes from the caramel, and a sharpness is added with the vinegar. Serve with roast duck.

Measure the sugar into a dry saucepan. Place over the heat and stir until the sugar has melted and becomes golden caramel brown. Draw the pan off the heat and add the water – take care, as the mixture will boil up furiously. Replace the pan over the heat and stir until the mixture has formed a thick syrup. Stir in the vinegar, the stock and the orange marmalade. Add the juice and flesh from one of the two oranges. Cover with a lid and simmer gently for 30 minutes.

Meanwhile cut a slice from the top and base of the remaining orange; using a sharp knife cut downwards round the orange to remove the peel entirely. Cut into the orange to remove the segments of flesh and reserve these. Cut away the white pith from the orange peel and shred the peel finely. Place the peel in a saucepan, cover with cold water and bring to the boil. Drain the peel, replace in the saucepan and re-cover with cold water. Bring to the boil and this time simmer until tender – about 20 minutes. When the peel is tender, drain and reserve.

When the stock and ingredients have simmered for 30 minutes, strain the stock and return to the saucepan. Blend the cornflour with the water and stir into the sauce. Stir over moderate heat until thickened and boiling. Add the reserved orange segments and the cooked peel and heat through.

Hot Cucumber Sauce

Serves 4 Time taken 15 minutes

½ cucumber	salt
25 g (1 oz) butter	freshly milled pepper
25 g (1 oz) flour	1 level teaspoon castor sugar
3 dl (½ pint) milk	1–2 tablespoons single cream

Peel and slice the cucumber in half lengthwise. Remove the centre seeds and chop up the flesh coarsely. Melt the butter in a saucepan, add the cucumber and cook over low heat, covered with a lid, for 5 minutes, or until the cucumber is softened. Sprinkle on the flour and gradually stir in the milk. Bring up to the boil, stirring all the time; then simmer gently for 2–3 minutes. Draw the pan off the heat, season well with salt and freshly milled pepper, stir in the sugar – cucumber sauce is nice sweetened a little – and add the cream. The sauce should be fairly thin.

Serve at once, while hot, with poached salmon.

Bearnaise Sauce

Serves 4 Time taken 15 minutes

little chopped fresh tarragon	2 egg yolks
freshly milled pepper	25 g (1 oz) melted butter
1 shallot	pinch salt
1 tablespoon white wine vinegar	juice of ½ lemon
2 tablespoons water	1 teaspoon fresh parsley

Place the tarragon, a good seasoning of pepper, the finely chopped shallot and vinegar in a small saucepan. Heat gently until the vinegar has boiled away, but take care not to burn the shallot. To the hot pan, add first the water and then the egg yolks. Whisk over gentle heat until thick and frothy. Draw the pan off the heat and whisk in the melted butter. Season with salt, and whisk in the lemon juice and chopped parsley. If necessary, this sauce can be kept warm for a short time by placing the base of the pan in a large roasting tin of gently simmering water.

Serve with grilled steak.

Hollandaise Sauce

Serves 4 Time taken 10 minutes

2 tablespoons wine vinegar	salt
3 tablespoons water	freshly milled pepper
4 egg yolks	juice of ½ lemon
100 g (¼ lb) melted butter	

Heat the vinegar in a saucepan over a moderate heat until reduced to half quantity. Draw off the heat, add first the water and then the egg yolks. Replace over low heat and whisk continuously until thick and light. Remove from the heat and gradually whisk in the melted butter. Season with salt and pepper and add the lemon juice to taste.

Serve with freshly cooked broccoli or cauliflower, poached salmon or poached turbot.

Blender Hollandaise

This lacks the sharp flavour of hollandaise made the correct way but is an acceptable substitute. Place 3 egg yolks in the blender with 2 tablespoons of lemon juice and a seasoning of salt and pepper. Cover and blend for a few seconds. Heat 100 g (¼ lb) butter until very hot. Switch blender speed to high and gradually pour the hot butter on to the egg yolks. Blend until thick and fluffy – about 30 seconds. Use as required.

Creole Sauce

Serves 4 Time taken 30 minutes

2 green peppers	salt
2 medium onions	freshly milled pepper
25 g (1 oz) butter	1 level teaspoon castor sugar
1 (425 g) (15 oz) tin tomatoes	1 level tablespoon cornflour

Halve, deseed and shred the green pepper. Peel and slice the onion. Heat the butter in a saucepan and stir in the prepared green pepper and onion. Cook gently, covered with a lid for 10 minutes until the vegetables are soft. Add the tin of tomatoes and a seasoning of salt and pepper and the sugar. Bring to the boil and simmer gently for a further 5 minutes. Blend the cornflour with a little water to make a smooth paste and stir into the vegetable mixture. Cook over moderate heat, stirring all the time until boiling and thickened. Check the seasoning.

Serve with omelettes, grilled or fried sausages, steaks or chops.

Cranberry Sauce

Serves 4–6 Time taken 15 minutes

175 g (6 oz) castor sugar   225 g (½ lb) fresh cranberries
1·5 dl (¼ pint) water

Measure the sugar and water into a saucepan. Stir over low heat to dissolve the sugar. Wash the cranberries, remove any soft berries and pick out any stalks. Add the berries to the pan and bring to the boil. Simmer gently for about 10 minutes until the berries are tender. Draw off the heat and serve warm.

Serve with roast capon, roast turkey or roast pork.

Cumberland Sauce

Serves 6 Time taken 30 minutes

2 oranges   approximately 2 heaped teaspoons
2 lemons   arrowroot
225 g (½ lb) redcurrant jelly   2 tablespoons cold water
1 wine glass red wine or port

Peel the rind from both the oranges and lemons, using a vegetable peeler. Squeeze the juice from the fruits and strain into a saucepan. Add the redcurrant jelly and stir over low heat until the jelly has melted.

Meanwhile, finely shred the peel and place in a small saucepan. Cover with cold water and bring up to the boil. Strain, re-cover with cold water and bring up to the boil again. Simmer for about 20 minutes or until the peel is tender. Drain and reserve.

Add the red wine or port to the sauce and bring up to the boil. Simmer for a few minutes, then draw off the heat and strain the mixture through a sieve. Rub any small pieces of redcurrant jelly through the sieve and then measure the sauce back into the saucepan. For each 3 dl (½ pint) of sauce, blend 1 heaped teaspoon of arrowroot with the cold water in a teacup. Stir into the hot mixture, replace over the heat and continue stirring until the sauce has thickened and is boiling.

Draw the pan off the heat and add the reserved cooked peel. Allow to cool, stirring occasionally to prevent any skin forming on the surface.

Serve with sliced cold gammon or ham.

Bread Sauce

Serves 4 Time taken 45 minutes–1 hour

3 dl (½ pint) milk	15 g (½ oz) butter
1 onion	salt
small bay leaf or blade mace	freshly milled pepper
50 g (2 oz) fresh white breadcrumbs	1 tablespoon cream
or 3 thick slices of bread	

Place the milk in a saucepan. Peel the onion leaving it whole. Add the onion and the bay leaf or mace to the milk. Bring almost to the boil, then draw off the heat, cover and allow to infuse for about 30 minutes.

Remove the onion and bay leaf or mace and add the breadcrumbs. If using bread slices, remove the crusts and break the bread into pieces. Add to the milk and allow to soak for about 10–15 minutes so that the bread softens. Stir with a wooden spoon or whisk to make a purée.

Place the bread sauce over the heat, add the butter and cook gently, stirring frequently until the mixture is fairly thick. Add salt and pepper to taste, and stir in the cream.

Serve with roast chicken or turkey.

Green Pepperonata

Serves 3–4 Time taken 1 hour

1 medium-sized onion	salt
2 tablespoons oil	freshly milled pepper
4 large tomatoes	1·5 dl (¼ pint) stock or water
2 large green peppers	1 teaspoon castor sugar
1 clove garlic	

Peel, halve and thinly slice the onion. Heat the oil in a frying pan, add the onion and fry over a moderate heat, until the onion is tender and lightly brown. Peel and slice the tomatoes and add to the pan. Lower the heat and continue to fry the mixture gently.

Cut the green peppers in half, deseed and shred the peppers finely. Lightly crush the garlic clove, remove the outer papery coating and then mash the garlic to a purée with a little salt. Add the shredded green peppers and the crushed garlic to the pan and season with freshly milled pepper. Stir in the stock or water. Cover and leave to cook very slowly for a further 35–40 minutes. Stir occasionally and remove the pan lid towards the end of the cooking time. When ready, most of the liquid will have evaporated and the peppers will be in a delicious spicy tomato sauce. Stir in the sugar.

Serve as a sauce on top of steaks, chops or omelettes. This sauce is also very nice cold.

Apple Sauce

Serves 4 Time taken 15 minutes

450 g (1 lb) cooking apples	25 g (1 oz) castor sugar
strip of lemon rind	15 g (½ oz) butter
2–3 tablespoons water	

Peel, core and slice the apples into a saucepan. Add the lemon rind and the water. Cover with a lid and stew gently for about 10 minutes or until the apples are soft. Add the sugar, then draw the pan off the heat. Rub the cooked apples through a sieve to make a purée then return to the saucepan. Add the butter, reheat and serve.

Serve with roast pork, duckling or goose and grilled or fried pork chops.

Chestnut Purée for Game

Serves 4–6 Time taken 1 hour

450 g (1 lb) chestnuts	salt
milk and stock	freshly milled pepper
40 g (1½ oz) butter	4–6 tablespoons single cream
1 onion	

Slit the chestnuts on the flat side and place in a saucepan. Cover with boiling water, reboil and simmer for about 10 minutes. Drain and peel away both the outer and inner skins. Replace the peeled chestnuts in the pan and add sufficient mixed milk and stock, or milk and water, to cover. Bring to the boil and simmer gently for about 20 minutes or until the chestnuts are tender. Meanwhile melt 25 g (1 oz) of the butter in a saucepan. Peel and finely chop the onion. Add to the pan and fry gently, until the onion is tender but not brown, and draw off the heat.

When the chestnuts are cooked, drain and add to the onion and butter. Mash them with a fork or a potato masher and then rub the mixture through a sieve to make a purée. Melt the remaining butter, add the chestnut purée and season with salt and lots of pepper. Stir in sufficient cream to make a smooth soft purée.

Serve with roast game.

Chaudfroid Sauce

Makes 6 dl (1 pint) Time taken 1–1½ hours

3 dl (½ pint) water	1 bay leaf
aspic jelly powder (see packet directions)	few parsley stalks
	peppercorns
3 dl (½ pint) milk	25 g (1 oz) butter
½ small onion	25 g (1 oz) flour

Heat the water almost to boiling. Draw off the heat and stir in sufficient aspic jelly powder to set 6 dl (1 pint) normal strength jelly (follow directions on the packet of aspic jelly used). The jelly must be made double strength since 3 dl (½ pint) of white sauce is to be stirred in later to make the chaudfroid sauce, and it must be strong enough to set over chicken or meat galantine. Pour this extra-strong jelly into a bowl and leave to cool while preparing the white sauce.

Measure the milk into a saucepan, add the onion, bay leaf, parsley stalks and peppercorns. Heat until almost boiling, then draw the pan off the heat and allow to infuse for 10 minutes. This flavours the milk and subsequently gives the sauce a good flavour. Melt the butter in a saucepan, stir in the flour and cook gently for 1 minute. Gradually stir in the strained milk and bring to the boil, stirring all the time to get a really smooth sauce. Simmer gently for 2 minutes, then draw off the heat; season well with salt and pepper and allow to cool. Stir occasionally to prevent a skin forming – this is important otherwise the final sauce will be lumpy.

When both aspic jelly and sauce are warm, mix the two together and pass through a fine sieve or muslin, into a clean mixing basin. Set aside until cool and almost on setting point – watch carefully at this stage as it must be used immediately it begins to set.

Use to coat beef galantine, poached chicken joints or whole chicken.

Remove the chicken skin and wipe the flesh with a hot wet cloth to remove any grease. Spoon the sauce generously over the food to be coated. It is always advisable to have too much rather than too little sauce, so that food can be evenly covered. If the sauce sets before it is used, simply warm it until it is liquid again and then allow it to cool to setting point before using.

Mint Sauce

Serves 4 Time taken 10 minutes

1 good handful fresh mint	1 tablespoon boiling water
1 teaspoon castor sugar	4 tablespoons vinegar

There are two schools of thought where mint sauce for lamb is concerned – some like it sharp, others prefer it sweet. The mint can be chopped or, better still, pounded with the sugar.

Strip the leaves from the mint and wash. Chop finely and put in a small basin with sugar. Add boiling water to dissolve the sugar and finally stir in the vinegar. This makes a sharp flavoured sauce.

Alternatively, put the chopped mint leaves in a mortar and sprinkle with sugar; use about 1 tablespoon, the quantity depends on how sweet you like it. Pound in the mortar with the pestle until fairly well crushed. Leave for ½ hour, and by this time the sugar will have extracted the juice from the mint. (The boiling water is not required when using this method.) Give a final pounding and add vinegar according to taste.

Sour-cream Horseradish Sauce

Serves 4–6 Time taken 5 minutes
Allow to stand for 1 hour

4 tablespoons prepared horseradish relish	salt
1 carton soured cream	freshly milled pepper
	dash Worcestershire sauce

Use the commercially prepared horseradish relish for this recipe. It gives a very good flavour.

In a basin mix together the horseradish relish and soured cream. Add a seasoning of salt and pepper and a dash of Worcestershire sauce. Allow to stand for 1 hour before serving, so that the flavour may develop.

Serve with hot or cold roast beef, with grilled steaks or with beef galantine.

DESSERT SAUCES

Custard Sauce

Makes 3 dl (½ pint) Time taken 15 minutes

3 dl (½ pint) milk
2 level tablespoons cornflour
25 g (1 oz) castor sugar

1 egg
few drops vanilla essence

Custard sauce is served with many hot puddings and pies. This is an economical recipe but, nevertheless, a very nice one.

Measure 2–3 tablespoons of the milk into a small basin, add the cornflour and blend thoroughly. Heat the remaining milk to just under boiling point. Draw off the heat and stir into the cornflour mixture. Blend well and pour back into the saucepan. Bring up to the boil stirring all the time until thickened. Simmer for 1–2 minutes, then draw off the heat. Stir in the sugar, the lightly mixed egg and a few drops of vanilla essence. Strain into a heated jug.

Serve hot with puddings or pies.

Caramel Sauce

Serves 4 Time taken 30 minutes

75 g (3 oz) granulated sugar
4 tablespoons cold water

1·5 dl (¼ pint) double cream

Measure the sugar into a dry saucepan. Place over moderate heat and stir until the sugar melts and turns to a golden caramel brown. Draw the pan off the heat. Measure the water into a teacup and pour all at once into the hot caramel. Take care, as the caramel will boil furiously with the addition of the cold liquid. Replace over the heat and stir until the caramel has dissolved and you have a thin caramel liquid. Pour into a basin and set aside until cold.

Very lightly whip the cream, add the caramel liquid and whisk the mixture together to make a smooth, creamy caramel sauce.

Serve with vanilla ice cream or over vanilla cream desserts.

Chocolate Sauce

Serves 4–6 Time taken 30 minutes

175 g (6 oz) granulated sugar
1·5 dl (¼ pint) water

50 g (2 oz) cocoa powder

An economical chocolate sauce with a very good flavour. This recipe is ideal to serve with ice cream or any cold dessert.

Dissolve the sugar in the water over low heat. Bring up to the boil and simmer for 1 minute. Draw the pan off the heat and whisk in the cocoa powder. Mix well until the sauce is smooth. The sauce will be quite thin at first but allow to cool for 10–15 minutes, stirring occasionally and it will thicken to a sauce consistency.

Serve with ice cream or with desserts.

Lemon Sauce

Serves 4 Time taken 15 minutes

100 g (4 oz) castor sugar
1 level tablespoon cornflour
pinch salt
·25 litre (½ pint) (1 teacupful) water

rind of 1 lemon
25 g (1 oz) butter
3 tablespoons lemon juice

Measure the sugar, cornflour and salt into a saucepan. Stir in the water and add the finely grated lemon rind. Mix well to blend the cornflour thoroughly.

Place over low heat and stir all the time, until the mixture has thickened and is boiling. Simmer for a moment, then draw off the heat and stir in the butter and lemon juice.

Serve hot or cold with cake or puddings.

Melba Sauce

Serves 4 Time taken 25 minutes

225 g (½ lb) fresh or frozen
   raspberries
3 good tablespoons redcurrant jelly

1½ level teaspoons cornflour
1 tablespoon water
squeeze lemon juice

Place the raspberries in a saucepan with the redcurrant jelly. Stir over low heat, mashing down the fruit until the jelly has melted and the fruit is quite soft. Draw off the heat. Blend together the cornflour and water and stir into the contents of the saucepan. Replace over low heat and stir all the time until boiling, thickened and clear. Strain through a sieve into a basin and add a squeeze of lemon juice to sharpen the flavour.

Serve warm or cold over vanilla ice cream or with fresh strawberries.

11 Hot Puddings

Hot warming puddings are always popular during cold weather. Many pudding recipes are traditional ones that have been popular for a long time and are likely to continue to be so. Our variable weather and uncertain climate have given them an essential place on the menu.

Some of these recipes can be baked along with a joint or a casserole, making maximum use of the oven. Fresh fruit, dried fruit and spices in various forms give puddings flavour. Serve them with delicious sauces, fresh cream or ice cream.

Soufflé au Grand Marnier

Serves 4 Time taken 1½ hours
Serve at once

1·5 dl (¼ pint) milk	5 large/standard eggs
75 g (3 oz) castor sugar	3–4 tablespoons Grand Marnier
2 pieces thinly pared lemon rind	
25 g (1 oz) butter	icing sugar
25 g (1 oz) plain flour	

Place the milk in a pan and add the sugar and pared lemon rind. Place over moderate heat, bring up to the boil. Draw off the heat and leave to infuse for 15 minutes, then remove the lemon peel.

Melt the butter in a large saucepan and stir in the flour. Cook gently for a few moments, then gradually beat in the hot milk. Bring up to the boil beating well all the time to get a smooth thick mixture. Draw off the heat, and allow the mixture to cool until the hand can be held comfortably against the pan sides.

Separate the eggs, cracking the whites into a bowl, but adding only four of the egg yolks one at a time to the pan. Beat each egg yolk in well. (All five egg whites should be in the bowl ready for whisking.) Beat in the Grand Marnier liqueur.

Whisk the whites until stiff, add to the mixture, fold in a small quantity first and then the remainder. Pour into a well-buttered and sugared, generous 1-litre (2-pint) soufflé dish. Place in the centre of a preheated moderate oven (180°C, 350°F or Gas No. 4) and bake for 1 hour. Dust the surface of the soufflé with icing sugar and serve at once with melba sauce (see page 182).

Hot Banana Soufflé

Serves 4 Time taken 1½ hours
Serve at once

25 g (1 oz) butter	50 g (2 oz) castor sugar
25 g (1 oz) plain flour	4 large eggs
1·5 dl (¼ pint) milk	
3 medium-sized bananas	icing sugar
juice of 1 large lemon	

Melt the butter in a large saucepan over low heat. Stir in the flour and cook gently for 1 minute. Gradually stir in the milk, beating well all the time. Bring the mixture up to the boil – at this stage the mixture will be very thick. Allow to cook for 1–2 minutes, then draw off the heat and cool until the hand can be held comfortably against the sides of the pan.

Mash the peeled bananas with the strained lemon juice and the sugar to a purée. Stir the banana purée into the sauce. Separate the eggs, stirring the yolks into the contents of the saucepan and placing the whites together in a mixing basin. Beat the egg whites until stiff and then, using a metal spoon, fold gently into the mixture. Pour into a buttered, generous 1-litre (2-pint) soufflé dish. Place in the centre of a moderate oven (180°C, 350°F or Gas No. 4) and bake for 45 minutes to 1 hour.

Dust with icing sugar and serve at once with hot chocolate sauce (see page 181) or cream.

Hot Lemon Soufflé

Serves 4 Time taken 1½ hours
Serve at once

25 g (1 oz) butter
25 g (1 oz) plain flour
1·5 dl (¼ pint) milk
rind and juice of 2 large
  lemons

100 g (4 oz) castor sugar
pinch salt
4 large eggs

icing sugar

Melt the butter in a large saucepan over low heat. It is important to use a large pan since the beaten egg whites have to be folded into the mixture at the end. Stir in the flour and cook very gently for 1 minute. Gradually stir in the milk, beating all the time to get a smooth, very thick mixture. Beat in the finely grated lemon rind and the strained juice and bring up to the boil. Draw the pan off the heat, stir in the sugar and salt and allow to cool, stirring occasionally until the hand can be held comfortably against the side of the pan.

Separate the eggs, beating the yolks into the mixture one at a time and placing the whites together in a large basin. Whisk the egg whites until stiff and, using a metal spoon, fold in gently but thoroughly. Any lumps of egg white left in the soufflé mixture will cause it to rise unevenly. Pour the mixture into a buttered generous 1-litre (2-pint) soufflé dish. Place in the centre of a preheated moderate oven (180°C, 350°F or Gas No. 4) and bake for 45 minutes to 1 hour. Dust the top with icing sugar and serve immediately with hot lemon sauce (see page 182).

Rum Bananas

Serves 4 Time taken 10 minutes
Serve at once

50 g (2 oz) butter
6 firm bananas
50 g (2 oz) soft brown sugar

pinch ground cinnamon
2–3 tablespoons rum

For the best results, choose bananas that are slightly under-ripe; they should be a little green at the stalk end.

Melt the butter in a large frying pan. Peel the bananas and cut in half lengthwise. Add to the hot butter in the pan and sprinkle with the mixed sugar and cinnamon. Fry gently for a few moments, until the bananas are lightly brown and the sugar has begun to caramelize, then turn the bananas over. Cook for a further few moments, then draw the pan off the heat and add the rum. Flambé – take care as this recipe burns quite fiercely for the first moment. Reheat gently, shaking the pan so that the flames spread over the entire contents.

Serve at once, with the liquid spooned from the pan and fresh cream.

Bakewell Tart

Serves 4–6 Time taken 1 hour

| 100 g (¼ lb) shortcrust pastry | lemon curd or raspberry jam |

For the Filling

50 g (2 oz) butter	25 g (1 oz) plain flour
50 g (2 oz) castor sugar	½ level teaspoon baking powder
1 egg	50 g (2 oz) ground almonds
few drops almond essence	1 tablespoon milk

On a lightly floured board, roll out the prepared pastry to a circle slightly larger than an 18-cm (7-inch) tart tin or flan ring set on a baking tray. Line with the pastry, prick the base with a fork and spread with a little lemon curd or raspberry jam. Set in a cool place while preparing the topping.

Cream together the butter and sugar until light. Beat up the egg and almond essence, add gradually to the creamed mixture, beating in each addition thoroughly. Sieve the flour and baking powder and add the ground almonds. Add half of this to the creamed mixture and blend lightly. Add the remaining almond mixture, and a little milk, if needed, to get a soft consistency.

Spread the almond mixture to fill the pastry case. Decorate with pastry leaves cut from the trimmings. Place above centre in a moderate oven (180°C, 350°F or Gas No. 4) and bake for about 30 minutes or until risen and firm.

Serve warm or cold with cream.

Apple Turnovers

Makes 8 turnovers Time taken 1 hour

| 225 g (½ lb) rough puff pastry | egg and milk |

For the Filling

| 450 g (1 lb) cooking apples | 50 g (2 oz) soft brown sugar |
| 15 g (½ oz) butter | pinch ground cinnamon |

Apple turnovers allowed to cool and dusted with icing sugar or glacé icing are a good item for a picnic basket.

Roll the prepared pastry out to an oblong about ·5 cm (¼ inch) thick. Trim the edges straight and then cut into eight squares. Leave the pastry to rest while preparing the filling.

Peel, quarter and core the apples. Cut in pieces and place the apple flesh in a pan with the butter. Cover with a lid and simmer gently for about 10 minutes until the apples are quite soft. Draw the pan off the heat and beat with a wooden spoon to make a purée. Add the sugar to sweeten and cinnamon to taste. Allow the filling to cool slightly.

Divide the filling evenly between the pastry squares, spooning the mixture into one triangular half. Damp the pastry edges and fold the other half over cornerwise. Press the two edges gently together to seal. Mark the edges with the floured prongs of a fork. Arrange the turnovers on a wetted baking tray and brush with mixed egg and milk. Place above centre in a very hot oven (220°C, 425°F or Gas No. 7) and bake for 10 minutes. Lower the heat to moderately hot (190°C, 375°F or Gas No. 5) and bake for a further 20 minutes.

Serve warm with cream.

Treacle Tart

Serves 4–6 Time taken 1½ hours

100 g (¼ lb) shortcrust pastry

For the Filling

4 rounded tablespoons golden syrup	rind of ½ lemon
4 heaped tablespoons fresh white breadcrumbs	1 tablespoon lemon juice

On a lightly floured board, roll out the prepared pastry to a circle slightly larger than an 18–20-cm (7- or 8-inch) tart tin or flan ring set on a baking tray. Line with the pastry and leave in a cool place while preparing the filling. Reserve any pastry trimmings.

Warm the syrup in a saucepan until thin and runny. Stir in the breadcrumbs and leave to stand for 10 minutes to allow the crumbs to absorb the syrup. Check the consistency and, if the mixture looks too stodgy, add a little more syrup. If it looks thin and runny, add a few more crumbs. Stir in the finely grated lemon rind and lemon juice to taste. Spread the mixture in the unbaked pastry case.

Re-roll any pastry trimmings and cut into thin strips. Use these to make a criss-cross lattice over the top. Place above centre in a hot oven (200°C, 400°F or Gas No. 6) and bake for 10 minutes. Lower the heat to moderately hot (190°C, 375°F or Gas No. 5) and bake for a further 15 minutes or until the tart is cooked – total baking time should be about 25 minutes.

Serve warm or cold with cream.

Pancakes with Lemon

Makes 12 pancakes Time taken 30 minutes

100 g (4 oz) plain flour	3 dl (½ pint) milk
pinch salt	1 tablespoon melted butter or oil
1 egg	sugar and lemons
1 egg yolk	50–75 g (2–3 oz) white vegetable fat

Sift together the flour and salt into a mixing basin and hollow out the centre. Add the egg, egg yolk and half the milk. Stir the ingredients, using a wooden spoon, and gradually draw in the flour from around the sides of the bowl. Beat well to form a smooth batter. Beat in the remaining milk and, just before using, stir in the melted butter or oil. Pour the batter into a jug ready for use.

Melt about 50–75 g (2–3 oz) white vegetable fat in a small saucepan. Pour a little of the hot fat into the pancake pan. Heat until smoking hot, gently swirl the fat around the side of the pan and pour back into the saucepan of melted fat. Quickly pour about 2 tablespoons of the batter into the centre of the hot pan. Tip the pan so that the batter runs over the surface to make a thin pancake. Cook over moderate heat to brown the underside, then toss or turn to cook the second side. Repeat the process with each pancake.

As the pancakes are prepared stack them neatly between two plates set over a pan of simmering water. Sprinkle each pancake with sugar and lemon juice. Roll up and serve with extra lemon quarters.

Golden Cap Pudding

Serves 6 Time taken 3 hours

175 g (6 oz) self-raising flour	1 level teaspoon baking powder
pinch salt	100 g (4 oz) shredded suet
75 g (3 oz) castor sugar	1 egg
75 g (3 oz) fresh white breadcrumbs	2 tablespoons marmalade
	2–3 tablespoons milk

For the Marmalade Sauce
3 heaped tablespoons marmalade
2 level tablespoons cornflour

juice of 1 lemon
3 dl (½ pint) water

Stir together the flour, baking powder and salt. Add the sugar, bread-crumbs and suet. Lightly mix the egg and 1 tablespoon of the marmalade and stir into the pudding mixture. Add sufficient milk to make a medium soft dropping consistency. Well-butter a 1-litre (1½- or 2-pint) pudding basin and place the remaining tablespoon of marmalade in the base.

Spoon in the pudding mixture and spread level. Cover with a double thickness of greased, greaseproof paper, fold a pleat across the centre to allow the pudding to rise. Tie tightly with string. Place in a proper steamer or in a saucepan on an upturned saucer with boiling water one third up the side of the basin. Steam briskly for 2–2½ hours. Turn out on to a hot dish and serve with marmalade sauce made as follows.

Place the marmalade in a saucepan. Blend the cornflour, lemon juice and water together in a basin and add to the marmalade. Place over the heat and stir until boiling. Simmer for 2–3 minutes, then pour into a jug and serve with the pudding.

Eve's Pudding

Serves 4 Time taken 1½ hours

450 g (1 lb) cooking apples
1–2 tablespoons water

75 g (3 oz) castor sugar

For the Cake Topping
100 g (4 oz) self-raising flour
50 g (2 oz) butter or margarine
50 g (2 oz) castor sugar
1 egg

pinch salt
milk to mix

castor or sifted icing sugar

Peel, core and slice the apples and place in the base of a buttered ·5–1-litre (1- or 1½-pint) baking or pie dish. Add the water and sugar. Set aside while preparing the cake topping.

Sift together the flour and salt. Cream together the butter or margarine and castor sugar until light and fluffy. Gradually beat in the lightly mixed egg. Fold in half the sifted flour, then the remaining flour along with enough milk to make a medium soft consistency. Spoon the cake mixture over the apples and spread evenly.

Place in the centre of a moderate oven (180°C, 350°F or Gas No. 4) and bake for 45 minutes or until the fruit is cooked and the top is well-risen and brown.

Dust with castor or icing sugar and serve hot with cream.

Rhubarb Crumble

Serves 4 Time taken 45 minutes

700 g–1 kg (1½–2 lb) rhubarb   ½ level teaspoon ground cinnamon
50 g (2 oz) castor sugar

For the Crumble
175 g (6 oz) self-raising flour   100 g (4 oz) Demerara sugar
100 g (4 oz) butter or margarine

Wash the rhubarb and trim away the leafy tops. Cut the stalks into 2·5-cm (1-inch) pieces and place in the base of a buttered, 1-litre (1½- or 2-pint) shallow baking dish. Sprinkle with the mixed castor sugar and cinnamon and set aside while preparing the crumble.

Sift the flour into a basin. Add the butter or margarine cut in pieces and rub into the flour until evenly mixed. Add the sugar and rub in again until the mixture becomes 'short' and crumbly. Sprinkle evenly over the rhubarb to cover, and press down lightly. At this stage the crumble may be kept for baking at a later stage. Place in the centre of a hot oven (200°C, 400°F or Gas No. 6) and bake for 30 minutes or until golden brown and crisp.

Serve hot or cold – either way it is delicious with cream.

Butterscotch Pudding

Serves 4 Time taken 30 minutes

100 g (4 oz) granulated or castor   few drops vanilla essence
   sugar   15 g (½ oz) butter
generous ·5 litre (1 pint) milk   chopped walnuts
40 g (1½ oz) cornflour

Measure the sugar into a dry saucepan. Set over moderate heat and stir until the sugar has turned to a caramel. At first, as the sugar melts on the base of the pan, the mixture will become lumpy, but continue stirring until all the sugar has dissolved. Allow the caramel to become a good golden-brown colour and then draw off the heat. Add all but 1·5 dl (¼ pint) of the milk. Replace over the heat and stir until the caramel has dissolved and flavoured the milk. With the addition of a cold liquid the caramel in the pan goes very hard, but it will re-soften as it is stirred over the heat. Reheat until almost boiling.

In a separate basin blend the cornflour with the reserved 1·5 dl (¼ pint) of cold milk. Stir in a little of the hot, flavoured milk. Blend well and return to the saucepan. Stir constantly over the heat until the mixture has come up to the boil and has thickened evenly. Draw off the heat and add the vanilla essence and the butter. Stir until the butter has melted, then pour into individual serving dishes. Decorate the top with a few finely chopped walnuts and set aside to cool.

Serve warm or cold with cream or with tinned pears.

Hot Spiced Peaches

Serves 4 Time taken 20 minutes
Serve at once

1 (850 g) (1 lb 14 oz) tin peach halves	1 level teaspoon ground cinnamon
50 g (2 oz) soft brown sugar	

Drain the peaches and reserve 1·5 dl (¼ pint) of the juice. Arrange the halves, cut-side up, in a small baking dish or roasting tin. Pour the reserved juice on to the base of the tin. Mix together the sugar and cinnamon and sprinkle evenly over the peaches. About 15 minutes before serving, place in the centre of a moderately hot oven (190°C, 375°F or Gas No. 5) and bake for 15 minutes. Serve hot with cream.

Chocolate Fudge Pudding

Serves 4 Time taken 1 hour

75 g (3 oz) self-raising flour	2 eggs
2 level tablespoons cocoa powder	½ teaspoon vanilla essence
pinch salt	1 tablespoon chopped walnuts
100 g (4 oz) butter or margarine	1–2 tablespoons milk
100 g (4 oz) castor sugar	

For the Sauce

100 g (4 oz) soft brown sugar	3 dl (½ pint) hot water
2 level tablespoons cocoa powder	

This chocolate pudding has a sauce that bakes underneath; it has a rich flavour and is popular with children.

Sift together the flour, cocoa powder and salt and set aside. Cream the butter or margarine and sugar until light. Lightly mix the eggs and vanilla essence and gradually beat into the creamed mixture. Add a little of the sifted flour with the last few additions of egg and then fold in the remaining flour, walnuts and enough milk to mix to a medium soft consistency. Spoon the mixture into a well-buttered, 1–1·25-litre (2- or 2½-pint) baking or pie dish and spread evenly. Set aside while preparing the sauce.

In a mixing basin, combine together the soft brown sugar and cocoa powder. Stir in the hot water and mix well. Pour over the top of the cake mixture. Place the pudding at once just above centre in a moderately hot oven (190°C, 375°F or Gas No. 5) and bake for 40 minutes. During baking the cake will rise to the top and the baked pudding will have a delicious chocolate sauce underneath.

Serve hot with cream or ice cream.

Queen of Puddings

Serves 4 Time taken 1 hour

1 inch thick slice cut from a large white loaf	1 level tablespoon castor sugar
	rind of ½ lemon
3 dl (½ pint) milk	2 egg yolks
15 g (½ oz) butter	2 tablespoons red jam

For the Meringue

2 egg whites	75 g (3 oz) castor sugar

Cut the crusts off the bread and cut the bread into large cubes – should be about 50 g (2 oz). Measure the milk and butter into a saucepan and bring just up to the boil. Draw off the heat and add the bread, sugar and finely grated lemon rind. Cover with a lid and allow to stand for 15 minutes. When the bread is quite soft, whisk to a purée and then stir in the egg yolks.

Pour the mixture into a well-buttered scant 1-litre (1½-pint) shallow baking dish. Place in the centre of a moderate oven (180°C, 350°F or Gas No. 4) and bake for 25 minutes or until the mixture has set firm. Carefully spread the jam over the surface of the pudding; if the jam is a little stiff, warm it first.

Whisk the egg whites until stiff, sprinkle in half the sugar and whisk again until thick and glossy. Then, using a metal spoon, lightly fold in the remainder of the sugar. Spoon the meringue over the pudding, swirling the surface roughly. Return to the centre of the oven and bake just long enough to brown the meringue – about 10 minutes.

Serve hot with cream.

Plum Cobbler

Serves 4–6 Time taken 1 hour

700 g (1½ lb) fresh plums	3 tablespoons water
175 g (6 oz) castor sugar	

For the Topping

225 g (8 oz) self-raising flour	1 egg
pinch salt	4 tablespoons milk
75 g (3 oz) butter	milk and granulated sugar
50 g (2 oz) castor sugar	

Bottle or canned fruits may be used, in which case the fruit should be drained and placed in the dish along with 2–3 tablespoons of the juice.

Wash, halve and stone the plums. Pack neatly in the base of a buttered, 1-litre (1½- or 2-pint) baking or pie dish. Add the sugar and water. Preheat the oven to hot (200°C, 400°F or Gas No. 6) and, when ready to assemble the topping, put the fruit in to warm for 5 minutes.

Sift the flour and salt together into a large mixing basin. Rub in the butter until it is evenly mixed and the mixture is crumbly, then add the sugar. Where possible, crack the egg into a measuring jug and make up to 1·5 dl (¼ pint) with milk; if this is not possible, 4 tablespoons of milk is approximately the correct quantity. Mix the egg and milk and add all at once to the dry ingredients. Using a fork, mix to a rough dough. Turn out on to a floured working surface and knead lightly until smooth.

Pat or roll out to about 1 cm (½ inch) in depth, then, using a floured round cutter, stamp out eight or nine scones. Place these overlapping on top of the warmed fruit. Brush with a little extra milk and sprinkle with granulated sugar.

Place above centre in the preheated hot oven (200°C, 400°F or Gas No. 6) and bake for 15 minutes. Then lower the heat to 190°C, 375°F or Gas No. 5 and bake for a further 15 minutes. Serve warm with cream or ice cream.

Gooseberry Stirabout

Serves 6 Time taken 45 minutes

100 g (4 oz) plain flour
pinch salt
2 eggs
3 dl (½ pint) milk
25 g (1 oz) sugar

225–350 g (½–¾ lb) green
  gooseberries
25 g (1 oz) butter

castor sugar

This is an old-fashioned batter pudding, nicest made with fresh green gooseberries, but it can also be prepared with chopped fresh rhubarb.

Sift the flour and salt into a mixing basin and hollow out the centre. Blend the egg yolks with the milk, placing the whites together in a separate basin. Add half the milk and egg mixture to the flour and, with a wooden spoon, stir the liquid gradually drawing in the flour from around the edges of the basin. Beat until smooth, then stir in remaining milk and egg mixture. Stir in the sugar and add the washed, topped and tailed, fresh gooseberries. At this stage the recipe can stand until ready for cooking.

Place the butter in a generous 1-litre (2-pint) shallow baking dish or small roasting tin. Set in the centre of a preheated hot oven (200°C, 400°F or Gas No. 6) and heat through for about 10 minutes until bubbling hot. Whisk the whites until stiff and, using a metal spoon, fold into the batter. Swirl the hot butter round the dish and at once pour in the prepared pudding. Replace in the hot oven just above centre and bake for 30 minutes or until risen and golden brown.

Dredge liberally with castor sugar and serve hot with cream.

Apple Charlotte

Serves 4 Time taken 1½ hours

100 g (4 oz) fresh white
  breadcrumbs

40 g (1½ oz) castor sugar
50 g (2 oz) shredded suet

For the Apple Mixture
450 g (1 lb) cooking apples
15 g (½ oz) butter
1 tablespoon water

50 g (2 oz) soft brown sugar
1 teaspoon golden syrup
rind of 1 lemon

For the Topping
1 tablespoon Demerara sugar

15 g (½ oz) butter

On other occasions rhubarb, plums or apricots chopped up can replace the apples in this recipe.

Measure the breadcrumbs, castor sugar and suet into a small basin and set aside. Peel, core and slice the apples into a saucepan. Add the butter and water and place over low heat. Cover with a lid and stew very gently until the apples are quite soft. Beat in the sugar, syrup and lemon rind and draw off the heat.

Well-butter a 1-litre (1½- or 2-pint) baking dish. Place two-thirds of the crumb mixture in the dish and press over the base and sides of the dish. Pour in the apple mixture and top with the remaining crumb mixture. Sprinkle with the Demerara sugar and dot with the butter, cut into small pieces. Place in the centre of a moderately hot oven (190°C, 375°F or Gas No. 5) and bake for about 45 minutes to 1 hour or until crisp and golden brown.

Serve hot with cream.

Apple Strudel

4–6 servings Time taken 1½ hours

100 g (4 oz) plain flour	2 tablespoons warm water
pinch salt	2 teaspoons oil
1 small egg	40 g (1½ oz) melted butter

For the Filling

450 g (1 lb) cooking apples	¼ level teaspoon cinnamon or
50 g (2 oz) walnuts	mixed spice
50 g (2 oz) sultanas	
50–75 g (2–3 oz) soft brown sugar	icing sugar

A strudel makes a wonderful hot pudding served with ice cream, or a cold sweet generously topped with whipped cream. Try a slice with morning coffee or afternoon tea.

Sift the flour and salt into a mixing basin and make a well in the centre. Mix together the egg, water and oil and pour into the centre of the flour. Mix to a soft dough, then turn out on to a clean working surface and rub down very thoroughly in the same way as for bread dough until the dough is smooth and elastic. Place the dough in a small basin, cover with a cloth and leave to rest for 30 minutes while preparing the filling.

Peel, core and slice the apples and coarsely chop the walnuts. Mix with the sultanas, sugar and cinnamon or mixed spice.

Roll out the strudel dough to an oblong shape and lift on to a clean tea cloth. Using the floured backs of the hands and knuckles, and working from the underside, pull and stretch the pastry gently in all directions. Keep the pastry spread out during working; if it is allowed to fall in folds, the surface will stick together. The odd hole will not matter but try to avoid making too many. When the pastry is ready it should be almost the size of a tea cloth and thin enough to see the pattern through. Brush generously with the melted butter and scatter the filling over the surface making a fairly generous layer of filling on the edge nearest to you.

Pick up the two nearest corners of the cloth and roll the strudel away from you. When rolled up flatten the two ends and trim away the edges. Roll over on to a greased baking tray and curl into a horseshoe shape. Brush all over with melted butter. Place in the centre of a hot oven (200°C, 400°F or Gas No. 6) and bake for the first 20 minutes, then reduce the heat to 190°C, 375°F or Gas No. 5, and bake for a further 10–15 minutes until the sides feel crisp. Dust lavishly with icing sugar. Run a palette knife under the strudel and lift on to a serving dish.

Serve hot, cut in slices with single cream or cold with whipped double cream.

Pineapple Meringue

Serves 4–6 Time taken 30 minutes

1 (225 g) (8 oz) tin of pineapple
    chunks
3 dl (½ pint) pineapple juice
25 g (1 oz) butter

25 g (1 oz) flour
25–50 g (1–2 oz) castor sugar
2 egg yolks

For the Meringue
2 egg whites
75 g (3 oz) castor sugar

reserved pineapple
angelica

Drain the pineapple chunks from the tin and set on one side. Make the juice up to 3 dl (½ pint) with water, if necessary. Melt the butter in a saucepan and stir in the flour. Cook over low heat for 1 minute. Gradually beat in the pineapple juice and bring up to the boil, stirring well all the time to make a smooth sauce. Add the sugar to taste, egg yolks and pineapple chunks, reserving a few for decoration. Remove from heat and pour into a buttered 1-litre (1½- or 2-pint) pie dish.

Beat the egg whites for the meringue until stiff and whisk in the sugar. Spoon the meringue on to the pudding surface and spread evenly. Top with the reserved pineapple chunks and pieces of angelica.

Place in the centre of a hot oven (200°C, 400°F or Gas No. 6) for 2–4 minutes or until golden brown. Serve hot.

Baked Apples with Cream

Serves 6 Time taken 1 hour

6 cooking apples	3 tablespoons water
6 tablespoons castor sugar	1·5 dl (¼ pint) single cream
40 g (1½ oz) butter	

Select apples of even size, wash and remove centre core leaving the apples whole. Run the tip of a sharp knife round the centre of the apple, just to cut through the skin. This allows the apples to puff-up when baking, without splitting the skins unattractively. Place the apples in a baking dish or roasting tin.

Fill the centre of each apple with castor sugar – takes about 1 tablespoon in each – and top with a nut of butter. Measure the water into the tin and place the apples in the centre of a moderate oven (180°C, 350°F or Gas No. 4). Bake for about 45 minutes or until the apples are puffy and soft. The water along with the sugar and butter in the apples will make a delicious syrup in the baking tin.

Serve the apples hot with the syrup from the tin spooned over them and the cream.

Apple Dumplings

Serves 4 Time taken 1¼ hours

225 g (½ lb) shortcrust pastry	milk
4 medium-sized cooking apples	
50 g (2 oz) castor sugar	extra castor sugar

Divide the prepared pastry into four and roll out each piece into a circle about 15 cm (6 inches) in diameter – approximately the size of a bread plate.

Peel and core the apples, keeping them whole. Put one on each round of pastry and fill its centre with sugar. Bring the edges of pastry together over the apples, trimming neatly and pressing well to a smooth shape. Turn over and put on a greased baking tray with the sealed pastry edge underneath. Make a hole in the top-centre of each, brush with milk and decorate each dumpling with small leaves cut from the pastry trimmings. Cut four pastry stalks from trimmings and set aside.

Bake in centre of a hot oven (200°C, 400°F or Gas No. 6) for 30 minutes. Remove from the heat, brush the apples with milk, sprinkle with sugar and return to the oven with the pastry stalks on the baking tray for a further 5–10 minutes, till lightly browned. Test to see that the apples are tender, before finally removing from the oven. Place the stalks in the holes on top of the dumplings.

Sprinkle with extra sugar and serve with cream.

Banana Fritters

Serves 4 Time taken 30 minutes

6 firm ripe bananas	oil for deep frying

For the Batter

75 g (3 oz) plain flour	2 tablespoons water
pinch salt	
1 egg	castor sugar
2 tablespoons milk	

The sugar for tossing the fritters can be varied. Try equal parts sweet chocolate powder and castor sugar, or a spicy finish using 1 level teaspoon cinnamon with 50 g (2 oz) castor sugar.

Select bananas that are not too over-ripe, or they will be too soft for fritters. Peel the bananas and cut in halves across. Dust with flour and pat off any surplus.

Sift the flour and salt for the batter into a mixing basin and make a well in the centre. Separate the egg, placing the yolk in a small basin or teacup and the white in a larger mixing basin. Using a fork, lightly mix the egg yolk with the milk and water. Add to the centre of the sifted ingredients and whisk until smooth. If the batter is very thick, add a little extra water just before using. Stiffly beat the egg white and fold in.

Dip the bananas into the prepared coating batter, allow excess to drain off, then place in hot, deep fat. Fry until crisp and golden brown, turning when necessary – takes 2–3 minutes.

Drain thoroughly on crumpled greaseproof paper, then toss in castor sugar and serve at once.

Spotted Dick

Serves 4 Time taken 2¼ hours

100 g (4 oz) self-raising flour	100 g (4 oz) fresh white
pinch salt	breadcrumbs
100 g (4 oz) shredded suet	rind of 1 lemon
50 g (2 oz) castor sugar	1·5 dl (generous ¼ pint) of milk
75 g (3 oz) cleaned currants	

Sift the flour and salt into a basin. Add the breadcrumbs, suet, sugar, currants and finely grated lemon rind and mix well. Stir in enough milk to mix to a medium dropping consistency. Spoon into a well-buttered, scant 1-litre (1½-pint) pudding basin – the mixture should fill three-quarters of the basin. Cover with buttered double-thickness greaseproof paper – buttered side inwards – fold in a pleat to allow the pudding to rise and tie securely. Steam gently for 2 hours, either in a proper steamer or on an upturned saucer in a saucepan with boiling water one-third up the sides of the basin. Top the pan up with boiling water as required. Remove the papers and turn out the pudding.

Serve hot with a custard sauce (see page 181).

Canary Pudding

Serves 6 Time taken 2½ hours

150 g (5 oz) self-raising flour	2 eggs
pinch salt	¼ teaspoon vanilla essence
100 g (4 oz) butter or margarine	2–3 tablespoons milk
100 g (4 oz) castor sugar	

For the Jam Sauce

3 heaped tablespoons raspberry jam	·25 litre (1 teacupful) cold water
2 level teaspoons cornflour	juice of ½ lemon

This mixture may be varied by adding different flavourings, such as orange or lemon peel, or by adding fruit such as sultanas, peel, ginger or glacé cherries.

Sift together the flour and salt and set aside. Cream the butter and sugar together until light and fluffy. Lightly mix the eggs and vanilla essence and gradually beat into the creamed mixture adding a little of the flour along with the last few additions, if necessary. Fold in half the flour, then the remaining flour and sufficient milk to mix to a medium soft consistency.

Well-grease a scant 1-litre (1½-pint) pudding basin. Spoon in the cake mixture and spread level. Cover with double thickness, greased greaseproof paper, fold in a pleat across the centre to allow the pudding to rise. Tie tightly with string. Place either in a steamer or in a saucepan or an upturned saucer with boiling water one-third up the sides of the basin. Cover and steam for 1½–2 hours. Top up with boiling water as required.

Turn out and serve with the jam sauce made as follows. Measure the jam into a saucepan – sieve the jam if there are any lumps of fruit. Blend the cornflour with the water and stir the jam along with the strained lemon juice. Bring up to the boil, stirring until thickened. Pour into a hot jug and serve with the pudding.

12 Cold Desserts

Desserts that are served cold have many advantages. They can be prepared well in advance of serving. This allows the texture of the recipe to set and the flavours to develop. The fresh flavour in desserts using fruit make a fitting end to any menu, particularly one with a rich or substantial main course. Custard and cream desserts are deliciously smooth and sophisticated and are ideal to choose for a special occasion.

Many of these recipes are set with gelatine and powdered gelatine is most commonly used. The proportions used are always 15 g ($\frac{1}{2}$ oz or 1 slightly rounded tablespoon) to set 6 dl (1 pint) of liquid. Where the gelatine is to be added to a hot liquid, it must first be soaked. To do this, measure out 3 tablespoons of cold water into a basin and sprinkle in the gelatine. Set aside for about 5 minutes during which time the granules will soak up the water. This 'cake' of soaked gelatine can then be added to the hot liquid or custard and stirred to dissolve. In a recipe where the gelatine is dissolved before adding, measure 4 tablespoons of water into a saucepan, sprinkle in the gelatine and set aside to soak as above. Then place over a low heat or, if in a basin, stand in a pan of hot water and stir gently until the gelatine has dissolved and the liquid is clear. On no account allow the mixture to boil, otherwise the setting properties will be impaired.

French leaf gelatine is a gelatine of very high quality and comes in thin brittle leaves. It is not widely available but is sometimes sold in specialist food shops. The proportions used are the same – approximately 5 thin leaves of gelatine equal 25 g (1 oz). In this case the gelatine must be soaked in cold water until pliable, then drained and squeezed out by hand before using. At this stage the gelatine leaves are quite soft and can be stirred into a hot liquid or custard until dissolved.

Where the gelatine is soaked and then added to a hot mixture, care is only necessary to see that the mixture is stirred over low heat to dissolve the gelatine. Sometimes the heat of the contents in the pan is sufficient to do this. Once soaked the gelatine dissolves very quickly and a few moments will be sufficient.

If, on the other hand, the dissolved gelatine is being added to an already partly cooled mixture, the procedure is slightly different and very important. Hold the pan of gelatine well above the basin and pour in a slow steady stream directly over the part of the mixture where whisking. Pouring slowly from a height helps to cool the gelatine mixture and pouring it over the part of the mixture where whisking helps to incorporate it immediately. This is important, otherwise the melted gelatine when coming in contact with a cold basin or mixture may set unevenly in lumps and become 'ropy'.

The next stage in any recipe is to ensure that the mixture, particularly those for creams, mousses or cold soufflés, is allowed to cool sufficiently before any beaten egg whites or cream are added. This is so that maximum volume and the best texture are maintained. One basic rule in cookery is that to get any ingredients to combine successfully together they must be of a similar consistency. For this reason, recipes nearly always say to leave the mixture until cool and beginning to set. The mixture concerned should be set aside in a cool place or, if liked, the base of the bowl may be placed in a larger basin containing ice cubes and water. Stir occasionally if in a cool place, or constantly if over iced water. When the consistency of the mixture changes noticeably and becomes 'lazy' – it appears to have the consistency of unbeaten egg white – the remaining ingredients should be folded in. There is no need to rush, unless the bowl has been placed over iced water, in which case the coldness of the basin is inclined to make the mixture set quickly. It is important, however, to have all remaining ingredients handy. Cream may already be lightly whipped but egg whites should not be beaten until the last moment. Add the ingredients, using a metal spoon that has a good cutting edge, and fold in the ingredients while slowly turning the bowl with the other hand.

Pour the mixture into a serving dish or mould and chill until set firm. Like many other foods the flavour of these desserts is best when not too cold. Always remove from the refrigerator at least 1 hour before serving. As long as the proportions of gelatine are correct the recipe will not soften, unless set in a warm place.

To Unmould Gelatine Desserts

Once the recipe has chilled and is quite firm it's ready to turn out; on the whole, 2–3 hours is long enough. First run the tip of a knife blade around the inside edge to loosen. Fill a large mixing basin with water as hot as the hand can comfortably bear. Holding the mould level, dip up to the rim in the water and hold it there for a few moments. Lift the mould out, dry the base and place the serving plate over the top. Hold the plate and mould firmly together, turn over right-side up and give a few firm, sharp shakes to loosen. If the mould does not turn out, repeat the procedure. It is a good idea to wet the plate first with a little cold water, as it will then be possible to move the mould slightly if it has not fallen in the centre of the plate.

Milanese Soufflé

Serves 6 Time taken 1 hour
Prepare in advance

15 g (½ oz) powdered gelatine	juice and rind of 3 lemons
3 tablespoons cold water	3 dl (½ pint) double cream
4 large eggs	chopped walnuts
100 g (4 oz) castor sugar	

Tie a band of double-thickness greaseproof paper around the outside of a 15–18-cm (6–7-inch) soufflé dish. The paper collar should stand at least 5 cm (2 inches) above the rim of the dish.

Sprinkle the gelatine over the water in a small saucepan and leave to soak for 5 minutes. Separate the eggs, cracking the yolks into a larger basin and the whites into a second smaller basin. Add the sugar and finely grated lemon rind to the yolks. Squeeze the lemons and strain the juice into the soaked gelatine. Place the saucepan over low heat and stir until the gelatine has dissolved – do not allow to boil. Draw off the heat and keep warm while preparing the rest of the recipe.

Set the basin with the egg yolks and sugar over a saucepan half-filled with hot water, and whisk until very thick. Remove from the heat and slowly pour in the dissolved gelatine, whisking all the time. Continue to whisk the mixture until cool and beginning to set. Whip the double cream until thick. Fold the whipped cream into the soufflé mixture along with the stiffly beaten whites. Blend, using a metal spoon, then pour into the prepared soufflé dish, and chill until set firm.

When ready to serve, run the tip of a knife around the inside edge of the paper collar. Detach the edge and gently peel away from the soufflé. Coat the sides of the soufflé with finely chopped walnuts and serve.

Strawberry Soufflé

Serves 6 Time taken 1 hour
Prepare in advance

900 g (2 lb) fresh strawberries	juice of 2 lemons
4 tablespoons cold water	3 egg whites
25 g (1 oz) powdered gelatine	3 dl (½ pint) double cream
250 g (9 oz) castor sugar	

Out of season this delicious recipe can be made using 2 (350 g) (12 oz) packets of frozen strawberries.

Tie a band of double greaseproof paper around an 18-cm (7-inch) soufflé dish. The paper should form a collar standing at least 5 cm (2 inches) above the rim of the dish.

Hull and wash the strawberries. Reserving a few for decoration, sieve the remainder and make about a scant 1 litre (1½ pints) purée. Measure the cold water into a cup. Sprinkle in the gelatine and set aside to soak for 5 minutes. Measure half the purée into a saucepan and add 175 g (6 oz) of the sugar, the soaked gelatine and strained lemon juice. Stir over gentle heat until the sugar and gelatine have dissolved, but do not allow to boil. Draw the pan off the heat, add the remaining purée and set aside until cold and beginning to thicken.

Whisk the egg whites until stiff, add the remaining castor sugar and beat until thick. Fold into the strawberry purée along with the lightly beaten cream. Blend well and pour into the prepared soufflé dish. Set aside in a cool place until firm.

When ready to serve, run the tip of a knife blade around the inside edge of the paper touching the soufflé. Pull away the paper. Decorate with the reserved, thinly sliced strawberries and serve.

Chocolate and Orange Mousse

Serves 4–6 Time taken 1 hour
Prepare in advance

175 g (6 oz) plain chocolate
4·5 dl (¾ pint) milk
rind and juice of 1 orange

15 g (½ oz) powdered gelatine
3 eggs
25 g (1 oz) castor sugar

Break the chocolate into a saucepan and add 1·5 dl (¼ pint) of the milk. Stir over low heat until the chocolate has melted and the mixture blended. Add the remaining milk and the finely grated orange rind and leave over low heat until the flavours infuse and the milk is hot but not boiling. Squeeze the juice from the orange and place in a small bowl. Sprinkle in the gelatine and leave to soak for 5 minutes.

Separate the eggs, placing the yolks in one basin and the whites together in a second basin. Add the sugar to the yolks and cream thoroughly. Gradually stir in the hot flavoured milk, blend well and return the mixture to the milk saucepan. Add the soaked gelatine and stir over low heat until the gelatine has dissolved – this will take only a few moments. Draw the pan off the heat and strain into a large bowl. Set aside to cool, stirring occasionally to prevent a skin forming. When cold and beginning to thicken, stiffly beat the egg whites and fold into the mixture. Pour into a serving dish and chill until set firm.

Serve with cream.

Prune Mousse

Serves 6 Time taken 1 hour
Soak prunes overnight   Prepare in advance

225 g (½ lb) prunes
cold tea (see recipe)
rind and juice of 1 lemon
50 g (2 oz) castor sugar

3 tablespoons water
15 g (½ oz) powdered gelatine
3 dl (½ pint) double cream

Place the prunes in a basin, cover generously with cold tea and leave to soak overnight. Next day place the prunes in a saucepan along with a measured 3 dl (½ pint) of the tea used for soaking and 2–3 strips of pared lemon rind. Simmer until tender – about 15–20 minutes. Draw off the heat, add the sugar, stir to dissolve and then strain the juice from the prunes and set aside. If necessary, make up to 3 dl (½ pint) with a little water.

Remove the stones from the prunes and either purée the prune flesh along with the reserved liquid in an electric blender or, alternatively, rub the prunes through a sieve to make a purée, using a little of the reserved juice to make it easier. Either way combine together the prune purée, reserved juice and strained lemon juice.

Measure the cold water into a small saucepan and sprinkle in the gelatine. Allow to soak for 5 minutes, then stir over low heat to dissolve the gelatine. Add the gelatine to the fruit purée, pouring it in a thin steady stream. Stir well all the time to blend the mixture evenly. Allow to cool for a few minutes then lightly whip the cream and fold into the mixture. Pour into a serving dish and chill for several hours before serving.

Note: to make a more economical recipe 1·5 dl ($\frac{1}{4}$ pint) double cream and 2 egg whites can be substituted for the double cream.

Apricot and Orange Mousse

Serves 4–6 Time taken 1 hour
Prepare in advance

225 g ($\frac{1}{2}$ lb) dried apricots	100 g (4 oz) castor sugar
6 dl (1 pint) boiling water	juice of 1 orange
4 tablespoons cold water	3 egg whites
15 g ($\frac{1}{2}$ oz) powdered gelatine	

Wash the apricots and place in a saucepan. Pour over the boiling water, cover with a lid and leave to soak for 2 hours. Place the pan over low heat, bring slowly to the boil then cover with a lid and simmer very gently until the apricots are quite soft. This should take about 35–40 minutes; stir occasionally to break up the fruit.

Measure the cold water into a teacup, sprinkle the gelatine in and allow to soak for 5 minutes. When the apricots are soft, draw the pan off the heat and add the soaked gelatine. Stir until dissolved – the heat of the pan should be sufficient to do this. Then stir in the sugar to sweeten. Pass the apricots and juice from the pan through a sieve into a basin to make a purée. Discard any pieces of skin left in the sieve. Add the strained orange juice to the purée and set aside to cool. Beat the egg whites until stiff and fold into the apricot mixture. Pour into a serving dish and chill until set.

Decorate with a little grated, plain chocolate, if liked, and serve with cream.

Blackberry Mousse

Serves 4–6 Time taken 1 hour
Prepare in advance

450 g (1 lb) blackberries
100 g (4 oz) castor sugar
15 g (½ oz) powdered gelatine
juice of 1 small lemon

3 tablespoons cold water
1·5 dl (¼ pint) double cream
2 egg whites

This mousse has a delicious flavour and is worth making when fresh blackberries are in season.

Wash and pick over the blackberries. Place in a saucepan along with the sugar and strained lemon juice. Place over low heat, cover and simmer gently for about 10 minutes – as the fruit heats the juices will form. Meanwhile, measure the water into a small basin, sprinkle in the gelatine, and set aside to soak for 5 minutes.

Draw the pan of cooked fruit off the heat, add the soaked gelatine and stir until dissolved – the heat of the fruit will do this. Pass the fruit and juice through a sieve into a large mixing basin to make a purée. Rub through as much of the fruit as possible and discard the pips left in the sieve. Set the purée aside until cold and beginning to thicken.

Lightly whip the cream and stiffly beat the egg whites; fold both into the fruit purée until evenly blended. Pour into a serving dish and chill until set firm.

Serve with a little extra single cream.

Lemon Mousse

Serves 4–6 Time taken 45 minutes
Prepare in advance

4 large eggs
175 g (6 oz) castor sugar
rind of 1 lemon

juice of 2 large lemons
1·5 dl (¼ pint) water
15 g (½ oz) powdered gelatine

Separate the eggs, cracking the yolks into one basin and the whites into a second, larger basin. Add the sugar to the yolks along with the grated lemon rind and lemon juice. To get the right lemon flavour in this recipe, you need about 3–4 tablespoons of lemon juice. Using a wooden spoon, stir the egg yolk mixture well to blend all the ingredients thoroughly.

Measure the water into a saucepan and sprinkle in the gelatine. Allow to stand for a few minutes, then place over low heat and stir until the gelatine has dissolved. Do not boil. Draw the pan off the heat, then holding it well above the mixing basin, add the gelatine to the lemon mixture pouring in a thin, steady stream. Stir well all the time to blend the gelatine into the mixture evenly. Allow the mixture to stand until it begins to thicken and set. Do not leave the mixture too long – it should not take longer than 30 minutes to set. Stiffly beat the egg whites and, using a metal spoon, fold into the lemon mixture. Pour into a serving dish and chill for several hours until firm.

Serve with cream.

Caramel Custards

Serves 4 Time taken 1½ hours
Prepare in advance

4 large eggs	vanilla essence
40 g (1½ oz) castor sugar	4·5 dl (¾ pint) milk

For the Caramel

3 rounded tablespoons granulated or castor sugar	1 tablespoon water

This same mixture can be baked as one caramel custard. Use a metal mould of about a scant 1-litre (1½-pint) capacity, a 15-cm (6-inch) deep cake tin would be ideal. Extend the baking time to 1½ hours.

First prepare the caramel for lining the moulds. Measure the sugar into a dry saucepan and place over moderate heat. Stir until the sugar melts and turns a golden brown. At first the sugar will become rough and lumpy, but continue stirring and it will finally melt. When golden brown, draw off the heat and add the water. Take care, the mixture will boil up with the addition of a cold liquid. Return the pan to the heat and stir until any bits of caramel have dissolved and you have a thick syrup. Pour a little into the base of four ungreased individual moulds – small ·25-litre (¼-pint) pudding moulds are ideal. Holding each mould in a cloth, tip slightly so that the caramel coats the inside. Set aside while preparing the custard.

Crack the eggs into a mixing basin, add the sugar and a few drops of vanilla essence. Whisk to break up the eggs, then whisk in the milk. Strain the mixture into a jug and then pour into each mould. Place the moulds in a shallow baking or roasting tin with cold water up to about 1 cm (½ inch). Place in the centre of a slow oven (150°C, 300°F or Gas No. 2) and bake for 1 hour. If the moulds are close together, allow 1¼ hours. Remove from the heat and leave until cold before serving.

Loosen the top edge of each custard with a knife and turn into individual serving glasses. A certain amount of the caramel will remain in the mould. This is quite in order since the caramel is only there to flavour and colour the custard.

Coffee Cream Mould

Serves 6 Time taken 1 hour
Prepare in advance

4 tablespoons cold water	75 g (3 oz) castor sugar
2 level tablespoons powdered gelatine	2 tablespoons coffee concentrate
6 dl (1 pint) milk	3 dl (½ pint) double cream
3 egg yolks	grated chocolate

Measure the water into a basin, sprinkle in the gelatine and set aside to soak for 5 minutes.

Heat the milk over low heat until almost boiling. Using a wooden spoon, cream the egg yolks and sugar in a basin until light. Gradually stir in the hot milk, blend well and then strain the milk back into the saucepan. Add the cake of soaked gelatine and stir over low heat just long enough to dissolve the gelatine. Do not allow the mixture to boil.

Draw the pan off the heat and pour into a basin. Add the coffee concentrate and set aside, stirring occasionally until the mixture is cold and beginning to thicken. In a separate basin, whisk the cream until thick, then gradually whisk in the coffee mixture. Blend well and then pour into a scant 1-litre (1½-pint) mould, or alternatively into a glass serving dish. Set aside in a cool place until the mould has set firm. Loosen the rim of the mould with a knife blade, then dip in water (hot as the hand can bear) for a few seconds and turn out on to a serving plate.

Decorate the dessert with grated chocolate and serve with single cream.

Praline Bavarois

Serves 4–6 Time taken 1 hour
Prepare in advance

4·5 dl (¾ pint) milk	50 g (2 oz) castor sugar
3 tablespoons cold water	3 dl (½ pint) double cream
15 g (½ oz) powdered gelatine	2 rounded tablespoons praline
4 egg yolks	(see page 342)

Measure the milk into a saucepan, set over low heat and allow to become quite hot. Measure the water into a small teacup, sprinkle in the gelatine and set aside to soak for 5 minutes.

Crack the egg yolks into a basin, add the sugar and, using a wooden spoon, beat the mixture until creamy and light. Gradually stir in the hot milk, blend well and return the mixture to the saucepan. Add the cake of soaked gelatine and stir over low heat, just long enough to dissolve the gelatine. Draw off the heat, strain into a basin and set aside to cool.

When the mixture is cold and beginning to thicken, lightly whip the cream and fold quickly into the mixture, together with the praline. Pour into a scant 1-litre (1½-pint) mould or six small individual moulds and chill until set firm. When ready to serve, loosen round the top edge of the mould with a knife. Dip in hot water (hot as the hand can bear) for a few seconds and turn out.

Serve with cream.

Pineapple Cheese Cream

Serves 6–8 Time taken 1 hour
Prepare in advance

1 level tablespoon powdered gelatine	rind and juice of ½ lemon
2 tablespoons cold water	350 g (12 oz) cottage cheese
2 eggs	1·5 dl (¼ pint) double cream
100 g (4 oz) castor sugar	angelica
1 (415 g) (14½ oz) tin pineapple rings	

Sprinkle the gelatine into the water and leave for 5 minutes. Separate the egg whites from the yolks. Add the sugar to the yolks and, using a wooden spoon, beat thoroughly until light. Drain the juice from the pineapple and make up to 1·5 dl (¼ pint) with water. Reserve the pineapple rings.

Bring the pineapple juice to the boil, then slowly beat into the egg and sugar mixture. Blend well, then return the mixture to the saucepan. Add the soaked gelatine and stir over low heat, just long enough to dissolve the gelatine. Draw off the heat and add the finely grated lemon rind. Pour into a basin and set aside to cool.

Sieve the cottage cheese into a bowl, and stir in the lemon juice and the cooled custard. Leave the mixture until it shows signs of setting, then fold in the lightly whipped cream. Finely chop 2–3 rings of the reserved pineapple and add along with the cream. Whisk the egg whites until stiff and fold into the mixture. Pour into a glass serving bowl and chill until set.

Decorate with a few remaining pineapple pieces and a little angelica, and serve.

Chocolate Pots de Crème

Serves 6 Time taken 1 hour
Prepare in advance

175 g (6 oz) plain chocolate	1 tablespoon dark rum
4·5 dl (¾ pint) milk	4 egg yolks
25 g (1 oz) castor sugar	

For the Decoration
1·5 dl (¼ pint) double cream   grated chocolate

Break the chocolate into a mixing basin. Set over a saucepan of hot, but not boiling water, and stir until softened and smooth. Pour the milk into a saucepan and warm gently. Remove the basin of chocolate from the heat and stir in the sugar and rum. Beat in the egg yolks one at a time. Blend the chocolate mixture well, then stir in the warm milk, and mix again very thoroughly. Strain into six individual baking or ramekin dishes.

Place the dishes in a roasting or baking tin, filled with 2·5 cm (1 inch) of cold water. Place in the centre of a very moderate oven (170°C, 325°F or Gas No. 3) and bake for 30–35 minutes or until firm.

Remove from the heat and leave to cool, then chill. Before serving, lightly whip the cream and spoon a little on top of each one. Sprinkle with grated chocolate and serve.

Blackberry Fool

Serves 6 Time taken 45 minutes
Prepare in advance

450 g (1 lb) fresh blackberries	juice of ½ lemon
100 g (4 oz) castor sugar	3 dl (½ pint) double cream

Select large juicy blackberries, rinse and place in a saucepan along with the sugar. Cover with a lid and place over low heat. As the fruit heats the juice will flow from the fruit. Bring up to the boil, then simmer gently for about 10 minutes or until the fruit is quite tender.

Draw off the heat and pass the fruit and juices from the pan through a sieve to make a purée. Discard the pips remaining in the sieve, add the lemon juice to the purée and set aside to cool.

Whip the cream until thick and fold in the fruit purée. Pour into a serving dish and chill for several hours before serving.

Serve with soft sponge fingers.

Lemon Syllabub

Serves 6 Time taken 10 minutes
Prepare in advance

3 dl (½ pint) double cream
100 g (4 oz) castor sugar
rind and juice of 1 large lemon

4 tablespoons medium dry sherry

sponge finger biscuits

Measure the cream, sugar, finely grated lemon rind, strained lemon juice and sherry into a mixing basin. Whisk all together until quite thick – this may take 2–3 minutes. Spoon into six serving glasses and chill for several hours.

Serve with sponge finger biscuits.

Creamed Lemon Rice

Serves 4–6 Time taken 1 hour
Prepare in advance

75 g (3 oz) round grain rice
6 dl (1 pint) milk
75 g (3 oz) castor sugar

2 eggs
rind and juice of ½ lemon

Creamed rice is an accepted favourite with children. The same recipe with lemon added for flavouring and egg for nourishment gives it a new interest.

Pick over and wash the rice grains. Bring the milk to the boil and stir in the rice. Reboil, then lower the heat and simmer very gently, stirring occasionally for 30–35 minutes or until the rice is creamy and very soft. Draw the pan off the heat and stir in the sugar.

Separate the eggs and stir the yolks one at a time into the creamed rice. Reserve the egg whites. Stir the finely grated lemon rind and lemon juice into the rice to taste. Take care not to make the lemon flavour too strong. Set the mixture aside until cold, stirring occasionally. Whisk the egg whites until stiff and then fold into the rice mixture. Spoon into a serving dish and chill until ready to serve.

Serve with fruit compote or ice cream.

Chestnut and Cream Dessert

Serves 6 Time taken 1 hour
Prepare in advance

450 g (1 lb) chestnuts	1 tablespoon rum
milk and water	3 dl (½ pint) double cream
vanilla pod	
100 g (4 oz) castor sugar	icing sugar
3 tablespoons water	

Slash the flat side of each chestnut and place in a saucepan. Cover with boiling water, bring back to the boil and simmer for 10 minutes. Drain and peel away both the inner and outer skins. Peel the chestnuts as quickly as possible before they cool. Replace the chestnuts in the saucepan and cover with equal parts milk and water. Add the vanilla pod and bring up to the boil. Simmer gently for 20 minutes or until the chestnuts are tender. Draw off the heat and drain. Using a wooden spoon, rub the chestnuts through a sieve into a basin to make a purée.

Measure the sugar and water into a saucepan. Stir over low heat to dissolve the sugar and then bring to the boil. Simmer for 1–2 minutes then remove from the heat. Stir the hot, sugar syrup into the sieved chestnuts stirring well to make a thick sweetened purée. Add the tablespoon of rum and set the mixture aside until quite cold.

Lightly whip the cream. This dessert is most effective if both mixtures are arranged in layers in a glass serving dish. Press a third of the chestnut mixture through a coarse sieve into the serving dish to make the first layer. Cover with a layer of whipped cream and then repeat the layers ending with a layer of chestnut. Dust with a little sieved icing sugar. Chill for several hours till the cream firms up.

Serve with a fruit compote.

Lemon Snow

Serves 6 Time taken 30 minutes
Prepare in advance

3 dl (½ pint) cold water	rind and juice of 2 lemons
15 g (½ oz) powdered gelatine	3 egg whites
100 g (4 oz) castor sugar	

Measure the water into a saucepan and sprinkle in the gelatine. Allow the gelatine to soak for 5 minutes. Add the sugar and thinly pared or grated rind of the lemons. Stir over low heat until the sugar and gelatine have both dissolved, but do not allow to boil. Draw off the heat and strain into a large mixing basin. Set aside until cold.

Add the strained lemon juice and the unbeaten egg whites. Whisk until thick and white. This may take up to 10 minutes – the mixture will not thicken until it begins to set. To speed up the process, place the base of the bowl in a larger one containing cold water and some ice cubes. The more the mixture is whisked as it comes up to setting point, the better the volume in the final dessert. When thick, white and stiff, pour the mixture into a serving dish and chill until set firm.

Serve with cream.

Iced Peaches

Serves 6 Time taken 30 minutes
Prepare in advance

4 medium-sized fresh peaches
1 tablespoon castor sugar
2–3 tablespoons Grand Marnier

3 dl ($\frac{1}{2}$ pint) double cream
Demerara sugar

This same recipe can be prepared using fresh raspberries.

Dip the peaches into boiling water for 30 seconds, drain and rub off the skins. Slice the fruit in half, remove the stone and then slice the flesh. Place the peach slices in the base of a fireproof serving dish – a porcelain white soufflé dish is ideal – sprinkle with the sugar and add the liqueur. Lightly whip the cream, pour over the fruit to cover completely, then chill in the refrigerator for several hours or overnight, until the cream is firm.

Sprinkle the top liberally with Demerara sugar and pass under a preheated, very hot grill just long enough for the sugar to melt and begin to caramelize. Cool so that the sugar topping becomes crisp, then serve.

Compote of Red Fruits

Serves 4–6 Time taken 30 minutes
Prepare in advance

450 g (1 lb) redcurrants
225 g ($\frac{1}{2}$ lb) dark red cherries
175 g (6 oz) castor sugar

225 g ($\frac{1}{2}$ lb) raspberries or
  loganberries

Wash the redcurrants, then strip the berries from the stems using a fork. Halve and stone the cherries. Place the redcurrants and cherries in a saucepan and add the sugar. Cover and place over low heat.

Shake the pan occasionally to help the sugar dissolve in the fruit juices. When the juices are just beginning to boil, draw the pan off the heat and allow to stand covered for about 5 minutes. This gives the fruit a chance to soften in the hot juices and, at the same time, avoids over-cooking them. Add the raspberries or loganberries and pour into a serving dish. Cool, then chill. Serve with cream.

Crème Brûlée

Serves 6 Time taken 1½–2 hours
Prepare in advance

6 egg yolks	6 dl (1 pint) single cream
100 g (4 oz) castor sugar	Demerara sugar

In this recipe the custard is best baked in advance and chilled before the caramel topping is added.

Crack the egg yolks into a basin. Add the sugar to the yolks and, using a wooden spoon, blend thoroughly. Bring the cream almost to the boil and pour slowly over the yolks, stirring well.

Strain the custard into a shallow, well-buttered, scant 1-litre (1½-pint) fireproof dish. This dessert looks pretty if baked in a white porcelain soufflé dish. Place in a shallow roasting or baking tin with 2·5 cm (1 inch) cold water up the sides of the dish. Set in a slow oven (150°C, 300°F or Gas No. 2) and bake for 1–1½ hours until the custard is set firmly. Remove from the heat and allow to cool, then chill.

About 1 hour before serving sprinkle the top with Demerara sugar to cover the surface. Brown quickly under a preheated hot grill. Turn the dish while browning so that the sugar melts evenly. Allow to cool and the sugar topping will become quite crisp. Serve with cream.

Rhubarb with Orange

Serves 4–6 Time taken 30 minutes
Prepare in advance

900 g (2 lb) rhubarb	225 g (8 oz) castor sugar
1·5 dl (¼ pint) water	rind and juice of 1 orange

Orange combines perfectly with the flavour of rhubarb. Here is an attractive way of serving this often badly prepared dessert.

Trim and wash the stalks of rhubarb, then cut into 2·5-cm (1-inch) lengths. Measure the water and sugar into a large saucepan. Stir over low heat until the sugar is dissolved, then bring up to the boil. Add the rhubarb, bring back to the boil, then lower the heat and simmer very gently, covered with a lid, for 3–5 minutes. Draw the pan off the heat and leave covered for a further 5–10 minutes until the rhubarb is quite soft but still in pieces. Add the finely grated rind and juice of orange. Pour into a serving bowl. Cool, then chill until ready to serve.

Sliced Oranges with Candied Peel

Serves 6 Time taken 1 hour
Prepare in advance

6 oranges	1·5 dl (¼ pint) water
175 g (6 oz) castor sugar	juice of ½ lemon

Slice both ends off each orange, then, standing the fruit upright, slice down and round the sides of the orange to remove both the peel and white pith, leaving only the orange flesh. Slice the oranges across, removing any pips, and place the slices in a serving dish.

Select the best pieces of orange peel. Cut away the white pith and finely shred the peel. Place the peel in a saucepan and cover with cold water. Bring up to the boil, drain immediately and re-cover with fresh cold water. This initial blanching removes the bitter taste from the peel. Reboil the peel, cooking for about 25–30 minutes or until tender. Drain and reserve.

Measure the sugar and water into a saucepan. Stir over low heat until the sugar has dissolved, then bring up to the boil. Add the cooked peel and simmer in the syrup for 2–3 minutes, or until the peel begins to look glazed and candied. Draw off the heat. Add the lemon juice to the syrup and then pour the hot syrup and candied peel over the oranges. Cool and then chill for several hours before serving.

Serve plain or with vanilla ice cream.

Fresh Fruit Salad

Serves 4–6 Time taken 30 minutes
Prepare in advance

2 dessert apples	2 bananas
2 ripe pears	2 oranges
225 g (½ lb) green grapes	

For the Syrup

100 g (4 oz) castor sugar	juice of ½ lemon
1·5 dl (¼ pint) water	1–2 tablespoons Kirsch or brandy

Strawberries, raspberries, cherries, peaches, plums and Chinese gooseberries, can be added to, or used in place of, the fruits in the recipe, depending on the time of year.

Prepare the syrup first and allow it to cool before adding the cut-up fruit. With lemon juice added to the syrup, all white fruits such as bananas, apples and pears will remain white and undiscoloured.

Measure the sugar and water into a small pan. Stir over low heat until the sugar has dissolved. Bring up to the boil and simmer for 1 minute. Draw the pan off the heat, add the lemon juice and pour into a basin. Leave to cool, then add the Kirsch or brandy if liked.

Peel, quarter and slice the apples. Peel and halve the pears, using a teaspoon to scoop out the core, and slice the flesh. Halve and deseed the grapes and peel and slice the bananas. Using a sharp knife, cut away the outer peel from the oranges and remove the orange sections individually. Add all the fruit, as it is prepared, to the syrup and stir well – especially when adding the white fruit. Chill for several hours before serving.

Apple and Blackberry Compote

Serves 6 Time taken 30 minutes
Prepare in advance

175 g (6 oz) sugar	450 g (1 lb) blackberries
3 dl (½ pint) water	1 level tablespoon cornflour
450 g (1 lb) dessert apples	

This compote makes a pleasant dessert in the middle of winter when the fresh fruit is out of season. Keep 450 g (1 lb) bags of the prepared fruit in the home freezer for this purpose.

Measure the sugar and water into a saucepan. Stir over low heat until the sugar has dissolved, then bring up to the boil and simmer for 1 minute. Meanwhile peel, core and slice the apples. Pick over and wash the blackberries. Add the apples to the saucepan and cover with a lid. Simmer gently for 1 minute, then add the blackberries. Bring back to the boil and draw the pan off the heat. Leave the pan covered with a lid to stand for about 15 minutes, or until the fruit is tender.

Either strain, or carefully remove, the fruit from the syrup using a perforated spoon. Place the fruit in a serving dish and return the juice to the saucepan. Blend the cornflour with a little cold water and stir into the fruit juice. Bring up to the boil, stirring until slightly thickened, shiny and clear. Pour the juice over the fruit. Cool, then chill well before serving.

Serve with cream.

Pears in Red Wine

Serves 4–6 Time taken 30 minutes
Prepare in advance

3 dl (½ pint) red wine
3 dl (½ pint) water
175 g (6 oz) castor sugar
1 small stick cinnamon

lemon rind
6 even-sized Conference pears
2 level tablespoons cornflour

Measure the wine and water into a large saucepan. Less wine and more water may be used, but the wine gives a delicious flavour and a good colour. Add the sugar, cinnamon stick and 2–3 pieces of thinly pared lemon rind, place over low heat and stir until dissolved.

Meanwhile peel the pears leaving them whole. Add the pears to the wine in the saucepan and arrange them as far as possible on their sides, so that they are almost submerged in the liquid. Bring up to simmering point, then cover with a lid and simmer for about 10–20 minutes or until the pears are tender – time taken will depend a little on the state of ripeness of the pears. Draw the pan off the heat, lift out the pears and arrange in a glass serving dish.

Blend the cornflour with a little liquid taken from the pan, then stir into the liquid remaining in the pan. Replace the pan over moderate heat and stir until the syrup has thickened, is boiling and has become clear. Simmer for 1 minute, then draw off the heat. Cool for a few moments, then strain the sauce over the pears. Cool, then chill for several hours.

Serve the pears with the red wine sauce and a little fresh cream.

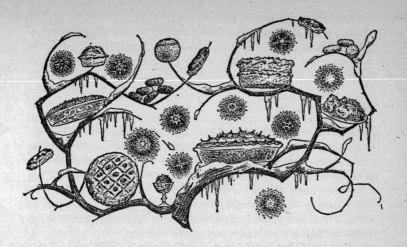

13 Cooking for the Freezer

A home freezer is rather like having another pair of hands in the kitchen or another day in the week; it allows a busy woman to shop when she wants and to cook when she has time. There are many ways in which a deep freeze can be used. Those in the country may use it largely to store surplus garden produce, whereas others in town may use it to store fresh or prepared goods, in order to cut down on endless shopping and cooking. There is nothing to be said in favour of freezing for the sake of freezing, but there is everything to be said for planned freezing that will save valuable time.

There are two points that are important to remember when freezing home-prepared foods. Firstly, food should be well protected. Freezing draws moisture and will dry unprotected food, causing freezer burn. Secondly, food should be frozen in suitable quantities for serving and, where possible, in containers in which it can be reheated. Chicken joints or chops, for instance, should be frozen in twos or fours according to how you plan to use them. Fruit should be stored in 225 g ($\frac{1}{2}$ lb), 450 g (1 lb) or 900 g (2 lb) packs, so that you know exactly how much you have and so that it can be used easily in recipes stating specific quantities. Creamed chicken, sliced beef and similar types of recipe can be frozen in foil containers ready for reheating.

Wrappings and Containers

These can be expensive and should be used economically. There is quite a selection to choose from, and only by trying the various kinds is it possible to determine which ones are the most practical. Always make a point of having suitable wrappings in stock: there is nothing more irritating than having items you wish to freeze and nothing suitable to put them in.

Polythene bags These are about the most useful of all. They come in various sizes and it is as well to have a selection. One great advantage is that they can be used over and over again. Once the chosen food is inside, press out as much air as possible from the bag, secure the opening with string, a rubber band or plastic wires, making the bag completely airtight, and put in the freezer. These are suitable for all items such as fruit, vegetables, meat, poultry, game, fish, bread or cakes. Baked pies in foil containers, or foods in moulds or dishes, can be placed inside a polythene bag before freezing.

Aluminium-foil sheets and containers Aluminium-foil is very suitable for wrapping food for the freezer, but can be a little expensive. If used, care should be taken to completely wrap and seal the items by turning the foil in on all open edges to make the package airtight. Foil dishes and containers are excellent. Pies and tarts can be baked in the dishes, and puddings baked or moulded in the basins. They should then be placed in polythene bags and sealed. Pies and tarts needing reheating or baking can be placed directly in the oven in the foil dishes.

Freezer paper This comes in wide rolls. It is moisture-proof and stands up to low temperatures without becoming brittle, as other papers do. The packages should be sealed with polytape.

Waxed tubs and cartons These are particularly useful for items that are likely to have juices, or recipes where there is a liquid, sauce or syrup. Remember never to fill the containers completely; leave 1 cm ($\frac{1}{2}$ inch) of space below the lid to allow for the expansion of any liquid ingredients when freezing.

Polythene boxes with airtight lids These come in different sizes and shapes and are extremely useful. Use them for ice creams, fruit or recipes with sauces. They are a little more expensive to buy in the first place but can be washed out and re-used indefinitely.

Polytape This is an indispensable item for wrappings. It should be used to seal packages and even in the low temperature of the freezer it does not unstick.

Always mark or label all foods for freezing. Use a waxed crayon or chinagraph pencil for marking. Remember that the areas around the sides of the cabinet and at the base freeze more quickly, so put new packs round the cabinet edges. Never freeze too many items at once since this will raise the temperature inside the cabinet. This is not only bad for the food already stored, but also causes the new packs to take longer to freeze.

Choose foods and recipes for the freezer with care. Best foods to freeze are those that are seasonal. Good too are those which take a long time to prepare or cook. Select recipes that require little time and attention once they have been thawed, and that can be served at once.

Pizza

Makes 3 pizza of 2 portions each Time taken 1½–2 hours

225 g (8 oz) plain flour	1 level teaspoon dried yeast
1 level teaspoon salt	¼ level teaspoon castor sugar
15 g (¼ oz) fresh yeast	1·5 dl (¼ pint) warm water
or	1 dessertspoon oil

For the Topping

1 tablespoon oil	freshly milled pepper
½ onion	1 tin anchovy fillets
1 (425 g) (15 oz) tin tomatoes	few black olives
pinch salt	50–100 g (2–4 oz) grated Cheddar
¼ level teaspoon castor sugar	cheese
pinch dried mixed herbs	

Pizza takes time to prepare, but freezes well and can be quickly reheated. Hot pizza makes an excellent cocktail party snack.

Sieve the flour and salt into a mixing basin. Blend the fresh yeast with the warm water. If using dried yeast, dissolve the sugar in the hand-hot water and sprinkle in the dried yeast. Stir to mix, then leave to stand in a warm place until frothy. Add the yeast mixture to the flour along with the oil. Mix to a soft dough then turn out on to a clean working surface and knead for about 5 minutes until the dough feels firm and elastic and is no longer sticky. Shape into a ball and replace in the basin. Place inside a polythene bag and leave to prove until double in size.

Meanwhile prepare the topping. Heat the oil in a saucepan. Peel and finely chop the onion. Add to a pan, cover and cook gently until the onion is soft. Stir in the tomatoes, salt, sugar, mixed herbs and a seasoning of pepper. Cover and simmer gently for about 30 minutes or until the mixture is fairly thick. Stir occasionally to prevent sticking, then remove from the heat and allow to cool.

Turn the risen dough on to a clean working surface and press firmly with the knuckles to knock out the air bubbles. Divide the dough into three equal pieces. Shape each piece into a ball and then roll out to a circle about 15 cm (6 inches) in diameter. Press each circle into a buttered 18-cm (7-inch) foil pie plate. Press the dough over the base and turn up the edges slightly. Brush each crust with a little oil.

Spoon the topping on to each pizza, spreading it to within 1 cm (½ inch) of the edges. Garnish with anchovy fillets and the halved and stoned black olives, and finely sprinkle with the cheese. Set aside for about 15 minutes or until the dough is slightly puffy. Place the pizza together in a very hot oven (220°C, 425°F or Gas No. 7) and bake for 15–20 minutes. Cool and then place each pizza (in the foil plate) in a polythene bag. Tie tightly and freeze.

To serve Thaw at room temperature for about 2 hours. Reheat in a hot oven (200°C, 400°F or Gas No. 6) for 10–15 minutes. Remove from the foil plates and serve with salad.

Melon in Ginger Syrup

Serves 6 Time taken 20 minutes

1 large ripe honeydew melon

For the Syrup

100 g (4 oz) castor sugar	1 tablespoon finely chopped stem
1·5 dl (¼ pint) water	ginger
juice of ½ lemon	

Where possible, scoop out the melon flesh using a vegetable baller. To do this, press the cutter into the melon flesh and twist round sharply.

Slice the melon in half, scoop out the seeds and cut the melon in quarters. Slice the melon flesh away from the skin and cut into small neat dice. Spoon the flesh and add any juice into a basin.

Measure the sugar and water into a saucepan. Stir over low heat until the sugar has dissolved and then bring up to the boil. Simmer for 2 minutes, then draw off the heat. Add the lemon juice and the chopped ginger. Leave until quite cold, then add the diced melon flesh. Spoon the mixture into one or more waxed or polythene containers, making sure that there is at least 1 cm (½ inch) of head space. Cover and freeze.

To serve Allow the fruit to thaw in the refrigerator for 1–2 hours. Serve in individual glasses while still well-chilled.

Salmon Fish Cakes

Serves 4 Time taken 30 minutes

1 (450 g) (1 lb) tin pink salmon
450 g (1 lb) potatoes
salt
freshly milled pepper
1 tablespoon finely chopped parsley

1 tablespoon tomato ketchup
squeeze of lemon juice
2 small eggs

toasted breadcrumbs

Drain the salmon from the tin, flake the flesh and remove the skin and small bones. Peel the potatoes and cook in boiling salted water until tender. Drain, return the potatoes to the hot pan and dry over the heat for a few moments. Sieve the potatoes into a bowl. Season well with salt and pepper. Add the salmon, parsley, tomato ketchup and lemon juice and mix with a fork. Lightly mix the eggs and add a little to the salmon mixture, sufficient to bind the mixture together. Check the seasoning in the mixture, adding a little more if necessary.

Pour the remaining eggs into a shallow dish and have the bread-crumbs for coating ready on a plate. Turn the salmon mixture out on to a lightly floured working surface and shape into a thick roll. Set aside in a cool place to firm up a little.

Divide the mixture into eight portions and shape them into neat fish cakes. Place them in turn in the egg and coat all over. Lift out, drain for a minute, then place in the bed of dry breadcrumbs and coat evenly. Pat the crumbs on firmly. Freeze unwrapped until firm, then place in polythene bags in suitable numbers for serving. Tie tightly and store in the freezer.

To serve   Heat 1 tablespoon of oil and 50 g (2 oz) butter in a frying pan. Add the frozen fish cakes and cook for 5 minutes each side, or until heated through and brown.

Meat Croquettes

Serves 4 Time taken 2–3 hours

225 g (8 oz) cooked meat
1 small onion
25 g (1 oz) butter
25 g (1 oz) flour
1·5 dl (¼ pint) stock
salt

freshly milled pepper
50 g (2 oz) grated Gruyère cheese
1 egg

toasted breadcrumbs

This is an excellent method of using up leftover meat from a joint. The croquettes can be prepared and frozen, ready to serve another day. Use Gruyère cheese; when hot and newly served the croquettes should have the delicious tacky texture that only Gruyère cheese can give.

Mince the meat. Peel and finely chop the onion. Melt the butter in a saucepan and add the onion. Cover and cook very gently for about 5 minutes, or until the onion is tender but not brown. Add the minced meat and cook for a further few moments. Stir in the flour and mix well, then gradually stir in the stock. Cook for several minutes until the mixture is very thick, then add a good seasoning of salt and pepper and stir in the cheese. Draw off the heat and spread the mixture about 1 cm ($\frac{1}{2}$ inch) thick on a plate. Cover with butter, foil or paper and leave until quite cold.

Divide the mixture into eight equal portions. Flour the hands and roll each portion first into a ball and then into a croquette shape. Coat in the lightly beaten egg and then in breadcrumbs. Freeze uncovered until hard. Place together in one or two lots of four in polythene freezer bags. Tie tightly and replace in the freezer.

To serve Allow to thaw at room temperature for 1–2 hours. Deep fry in hot fat for 5 minutes, then serve.

Danish Liver Pâté

Serves 6 Time taken 2$\frac{1}{4}$ hours

3 dl ($\frac{1}{2}$ pint) milk
1 peeled onion
1 bay leaf
175 g (6 oz) fat bacon
450 g (1 lb) lambs' liver
1 clove garlic
3–4 fillets of anchovy
 or

1 teaspoon anchovy essence
1 level teaspoon salt
freshly milled pepper
25 g (1 oz) butter
1 level tablespoon flour
5–6 rashers streaky bacon

Measure the milk into a saucepan and add the onion and bay leaf. Bring up to the boil, then draw off the heat and allow to infuse for 15 minutes. Strain and reserve the milk.

Trim any rind from the fat bacon (streaky bacon rashers can be used instead) and mince twice, together with the liver, peeled garlic and anchovy fillets. If anchovy essence is used, add after mincing the ingredients. Season with the salt and pepper.

Melt the butter in a saucepan, add the flour and cook for a few moments without browning. Gradually stir in the strained milk, beating well all the time. Bring up to the boil, cook for a few moments, then draw off the heat and pour into a basin. Blend in the minced liver mixture.

Line a large 23 × 13 × 5-cm (9 × 5 × 2-inch) loaf tin with the streaky bacon rashers. Pour in the pâté mixture. Fold any edges of bacon rashers in over the top. Cover with a buttered paper and a lid or foil, and stand the dish in a roasting or baking tin filled with 2·5 cm (1 inch) of cold water. Place in the centre of a very moderate oven (170°C, 325°F or Gas No. 3) and bake for 1½–2 hours. Remove from the heat, cover with a fresh buttered paper and a weight. Leave until quite cold, preferably overnight. Turn the pâté out and wrap in foil. Or slice into individual portions and wrap each portion in foil. Fold in the edges of the foil securely and freeze.

To serve Thaw whole pâté overnight or 6–8 hours in the refrigerator. Thaw the slices for 2–3 hours. Keep chilled until ready to serve. Serve with hot toast and butter.

Sautéed Pork Fillet with Lemon

Serves 4 Time taken 15 minutes

450–700 g (1–1½ lb) pork fillets toasted breadcrumbs
seasoned flour
1 egg, lightly beaten

This is an example of a recipe that can be put ready for cooking and then placed in the freezer. Portions of turkey breast or boned chicken breast can be treated in the same way.

Using a sharp knife, trim away any fat, skin and sinew on the outside of the pork fillet. Cut the meat across into 5-cm (2-inch) pieces. Place each slice on end, that is with one cut-side facing upwards. Place each piece, one at a time, between two squares of wetted greaseproof paper and beat with a rolling pin until quite thin and flat. The wetted paper prevents the meat from sticking to either the board or the pin.

Dip each piece of pork on both sides in lightly beaten egg, then in brown breadcrumbs. Shake away any loose crumbs and pat the remainder on firmly. Stack in a suitable quantity for serving, either two portions of two, or one portion of four, servings. Place a square of waxed paper between each slice of pork fillet. Wrap in foil and place inside a freezer polythene bag, tie tightly and freeze.

To serve Separate the portions of meat and cook while still frozen. Melt 50–75 g (2–3 oz) butter in a frying pan and add the pieces of pork. Fry gently for 3–5 minutes on each side or until heated through and brown. Draw the pan off the heat and squeeze over the juice of ½ lemon. Serve at once with the butter and juices from the pan.

Croquette Potatoes

Makes 24   Time taken 45 minutes

900 g (2 lb) potatoes	freshly milled pepper
15 g (½ oz) butter	
2 eggs	toasted breadcrumbs
salt	

Peel the potatoes and place in a saucepan with sufficient cold, salted water to cover. Bring to the boil, then simmer for 15–20 minutes or until tender, but do not overcook. Drain the potatoes well, return to the hot pan and dry thoroughly over low heat for a few moments. Rub the potatoes through a sieve to get rid of all the lumps.

Rinse out the cooking pan and return to the heat with the butter. Warm, just to melt the butter, then draw off the heat. Add the potatoes and beat well to mix. Add a good seasoning of salt and freshly milled pepper. Separate the eggs and beat the yolks into the potato mixture. Place the whites in a shallow dish and mix lightly with a fork.

Turn the potato mixture out on to a lightly floured working surface and shape into a thick roll. Divide into 24 equal portions, then, using lightly floured hands, shape each portion into a neat croquette. Roll each croquette first in the lightly mixed egg white and then in the toasted breadcrumbs.

Place the shaped croquettes on a tray or baking sheet and place in the freezer, uncovered, until quite hard. They are now easily packed and will not stick together. Pack in polythene bags and store in the freezer.

To serve   Allow the croquettes to thaw at room temperature for 2–3 hours. Fry in hot, deep fat until golden brown.

Red Cabbage with Apple

Serves 4–6   Time taken 2 hours

1 small red cabbage	2 large cooking apples
salt	boiling water
25 g (1 oz) butter	3 tablespoons vinegar
1 onion	25 g (1 oz) castor sugar

Red cabbage freezes and reheats exceptionally well.

Remove outer, damaged leaves and cut the cabbage into quarters. Cut away the centre core and shred the cabbage finely. Cover with cold salted water and leave to soak for 1 hour.

Melt the butter in a large saucepan. Peel and chop the onion. Add the onion and fry gently for about 5 minutes or until soft. Add the red cabbage lifted straight from the salt water. Peel, core and chop the apple, add to the pan and pour in sufficient boiling water to cover the base of the saucepan generously. Add the vinegar and sugar. Cover with a lid and bring up to the boil. Simmer gently for about 45 minutes or until the cabbage is tender. Stir or press the cabbage with a potato masher occasionally, to help pulp the apples. Add a little extra water only if necessary, the mixture should not be too moist. Check the seasoning and flavour. Cool the cabbage as quickly as possible, then spoon into one or more polythene freezer bags. Tie tightly and freeze.

To serve While still frozen, place in a saucepan along with 15 g (½ oz) butter. Heat gently, breaking the block of cabbage up with a fork as it heats. Heat through until simmering. Serve with roast pork, roast duck or game.

Creamed Chicken

Serves 4 Time taken 8 hours

1 (1·5 kg) (3 lb) oven-ready chicken	40 g (1½ oz) butter
1 tablespoon salt	40 g (1½ oz) flour
few peppercorns	salt
1 onion	freshly milled pepper
1 clove	2 egg yolks
2–3 stalks of celery	2–3 tablespoons double cream
1 bay leaf	15 g (½ oz) butter
4·5 dl (¾ pint) chicken stock	squeeze of lemon juice

The chicken stock left over from cooking this recipe may be used for soup.

Place the chicken, breast downwards, in a large saucepan. Add sufficient water to cover. Add the salt, peppercorns, the peeled onion stuck with the clove, the stalks of celery cut up, and the bay leaf. Cover and bring to the boil. Simmer the chicken gently for 1 hour then draw off the heat. Remove the flavouring vegetables and leave the chicken to cool in the liquor.

Remove the chicken and strain the stock. Remove the fat from the surface and measure out 4·5 dl (¾ pint) of stock. Melt the butter in a saucepan and, over low heat, stir in the flour. Cook gently for 1–2 minutes, then gradually stir in the measured stock. Bring up to the boil stirring all the time to get a smooth sauce. Check the seasoning with salt and pepper. Allow to simmer gently for about 5 minutes, then draw off the heat. Mix the egg yolks and cream in a bowl. Stir into the sauce. Add the butter and the lemon juice to taste. Strain into a basin and cool, but continue to stir frequently to prevent a skin from forming.

Lift the chicken flesh from the carcass and cut the flesh into chunky pieces. Place in one or more containers of a suitable size. Pour over the sauce, tap the container gently so that the sauce runs to the base. Make sure there is at least 1 cm ($\frac{1}{2}$ inch) of space at the top. Cover and freeze.

To serve Loosen and turn out the frozen mixture into the top of a double boiler. As the mixture thaws over the heat, break the pieces of chicken apart with a fork. Heat through thoroughly for 30 minutes.

Sprinkle with chopped parsley and serve with rice.

Cottage Pie

Serves 4 Time taken 1$\frac{1}{2}$ hours

25 g (1 oz) dripping or vegetable fat	freshly milled pepper
1 onion	1 level tablespoon flour
450 g (1 lb) lean minced beef	1 (65 g) (2$\frac{1}{2}$ oz) tin tomato purée
1 level teaspoon salt	3 dl ($\frac{1}{2}$ pint) stock

For the Topping

700 g (1$\frac{1}{2}$ lb) potatoes	25 g (1 oz) butter
salt and pepper	
little warm milk	chopped parsley

Heat the dripping in a large saucepan. Peel and slice the onion and add to the pan. Fry gently for 5 minutes to soften, then add the minced beef, salt and freshly milled pepper. Continue to fry a little more quickly to brown the meat. Sprinkle the flour over the mince, stir in the tomato purée and stock. Bring up to the boil, then lower the heat, cover the pan with a lid and simmer gently for $\frac{1}{2}$–1 hour. Draw the cooked meat off the heat, check the seasoning and pour into one large foil container or two smaller ones. Allow to cool.

Peel and cut up the potatoes. Cover with cold salted water and bring up to the boil. Cook quickly until potatoes are tender – about 20 minutes – then drain and mash them thoroughly. Season well with salt and pepper, add a little warm milk and half the butter and beat thoroughly with a wooden spoon until the potatoes are creamy and smooth.

Spoon the potato topping over the meat and, using a fork, spread evenly. Allow the mixture to become quite cold. Dot the surface of the potato with the remaining butter in pieces. Freeze unwrapped until firm. Then wrap in foil or place in polythene bags. Tie tightly and freeze.

To serve Allow to thaw for 3–6 hours at room temperature. Place above centre in a moderately hot oven (190°C, 375°F or Gas No. 5) and bake for 20–30 minutes or until bubbling hot and brown.

Chicken Pies

Makes 2 pies of 4 portions each Time taken 1½ hours

350 g (¾ lb) shortcrust pastry

For the Filling

6 chicken joints	salt
100 g (4 oz) butter	freshly milled pepper
50 g (2 oz) plain flour	350 g (¾ lb) mushrooms
6 dl (1 pint) chicken stock	

Prepare the shortcrust pastry and set aside to rest while preparing the filling.

Put the chicken joints in a roasting tin. Add 25 g (1 oz) of the butter and cover with a buttered paper. Cook in a moderate oven (180°C, 350°F or Gas No. 4) for 1 hour, until tender. Meanwhile, melt 50 g (2 oz) of the remaining butter in a saucepan over low heat. Stir in the flour and cook gently for 1 minute. Gradually stir in the stock and bring to the boil, beating well all the time. Season with salt and pepper and cook gently for a few minutes, then draw off the heat.

Remove the chicken from the oven and leave until cool enough to handle. Remove the skin and lift the flesh from the bones. Add the chicken flesh to the sauce. Trim and slice the mushrooms and lightly fry in the remaining 25 g (1 oz) of butter. Add to the chicken filling. Spoon the mixture into two 20-cm (8-inch) foil pie cases, filling the dishes. Set aside to cool. When cold, lightly grease the edge of each dish.

Divide the pastry in half and roll out two circles, large enough to cover the pies. Line the edges of the dish with pastry trimmings, dampen with water and cover each pie with a pastry circle. Seal the edges well. Do not cut slits in the pie top. Put each pie in a polythene bag or wrap in foil and freeze.

To serve Unwrap the pie and thaw for 2–3 hours at room temperature. Cut a few slits in the top. Bake in a preheated, moderately hot oven (190°C, 375°F or Gas No. 5) for 45–50 minutes. Serve hot.

Chicken with Spanish Rice

Serves 4   Time taken 1½ hours

4 chicken leg joints	1 (425 g) (15 oz) tin tomatoes
50 g (2 oz) butter	salt
1 onion	freshly milled pepper
1 green pepper	2 level teaspoons castor sugar
175 g (6 oz) long grain rice	1 small packet frozen peas
4·5 dl (¾ pint) chicken stock	

Trim the chicken legs and remove any loose skin. Cut each one in half through the leg joint to make two pieces. Melt the butter in a large frying pan, add the chicken pieces and fry gently for about 5 minutes browning on both sides. Lift the pieces from the pan and place in a large casserole dish.

Peel and slice the onion. Halve, deseed and shred the green pepper. Add the sliced onion and green pepper to the hot fat in the frying pan, cover and fry gently for about 5 minutes until the onion is softened. Add the rice, stir to mix with the vegetables and then stir in the hot stock. Stir in the tomatoes and liquid from the tin. Season well with salt and freshly milled pepper and add the sugar. Bring up to the boil, then draw off the heat and spoon or pour over the chicken joints.

Cover the casserole and place in the centre of a moderate oven (180°C, 350°F or Gas No. 4) and cook for 1 hour. After 45 minutes, give the contents of the casserole a stir and add the peas. When cooked, the rice will have absorbed all the liquid. Check the seasoning and allow to cool. Spoon into a suitable container, cover and freeze. *To serve* Thaw for 3–4 hours at room temperature. Place in a casserole set in the centre of a moderate oven (180°C, 350°F or Gas No. 4) and cook for 30–35 minutes to heat through. Stir the ingredients with a fork and serve hot.

German Pastry for Tart or Flan Cases

Makes four 20-cm (8-inch) flan cases   Time taken 1½ hours

450 g (1 lb) plain flour	275 g (10 oz) butter
150 g (5 oz) castor sugar	1 egg

This is a pastry that deep freezes very well. Flan cases baked and then deep frozen ready for use can be very handy.

Sift the flour into a mixing basin, add the sugar and the butter cut in pieces. Rub in the butter, just enough to blend into the mixture, then add the egg and knead by hand to a smooth dough. Cover and place in the refrigerator for 30 minutes.

Divide the dough into four portions; while working with each piece keep the rest in the refrigerator. Knead the portion of dough slightly to soften, then, on a floured working surface, roll out to a circle slightly larger than a 20-cm (8-inch) flan ring, set on a baking tray. Line the ring with the pastry, trim the edges and prick the base. Fill with a piece of crumpled kitchen foil to keep the shape while baking. Place in the centre of a moderately hot oven (170°C, 325°F or Gas No. 5) and bake for 10–12 minutes. Remove the foil a few minutes before the end of baking time. Repeat this procedure with each piece of dough, baking four flan cases. Allow to cool, then place together in one large polythene freezer bag. Tie tightly and freeze.
To serve Remove the pastry as required, allow to thaw – takes about 30 minutes – then use in dessert recipes.

Chocolate Charlotte Russe

Serves 6 Time taken 1½ hours

1 packet of 8 trifle sponge cakes

For the Chocolate Filling

175 g (6 oz) plain chocolate	3 egg yolks
4·5 dl (¾ pint) milk	25 g (1 oz) castor sugar
3 tablespoons cold water	½ teaspoon vanilla essence
15 g (½ oz) powdered gelatine	1·5 dl (¼ pint) double cream

Line the base of a deep, round 15-cm (6-inch) cake tin with a circle of greaseproof paper. Slice each sponge cake in half, setting aside the more attractive tops for lining the sides of the tin. Cut the base of each sponge cake into a triangle and fit them close together round the base of the cake tin, with the narrow tips inwards towards the centre. Trim the edges of the remaining top pieces of cake straight and, keeping the best sides outwards, fit them upright and fairly tightly round the inside of the tin. Set aside while preparing the filling.

Break the chocolate into a saucepan and add 1·5 dl (¼ pint) of the milk. Stir over low heat until the chocolate has melted and the mixture is blended. Measure the cold water into a teacup and sprinkle in the gelatine. Leave to soak for 5 minutes. Add the remaining milk to the chocolate mixture and bring to the boil. Meanwhile, in a basin, cream the egg yolks and sugar together, then stir in the hot, chocolate-flavoured milk. Blend well and return the mixture to the saucepan. Add the soaked gelatine and replace the pan over a low heat. Stir only until the gelatine has dissolved, then draw off the heat. Add the vanilla essence and strain the mixture into a large basin. Set aside to cool, stirring occasionally.

When the mixture is cold and beginning to thicken, lightly whip the cream and fold into the mixture. Pour into the prepared cake tin and chill until set firm. Trim the edges of the sponge cake level, and place the dessert, still inside the tin, in a polythene bag. Tie closed and freeze.

To serve Remove the dessert from the polythene bag and allow to thaw overnight in a refrigerator, or at room temperature for about 5 hours. Gently remove from the mould and remove the greaseproof paper circle from the base. Serve with cream.

Apple Crumble

Makes 2 serving portions of 4 Time taken 45 minutes

1·5 kg (3 lb) cooking apples	175 g (6 oz) soft brown sugar
2 tablespoons water	pinch mixed spice
25 g (1 oz) butter	

For the Crumble Topping

175 g (6 oz) plain flour	50 g (2 oz) castor sugar
100 g (4 oz) butter	

Peel the apples, then quarter and core them. Cut up finely and place in the saucepan along with the water and butter. Cover with a lid and cook very gently, stirring or shaking the pan occasionally, until the apples are soft – takes about 15 minutes. Draw the pan off the heat and beat the apples to a pulp. Stir in the sugar and mixed spice. Dividing the mixture equally, spoon into two suitable-sized foil trays. Set aside until quite cold.

Meanwhile prepare the crumble topping. Sift the flour into a mixing basin. Add the butter cut in pieces and rub into the flour. Add the sugar and continue rubbing in until the mixture clings together in large crumbs. When the apple base is cold, cover with a layer of the crumble mixture dividing it equally between the two trays. Pack down lightly. Place each one inside a polythene freezer bag or wrap in foil. Tie tightly and freeze.

To serve Remove from wrappings and allow to thaw at room temperature for 1–2 hours. Place above centre in a hot oven (200°C,

400°F or Gas No. 6) and bake for 15 minutes. Lower the heat to moderately hot (190°C, 375°F or Gas No. 5) and bake for a further 15 minutes. Serve hot with cream.

Chocolate Eclairs

Makes 12 Time taken 1½ hours

1·5 dl (¼ pint) water	4 eggs
50 g (2 oz) butter	3 dl (½ pint) double cream
100 g (4 oz) plain flour	

For the Chocolate Icing

1 rounded tablespoon cocoa powder	3 tablespoons water
25 g (1 oz) castor sugar	175 g (6 oz) icing sugar, sieved

Measure the water into a saucepan and add the butter cut in pieces. Sieve the flour on to a square of paper. Bring the water and butter to a brisk boil, making sure the butter is melted, then quickly tip in the flour all at once. Using a wooden spoon, beat for 1 minute over the heat, then draw off the heat and beat for about 5 minutes, the mixture should leave the sides of the pan clean. Beat in the eggs one at a time, beating each one in thoroughly before adding the next. Take care not to add too much egg, especially if the eggs are large ones – the mixture should be smooth and glossy and stiff enough to hold its shape when piped.

Spoon the mixture into a cotton or nylon piping bag fitted with a 1-cm (½-inch) plain tube. Pipe out 7·5-cm (3-inch) lengths of the mixture on to greased baking trays. Allow about 6 eclairs per tray and do not pipe too closely together. Place above centre in a preheated hot oven (220°C, 425°F or Gas No. 7) and bake for 20 minutes or until dry and crisp. Allow to cool.

Split the sides of each and fill with lightly whipped cream. This can be done neatly by making a small slit and piping in the cream using the bag and a small nozzle.

Measure the cocoa powder, castor sugar and water into a saucepan. Stir to dissolve the sugar then bring back to the boil. Draw off the heat and stir in the icing sugar. Dip the smoothest side, often the flat base is best, of each eclair in the chocolate icing. Allow any surplus to run off and set the eclairs aside until the icing is firm.

Freeze the unwrapped eclairs until hard, then arrange in suitable containers for extra protection. Wrap in foil or polythene and freeze.

To serve Thaw 1–2 hours at room temperature. Serve as soon as possible after thawing since they are inclined to become soft.

Fresh Strawberry Sauce

Makes 6 dl (1 pint) Time taken 10 minutes

450 g (1 lb) fresh strawberries   strained juice of 1 lemon
175 g (6 oz) castor sugar

This is an excellent method of using up quantities of strawberries, particularly towards the end of the season when they are less expensive.

Strawberries that are not quite perfect can be used so long as any bruised parts are cut away. Hull and wash the fruit. Either sieve the fruit to make a purée and then add the sugar and lemon juice, stirring until the sugar dissolves, which it will do in the juice from the fruit; or, better still, place the fruit in the glass container of an electric blender along with the sugar and lemon juice, then cover and blend until the fruit is puréed.

Pour the mixture into a container making sure that there is a 1-cm (½-inch) space left at the top for the mixture to freeze and expand. Cover and freeze.

To serve Allow the sauce to thaw out, then serve chilled over ice cream or light desserts such as a vanilla bavarois or fruit mousse.

Coffee Walnut Cake

Makes one 20-cm (8-inch) sponge layer cake Time taken 1 hour

225 g (8 oz) self-raising flour   1 tablespoon coffee essence
pinch salt   3 eggs
175 g (6 oz) butter   50 g (2 oz) chopped walnuts
175 g (6 oz) soft brown sugar   1–2 tablespoons milk

For the Coffee Butter Cream
100 g (4 oz) butter or margarine   few walnut halves
175 g (6 oz) icing sugar
2–3 teaspoons coffee essence

Always use butter cream to frost layer cakes that are to go in the freezer.

Sift the flour and salt together and set aside. Cream the butter and sugar together until light, then beat in the coffee essence. Lightly mix the eggs and beat into the butter mixture a little at a time beating each addition in well before adding the next. Using a metal spoon, lightly fold in the flour and chopped walnuts, adding only enough milk to make a medium soft consistency.

Divide the mixture between two 20-cm (8-inch) sponge sandwich tins lightly greased and with the bases lined with circles of grease-proof paper. Spread the mixture evenly, hollowing out the centres slightly. Bake in the centre of a moderately hot oven (190°C, 375°F or Gas No. 5) for about 25 minutes, or until risen and brown and slightly shrunk from the sides of the tin. Allow the cake layers to cool in the tins for 2–3 minutes, then turn out, remove the papers and leave to cool while preparing the coffee butter cream.

Cream the butter or margarine until soft. Beat in the sieved icing sugar a little at a time. Beat in the coffee essence to taste. Use half of the cream to sandwich the cake layers together and the remainder to forst the top of the cake. Decorate with a few walnuts halves. The cake can be left whole, or cut in two halves. Freeze the cake un-covered until the icing is hard and firm, then wrap in foil and replace in the freezer.

To serve Allow the cake to thaw at room temperature for about 2 hours.

Orange Water Ice in Orange Shells

Serves 6 Time taken 1–1½ hours
Freeze overnight before finishing recipe

100 g (4 oz) castor sugar	1 egg white
3 dl (½ pint) water	6 small oranges
1 (175 g) (6¼ oz) tin frozen orange juice concentrate	

Start preparing this recipe at least 24 hours before serving, to allow not only time to prepare the water ice but also for it to freeze quite firm in the orange shells.

Measure the sugar and water into a saucepan and stir over low heat until the sugar has dissolved. Bring up to the boil and simmer for 5 minutes. Draw the pan off the heat, add the concentrated orange juice and allow to cool.

Stir in the unbeaten egg white and pour the syrup into a 1-litre (1½–2-pint) polythene container. Place in the freezer. Allow to freeze until almost firm, then quickly scoop all the frozen mixture into a basin. Using a hand-whisk, beat until smooth and light in colour.

Return to the container, cover with the lid and re-freeze until quite firm. This takes several hours.

To prepare the oranges, slice the tops off each and reserve. Using a teaspoon, scoop some of the orange flesh from inside each orange into a basin. Then work the fingers round the inside of the orange shells between the rind and the orange flesh; you will then be able to pull away all the inside flesh, including the thin white skin, leaving the shells quite clean. Place the shells in the freezer to get quite cold before filling with the water ice. It does not matter if they freeze quite hard. When the water ice is ready, spoon into the prepared orange cups. Remove any orange flesh from the lids and cover each one. Replace in the freezer and leave for several hours. Do not remove from the freezer until ready to serve.

Lemon Ice Cream

Serves 6–8 Time taken 1½–2 hours

8 egg yolks	juice of 2 large lemons
225 g (8 oz) castor sugar	3 dl (½ pint) double cream

Smooth and very lemony in flavour, this ice cream is lovely as a dinner party dessert.

Crack the egg yolks into a medium-sized mixing bowl and add the sugar. Whisk until thick and light, then stir in the strained lemon juice. Lightly whip the cream and fold into the lemon mixture.

Pour the mixture into a generous 1-litre (2-pint) polythene container. Place in the freezer and leave until the mixture is partially frozen, then turn out into a chilled mixing bowl and whisk until creamy and smooth. Return quickly to the container, cover with the lid and re-freeze for several hours, or overnight, until quite firm. Store in the container.

Raspberry Water Ice

Serves 4–6 Time taken 3–4 hours
Make in advance

450 g (1 lb) fresh raspberries	juice of 1 lemon
175 g (6 oz) castor sugar	juice of 1 orange
3 dl (½ pint) water	2 egg whites

Press the raspberries through a nylon sieve to make a purée. Discard the pips remaining in the sieve. Measure the sugar and water into a saucepan. Set over low heat and stir until the sugar has dissolved. Bring up to the boil and simmer for 5 minutes. Draw the pan off the heat and stir in the fruit purée. Add the strained lemon and orange juice, pour the mixture into a bowl and allow to cool.

Pour into a generous 1-litre (2-pint) polythene container and leave until the mixture is partially frozen. Whisk the egg whites until stiff, then gradually whisk in the partially frozen water ice, spoonfuls at a time. Return quickly to the container, cover and replace in the freezer. Freeze for several hours or until the water ice is quite firm.

Serve with wafers or macaroons.

Rum Parfait

Serves 4–6 Time taken 15 minutes
Freeze for several hours

4 eggs	1·5 dl (¼ pint) double cream
75 g (3 oz) castor sugar	
2 tablespoons rum	few glacé cherries
50 g (2 oz) toasted flaked almonds	

Separate the eggs, cracking the yolks into a large mixing basin and the whites into a second basin. Add the sugar to the egg yolks and, using a wooden spoon, beat until light and creamy. Stir in the rum and the toasted almonds. Lightly whip the cream and stiffly beat the egg whites. Fold the cream and then the egg whites into the mixture. Blend gently but thoroughly. Pour into a generous 1-litre (2-pint) polythene container. Cover and freeze for 5–6 hours or overnight.

When ready to serve, spoon into individual glasses and decorate with glacé cherries. Serve with macaroons or small meringues.

Chocolate Ice Cream

Serves 6 Time taken 1½–2 hours

100 g (4 oz) plain chocolate	½ teaspoon vanilla essence
1 small tin condensed milk	3 dl (½ pint) double cream
4 tablespoons water	

An unusual recipe for ice cream, but one with a good flavour and a very smooth texture.

Break the chocolate into pieces and place in a basin with the condensed milk. Set over a saucepan of simmering water. Stir occasionally until the mixture is melted and thickened – takes about 10 minutes. Remove from the heat.

Gradually stir in the water and vanilla essence, the mixture at this stage will become thin, then put to chill. When cold, lightly whip the cream and blend into the chocolate mixture. Pour into a 1-litre (1½–2-pint) polythene container. Place in the freezer and leave until the mixture is partially frozen. Then turn into a chilled basin, and whisk until creamy and smooth. Return to the container, cover with the lid, and replace quickly in the freezer. Freeze for several hours, or overnight, until firm. Store in the container.

French Vanilla Ice Cream

Serves 6 Time taken 1½–2 hours

3 dl (½ pint) single cream	pinch salt
4 egg yolks	3 dl (½ pint) double cream
100 g (4 oz) vanilla sugar	

The very best ice creams are made using cream only. They have a rich smooth texture and are less trouble, since they require to be stirred only once during freezing. Vanilla sugar, used here, gives a much better flavour than vanilla essence in ice cream. All flavouring essences tend to deteriorate in flavour during freezing, and it is so easy to keep a vanilla pod in a jar with castor sugar. As the sugar is used, simply top up the jar.

Place the single cream in a saucepan, set over moderate heat and bring up just to the boil. Meanwhile, using a wooden spoon, stir the egg yolks, vanilla sugar and salt together in a basin. Pour the hot cream slowly into the egg mixture, stirring all the time. Return the mixture to the pan and heat through for a moment to cook the custard, but do not boil. Pour into a basin and leave until cold. Stir occasionally to prevent a skin forming.

Whip the cream until thick, and fold in the custard mixture. Pour into a generous 1-litre (2-pint) polythene container. Place in the freezer. Freeze until the mixture is partially frozen, then turn out into a chilled basin and whisk quickly until smooth. Return to the container, cover with the lid and re-freeze until firm. The ice cream should be stored in the container and will keep for several weeks.

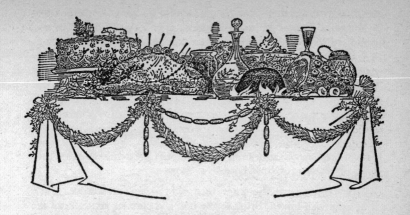

14 Cooking for Christmas

Advance preparation and good planning are undoubtedly the key to a calm and happy Christmas. Some of the preparation for Christmas should be completed in November – a good time to make the Christmas cake, puddings and mincemeat. Allow cakes and puddings to become quite cold before storing. Wrap cakes in foil and re-cover puddings with fresh greaseproof papers. Store both in a cool dry cupboard. Mincemeat is time-consuming to prepare and usually more expensive than to buy. Nevertheless, home-made mincemeat is delicious. If it dries out during storage, stir in a little rum or brandy.

With the exception of the important Christmas Day lunch, meals over the holiday can be fairly flexible and menus should be planned accordingly. Have plenty of cold foods prepared in advance: cooked gammon or tongue with Cumberland sauce, chicken liver or duck pâté or a beef galantine. Prepare some cold desserts that could be served any time: compôte of oranges with candied peel, prunes in claret or caramel custards. Make good use of the freezer with mince-pies, drop scones, coffee walnut cake, croquette potatoes or red cabbage with apple all made ready for serving.

For Christmas lunch, one of the most important meals of the year, serve a traditional roast turkey and all the trimmings, or a roast goose. For a smaller family, choose a roast capon with lemon and parsley stuffing or sugar-baked gammon. These will usually be large enough to serve cold on Boxing Day, so buy in plenty of ingredients for interesting salads. When frozen oven-ready birds are used they should be allowed to thaw slowly over a period of 24 hours for birds up to 5 kg (12 lb) and of 48 hours for birds over 5 kg (12 lb). Slow and complete thawing is most essential for both texture and flavour. Fresh birds should be ordered well in advance. Once drawn, poultry will not keep and should be collected on Christmas Eve. A small joint is a useful reserve for later in the holiday.

Apricot Glaze

Covers one 20- or 23-cm (8- or 9-inch) cake Time taken 10 minutes

1 heaped tablespoon castor sugar	2 heaped tablespoons sieved apricot
1 tablespoon water or lemon juice	jam

Dissolve the sugar in the water, then add the jam and stir over gentle heat until well mixed. Bring to the boil and simmer gently until the glaze hangs in heavy drops from the spoon, takes 3–5 minutes. Draw the pan off the heat and brush the glaze while still hot over the surface of the cake.

Almond Paste

Covers one 20- or 23-cm (8- or 9-inch) cake Time taken 10 minutes

175 g (6 oz) icing sugar	juice of half a lemon
175 g (6 oz) castor sugar	1 large egg
350 g (12 oz) ground almonds	½ teaspoon vanilla or almond essence

This first stage in the decoration of a Christmas cake is very important, as a flat, even base must be provided for the final icing. The cake is first brushed with apricot glaze, which holds down any loose cake crumbs and helps the almond paste stick to the cake.

Sieve the icing sugar into a large mixing basin, add the castor sugar and ground almonds. Lightly mix the lemon juice, egg and flavouring. Pour into the dry ingredients and, using a fork, mix to a fairly stiff paste. Turn out on to a working surface, lightly dusted with castor sugar, and knead lightly by hand to a smooth dough.

Avoid over-mixing, as the warmth of the hands can cause the oil to come out of the almonds, making the paste difficult to roll out. If the paste is a little sticky, work in more sugar, or a little more lemon juice if too stiff. Set the finished almond paste aside until ready to use.
Covering the cake with almond paste The cake should be as level and as even in shape as possible. Slight irregularities in the shape can be made up with the almond paste, but any high dome in the centre of

the cake should be trimmed level – use a saw-edged knife and slice across.

Divide the almond paste into two portions, one-third for the top of the cake and two-thirds for the sides. Dusting your working surface with more castor sugar, roll out the smallest portion of the almond paste to a circle the size of the top of the cake. If preferred take a professional tip and reverse the cake using the flat base as the top. Brush the 'top' of the cake with hot apricot glaze and *turn over* on to the circle of rolled out almond paste. Press down firmly, and trim away the surplus paste from the sides. Add these pieces to the remaining almond paste.

Using a piece of string, measure the circumference of the cake and cut to the exact length – keep this for measuring. Roll out the remaining almond paste to a length long enough to fit the sides. This is most easily done if you first shape the almond paste with your hands into a long rope the circumference of the cake – use string for measuring. Then flatten this 'rope' with your rolling pin to the depth of the cake. Trim and neaten one edge of the strip. Brush round the cake with hot apricot glaze, then turn the cake on its side and lift carefully on to the paste so that the trimmed edge is level with the top of the cake. Roll the cake along the strip until the side is completely covered. Trim away any extra paste and turn the cake back with the almond paste top *downwards* on the sugared working surface.

Trim any paste away from the base or sides and neaten any joins. Roll a straight-sided jar or tin round the sides so the paste sticks firmly to the cake. Turn the cake back over – right side up – and place on an upturned plate. Cover lightly with greaseproof paper and put the cake away in a cool dry place for 3–7 days. The almond paste should be allowed to dry out before the royal icing is put on, especially if the finished iced cake is likely to be kept for some time. If this is not done, the oil from the almonds can stain a white icing yellow.

Royal Icing

Sufficient to ice and decorate one 20- or 23-cm (8- or 9-inch) cake
Time taken 20–30 minutes   Allow to stand for 1 hour

900 g (2 lb) icing sugar
whites of 4 large eggs

1 teaspoon lemon juice
2 teaspoons glycerine or clear honey

Sift icing sugar through a fine sieve on to a large square of greaseproof paper. Break the egg whites into a mixing basin and beat lightly until just frothy. Use eggs that are at room temperature and not straight from the refrigerator. Using a wooden spoon, gradually beat in about half the quantity of sifted sugar; taking care to beat in each addition well before adding the next.

Continue beating until the mixture becomes light and fluffy – it may take from 5 to 10 minutes, but it's worth the effort. Then add lemon juice, glycerine or honey and the remaining icing sugar, stirring in a little at a time. Sufficient sugar has been added when the icing holds up in peaks on the spoon – the quantity will depend on the volume of the egg whites. If you leave the icing at any time during beating, cover it with a damp cloth. Leave the icing for at least one hour before using. After this you may find it is necessary to add a little more sugar as the icing may have softened a little while it has been standing.

Using an electric mixer A mixer is a great asset for preparing icing. Crack the egg white into the bowl, and turn the mixer on to low speed to break up the whites. Then add half the quantity of icing sugar gradually, still on the lowest speed. Increase to speed 2 or 3 and beat for 5–8 minutes until light and fluffy. Remove the basin from the mixer and beat in the lemon juice, glycerine or honey and the remaining icing sugar by hand. It's important not to overmix the icing, otherwise too many air bubbles will spoil the surface finish. Allow the icing to stand, covered with a damp cloth for 1½–2 hours before using.

To ice the cake With the tip of a knife, spread a little icing on the base of the cake and place on a silver board of a suitable size. Place the cake, now stuck to the silver board, on an upturned plate – this makes an excellent turntable for easy icing. Reserve a small amount of icing for the decoration, and spoon the remainder on top of the cake. With a spatula or flat knife spread the icing over the top and round the sides of the cake, as evenly as possible. Even the sides off for a professional look, using a plastic icing scraper. Holding the scraper at an angle and upright against the edge of the cake, run the scraper round the side of the cake in one easy sweep – don't press too hard, otherwise you may go through to the almond paste. If the first attempt is not successful, spread the icing evenly and try again. Flatten the top surface of the cake using a knife blade dipped in boiling water. Warm the knife blade in a jug of boiling water, shake away any drips and, using the flat side, smooth out any rough surfaces. Allow the base coat of icing to dry out before decoration.

Choose simple decoration, as this often looks much more effective than a very elaborate design.

American Frosting

For one 20-cm (8-inch) cake Time taken 30 minutes

450 g (1 lb) granulated sugar	2 egg whites
6 tablespoons cold water	

American frosting makes a popular alternative to royal icing for a Christmas cake. The icing should be swirled in peaks over the cake and a sprig of holly adds sufficient decoration.

Measure the sugar and water into a saucepan. Place over low heat and stir until the sugar has dissolved. Wash down the sides of the pan with a clean pastry brush dipped in water to remove every grain of sugar that might remain. Replace over the heat and bring up to the boil. Boil rapidly to a temperature of 116°C (240°F) on a sugar thermometer or until a little dropped in a saucer of cold water forms a soft ball. Have the egg whites ready cracked in a basin. When the sugar syrup has almost reached the required temperature, whisk the egg whites until quite stiff.

Draw the pan off the heat and, holding the pan high above the basin, slowly pour the sugar syrup on to the egg whites. The syrup should cool slightly as it falls into the mixture. Whisk all the time, and pour over the point where continuously whisking. Once all the syrup has been added, continue whisking for several minutes; the frosting will gradually get thicker but is not ready until it clearly changes texture and appearance from a shiny soft mixture to a dull, very light texture, rather like cotton wool. At this stage spread quickly over the cake and rough up the surface. Add any decoration. Set aside until the icing is cold and has set.

Christmas Pudding

Makes one 1·5-kg (3-lb) pudding – serves 8 Time taken 5½–6 hours

100 g (4 oz) self-raising flour	225 g (8 oz) sultanas
1 level teaspoon mixed spice	225 g (8 oz) seedless raisins
1 level teaspoon ground cinnamon	50 g (2 oz) chopped mixed peel
pinch salt	rind of 1 orange
100 g (4 oz) shredded beef suet	3 eggs
100 g (4 oz) fresh white breadcrumbs	1 tablespoon treacle
100 g (4 oz) soft brown sugar	4–5 tablespoons ale or milk
50 g (2 oz) ground almonds	1 tablespoon rum or brandy
100 g (4 oz) currants	

Sieve the flour, spices and salt into a large mixing basin. Add the suet, breadcrumbs, sugar, ground almonds, prepared fruit and peel. Mix well, then add the finely grated orange rind and stir in the lightly mixed eggs and treacle. Add enough ale or milk to mix to a medium soft consistency.

At this stage any small charms, wrapped neatly in small squares of greaseproof paper, may be added. Spoon the mixture into a well-buttered 1·5-litre (3-pint) pudding basin. The mixture should three-quarters fill the basin. Cover with buttered papers and fold in a pleat across the top to allow the pudding to rise. Tie the papers tightly with string and, if liked, the pudding may be covered with an additional layer of kitchen foil or an old-fashioned pudding cloth, knotted at the top to make the cooked pudding easier to lift out.

Steam gently, preferably in a proper steamer; failing that, put the pudding on an upturned saucer in a large saucepan. Simmering water should come one-third up the side of the basin. Steam for 5 hours, making sure that the pan is never allowed to boil dry. Top up, if needed, with boiling water.

Allow the cooked pudding to cool in the basin. Remove the papers and pour the rum or brandy over it. Re-cover with fresh ungreased paper and store in a dry, airy place until Christmas.
Note: do not make the covers airtight, as mould may develop.
On Christmas Day Re-cover with greaseproof paper and steam for 2 hours. Serve with rum or brandy butter (pages 246-7).

Traditional Christmas Cake

Makes one 20-cm (8-inch) cake Time taken 4½–5 hours

275 g (10 oz) plain flour	100 g (4 oz) glacé cherries
1 level teaspoon mixed spice	225 g (8 oz) currants
1 level teaspoon salt	225 g (8 oz) sultanas
225 g (8 oz) butter	225 g (8 oz) seedless raisins
225 g (8 oz) soft brown sugar	100 g (4 oz) chopped candied peel
4 large eggs	50 g (2 oz) blanched chopped
1 tablespoon black treacle	almonds
½ teaspoon vanilla essence	2 tablespoons brandy or milk

Sieve together the flour, spice and salt and set aside. Cream together the butter and sugar until very soft and light. Lightly mix the eggs treacle and vanilla essence together, then gradually beat into the creamed mixture a little at a time. Add some of the flour along with the last few additions of egg.

Rinse the cherries in warm water to remove the outer sugary coating. Pat dry and cut into quarters. Place in a basin with the currants, sultanas, seedless raisins, chopped candied peel and chopped almonds. Add 1–2 spoonfuls of the sieved flour to the fruit and mix well. Using a metal spoon, fold in the remaining sieved flour, then the fruit mixture and brandy or milk.

Spoon the mixture into a greased and lined 20-cm (8-inch) round, deep cake tin, and hollow out the centre slightly. Place on the shelf below centre of a preheated slow oven (150°C, 300°F or Gas No. 2) and bake for 1½ hours. Then lower the heat to slow (140°C, 275°F or Gas No. 1) and bake for a further 2½ hours. Cool the baked cake in the tin before wrapping and storing.

Golden Christmas Cake

Makes one 20-cm (8-inch) cake Time taken 3–4 hours

100 g (4 oz) crystallized pineapple	½ level teaspoon salt
100 g (4 oz) glacé cherries	175 g (6 oz) butter
100 g (4 oz) chopped walnuts	175 g (6 oz) castor sugar
350 g (12 oz) seedless raisins or sultanas	3 large eggs
250g (9oz) self-raising flour	2–3 tablespoons sherry or milk

Rinse the crystallized pineapple and glacé cherries in warm water to remove the outer sugary coating. Pat dry, chop the pineapple and the cut cherries into quarters. Place in a basin with the chopped walnuts and seedless raisins or sultanas. Sift together the flour and salt and set aside. Cream together the butter and sugar until very soft and light. Lightly mix the eggs and vanilla essence, then gradually beat into the creamed mixture a little at a time. Add some of the flour along with the last few additions of egg. Fold in the sifted flour mixture alternately with the sherry or milk and then finally fold in the prepared fruit and nuts.

Turn the mixture into a greased and lined, 20-cm (8-inch) round, deep cake tin. Spread the mixture level and hollow out the centre slightly. Place in the centre of a preheated, very moderate oven (170°C, 325°F or Gas No. 3) and bake for 1 hour. Lower the heat to 150°C, 300°F or Gas No. 2 and bake for a further 1½–2 hours. To test the cake, push a warmed skewer into the centre. It should come out clean with no traces of uncooked mixture. Allow the cake to cool in the tin.

To decorate Brush the cake with apricot glaze and cover with almond paste. When the paste has dried out, decorate with royal icing (see pages 241–2).

Mincemeat

Makes 7 lb Time taken 45 minutes

450 g (1 lb) stoned or seedless raisins
450 g (1 lb) sultanas
450 g (1 lb) currants
100 g (4 oz) blanched almonds
175 g (6 oz) whole candied peel
450 g (1 lb) firm tart apples
350 g (12 oz) shredded beef suet

450 g (1 lb) soft brown sugar
1 level teaspoon ground cinnamon
½ level teaspoon grated nutmeg
rind and juice of 1 lemon
2 liqueur glasses brandy, rum or sherry

This mincemeat will keep for several months, but may need a little more moisture stirred into it before using.

Clean and dry the fruit, then chop the raisins and sultanas roughly and add the currants. Mince the blanched almonds and the candied peel finely and add to the fruit. Peel, core and chop the apples and add along with the suet and the sugar. Stir in the spices, finely grated lemon rind, strained lemon juice and the brandy, rum or sherry. Cover with a cloth and leave overnight.

Mix thoroughly and pack the mincemeat into clean dry jars. Cover and store in a very cool place.

Rum Butter

Serves 8 Time taken 10 minutes

175 g (6 oz) unsalted butter
175 g (6 oz) soft brown sugar

1–2 tablespoons rum

A soft creamy sauce which some people prefer to brandy butter (see below).

Beat the butter until soft and light. Gradually beat in the soft brown sugar, then beat in the rum. Pile into a dish and chill.

Serve with the Christmas pudding or hot mincepies.

Brandy Butter

Serves 8 Time taken 10 minutes

175 g (6 oz) unsalted butter   2 tablespoons brandy
225 g (8 oz) sieved icing sugar

Cream the butter until soft, then gradually beat in the icing sugar.
Beat in the brandy very thoroughly. Pile roughly into a serving dish
and chill well.

Serve with the Christmas pudding or hot mincepies.

Lemon Mincemeat

Makes 2 kg 250 g (5 lb) Time taken 1 hour

6 large lemons   700 g (1½ lb) castor sugar
450 g (1 lb) sultanas   ½ level teaspoon ground mixed spice
225 g (8 oz) candied peel or   ½ level teaspoon nutmeg
  crystallized ginger and pineapple   ½ level teaspoon cinnamon
50 g (2 oz) blanched almonds   1·5 dl (¼ pint) brandy
225 g (8 oz) shredded suet

A recipe with an unusual tangy flavour. It can be used immediately
but does improve on storage.

Halve and squeeze the juice from the lemons. Reserve the juice.
Quarter the lemon peel and remove the excess white pith and flesh.
Place the lemon skins in a small saucepan, cover with cold water and
bring up to the boil. Drain away the water, then re-cover with fresh
cold water and repeat the procedure twice more. After finally drain-
ing, pass them through the fine blade of a mincer along with the
sultanas, crystallized fruits and almonds. Add the suet, sugar and
strained lemon juice and mix well. Add the spices and then stir in the
brandy. Pack into 450-g (1-lb) jam jars, cover and seal.

Mincemeat Pies

Makes 2 dozen Time taken 1 hour Can be made in advance

275 g (10 oz) plain flour   rind of ½ lemon
25 g (1 oz) ground almonds   1 egg yolk
175 g (6 oz) butter   3 tablespoons milk
75 g (3 oz) castor sugar

For the Filling
450 g (1 lb) mincemeat   icing sugar
1–2 tablespoons brandy

Sift the flour into a mixing basin and add the ground almonds. Add the butter, cut in small pieces, and rub into the mixture evenly. Add the sugar and grated lemon rind. Lightly mix the egg yolk and milk, and stir into the dry ingredients. Mix to a fairly firm dough, turn out on to a lightly floured board and knead until smooth. Chill for 30 minutes before using.

Roll the pastry out on a lightly floured working surface and, using a floured plain or fluted cutter, stamp out forty-eight circles of pastry.

Place twenty-four in lightly greased tartlet tins – prepare in batches if necessary. Mix the mincemeat with the brandy and place a tea-spoonful of the mixture in the centre of each pastry circle. Take care not to overfill the pies. Damp the edges of the pastry and cover each one with a pastry top. Seal the edges and then, using scissors, snip two slits in the top of each. Place in the centre of a hot oven (200°C, 400°F or Gas No. 6) and bake for 15–20 minutes or until golden brown.

Dust with icing sugar and serve hot with brandy butter or cream.

Mulled Wine

Serves 12 glasses Time taken 15–20 minutes

Serve at once

1 small lemon	½ bottle inexpensive port
6 cloves	1 cinnamon stick
3 dl (½ pint) water	little nutmeg
175 g (6 oz) castor sugar	
1 bottle claret	lemon slices

The simplest mulled wines are made by dissolving sugar in a little water, about 100 g (4 oz) sugar to 1·5 dl (¼ pint) water for each bottle of wine. Bring to the boil. Add the wine and bring up to boiling point but no more. Draw off the heat. Grate a little nutmeg over the top and serve very hot. The following recipe is a good one for a party.

Pare the rind very thinly from the lemon and put it into the pan. With a very sharp knife cut away the thick, white, outer pith from the lemon and discard it. Stud the pared lemon with the cloves and add to the pan, together with the water and sugar. Stir over heat till the sugar has dissolved. Add the claret and port. Stir with the cinnamon stick till *just* boiling. Remove from the heat and strain.

Serve at once, very hot, with a little nutmeg grated on top and a slice of lemon in each mug.

The Bishop

Serves 12 glasses   Time taken 45 minutes
Serve at once

2 lemons
few cloves
50 g (2 oz) lump sugar

1½ bottles inexpensive port
6 dl (1 pint) water
pinch mixed spice

A traditional Christmas recipe. Served warm this is a wonderful drink for a party.

Stick one of the two lemons with cloves and roast in a moderate oven (180°C, 350°F or Gas No. 4) for 30 minutes. Rub the lump sugar over the remaining lemon to take up the oils from the skin. Place the sugar in a large serving bowl along with the juice squeezed from the lemon. Put the port into a saucepan and bring it almost to the boil. In a separate saucepan bring the water with the spices added, up to the boil. Add the boiling water to the hot port and pour into the serving bowl. Add the roasted lemon and serve as hot as possible.

Apple Mincemeat Jalousie

Serves 6   Time taken 45 minutes
Can be made in advance

225 g (½ lb) homemade puff pastry
  or
1 (350 g) (12 oz) packet frozen puff
  pastry
100–175 g (4–6 oz) mincemeat
1 large apple

1 tablespoon sugar
2 teaspoons rum or brandy
milk and sugar

icing sugar

Roll the pastry out thinly to an oblong strip 15 or 18 cm (6 or 7 inches) wide and about 45 cm (18 inches) long. Cut in half across to make two 23-cm (9-inch) long strips. Flour one strip lightly and fold in half lengthwise. Using a sharp knife, cut a series of slits through the folded edge to within 2·5 cm (1 inch) of the trimmed edge.

Place the plain strip on a wetted baking tray and spread the mincemeat over it to within 2·5 cm (1 inch) of the border all round. Thinly slice the apple and place on top of the mincemeat; sprinkle with the sugar and rum or brandy. Damp the pastry edge all round. Open out the slashed strip of pastry and place over the filling to cover both the base and filling. Seal the edges, trim with a sharp knife, and flute –

as for a fruit pie. Brush the top with a little milk and sprinkle with sugar.

Place just above the centre of a very hot oven (220°C, 425°F or Gas No. 7) and bake for 25–30 minutes or until risen and brown. Reduce the heat after 20 minutes if the pastry colours too much.

Dredge with icing sugar, cut in slices and serve hot with brandy butter.

Slow Roast Turkey

Serves 12–14   Time taken 4–6 hours

1 (7 kg) (15 lb) turkey	watercress
traditional forcemeat	225 g ($\frac{1}{2}$ lb) back bacon for rolls
savoury sausage meat stuffing	450 g (1 lb) chipolata sausages
coarse salt	giblet gravy
50–75 g (2–3 oz) dripping or butter	cranberry sauce (page 176)
100 g ($\frac{1}{4}$ lb) streaky bacon rashers	

Have the turkey drawn and cleaned by the butcher and check weight so that cooking time may be calculated. If you have a frozen oven-ready turkey, allow to thaw slowly for up to 48 hours and do not remove from the vacuum sealed bag until you are ready to stuff and roast it.

Prepare the necessary stuffings, as given on pages 252–3. Rinse the inside of the turkey with cold water and pat dry with a clean cloth. Stuff the neck cavity with the prepared forcemeat stuffing. Don't pack too tightly, the stuffing will swell a little during cooking. Pull the neck tight under the front of the bird and fix underneath with a skewer. Stuff the body cavity with savoury sausage meat stuffing, skewer the end closed and tie the legs firmly together.

Preheat the oven to a low temperature (170°C, 325°F or Gas No. 3). Experiments have shown that low temperature roasting gives excellent results. At this heat the bird will slow roast and will be tender and juicy when finished. Add about 900 g (2 lb) to the weight of the bird to allow for stuffing and calculate the cooking time as follows:

3–4·5 kg (7–10 lb) bird needs 3–3$\frac{1}{2}$ hours
4·5–6·5 kg (10–14 lb) bird needs 3$\frac{1}{2}$–4 hours
6·5–9 kg (14–20 lb) bird needs 4$\frac{1}{2}$–5 hours

Rub the turkey skin with coarse salt and smear with dripping or soft butter. Cover the breast with trimmed rashers of streaky bacon and loosely cover the whole bird with kitchen foil. Place in a large roasting tin with a little extra fat. Set the tin on a low shelf in the oven and leave to cook for the required time. Baste occasionally with a little hot fat from the tin; to do this lift the foil but do not remove the bacon rashers. Towards the end of the cooking time, remove the foil and bacon. Baste the breast and dredge with a little flour. Replace in the oven and raise oven heat to 190°C, 375°F or Gas No. 5 and complete the browning of the bird.

Garnish the turkey with watercress and serve with bacon rolls and chipolata sausages, giblet gravy and cranberry sauce, using the recipes given below and on page 176.

Bacon Rolls

Trim the back bacon rashers and stretch, using the flat blade of a knife and pressing the rasher out along a working surface. Cut each rasher in half and roll up each piece and fix on a skewer. Grill for 2–3 minutes, turning, until ready to serve.

Small Sausages

Separate the chipolata sausages and, holding each sausage in the centre, twist the ends in opposite directions to make two small sausages. Snip in half and place in a small baking or roasting tin with a knob of dripping. Place on the top shelf of the oven over the turkey and cook with the turkey for the last 30 minutes. Turn them occasionally until they are brown.

Giblet Gravy

The nicest gravy is made in the roasting tin, after straining off the fat. Retain all the brown bits from the bird and add 6 dl (a generous pint) of giblet stock – prepare this in advance by covering the giblets with cold water, bringing up to the boil and simmering for ½ hour. Stir the gravy briskly over the heat for several minutes. Season and strain into a hot gravy boat. If you like a slightly thickened gravy, add 1 level dessertspoon cornflour blended with ½ teacup cold water, stock or wine. Stir until boiling to ensure even thickening.

Chestnut Stuffing

Sufficient to stuff a 7–9 kg (15–20 lb) turkey Time taken 1 hour

900 g (2 lb) fresh chestnuts
 or
700 g (1½ lb) dried chestnuts
turkey liver
700 g (1½ lb) pork sausage meat
pinch mixed spice

salt
freshly milled pepper
75 g (3 oz) butter
1 small onion
2 tablespoons brandy

This stuffing can be used in place of the savoury sausage meat stuffing.

Slit the skins on the flat side of the chestnuts and place in a roasting tin. It is better to prepare these a few at a time since they peel better when they are hot. Place the chestnuts in a hot oven (200°C, 400°F or Gas No. 6) for 10 minutes or until the skins crack, then peel away both outer and inner skins. Alternatively, cover the dried chestnuts with cold water and leave to soak overnight, then drain.

Place the chestnuts in a saucepan and cover with cold water. Bring up to the boil and simmer for 15 minutes or until tender. Drain, then pass the cooked chestnuts through the mincer along with the turkey liver, into a large mixing basin. Add the pork sausage meat, mixed spice and a good seasoning of salt and pepper.

Heat the butter in a small saucepan. Finely chop the onion and add to the pan. Cover with a lid and sauté gently for 5 minutes until the onion is soft but not browned. Add to the stuffing ingredients along with the brandy and mix well – easiest using the hands. Use to stuff the body cavity of the turkey.

Traditional Forcemeat

Stuffing for a 5·5–7 kg (12–15 lb) Turkey Time taken 15 minutes

100 g (4 oz) butter
225 g (8 oz) fresh white breadcrumbs
4 tablespoons finely chopped parsley
½ level teaspoon thyme and mixed
  herbs

1 level teaspoon salt
freshly milled pepper
1 lemon
2 eggs

Melt the butter in a large saucepan over low heat. Draw off the heat and add the breadcrumbs, parsley, herbs, seasoning and finely grated lemon rind. Mix with a fork until the butter is all absorbed. Add the juice of a quarter of the lemon and the lightly mixed eggs and mix well until evenly moist. Use to stuff the breast of the turkey.

Savoury Sausage Meat Stuffing

Stuffing for a 5·5–7 kg (12–15 lb) turkey body Time taken 15 minutes

100 g (¼ lb) streaky bacon rashers	900 g (2 lb) pork sausage meat
1 large onion	1 level teaspoon finely crushed
15 g (½ oz) butter	rosemary or powdered sage

Trim and chop the bacon into small pieces. Add along with the finely chopped onion to the hot butter melted in a saucepan. Fry gently until soft but not browned. Meanwhile place the sausage meat in a basin, sprinkle in the herbs, add the ingredients from the saucepan and mix well. Use to stuff the body of the turkey.

Roast Goose with Prune Stuffing and Spiced Apples

Serves 8 Time taken 4–5 hours

1 (4·5 kg) (10 lb) oven-ready goose	a little flour

For the Prune Stuffing

225 g (½ lb) soaked prunes	¼ level teaspoon powdered mace
liver from the goose	salt and freshly milled pepper
175 g (6 oz) fresh white breadcrumbs	75 g (3 oz) butter

For the Spiced Apples

6 apples	1 teaspoon mixed spice
100 g (4 oz) sultanas	100 g (4 oz) butter
100 g (4 oz) soft brown sugar	few whole cloves

Wipe the goose and remove the giblets from the inside. If a frozen oven-ready goose is used, allow to thaw slowly over a period of at least 24 hours. Meanwhile prepare the stuffing.

Simmer the prunes in the liquid they soaked in for about 10 minutes until tender but not soft. Drain the prunes, remove the stones and rub the flesh through a sieve to make a purée. Cover the goose liver with cold water and bring up to the boil. Simmer for about 5 minutes, then drain. Chop finely and then pound to a paste. Using a fork, mix the prune purée, the liver paste, the breadcrumbs and mace together. Season with salt and pepper. Melt the butter over low heat, then, using a fork, stir into the stuffing. Pack the stuffing into the tail-end of the bird and skewer closed.

Rub the skin of the goose over with flour and then, using the prongs of a fork, prick the breast of the goose well. Place in a roasting tin and cover with a sheet of buttered greaseproof paper or foil. Set the bird in the centre of a hot oven (200°C, 400°F or Gas No. 6) and roast for 30 minutes, then lower the heat to 190°C, 375°F or Gas No. 5 and roast for the remaining time allowing 20 minutes per 450 g (1 lb) plus 20 minutes over. Remove the paper or foil after 45 minutes' cooking time to allow the bird to brown. During the roasting time remove some of the fat from the tin, if it becomes rather full.

While the bird is roasting, prepare the spiced apples. Wash and remove the cores from the apples, keeping the apples whole. Run the top of a sharp knife blade round the centre of each apple just to pierce the skin. This helps to prevent the apple skins from splitting during baking. Wash and chop the sultanas and mix in a bowl with the sugar and half the spice. Heat the butter in a saucepan until melted, then draw off the heat and stir in the remaining spice. Pour half the spiced butter into an ovenproof baking dish or small roasting tin. Place the apples in the tin and fill the centre of each one with the fruit and sugar mixture. Stick each apple with two cloves and then pour over the remaining spiced butter. About 40 minutes before the end of the cooking time for the goose, place the apples in the oven to bake along with the goose. Baste the apples occasionally with the butter in the dish.

When the goose is ready, lift from the tin and remove any skewers. Arrange on a serving dish and surround with the spiced apples and serve with a thin gravy.

Sugar Glazed Gammon

Serves 6 Time taken 2½ hours
Soak gammon overnight

1·5–2 kg (3½–4 lb) piece of corner gammon	1 onion
	1 clove
bay leaf	French mustard
sprig of rosemary	
1 carrot	Demerara sugar

A mild cured bacon is the best to choose if you intend to bake the joint. If you have any doubts as to the saltiness of the joint, then soak for 24 hours. Change the water once or twice.

Cover the gammon with cold water and soak overnight. According to whichever method is the most convenient, the gammon can be either baked or boiled.

To bake Wrap completely in foil, adding a bay leaf or sprig of rosemary for flavour. Set in a roasting tin and bake in a moderate oven (180°C, 350°F or Gas No. 4) allowing 30 minutes per 450 g (1 lb).

To boil Place in a large saucepan with cold water to cover. Add a bay leaf or sprig of rosemary, 1 carrot and 1 small onion, peeled and stuck with a clove. Cover with a lid and simmer, allowing 30 minutes to 450 g (1 lb).

To finish off Using a small sharp knife, peel the rind away. Spread the fat generously with French mustard, then coat generously with Demerara sugar. Stand the joint on a trivet in a roasting tin and crisp off in a hot oven (200°C, 400°F or Gas No. 6) for 10–15 minutes.

Chicken à la King

Serves 4 Time taken 1½ hours

350 g (12 oz) left-over cooked chicken
  or 4 fresh chicken joints

For the Sauce

50 g (2 oz) butter	1·5 dl (¼ pint) milk
1 green pepper	1 level teaspoon salt
100 g (4 oz) button mushrooms	freshly milled pepper
1 rounded tablespoon flour	1·5 dl (¼ pint) single cream
3 dl (½ pint) chicken stock	2 egg yolks

This recipe is very suitable for using up left-over chicken or turkey. On the other hand, it has such a delicious flavour that it is worth cooking four chicken joints specially.

If chicken joints are used, place them in a roasting tin with a little butter and cover with a buttered paper. Place in a moderate oven (180°C, 350°F or Gas No. 4) and cook for 45 minutes to 1 hour. Test by piercing the chicken joints with a sharp knife; the juices that run out should be quite clear with no tinges of pink. Remove any skin and bones and cut the chicken flesh into chunky pieces. Set aside while preparing the sauce.

Melt the butter in a medium-sized frying pan. Halve, deseed and shred the green pepper. Add the green pepper and sauté gently for about 5 minutes to soften. Trim and slice the mushrooms, add to the pan and fry for a further few moments. Draw the pan off the heat and stir in the flour. Gradually stir in the chicken stock and then the milk. Replace the pan over the heat and cook until the mixture thickens and comes to the boil, stirring all the time to make a smooth sauce. Season with the salt and pepper, add the pieces of chicken and heat thoroughly.

Blend together the cream and egg yolks and stir into the sauce. This enriches the sauce and gives it a light attractive appearance. Heat gently but do not boil. Draw off the heat and serve either with plain, boiled rice or spoon into hot, baked, vol-au-vent cases.

Apricots with Brandy and Cream

Serves 4–6 Time taken 20 minutes
Serve at once

25 g (1 oz) butter	1 tablespoon brandy
50 g (2 oz) castor sugar	finely grated orange rind
juice of 1 orange	1·5 dl (¼ pint) double cream
1 (825 g) (1 lb 13 oz) tin apricot halves	

This useful recipe can be put together very quickly. Hot apricots with a hint of orange and brandy are delicious. Serve them with soft sponge fingers.

Melt the butter in a large frying pan and add the sugar. Using a wooden spoon, stir over the heat until the sugar has melted and the mixture is a golden, caramel brown. Stir fairly constantly so that the mixture browns evenly. Add the orange juice, then stir until the caramel in the pan has dissolved and a syrup has formed. Drain the apricots from the juice and add to the pan. Stir and turn the apricots gently and allow them to become glazed with syrup. Add the brandy and flame. Draw the pan off the heat, add a little finely grated orange rind and pour over the cream. Stir to blend the sauce and serve the apricots hot.

Sherry Trifle

Serves 8 Time taken 45 minutes
Chill for several hours

6 trifle sponge cakes	100 g (4 oz) ratafias
raspberry jam	1·5 dl (¼ pint) sweet sherry

For the Custard

6 egg yolks	few drops vanilla essence
50 g (2 oz) castor sugar	
2 level teaspoons cornflour	toasted flaked almonds
6 dl (1 pint) double cream	

Custard for a Christmas trifle should be made with eggs and cream. This is an extravagant recipe but one with a delicious flavour and suitable for a special occasion.

Split the sponge cakes and spread with jam. Cut in pieces and place in the base of a large, glass serving dish. Add the ratafias and pour over the sherry. Set aside for 30 minutes to soak while preparing the custard.

Crack the egg yolks into a basin. Add the sugar and cornflour. Whisk thoroughly to blend the ingredients. Heat the cream in a saucepan until very hot, then draw off the heat and gradually stir into the egg mixture. Blend well and then strain the custard back into the saucepan. Replace over low heat and stir constantly until the custard thickens and coats the back of a spoon, but do not allow the custard to boil. Draw off the heat, add the vanilla essence and allow to cool for a few moments. Pour over the soaked sponge cakes and leave until cold. Chill for several hours. Then sprinkle with the toasted flaked almonds before serving.

Prunes in Claret

Serves 6 Time taken 30–40 minutes
Soak the prunes overnight

450 g (1 lb) prunes	small stick of cinnamon
3 dl (½ pint) claret	100–175 g (4–6 oz) castor sugar
3 dl (½ pint) water	2 level tablespoons cornflour
few pieces thinly pared lemon rind	walnut halves

Soak the prunes overnight in the mixed claret and water. Place the prunes and the liquid in a saucepan and add the pared lemon rind and cinnamon. Bring up to the boil and simmer gently for 10–20 minutes or until the prunes are just tender. Strain the prunes from the liquid and spread them out to cool for a few moments so that they may be handled easily.

Return the wine and water to the pan and add the castor sugar. Stir over low heat to dissolve the sugar. Blend the cornflour with a little water to make a smooth paste. Add a little of the hot wine mixture, blend well and pour it into the contents of the saucepan. Stir over the heat until the mixture has come up to the boil and thickened very slightly.

Slit the prunes and carefully remove the stone in each one without breaking up the prune. Replace the stone in each prune with a piece of walnut and reshape the prunes. Place the prunes in a serving dish and pour the wine mixture over them. Cool, then chill until ready to serve. Serve with fresh cream.

Chocolate Roulade

Serves 8 Time taken 45 minutes
Bake the day before serving.

175 g (6 oz) Chocolat Menier or plain chocolate	3 tablespoons hot water
	icing sugar
5 eggs	3 dl (½ pint) double cream
175 g (6 oz) castor sugar	

This recipe needs to be baked in a large, shallow tin. Use a biscuit tin approximately 33 by 24 cm (13½ by 9½ inches) in size.

Brush the tin with oil and line with a sheet of greaseproof paper. Break the chocolate into a small basin and place over a pan of hot, but not boiling, water, Stir occasionally until melted. Separate the eggs, cracking the yolks into a large basin and the whites into a second smaller basin. Add the sugar to the yolks and, using a wooden spoon, beat thoroughly until pale in colour.

When the chocolate has melted, remove from the heat and stir in the hot water – take this from the pan below the chocolate. Stir thoroughly to get a smooth mixture, then beat into the egg yolks and sugar. Whisk the egg whites until stiff, then fold gently but thoroughly into the chocolate mixture. Pour into the prepared tin spreading the mixture evenly. Place in the centre of a moderate oven (180°C, 350°F or Gas No. 4) and bake for 15 minutes. Remove from the heat, cover with a sheet of greaseproof paper and a damp cloth and leave overnight.

Turn the roulade out on to a sheet of greaseproof paper that has been well-dusted with icing sugar. Peel away the baking paper. Lightly whip the cream and spread evenly over the surface of the roulade. Roll up like a Swiss roll using the sugared paper to help. Put to chill for several hours. When ready to serve, dust the surface with a little extra icing sugar and using a sharp knife cut into slices diagonally.

15 Party Snacks & Drinks

Well-flavoured dips are ideal to serve along with drinks at a party.
Serve the bowl of dip surrounded with a selection of salty biscuits
and potato crisps. Make sure that the dip is soft in consistency, as
fragile biscuits will break in a very stiff mixture and leave the dip
looking unattractive. Where necessary thin down the dip with cream,
lemon juice or oil and vinegar dressing, according to the recipe. Fresh
cream cheese or 75 g (3 oz) packets of full fat cheese may be used in
any of the recipes given here.

Serve food in small bite-sized pieces that are easy to handle –
stuffed celery sticks, small hot sausages, grilled oysters with bacon or
tiny meat balls. Prepare interesting mixtures in the form of taramasalata, potted cheese and chicken liver pâté. Spread these on small
cocktail biscuits or fingers of toast and garnish with slices of olive,
hard-boiled egg and cucumber or chopped parsley, anything, in fact,
that looks attractive and goes with the mixture. Welcome friends
with a warming wine punch or a wine cup; these are often less
expensive to serve than short drinks.

PARTY SNACKS

Avocado Dip

Serves 10–12 Time taken 10 minutes

2 ripe avocado pears
225 g (8 oz) fresh cream cheese
juice of ½ lemon
1 teaspoon finely chopped onion

1 level teaspoon salt
dash Worcestershire sauce
2 tablespoons cream

Halve the avocado pears, remove the stones and scoop out the flesh.
Mash well with a fork and add to the cream cheese along with remaining ingredients. Beat well until smooth and quite soft, or, for
best results, blend to a purée in an electric blender.

Serve with salted biscuits.

Horseradish Dip

Serves 10–12 Time taken 10 minutes
Allow to stand for 1 hour

225 g (8 oz) fresh cream cheese
2–3 tablespoons single cream
3 tablespoons prepared horseradish
  relish

¼ teaspoon Worcestershire sauce
pinch salt

Measure the cream cheese, single cream and horseradish relish into a
basin. Beat well to mix the ingredients, then add the Worcestershire
sauce and salt to taste. Mix again, leave to stand for an hour or more
for flavours to develop.

Serve this dip with trimmed cauliflower sprigs and carrot sticks for
dipping.

Party Dip

Serves 10–12 Time taken 10 minutes

2 tablespoons prepared oil and
  vinegar dressing
225 g (8 oz) fresh cream cheese

2 tablespoons tomato ketchup
2 teaspoons finely chopped onion
1 teaspoon anchovy essence

Gradually beat the oil and vinegar dressing into the cream cheese.
Blend well and then beat in the tomato ketchup, onion and anchovy
essence to taste.

Serve with salted biscuits or potato crisps.

Cheese Straw Bundles

Makes 25 bundles Time taken 40 minutes

225 g (8 oz) plain flour	100 g (4 oz) grated Parmesan cheese
salt and pepper	beaten egg
100 g (4 oz) butter	paprika pepper

Sift together the flour and seasoning. Rub in the butter until the mixture is fine and crumbly. Add the Parmesan cheese and mix well. Stir in sufficient beaten egg to mix to a rough dough. Turn the dough out on to a lightly floured board and knead until smooth. Roll out to approximately ·5 cm (¼ inch) thick and, using a 3·5-cm (1½-inch) round cutter, cut out twenty-five circles from a portion of the dough. Cut the remainder into cheese straws. Using a 2·5-cm (1-inch) cutter remove the centres of the pastry circles to form twenty-five rings (these small circles cut from the centre may be baked and eaten as cheese biscuits).

Place the circles and straws on lightly greased baking sheets. Bake above centre in a hot oven (200°C, 400°F or Gas No. 6) for 8–10 minutes until pale golden brown. Allow to cool on a wire cooling tray and, while still warm, dip the ends of the straws in the paprika pepper. When cold fit the straws through the rings to make bundles. *Note* Always prepare these in advance.

Fondue

Serves 8 Time taken 20 minutes
Serve at once

1 clove garlic	1 small liqueur glass kirsch
3 dl (½ pint) white wine	freshly milled pepper
700 g (1½ lb) grated Swiss cheese	nutmeg
2 rounded teaspoons cornflour	

Fondue is traditionally made in a special pan known as a 'caquelon' but any fireproof dish will do as well. Use Swiss Gruyère or Emmental cheese.

Rub the inside of the fondue pan with the garlic, put the pan on the heat and warm the wine in it. Stirring all the time, add the grated cheese, and, as soon as the mixture starts to bubble, add the cornflour which has been blended with the kirsch. Season with pepper and nutmeg to taste and bring up to the boil.

Have everything ready: a basket of bread cubes, a fondue fork for each guest. Place the fondue on a spirit cooker to keep it hot and simmering gently.

A bread cube should be placed on the end of the fork and each guest should stir this in the fondue so that the bread becomes completely coated. Keep the fondue well-stirred all the time to prevent the cheese at the base of the dish turning brown.

Traditionally a glass of kirsch is also served with the fondue.

Salted Almonds

Serves 4–6 Time taken 15–20 minutes

100 g (¼ lb) unblanched almonds   15 g (½ oz) butter
kitchen or sea salt

Where possible use ground sea salt for salted almonds. The flavour is nicer and you can afford to be more generous with it.

Place the almonds in a bowl and cover with boiling water. Allow to stand for about 3 minutes, then drain and remove the brown skins. Dry the almonds thoroughly in a clean cloth.

Have ready a sheet of greaseproof paper sprinkled with kitchen salt or ground sea salt. Melt the butter in a frying pan, add the almonds and fry, turning them occasionally until lightly browned. Remove from the pan and toss in the salt. When cool, pile them in a dish for serving.

Stuffed Celery Sticks

Makes 25–30 Time taken 10 minutes

1 head of celery   1 tablespoon cream or milk
3 packets Demi-sel cheese   paprika pepper
100 g (4 oz) Roquefort cheese

Celery sticks are also delicious stuffed with cream cheese seasoned with salt and pepper and lemon juice with smoked salmon added, or with taramasalata (see page 266).

Wash the celery stalks thoroughly in cold water to clean and crispen. (There are approximately nine in a head.) Trim off the leafy ends and the base. Blend together the cheese and cream until smooth.

Fill the hollow celery stalks with this cheese filling, and sprinkle with a little paprika pepper. Cut crosswise into 3-cm (1½-inch) pieces. Serve as an appetizer with drinks.

Angels on Horseback

Makes 12   Time taken 15 minutes

1 dozen oysters	few drops lemon juice
12 small rashers of streaky bacon	
freshly milled pepper	cocktail sticks

Better known as an after-dinner savoury, these bacon-wrapped oysters, impaled on cocktail sticks, make wonderful party snacks.

Poach the oysters in their own liquor very gently for 2 minutes only. Meanwhile, trim and stretch the bacon rashers by pressing them flat with a knife blade. Drain the oysters. Dust with freshly milled pepper and sprinkle with a few drops of lemon juice. Wrap each oyster in a bacon rasher and thread on skewers.

Grill both sides under a preheated grill to crispen and cook the bacon. Push off the skewer and impale each one on a cocktail stick. Serve hot.

Hot Sausages with Mustard Mayonnaise

Serves 12   Time taken 30–35 minutes

450–700 g (1–1½ lb) cocktail sausages   25 g (1 oz) lard or dripping
  or chipolata sausages

For the Mustard Mayonnaise

1 level teaspoon ready-mixed mustard	1 level teaspoon castor sugar
¼ level teaspoon salt	2 egg yolks
pinch of curry powder	3 dl (½ pint) vegetable or corn oil
freshly milled black pepper	1 level teaspoon tomato purée
1 teaspoon lemon juice	1 tablespoon wine vinegar
2 teaspoons cream	

Separate the sausages; if chipolatas are used twist them in half to make smaller ones. Put the sausages in a roasting tin with a little dripping or lard and set aside until ready to cook.

Prepare the mustard mayonnaise. Measure the mustard, salt, curry powder, pepper, lemon juice, castor sugar and egg yolks into a medium-sized mixing basin. Blend together with a whisk. Add the oil, drop by drop at first, whisking all the time until the mixture begins to thicken a little. Then add it faster, whisking continuously, until all the oil is added. Stir in the tomato purée and vinegar. Stir in the cream just before use.

About 30–35 minutes before serving, place the tin of sausages above centre in a hot oven (200°C, 400°F or Gas No. 6). Turn frequently to brown the sausages evenly. Drain, stir with cocktail sticks and serve hot, along with the mustard mayonnaise for dipping.

Miniature Meat Balls

Makes 25–30 Time taken 30 minutes

450 g (1 lb) lean chuck steak	1 level teaspoon salt
1 medium onion	¼ level teaspoon black pepper
1 clove garlic	seasoned flour
1 egg	50 g (2 oz) butter

Can be made in advance ready for last-minute cooking. This recipe makes 25–30 small meat balls and is very economical.

Trim fat and gristle from the steak and peel and quarter the onion. Pass the meat through a fine mincer along with the onion. Crush and chop the garlic very finely. Beat the meat, garlic, egg and seasoning thoroughly together.

Using lightly oiled fingers, divide the mixture into pieces and roll into meat balls the size of large marbles. Roll them in seasoned flour. Melt the butter in a frying pan. Add the meat balls a few at a time and fry until lightly browned on all sides.

Serve hot or cold, speared with cocktail sticks. Dip into a spicy sauce.

Bacon Savouries

Makes enough to serve 18–20 Time taken 30 minutes

30 rashers of streaky bacon	20 cocktail sausages
20 tenderized (pitted) prunes	50–75 g (2–3 oz) melted butter
20 chicken livers	
or	

These are easy to prepare and, if they are all threaded close together on long skewers ready for grilling, very quick to cook.

Trim the rinds from the bacon rashers, stretch the rashers slightly by pressing them flat along the working surface with a knife. Cut each rasher in half and roll a portion of one of the three fillings in each piece of bacon.

Push the prepared savouries close together on to long skewers ready for grilling, then brush with a little melted butter.

Place under a preheated hot grill and cook for 3–5 minutes. Turn the complete skewer of savouries over, to cook both sides. When ready push off the savouries using a fork. Spike each one with a cocktail stick and serve hot.

Cream Cheese with Garlic and Chives

Serves 4–6 Time taken 10 minutes
Allow to stand for several hours

225 g (½ lb) fresh cream cheese
1 clove garlic
salt

1–2 tablespoons finely chopped
    chives or parsley

Blend the cheese in a bowl until soft. Crush the garlic lightly and remove outer papery coating. Using a knife blade, mash the garlic with a little salt to a paste. Add the mashed garlic to the cheese – no extra salt for flavouring will be needed. Add the chopped chives or parsley and mix thoroughly.

Spoon the mixture into a small serving pot and fork the top attractively. Sprinkle with a little extra chopped herbs. Chill for several hours, to let flavours develop before serving.

Serve as a spread for canapés. Serve on a tray with a selection of cheeses and crisp French bread.

Liptauer Cheese

Serves 4–6 Time taken 10 minutes
Allow to stand for several hours

100 g (4 oz) butter
225 g (½ lb) fresh cream cheese
½ level teaspoon sweet paprika
½ level teaspoon caraway seeds
1 teaspoon finely chopped chives

½ level teaspoon French mustard
salt
freshly milled pepper
1 teaspoon finely chopped capers
1 teaspoon finely chopped parsley

This is a delicious savoury cheese mixture made using cream cheese and spices. Note that the flavour develops if allowed to stand a few hours.

Cream the butter until soft, then add the cream cheese, paprika, mustard and a seasoning of salt and pepper. Beat well until smooth and well-blended. The ingredients state sweet paprika because paprika peppers do vary in strength and a sweet or mild paprika is preferable in this case. Stir in the caraway seeds, chives, capers and parsley. Mix well and then spoon into a 3-dl (½-pint) pot. Cover and chill until required.

Serve on a tray with a selection of other cheeses and French bread or with crackers. Or serve as a spread on cocktail biscuits.

Cream Cheese with Smoked Oysters

Enough for 2–3 dozen cocktail biscuits Time taken 10 minutes

2 tablespoons lemon juice
1 tablespoon finely chopped onion

225 g (½ lb) fresh cream cheese
2 (90 g) (3¼ oz) tins smoked oysters

Measure the lemon juice, chopped onion and cream cheese into a mixing basin. Beat until smooth and blended, using a wooden spoon. Drain the oysters from the tins, mash thoroughly with a fork and then beat into the mixture. Season if liked with a little freshly milled pepper.

Serve as a spread on cocktail biscuits.

Taramasalata

Serves 6 Time taken 15 minutes
Allow to stand for several hours

225 g (½ lb) smoked cod's roe
1 small clove of garlic
2 small slices white bread
2 tablespoons milk

6 tablespoons oil
2 tablespoons lemon juice
freshly milled pepper
1 teaspoon finely chopped parsley

Taramasalata can be mixed in an electric blender; it makes a smoother pâté. Add the seasoning to taste and parsley afterwards.

Scoop the cod's roe out of the skin, using a teaspoon, and place in a mixing basin. Peel and finely chop the garlic. Add to the cod's roe and beat the mixture with a wooden spoon until smooth. For a milder garlic flavour simply rub the inside of the pot to be used for serving with the whole crushed garlic and then discard the clove.

Trim the crusts from the bread and soak for 2–3 minutes with the milk. Squeeze the bread, extracting as much milk as possible and add the bread to the cod's roe. Mix thoroughly, then beat in the oil, one tablespoon at a time. Alternate the additions of oil with a little of the lemon juice. Season with pepper and beat in the chopped parsley. Spoon into a small covered pot and chill until ready to serve.

Use as a spread on canapés, or use to stuff celery stalks. This mixture can also be served with hot toast and butter.

Potted Cheese

Serves 4–6 Time taken 10 minutes

100 g (¼ lb) grated Cheddar cheese
50 g (2 oz) soft butter
freshly milled pepper

pinch ground mace
2 tablespoons sherry

Pound the cheese with the butter, pepper and mace. Add the sherry and mix thoroughly. Spoon into a small pot, cover and store in the refrigerator. This mix will keep for several weeks and makes a useful spread for toast, on biscuits or cocktail canapés. It is an excellent method of using up left-over bits of cheese.

Smoked Haddock Pâté

Serves 6 Time taken 20–25 minutes
Prepare in advance and chill

350 g (¾ lb) smoked haddock fillet
50 g (2 oz) melted butter
1·5 dl (¼ pint) double cream
2 teaspoons lemon juice

1 teaspoon Worcestershire sauce
freshly milled pepper
cayenne pepper
2–3 tablespoons melted butter

Poach the haddock fillet for 10 minutes in enough boiling water to cover. Drain the fish, remove the skin and flake the flesh. Mash the fish with the melted butter and pass through a sieve, or blend in an electric blender to make a purée. Lightly whip the cream and fold into the fish adding the lemon juice, Worcestershire sauce and seasoning to taste. Pour into a small serving pot and chill for several hours until firm. Cover the top with melted butter and replace in the refrigerator for the butter to set.

Serve as a spread on canapés or cocktail biscuits. This mixture can also be served with hot toast and butter.

Quick Chicken Liver Pâté

Serves 6 Time taken 20 minutes
Make in advance and chill

225 g (½ lb) chicken livers
100 g (4 oz) butter
1 tablespoon brandy or dry sherry

salt
freshly ground black pepper
grated nutmeg

Trim the chicken livers and set aside. Melt half the butter in a saucepan, add the chicken livers, cover and fry gently for 5 minutes.

Draw the pan off the heat and pass the livers and juices from the pan through the fine blade on a mincer or blend the ingredients in an electric blender. Add the brandy or sherry.

Cream the remaining butter in a mixing basin. Add the liver mixture and beat thoroughly with a seasoning of salt, freshly milled pepper and a little grated nutmeg. Spoon the mixture into a small covered dish and chill.

Serve as a spread on canapés or cocktail biscuits. This mixture can also be served with hot toast and butter.

PARTY DRINKS

Sangria

Serves 12–14 Time taken 10 minutes

1–2 lemons	1–2 glasses inexpensive brandy
2–3 oranges	2 bottles red wine
1–2 apples	1 bottle lemonade or soda water

A most refreshing summer drink for which there are many variations; here's a simple and very acceptable one.

Place lots of ice cubes in the base of a large bowl. Add the sliced or roughly cut up lemons and oranges, and the cored and sliced apples. Stir in the brandy and then add the red wine and lemonade or soda water. (Ordinary bottled lemonade is already sweetened, in which case the Sangria may be sufficiently sweet. Where soda water is used, 2–3 tablespoons castor sugar should be added to the fruit.) Stir well and then pour with the fruit into jugs.

Serve as a summer drink at a lunch or supper party.

Hock Sparkler

Serves 35 glasses Time taken 10 minutes
Marinate fruit and wine for 1 hour

450 g (1 lb) fresh melon cubes or strawberries or peaches	1 bottle sparkling hock
	1 liqueur glass brandy
sugar to taste	3 liqueur glasses Curaçao or
3 bottles hock	Cointreau

This is a particularly lovely summer party drink. The wine takes the flavours from the fruit and it looks so attractive.

Place the melon cubes, the sliced strawberries or peaches in a bowl. Add sugar to sweeten – about 2–3 tablespoonfuls – and one bottle of hock. Leave for 1 hour, stirring occasionally to blend the flavours and dissolve the sugar. Chill the remaining wine.

Add the chilled wine, the brandy and the orange liqueur. Mix well and serve with a little of the fruit in each glass.

Gluhwein

Serves 8 glasses Time taken 25 minutes
Serve hot

3 dl (½ pint) water	2 cloves
rind and juice of 1 lemon	175 g (6 oz) castor sugar
little grated nutmeg	1 bottle red wine
2·5 cm (1 inch) cinnamon stick	

This is a warming drink to serve at a winter party.

Put the water, finely pared lemon rind and juice, grated nutmeg, cinnamon stick, cloves and sugar into a saucepan. Bring slowly up to the boil, stirring to dissolve the sugar. Infuse gently over low heat for 15 minutes. Strain the liquid and return to the saucepan along with the wine. Reheat but do not allow to boil.

Serve hot in small mugs or heat-resistant glasses.

Summer Wine Cup

Serves 18–20 glasses Time taken 1 hour

225 g (½ lb) fresh strawberries	juice of 3 lemons
2 liqueur glasses brandy	1 bottle Sauternes
1 miniature bottle Cointreau	3–6 dl (½–1 pint) soda water
1 bottle Beaujolais	few sprigs fresh mint
1 tablespoon sugar	

This recipe makes a delightful, refreshing summer drink.

Wipe the strawberries and slice them into a bowl. Add the sugar, lemon juice, brandy and Cointreau and leave to chill for a little while. Add the chilled Beaujolais and Sauternes, then, immediately before serving, add some ice cubes and the soda water.

Garnish with a few sprigs of mint.

White Wine Cup

Serves 12 glasses Time taken 15 minutes

12 lumps of sugar
1 lemon
2 bottles dry white wine

1·5 dl (¼ pint) sherry
6 dl (1 pint) soda water

Rub the lumps of sugar over the rind of the well-washed lemon until the sugar is yellow and full of the lemon zest. Place in the base of a large bowl or jug and crush the sugar. Add the strained lemon juice and stir to dissolve the sugar. Add wine and the sherry.

Just before serving add a few ice cubes and slices of cucumber for decoration.

Rum Punch

Serves 10–12 glasses Time taken 15 minutes
Serve hot

15 g (½ oz) China tea
generous 1 litre (2 pints) boiling
  water

3 large lemons
450 g (1 lb) granulated sugar
3 dl (½ pint) rum

Put the China tea into a bowl and pour over the boiling water. Add the very thinly pared rind of one of the lemons and leave to infuse for 10 minutes. Strain through muslin into a saucepan and add the sugar. Stir over low heat until the sugar has dissolved. Add the rum and the squeezed juice of the pared lemon. Bring almost to the boil and then draw off the heat. Slice the remaining two lemons and add.

Serve hot with slices of lemon floating on the top.

16 Eating out of Doors

BARBECUES

Eating out of doors has great appeal for almost everyone and, given the right weather, a barbecue can be great fun. Keep the menu simple with grilled or fried foods; avoid lavish sauces and instead use spicy marinades or bastes to give a variety of flavours. Crisp unusual salads, hot breads and baked potatoes take the place of vegetables. Prepare as much in advance as possible, leaving only the salads to be tossed, bread to be heated through, and the main dish to be cooked over the barbecue.

When Grilling over Charcoal remember:
1 A charcoal fire takes some time to become hot enough to cook over – remember to light the fire well in advance. Only when the flames have died down and the coals have a red glow are they hot enough.
2 Meat for barbecueing should be at room temperature, especially thick steaks. Remove any steaks for grilling from the refrigerator at least 1 hour before cooking.

3 Place young halved chickens, either small *poussins* split in half or chicken joints, on the grill boney-side down. The bone helps to act as a heat conductor. Brush with oil or baste, then turn the chicken over to the fleshy side to finish cooking.

4 Spear fat trimmings. or a piece of bacon fat, and rub over the grill bars before cooking to prevent meat or poultry from sticking.

5 Use a narrow paint brush to brush melted butter on meat before grilling, or for basting foods with a special baste.

6 Baste food with a tomato-flavoured baste towards the end of cooking time, otherwise it is inclined to burn.

7 Use any of the bastes given for cooking the kebabs for other meats. Butter baste goes well with steaks or hamburgers, mustard bastes go well with gammon steaks or chicken joints.

8 Make sure you have a sharp knife, a long-handled fork or meat tongs, gloves to protect your hands from the heat, and pot holders. Have a sprinkler bottle of water handy to put out any spurt of flame from fat drippings in the fire.

Food to Choose for the Outdoor Barbecue

Steaks Choose good quality steak cut fairly thick: rump steak, T-bone steak, a thick slice cut from the sirloin or porterhouse steak. It is best to grill large rump and T-bone steaks in one piece and then cut them up after grilling. Rub the meat over with a cut clove of garlic, or soak in spicy marinade before cooking. Brush with melted butter before grilling then, when one side is brown, turn and season with salt and pepper. Season the second side as you take it from the grill. Cooking time: Steak about 2·25 cm (1 inch) thick takes 15 minutes to cook for rare or 20 minutes for well done.

Chicken joints Split small *poussins* or spring chickens down the back bone and open out, or use chicken joints. Brush with oil or melted butter and grill. Baste with the mustard baste during cooking, if liked. Cooking time: cook for 20–30 minutes, turning occasionally. To test, pierce the thickest part of the chicken with a sharp knife. If the juices are clear with no tinge of pink the joints are ready.

Pork chops Choose nice loin chops. Rub each side of the chop with a mixture of equal parts dry mustard and castor sugar for a delicious, spicy, sweet flavour. Brush with melted butter. Cooking time: cook for about 15 minutes, turning occasionally.

Gammon rashers Choose nice thick gammon rashers and score the edges of the fat with a sharp knife in several places, so that they will not curl up when cooking. Brush with oil or melted butter. Cooking time: about 5 minutes each side, turning once.

Sweetcorn Remove the outer husks and silks from whole heads of sweetcorn. Spread with melted butter and sprinkle with salt and pepper. Wrap securely in foil. Cook over the hot coals for 15–20 minutes, turning once.

Baked potatoes Scrub large potatoes and rub the skins with salt – if soft skin is preferred, rub with butter. Wrap completely in foil and bake at the edges of the barbecue grill for 45–60 minutes, turning occasionally. If space is limited, the potatoes can be baked in a hot oven (200°C, 400°F or Gas No. 6) for 1 hour. When ready, cut a crisscross in each potato through the foil and squeeze the sides of the potato to push the middle up. Serve topped with butter or, better still, with sour cream and snipped chives.

Kebabs

Food on skewers can include a whole variety of items. Choose lean meat that cooks quickly and, where vegetables are included, items like small whole onions should be par-boiled first to speed up cooking. Otherwise most suitable vegetables such as tomatoes, green peppers, mushrooms and courgettes will cook quickly enough along with the meat. Select foods which go well together and baste with oil, or a special baste, while cooking. Have ready hot finger rolls and, when each skewer is cooked, enclose the food in the roll and draw out the skewer. Serve the rolls hot at once. Serve the food on skewers with baked potatoes or hot bread and a crisp salad.

Choice of Foods for Kebabs

Cubes or beef, lamb or pork Buy rump steak, leg or neck fillet of lamb or pork fillet (tenderloin). Trim the meat and cut into even-sized cubes. Marinate lamb or beef for 1 hour in a marinade using the following proportions – 4 tablespoons oil, 2 tablespoons white wine vinegar, 1 tablespoon white wine, pinch mixed herbs, little crushed garlic, and a seasoning of salt and freshly milled pepper.

Green peppers Halve, deseed and cut the peppers into chunky pieces. To help prevent splitting on skewers, blanch in boiling water for 1 minute, then drain and cool.

Whole onions Select small onions. Peel, leaving them whole, and par-boil for about 5 minutes. Drain and cool.

Tomatoes Select small firm tomatoes – leave whole or cut in half.

Chicken livers Separate the livers; trim and roll up each one in a trimmed bacon rasher.

Sausages Choose beef or pork chipolatas. Place fingers in the centre of each sausage and twist in opposite directions to make smaller sausages.

Cheese Cut neat chunks of Cheddar cheese and wrap each one in a trimmed bacon rasher.

Mushrooms Wipe, remove stalks and blanch mushrooms for 1 minute in boiling water. Place the mushrooms towards the tip of the skewers; if pushed too far up they are inclined to break.

Pineapple Drain chunks from a tin.

Kebabs of Lamb

Serves 4 Time taken 1½ hours

700 g (1½ lb) neck fillet of lamb	salt
2 small onions	freshly milled pepper
100 g (¼ lb) small mushrooms	oil
1 bay leaf	Worcestershire sauce

Trim any fat or skin from the meat, then cut into twelve pieces. Peel the onions, cut into quarters and separate the pieces. Wash the mushrooms and trim the stalks level with the caps. Place the meat and onions in a shallow dish together with the crushed bay leaf. Season well with salt and pepper and sprinkle with oil and a few drops of Worcestershire sauce. Leave for 1 hour to marinate, turning occasionally.

Thread the pieces of meat on to four skewers alternately with pieces of onion and mushrooms. Roll the kebabs in the oil in the dish to coat well, then place over glowing coals. Cook turning once for 10 minutes.

Serve the kebabs with rice pilaff and tossed salad.

Liver and Bacon Kebabs

Serves 4 Time taken 30 minutes

100 g (¼ lb) bacon rashers	4 tomatoes
225 g (½ lb) chicken livers	4 chipolata sausages

For the Butter Baste

100 g (4 oz) butter	3 tablespoons tomato ketchup
4 tablespoons meat sauce	

Cut the rinds from the bacon rashers and cut the rashers in half. Separate and trim the chicken livers. Wrap a piece of bacon round each piece of liver. Cut the tomatoes in half. Separate the sausages, nip each one in the centre and twist the ends in opposite directions to make two smaller sausages. Thread the liver, tomatoes and sausages alternately on to four long skewers. Set aside while preparing the baste.

Melt the butter in a saucepan over low heat. Stir in the meat sauce and tomato ketchup. Blend well and draw off the heat.

Brush the skewers with a little of the baste, place over the glowing coals and cook for 5–10 minutes, basting and turning occasionally.

Trout in Foil

Serves 4 Time taken 45 minutes

4 trout	50 g (2 oz) butter
salt	1 tablespoon finely chopped parsley
freshly milled pepper	1 lemon

Trout (also salmon steaks) cooked in foil packets are particularly delicious baked over hot glowing charcoal.

Gut the trout leaving on the head. Wipe dry and place each one in the centre of a large square of buttered foil. Season with salt and pepper and place 15 g ($\frac{1}{2}$ oz) butter in small pieces on each one. Sprinkle with chopped parsley. Thinly slice the lemon and place 1–2 lemon slices on top of each fish.

Close the paper carefully to seal in all the juices while cooking. Draw opposite sides of the foil together over the fish and fold closed. Then turn up both ends to seal completely. Place the package over the glowing coals and cook for 25–30 minutes turning occasionally.

Serve the trout from the package with the juices and melted butter poured over.

Hot Garlic Bread

Serves 4–6 Time taken 30–40 minutes

2 Vienna loaves

For the Garlic Butter

100 g (4 oz) butter	salt
1 dessertspoon hot water	2 tablespoons chopped parsley
1 clove garlic	

Diagonally slice the Vienna loaves into 5-cm (2-inch) slices, cutting almost through the bread but leaving the bottom crust whole.

Cream the butter with the hot water until soft. Crush the garlic, remove the outer papery coating and mash the garlic to a pulp with a little salt. Add the garlic and half the parsley to the butter and beat until blended. Check the flavour, but no extra salt should be needed. Spread the garlic butter generously between each slice of bread. Any left over should be spread over the top of the loaves. Sprinkle with the remaining parsley and wrap each loaf in kitchen foil.

Place in the centre of a very hot oven (220°C, 425°F or Gas No. 7) and bake for 20 minutes. Unwrap and serve hot – if kept wrapped the loaves will keep hot for some time.

Onions in Sour Cream

Serves 4 Time taken 2–3 hours

2 medium onions	¼ level teaspoon salt
1 carton soured cream	1 teaspoon lemon juice

Peel the onions, slice into rings and place in a mixing basin. Cover with boiling water and allow to soak for 2 minutes. Drain and chill for several hours.

When ready to serve, mix together the soured cream, salt and lemon juice. Add the onion rings and toss well to mix.

Excellent served with grilled steaks, chicken or gammon.

Pork and Pineapple Kebabs

Serves 4 Time taken 45 minutes

1 pork fillet or tenderloin	4 courgettes
1 (225 g) (8 oz) tin pineapple rings	225 g (½ lb) back bacon rashers

For the Mustard Baste

50 g (2 oz) butter	2 tablespoons clear honey
2 level tablespoons prepared mustard	2 level tablespoons soft brown sugar

Trim the pork fillet and cut into neat cubes. Drain the pineapple from the tin and cut the rings into chunky pieces. Wash and slice the courgettes. Place the courgettes in a saucepan, cover with cold water and bring to the boil. Simmer for 1 minute and drain, this removes the slightly acid flavour from the skins. Cut the bacon rashers in half and wrap round the pieces of pork fillet. Fix the pork fillet on four skewers alternately with the courgettes and chunks of pineapple. Set aside while preparing the glaze.

Melt the butter in a small saucepan and add the mustard, honey and sugar. Stir over low heat until the mixture is blended and just coming to the boil. Draw off heat and use. Brush the skewers with a little of the baste and place over the glowing coals. Cook for 10–15 minutes, basting and turning occasionally.

Hamburgers

Serves 4 Time taken 30 minutes

450 g (1 lb) lean steak, minced
1 level teaspoon salt
freshly milled pepper
pinch dried mixed herbs

1 small egg
50 g (2 oz) softened butter
4 soft rolls for serving

The better the quality of the steak chosen for hamburgers the tastier and more succulent they are. The steak should be minced coarsely and only once. Place the minced steak, seasoning and herbs in a mixing basin. Using a fork, stir in sufficient lightly mixed egg to make a soft but not sticky mixture. The mixture should cling together when gently pressed into shape. Turn the mixture out on to a clean working surface and divide into four portions. Oil the fingers to prevent the meat sticking to them, then, using a spatula or a knife, lightly shape each portion of meat into a flat round, about 2·5 cm (1 inch) thick. Set aside in the refrigerator until ready to cook.

Spread each hamburger on both sides with softened butter. Grill over glowing coals for 8–10 minutes, turning once. As each hamburger is cooked, place in a split, toasted, soft roll. Season with salt and pepper, add tomato ketchup or fried onions if liked, and serve.

Talatourie

Serves 4 Time taken 10 minutes
Chill before serving

1 cucumber
½ onion
1 carton plain yogurt

salt
freshly milled pepper
1–2 teaspoons finely chopped mint

A delicious recipe from Cyprus, where it is served with all grilled kebabs.

Peel the cucumber and cut in half lengthwise. Remove centre seeds and dice the flesh. Place in a bowl with the peeled and finely chopped onion. Add the yogurt, a seasoning of salt and pepper and the mint. Mix well and serve with grilled steaks or kebabs.

Beef and Onion Kebabs

Serves 4 Time taken 45 minutes

350 g (¾ lb) rump steak

2 green peppers

225 g (½ lb) small whole onions

4 tomatoes

For the Barbecue Baste

4 tablespoons oil

1 medium size onion

1 clove garlic

1 (65 g) (2½ oz) tin tomato purée

4 tablespoons soft brown sugar

2 tablespoons vinegar

juice of ½ lemon

1 level teaspoon salt

1 level teaspoon chilli powder

1 level tablespoon dry mustard

Trim any fat from the steak and then cut it up into neat cubes. Halve, deseed and cut the green peppers into pieces. Peel the onions, leaving them whole, place in a saucepan, cover with cold water and bring to the boil. Simmer for 10 minutes to partly cook. If small onions are difficult to find, use two large onions peeled and cut in quarters but do not par-boil. Cut the tomatoes in half. Fix the chunks of meat on to four skewers alternating the meat with the green peppers, onions and tomato halves. Set aside while preparing the baste.

Heat the oil in a small saucepan. Peel and finely chop the onion and the garlic. Add the onion and cook gently for 5 minutes until tender but not brown. Add the garlic and fry for a moment, then stir in the remaining ingredients. Stir well and bring to the boil. Simmer gently for 10 minutes stirring occasionally. Draw off the heat and the baste is ready for use.

Brush the skewers with a little of the baste and place over the glowing coals. Cook for 10–15 minutes, basting and turning occasionally.

New Potato Salad

Serves 4 Time taken 20 minutes
Cool before serving

450–700 g (1–1½ lb) new potatoes

1 bunch spring onions

1 tablespoon finely chopped parsley

1 tablespoon finely chopped mint

4–6 tablespoons prepared oil and
 vinegar dressing

Tossing the potatoes in the dressing while they are still hot, considerably improves the flavour of the potato salad.

Select even-size potatoes, scrape and add whole to boiling salted water. Reboil and simmer for about 15 minutes or until just tender, depending on the size of the potatoes. Drain and leave until cool enough to handle, then slice thickly into a salad bowl. Wash and trim the spring onions. Shred the white base of each and add to the potatoes along with the chopped parsley and mint.

Pour the oil and vinegar dressing over the potatoes while they are still hot, then leave until cold before serving.

Pineapple Coleslaw

Serves 6 Time taken 45 minutes

½ small white summer cabbage
225 g (½ lb) seedless green grapes

1 small pineapple

For the Dressing
4–5 tablespoons prepared oil and
vinegar dressing

3 tablespoons mayonnaise
4 tablespoons single cream

Discard any outer, bruised leaves from the cabbage, cut half the cabbage into quarters and remove the hard stalk. Shred the cabbage finely and wash well in salted water. Drain thoroughly and place in a salad bowl. Pick the grapes from the stem, wash thoroughly, cut in half and add to the cabbage.

Slice the leafy top and the base from the pineapple then cut downwards round the sides to remove the outer peel. Remove any eyes and cut the pineapple into slices. Cut away any hard core and shred the pineapple and add. Pour the oil and vinegar dressing over the prepared ingredients and toss well to mix through the salad.

Thin down the mayonnaise with the cream and pour over the salad. Toss to mix again and then serve. It is advisable to mix the salad in a mixing basin, if a wooden salad bowl is to be used for serving, as the bowl is inclined to get stained when tossing the salad in the mayonnaise dressing.

This salad is delicious with grilled fish, poultry, roast pork, grilled steak or chops.

Salade Niçoise

Serves 4 Time taken 20 minutes

1·5 dl (¼ pint) prepared oil and
vinegar dressing
1 lettuce heart
225 g (½ lb) cooked French beans
1 green pepper
½ onion

1 (225 g) (8 oz) tin tuna fish
6–8 black olives, stoned
8 anchovy fillets
3–4 firm tomatoes
2 hard-boiled eggs

This particular salad makes an excellent start to a meal, it looks attractive and is very easy to prepare.

Pour half the prepared dressing into the base of a salad bowl – the one to be used for serving. Separate the lettuce leaves and wash them, tearing any large ones in half. Add the lettuce and the cooked beans to the dressing in the bowl, and toss to mix with the dressing. Halve, deseed and shred the green pepper. Peel and slice the onion into rings. Arrange the tuna fish, drained from the tin and broken in pieces, the olives, shredded green peppers, anchovy fillets and onion rings on top of the salad. Cut the tomatoes and shelled, hard-boiled eggs in quarters and arrange around the sides of the bowl.

Sprinkle with the remaining oil and vinegar dressing and serve.

Spinach Flan

Serves 4–6 Time taken 1 hour

100 g ($\frac{1}{4}$ lb) shortcrust pastry

For the Filling

450 g (1 lb) fresh spinach	4 tablespoons single cream
1 (225 g) (8 oz) carton cottage cheese	salt
3 eggs	freshly milled pepper
25 g (1 oz) grated Parmesan cheese	pinch nutmeg

Roll the prepared pastry out thinly and use to line a 20-cm (8-inch) quiche tin or a flan ring set on a baking tray. Trim the edges and prick the base of the flan with a fork. Fill the centre with a piece of crumpled kitchen foil to hold the shape while baking. Place above centre in a hot oven (200°C, 400°F or Gas No. 6) and bake for about 10 minutes. Remove the foil a few minutes before the end of the cooking time.

Meanwhile, wash the spinach in several lots of cold water to clean thoroughly. Tear away the centre stalk from each leaf and place the spinach in a saucepan. Cover and cook over moderate heat for about 10–15 minutes, or until tender. No water is required, sufficient will be clinging to the spinach leaves. Drain the cooked spinach well and press to get rid of excess moisture. Chop the spinach finely. Sieve the cottage cheese into a mixing basin and add the spinach, eggs, Parmesan cheese and cream. Mix well and season to taste with salt and pepper and add the nutmeg.

Spoon the mixture into the pastry case and spread evenly. Replace in the oven at moderately hot (190°C, 375°F or Gas No. 5) and bake for 30 minutes or until the filling is set and lightly browned.

Serve warm with sliced tomatoes tossed in oil and vinegar dressing.

Cheese and Tomato Quiche

Serves 4 Time taken 1 hour

100 g (¼ lb) shortcrust pastry

For the Filling

225 g (½ lb) tomatoes
2 eggs
1·5 dl (¼ pint) single cream
50 g (2 oz) grated Cheddar cheese
1 teaspoon chopped fresh parsley or
  chervil

½ level teaspoon salt
freshly milled pepper
cayenne pepper

On a lightly floured working surface roll the pastry out to a circle slightly larger than a 20-cm (8-inch) quiche tin or flan ring set on a baking try. Line with the pastry and set aside while preparing the filling.

Plunge the tomatoes into boiling water for 1 minute, then drain and peel away the skins. Slice and arrange over the base of the flan.

In a mixing basin, blend together the eggs, cream, grated cheese, herbs and a seasoning of salt and pepper. Pour into the flan case and place in the centre of a fairly hot oven (190°C, 375°F or Gas No. 5) and bake for 40 minutes or until set.

Serve warm with salad.

Pissaladière

Serves 4 Time taken 1½ hours

100 g (¼ lb) shortcrust pastry

For the Filling

450 g (1 lb) tomatoes
1 onion
1 clove garlic
15 g (½ oz) butter
3 sprigs parsley
3 sprigs thyme
2 tablespoons tomato purée

2 eggs
100 g (4 oz) grated cheese
salt
freshly milled pepper

12 anchovy fillets
black olives

Traditionally a Pissaladière is made using a bread dough; in this recipe use a shortcrust pastry made with self-raising flour to get a similar soft crust.

Roll out the pastry and use to line a 20-cm (8-inch) quiche tin, or flan ring set on a baking tray. Trim the edges neatly and set aside while preparing the filling.

Nick the skins of the tomatoes. Place together in a mixing basin and cover with boiling water. Stand for 1 minute, then drain and peel away the skins. Halve the tomatoes, remove the seeds and chop the tomato flesh coarsely. Peel and finely chop the onion; peel the garlic and crush to a paste with a little salt. Melt the butter in a saucepan and add the tomatoes, onion, garlic, parsley, thyme and tomato purée. Cover with a lid and cook very gently for 30 minutes.

Draw the pan off the heat, cool for a moment and then beat in the eggs, cheese and a seasoning of salt and pepper. Pour into the prepared pastry case. Arrange a lattice work of anchovy fillets over the top and decorate with halved and stoned black olives. Place above centre in a moderately hot oven (190°C, 375°F or Gas No. 5) and bake for 40 minutes.

Serve warm with salad.

Fresh Strawberry Tart

Serves 6–8 Time taken 1–1½ hours

225 g (½ lb) rich shortcrust pastry   450–700 g (1–1½ lb) strawberries

For the Custard
3 dl (½ pint) milk   1 level tablespoon flour
3 egg yolks   25 g (1 oz) butter
50 g (2 oz) vanilla sugar

For the Glaze
3 tablespoons raspberry jam or   juice of ½ lemon
  redcurrant jelly

Roll the prepared pastry out and use to line a 26-cm (10-inch) tart tin with a loose base, or a flan ring set on a baking tray. Trim the edges neatly and fill the centre with a piece of crumpled kitchen foil to hold the shape of the pastry while baking. Place in the centre of a hot oven (200°C, 400°F or Gas No. 6) and bake for 10–12 minutes, removing the foil a few minutes before the end of the cooking time. Allow the pastry case to cool while preparing the custard filling.

Measure the milk into a saucepan and heat gently until hot. In a basin, beat together the egg yolks, vanilla sugar (this is simply castor sugar kept in a jar along with a vanilla pod) and the flour. Gradually stir the hot milk into the egg mixture. Blend well and return to the saucepan. Stir constantly until the custard has thickened and is boiling. Cook gently for a few minutes then draw off the heat. Add the butter and beat in. Pour the custard into a bowl and stir fairly often as it cools to prevent a skin forming.

Spread the cooled custard over the base of the baked pastry case. Arrange the washed, whole or sliced strawberries over the top. Sieve the jam for the glaze into a saucepan and add the lemon juice. Stir until melted, blended and boiling. Draw off the heat and spoon over the fruit to glaze.

Serve cold with cream.

Continental Cheesecake

Makes one 20-cm (8-inch) cake Time taken 2 hours
Bake the day before serving

25 g (1 oz) butter	3 large eggs
6 digestive biscuits	½ teaspoon vanilla essence
1 (225 g) (8 oz) carton cottage cheese	25 g (1 oz) cornflour
225 g (8 oz) fresh cream cheese	1 carton soured cream
100 g (4 oz) castor sugar	

Leave this cheesecake to stand for 24 hours before cutting if possible, as this will improve the texture and flavour.

Melt the butter in a small saucepan and draw off the heat. Crush the biscuits to crumbs and, using a fork, stir into the butter. Blend the mixture well, then spoon into the base of a buttered, 20-cm (8-inch) round cake tin. It is essential to choose a tin with a spring-clip side. Spread the crumbs evenly over the base of the tin and press down firmly.

Rub the cottage cheese through a sieve into a large mixing basin, add the cream cheese and beat well to mix. On no account should a processed cream cheese be used in a recipe such as this. Add the sugar and beat again. Separate the eggs, adding the yolks to the cheese mixture and placing the whites in a separate basin. Beat the yolks into the mixture along with the vanilla essence. Sift the cornflour over the surface and fold in, then add the soured cream. Beat the whites until stiff and then fold in gently and thoroughly.

Pour the mixture into the prepared tin. Place just below centre of a slow oven (150°C, 300°F or Gas No. 2) and bake for 1½ hours. If possible, turn off the oven and leave the cheesecake in the oven until cold. Otherwise remove from the oven and put to cool away from a draught. The cheesecake will rise on baking but should fall level on cooling. Loosen the sides of the cheesecake and lift out of the tin.

Scandinavian Strawberry Cake

Serves 6 Time taken 1 hour
Chill before serving

225 g (½ lb) rich shortcrust pastry
3 tablespoons raspberry jam or
  redcurrant jelly

450–700 g (1–1½ lb) strawberries
juice of ½ lemon
1·5 dl (¼ pint) double cream

Roll the prepared pastry out to a circle about ·5 cm (¼ inch) thick and 26 cm (10 inches) in diameter – use a saucepan lid as a cutting guide. Transfer the pastry base into a greased baking tray and prick all over with a fork. Place in the centre of a hot oven (200°C, 400°F or Gas No. 6) and bake for 15 minutes, or until pale golden brown. Allow to cool and then place on a larger serving plate or wooden board.

Spread 1 tablespoon of the jam or jelly over the centre and arrange the whole strawberries close together over the surface, leaving about 2·5 cm (1 inch) around the edge.

Sieve the remaining jam or jelly into a saucepan and add the lemon juice. Stir over the heat until melted, blended and boiling. Draw off the heat and spoon over the fruit to glaze it completely. Lightly whip the cream and spoon or pipe around the edge of the pastry circle. Chill for about 1 hour.

Iced Coffee

Serves 6 Time taken 25 minutes
Chill before serving

50 g (2 oz) medium ground coffee
6 dl (1 pint) boiling water

3 tablespoons sugar
5 dl (¾–1 pint) chilled milk

Measure the coffee into a saucepan. Add the boiling water, stir well and bring slowly to the boil. Draw off the heat, cover with a lid and infuse for 15 minutes. Strain through muslin into a bowl, add the sugar to taste and stir well. Cool, then chill until required.

When ready to serve, pour the chilled coffee into a tall jug. Add plenty of ice cubes and sufficient chilled milk to dilute to taste, then serve.

PICNICS

Where eating out of doors concerns a picnic, choose foods that are moist and easy to carry, and include plenty of salad ingredients and fresh fruits. Meat is by no means an impossibility – cold fried chicken legs or duck portions are excellent; cold cooked sausages or small cutlets taken from the best end of neck of lamb roasted and eaten cold are delicious, and slices of any cold roast meat carry well. Eggs can be hard-boiled and stuffed with a variety of ingredients. Also excellent are cold cooked open omelettes. Make them rather firmer than when they are eaten hot and add chopped fried onion or thinly sliced fried mushrooms. Cold Spanish omelette is another good choice.

Sausage Rolls

Makes 8–12 rolls Time taken 45 minutes–1 hour

100 g (¼ lb) flaky pastry	salt and pepper
175 g (6 oz) sausage meat	egg and milk

Larger sausage rolls are delicious for supper, particularly if you heat them gently in the oven just before you serve them.

On a floured board, roll the pastry out thinly to an oblong about 30 by 15 cm (12 by 6 inches). Trim the edges and cut in half lengthwise. Leave the rest in a cool place.

Season the sausage meat and divide into two. Then lightly flour your hands and roll each portion of sausage meat out to a rope as long as each pastry strip. Place one rope of sausage meat down the centre of each piece of pastry. Damp one long edge of the pastry, fold this over the sausage meat and seal it to the opposite edge. With a sharp knife, cut each long roll into four or six sausage rolls.

Place the sausage rolls on a baking sheet which has been rinsed in cold water and make one or two diagonal slashes on top of each roll. Brush with a little beaten egg and milk. Place above centre in a very hot oven (220°C, 425°F or Gas No. 7) and bake for 20 minutes.

Scotch Eggs

Serves 4 Time taken 45 minutes
Cool before serving

4 eggs	pinch powdered sage
seasoned flour	lightly beaten egg
225 g (½ lb) sausage meat	toasted breadcrumbs

Hard-boil the eggs, drain and allow to cool. Remove the shells; roll the eggs in seasoned flour and pat off any surplus flour. Flavour the sausage meat with a little powdered sage and divide into equal portions. Pat out each portion on a well-floured working surface to an oblong about 7·5 by 13 cm (3 by 5 inches). Place one egg across the centre of each portion of sausage meat and mould the sausage meat around the eggs without any cracks.

Coat with lightly beaten egg and then roll in toasted breadcrumbs. Fry in hot deep fat or oil for about 4–5 minutes. Drain and leave until cold. Cut in half and serve with salad.

Quiche of Bacon and Leeks

Serves 4 Time taken 1¼ hours

100 g (¼ lb) shortcrust pastry

For the Filling

450 g (1 lb) leeks	100 g (¼ lb) lean bacon rashers
40 g (1½ oz) butter	2 eggs
salt	1·5 dl (¼ pint) cream
freshly milled pepper	

Roll the pastry out to a circle slightly larger than a 20-cm (8-inch) quiche tin or flan ring set on a baking tray. Line the tin with the pastry, and trim the edges neatly. Set aside in a cool place while preparing the filling.

Trim away the base of the leeks and remove the outer damaged leaves. Cut the green leaves down to within 2·5 cm (1 inch) of the white part. Slit the leeks open and wash well under running cold water. Shred the leeks finely. Trim away the rinds and cut up the bacon rashers. Melt the butter in a frying pan and add the bacon. Stir for a moment and then add the shredded leeks. Season with salt and pepper, stir to mix and then cover with a lid. Lower the heat and sauté very gently for about 20 minutes or until the leeks are quite soft, but not brown.

Draw the pan off the heat and spoon the leek and bacon mixture into the prepared pastry case. Leave behind any juices in the pan. Lightly mix the eggs and cream and pour over the leek and bacon mixture. Place above centre in a moderately hot oven (190°C, 375°F or Gas No. 5) and bake for 40 minutes.

Serve warm or cold with salad.

Chicken Liver and Bacon Pasties

Makes 12 Time taken 45 minutes

225 g (½ lb) chicken livers
6 rashers lean bacon
225 g (½ lb) flaky or puff pastry

egg and milk

Clean the livers in cold salted water, drain well and then trim and divide into twelve portions. Trim the bacon rashers and cut each in half. Stretch with the back of a knife. Place a portion of chicken livers at one end of each bacon rasher, roll up and set aside.

Roll the prepared pastry out to a long strip about 26 cm (10 inches) wide and 38 cm (15 inches) long. Cut in half lengthways and then evenly place six of the bacon rolls down one side of each pastry strip, about 1 cm (½ inch) from the edge. Brush the pastry lightly with the egg and milk, down the edges and between each bacon roll, then fold the pastry over the bacon rolls to cover and seal down the opposite edge. Using a sharp knife, cut between each roll and seal round the other two edges. Knock up the edges with the blade of a knife.

Place the pasties on a wetted baking tray. Make two cuts across the top of each pasty and then brush with egg and milk, place above centre of a hot oven (220°C, 425°F or Gas No. 7) and bake for 20–25 minutes or until the pastry is golden brown.

Serve with a salad.

Dutch Apple Cake

Serves 6 Time taken 1 hour
Cool before serving

175 g (6 oz) self-raising flour
1 level teaspoon baking powder
75 g (3 oz) castor sugar

1 large egg
6 tablespoons milk
25 g (1 oz) melted butter

For the Topping
25 g (1 oz) melted butter
450 g (1 lb) cooking apples

75 g (3 oz) castor sugar
1 level teaspoon cinnamon

Sift the flour and baking powder into a bowl and add the sugar. Mix together the egg, milk and melted, but not hot, butter. Pour into the centre of the flour and, using a wooden spoon, beat the mixture gently, gradually drawing in the flour. Then beat thoroughly for a moment to make a smooth, fairly soft, mixture. Spoon the mixture into a small, well-buttered roasting tin, or shallow baking tin, approximately 28 by 18 cm (11 by 7 inches). Spread the mixture level, and prepare the topping.

Brush the top all over with the melted butter. Peel, core and thinly slice the apples. Arrange the apples over the surface of the cake, laying them in overlapping rows for the prettiest effect. Mix together the castor sugar and cinnamon and then generously sprinkle the mixture over the apple slices. Place in the centre of a hot oven (200°C, 400°F or Gas No. 6) and bake for 35 minutes, or until the apples are tender and golden.

Cool, then cut in squares.

Streusel Cake

Makes one 23-cm (9-inch) cake Time taken 1 hour
Cool before serving

225 g (8 oz) self-raising flour
1 level teaspoon baking powder
75 g (3 oz) butter

75 g (3 oz) castor sugar
1 egg
1·5 dl ($\frac{1}{4}$ pint) milk

For the Streusel Topping
25 g (1 oz) self-raising flour
50 g (2 oz) soft brown sugar

25 g (1 oz) melted butter

This delicious cake with a crunchy, sweet topping is quickly and easily made at short notice.

Sift together the flour and baking powder. Add the butter, cut in pieces, and rub into the mixture. Stir in the sugar. Lightly mix the egg and milk and add all at once. Stir with a wooden spoon until the ingredients are blended, then beat well to get a smooth batter. Spoon into a greased, 23-cm (9-inch), loose-bottomed cake tin or spring-clip sided cake tin. Spread the mixture level.

Mix the flour and sugar for the topping in a basin. Add the melted, but not hot, butter. Mix, using a fork, until crumbly. Sprinkle all over the top of the cake. Place in the centre of a moderately hot oven (190°C, 375°F or Gas No. 5) and bake for 40 minutes. Allow to cool for 5 minutes then remove from the tin. Leave until cold.

17 Cakes, Teabreads & Biscuits

Successful cakes are the direct result of careful preparation and accurate baking. Collect and weigh out all the ingredients to be used before starting. Bring fat and eggs out of the refrigerator or cold larder well in advance.

Creamed Mixture

The temperature of the ingredients is important when you mix these cakes. Fat which is too cold will not cream easily; this particularly applies to butter. Cold eggs will quickly curdle a creamed butter and sugar mixture and the cake will lose in lightness and texture. To avoid this always bring the fat and eggs out of the refrigerator or cold larder some time in advance. While weighing out or preparing other ingredients, fill the mixing bowl you are going to use with warm water and place the eggs in it to warm them. By the time everything else is ready, the eggs will be the right temperature for cracking and the bowl pleasantly warm when the fat and sugar are put into it for creaming. Any additional ingredients such as fruit and nuts should be prepared ready for use. Fruit should be cleaned, and glacé fruits such as cherries rinsed in warm water to remove the outer syrupy coating, then halved and patted dry. Always mix any added fruit with a little of the flour taken from the measured ingredients.

Before starting on the recipe, have all cake tins lined and ready.

Set the oven to the correct temperature and preheat for at least 15 minutes. Make sure the oven shelves are at the correct level; small cakes can be baked a little above centre, sandwich layer cakes on the centre shelf, and larger cakes below centre. The success of these cakes lies largely in the preparation of the recipe. Butter or margarine and sugar should be well creamed until light and fluffy – this takes a good 5 minutes. This creaming incorporates some air and it breaks down the sugar crystals by friction. The warmed eggs should be added a little at a time. Each addition should be well beaten in before adding the next; the time taken to add the eggs should be about 5 minutes. If the mixture is well-creamed and the eggs beaten in slowly, all the egg can be incorporated without curdling the mixture. The flour should be added in two additions, each one gently folded in with the cutting edge of a metal spoon. This retains as much of the air in the mixture as possible.

When baked, layer cakes should be evenly brown and slightly shrunk from the sides of the tin. Test by touching the centre with the tips of the fingers. The cakes should feel firm to the touch and the marks of the finger should disappear. When larger cakes are taken out of the oven and held close to the ear, there should be no hissing sound. Experience is needed to check by this method, and generally the best test is to see if a warmed skewer pushed into the centre of the cake comes out clean. If it does the cake is ready. Warm the skewer by first placing it down the side of the cake, between the tin and paper.

Whisked Egg and Sugar Mixture

A whisked egg and sugar mixture for a sponge should be placed over a saucepan half-filled with hot, but not boiling, water. The eggs and sugar should be whisked until the mixture leaves a 'trail'. This means that when a little of the mixture is dropped from the whisk on to the surface of the remainder in the bowl, it should hold its shape for a moment before disappearing into the rest of the mixture.

When flour is added to the mixture it should be gently folded in with the sharp cutting edge of a metal spoon. Only mix for long enough to blend the ingredients – over-mixing after the flour is added can be disastrous with whisked sponges.

A newly baked cake is fragile. Allow layer cakes to stand for 1–2 minutes before turning out. Larger rich fruit cakes may be left in the tin until cold; this helps to keep the crust soft. In any case, the paper round a rich cake, particularly a Christmas cake, should be left on until ready for using or icing. No cake should be stored before it is quite cold; then place in tightly lidded tins. The flavour of a Christmas cake will be greatly improved if the surface is pricked over with a skewer and the cake sprinkled with rum or brandy before storing. If they are very large, wrap fruit cakes in foil for storing.

Note: All tins used for baking are standard size. Metric measures and equivalent sizes can be found on page viii.

Victoria Sponge Cake

Makes one 20-cm (8-inch) cake Time taken 1 hour

100 g (4 oz) butter or margarine
100 g (4 oz) castor sugar
2 large/standard eggs

few drops vanilla essence
100 g (4 oz) self-raising flour

For perfect results all ingredients should be at room temperature before starting.

Cream the butter or margarine and sugar together for a full 5 minutes, until light and creamy. Lightly mix the eggs and vanilla essence. Beat the eggs into the creamed mixture a little at a time; beat well after each addition. Add a little of the sifted flour along with the last few additions of egg. Using a metal spoon, fold in the remaining flour.

Place the mixture in a greased and lined 20-cm (8-inch) sandwich cake tin and smooth level. Place in the centre of a very moderate oven (170°C, 325°F or Gas No. 3) and bake for 35–40 minutes. Allow the cake to cool in the tin for 2 minutes, then turn out.

When cold fill with buttercream or fresh cream and jam.

Chocolate Layer Cake

Makes one 18-cm (7-inch) layer cake Time taken 1½ hours

100 g (4 oz) self-raising flour
1 rounded tablespoon cocoa powder
2 tablespoons boiling water
100 g (4 oz) butter

100 g (4 oz) castor sugar
2 large/standard eggs
½ teaspoon vanilla essence

For the Chocolate Frosting
75 g (3 oz) icing sugar
25 g (1 oz) cocoa powder
40 g (1½ oz) butter

2 tablespoons water
50 g (2 oz) castor sugar

Sift the flour on to a plate and set aside. Measure the cocoa powder into a small basin, add the boiling water and stir until the mixture is smooth and blended. Cream the butter and sugar until light and then beat in the chocolate mixture. Lightly mix the eggs and vanilla essence, then beat into the creamed mixture, a little at a time. Add some of the flour, along with the last few additions of egg mixture, then fold in the remaining flour.

Divide the mixture equally between two buttered and lined, 18-cm (7-inch), shallow, sponge cake tins. Spread the mixture evenly and hollow out the centre slightly. Place in the centre of a moderate oven (180°C, 350°F or Gas No. 4) and bake for 25 minutes. Remove from the tins and cool, while preparing the chocolate frosting.

Sift the icing sugar and cocoa powder into a mixing basin. Measure the butter, water and sugar into a saucepan. Set over low heat and stir well, until the sugar has dissolved and the butter melted. Bring just to the boil, then draw off the heat and pour at once into the sifted ingredients. Beat with a wooden spoon until the mixture is smooth; then allow to cool, stirring occasionally, until the frosting is thick enough to coat the back of a wooden spoon.

Spread a little of the frosting between the layers and sandwich together. Pour the remainder over the whole cake, spreading it over with a knife to coat both top and sides. Leave until cold and set firm.

Cherry and Almond Cake

Makes one 20-cm (8-inch) cake   Time taken 2 hours

175 g (6 oz) self-raising flour	175 g (6 oz) butter
pinch salt	175 g (6 oz) castor sugar
100 g (4 oz) ground almonds	3 large/standard eggs
225 g (8 oz) glacé cherries	few drops vanilla essence

Sift the flour and salt together and add the ground almonds. Rinse the cherries in warm water to remove the sugary coating. Cut in half, then pat dry in a clean cloth. Place in a mixing basin and add to 2 tablespoons of the sifted flour mixture. Toss the cherries to coat well and set aside.

Cream the butter and sugar until light. Lightly mix the eggs and vanilla essence, then gradually beat into the creamed butter and sugar. Beat each addition of egg in well, before adding the next. Add a little of the sifted dry ingredients along with the last few additions of egg. Then, using a metal spoon, fold in the remaining flour and the cherries, and mix to a medium soft consistency.

Spoon the mixture into a 20-cm (8-inch), round, deep cake tin greased and lined with greaseproof paper. Place in the centre of a slow oven (170°C, 325°F or Gas No. 3) and bake for 1½ hours. Allow the baked cake to cool in the tin for 30 minutes before turning out.

Chocolate Swiss Roll with Vanilla Cream

Cuts into 8 slices   Time taken 40 minutes
Fill when cold

50 g (2 oz) self-raising flour	3 large/standard eggs
25 g (1 oz) cocoa powder	90 g (3½ oz) castor sugar

For the Cream Filling

50 g (2 oz) butter or margarine	6 teaspoons cold milk
50 g (2 oz) castor sugar	few drops vanilla essence
4 teaspoons hot water	icing sugar

To make a plain Swiss roll follow the recipe using 75 g (3 oz) self-raising flour and omitting the cocoa.

Preheat the oven to hot (220°C, 425°F or Gas No. 7). Lightly grease a Swiss roll tin approximately 26 by 35 cm (10 by 14 inches) and line lengthwise with a strip of grease-proof paper, cut the width of the base of the tin and long enough to overlap the ends by about 5 cm (2 inches) either end.

Sift the flour and cocoa powder together several times. Sift finally on to a square of greaseproof paper and set aside, in a warm place. Whisk the eggs and sugar together in a mixing basin set over a pan of hot water. Draw the pan of hot water off the heat while whisking and beat the mixture until it is thick and light. Remove the basin from the heat and beat a further 2–3 minutes. Set the basin on a damp cloth to hold it still.

Sift the flour over the surface of the beaten mixture, and, using a metal spoon, gently fold into the mixture. Pour the mixture into the prepared Swiss roll tin and spread evenly, paying particular attention to the corners of the tin. Place above centre in the preheated hot oven and bake for 8–12 minutes or until risen and springy to the touch. Remove from the oven, loosen the sides with a knife and turn the tin over on to a clean tea cloth, lightly sprinkled with castor sugar. Lift off the tin and peel away the lining paper. Using a sharp knife, cut away the crisp edges of the cake. Roll up immediately, rolling the cloth on which the Swiss roll is lying, inside the cake. Set aside until quite cold. To fill a Swiss roll with a cream filling the cake must be allowed to cool first; the cloth inside prevents the cake from sticking together and means that it can be unrolled for filling.

While the cake is cooling, prepare the vanilla cream. Cream the margarine or butter and sugar together until light. Then beat in the hot water, one teaspoonful at a time. This softens the filling. Then beat in the cold milk in the same way. The cold milk will make the filling firm up again but stay light and fluffy. Flavour with vanilla essence. Very gently unroll the cold Swiss roll sufficiently to spread the filling inside. Re-roll neatly, then chill, so that the filling sets firmly. Trim the ends neatly and dust with icing sugar before serving. This same method can be used when filling a plain Swiss roll with fresh whipped cream and fruit; it can then be served as a dessert.

Orange and Walnut Cake

Makes one 18-cm (7-inch) cake Time taken 2 hours
Decorate when cold

225 g (8 oz) self-raising flour	rind of 1 large orange
¼ level teaspoon salt	25 g (1 oz) chopped mixed peel
175 g (6 oz) butter	50 g (2 oz) chopped walnuts
175 g (6 oz) castor sugar	1 tablespoon orange juice
3 large/standard eggs	

For the Orange Icing
225 g (8 oz) icing sugar   2–3 tablespoons orange juice

Sift together the flour and salt on to a plate and set aside. Cream together the butter and sugar until light. Gradually beat in the lightly mixed eggs and finely grated orange rind. Add a little of the sieved flour along with the last few additions. Using a metal spoon, fold in remaining flour along with the chopped peel, walnuts and orange juice. Spoon the mixture into a greased and lined, 18-cm (7-inch), round, deep cake tin. Spread the mixture level, hollowing out the centre slightly. Place in the centre of a moderate oven (180°C, 350°F or Gas No. 4) and bake for 1¼ hours. Allow baked cake to cool 5–10 minutes in the tin before turning out. Leave until cold before decorating.

Sieve the icing sugar into a mixing basin, add the strained orange juice and mix to a smooth paste. Pour into a small saucepan and warm gently over a low heat beating well until a good pouring consistency is obtained. On no account allow the icing to become too hot, otherwise the finished glaze will be dull rather than shiny. Pour the warm icing over the cake all at once and, using a knife, spread over the top surface and allow to run down the cake sides. Set aside to cool and set firm.

Honey Snap Cake

Makes one 18-cm (7-inch) layer cake Time taken 2 hours
Assemble cake when cold

75 g (3 oz) self-raising flour   100 g (4 oz) castor sugar
3 large/standard eggs

For the Butter Cream
3 egg yolks   225 g (8 oz) softened butter
6 level tablespoons clear honey

For the Honey Snaps
40 g (1½ oz) plain flour   40 g (1½ oz) butter
¼ level teaspoon mixed spice   40 g (1½ oz) castor sugar
¼ level teaspoon ground ginger   3 level dessertspoons clear honey

This cake is a pretty, special-occasion or party-time cake. It is essential that the cake layers, the filling and decoration are all prepared before the cake is finally assembled.

Line the base of two greased 18-cm (7-inch) sponge cake tins with buttered greaseproof paper and dust the insides of both tins with a little extra flour. Sift the flour on to a plate or square of paper and set aside. Crack two of the eggs and one yolk into a medium-sized mixing basin. Reserve the egg white. Add the sugar to the eggs and place the bowl over a saucepan half-filled with hot water. Whisk until the mixture is thick and light – takes about 6–8 minutes – then remove the bowl from the heat. Whisk the reserved egg white until stiff, then, using a metal spoon, fold into the beaten egg mixture with the sifted flour.

Dividing the mixture equally, pour into the two prepared tins. Place in the centre of a moderately hot oven (190°C, 375°F or Gas No. 5) and bake for 20 minutes. Cool in the tins for 5 minutes before turning out.

To make the butter cream, place the egg yolks in a basin and whisk lightly to mix. Put the honey into a small pan and, over a very low heat, bring slowly to the boil. Boil for 1 minute only, then remove from the heat and pour the honey in a steady stream on to the egg yolks, whisking all the time. Continue whisking until the mixture becomes cool and thick, then whisk in the soft (but not melted) butter, a little at a time. Set the butter cream aside until required, but do not chill.

For the honey snaps, sift the flour and spices on to a square of paper and set aside. Measure the butter, sugar and honey into a small pan and, over a very low heat, melt the ingredients, stirring until blended. Draw the pan off the heat and stir in the flour mixture. Line two baking trays with silicone paper and then drop small tea-spoonfuls of the mixture about 5 cm (2 inches) apart on to the lined tins. Bake the honey snaps, one tray at a time, above centre of a moderately hot oven (190°C, 375°F or Gas No. 5) for 7–10 minutes, or until beginning to brown at the edges. Remove from the oven and allow to cool slightly, then slide a knife underneath and lift off, rolling the honey snaps around greased cream-horn tins or the thin, greased handle of a wooden spoon. Leave a few moments then remove.

Sandwich together the cake layers with a little of the butter cream and then spread the remainder smoothly over and around the sides of the cake until completely covered. Reserve best honey snaps for decoration, then finely crush 6 or 8 of the remainder between sheets of greaseproof paper. Press these crumbs round the sides of the cake and arrange the reserved snaps evenly over the top of the cake, cart-wheel fashion.

Fresh Gooseberry Cake

Serves 6 Time taken 1½ hours

450 g (1 lb) green gooseberries

For the Crumble Topping

100 g (4 oz) self-raising flour	1 tablespoon water
75 g (3 oz) castor sugar	icing sugar
75 g (3 oz) butter	

For the Cake Base

175 g (6 oz) self-raising flour	2 eggs
pinch salt	½ teaspoon vanilla essence
100 g (4 oz) butter	milk to mix
100 g (4 oz) castor sugar	

This attractive fresh fruit cake comes from Germany. The sharpness of the fruit combines perfectly with the sweet cake mixture.

Top and tail the gooseberries. Wash the fruit and pat dry. For the crumble topping, sift the flour into a mixing basin and add the sugar. Add the butter in pieces and rub into the mixture until fine and crumbly. Set aside while preparing the cake base.

Sift the flour and salt on to a plate. Cream the butter and sugar in a mixing basin until soft and light. Lightly mix the eggs and vanilla essence and beat into the creamed mixture a little at a time. Add a little of the sifted flour along with the last few additions of egg. Using a metal spoon, gently fold in the remaining sifted flour and sufficient milk to make a medium soft consistency.

Spoon the mixture over base of a buttered 20- or 23-cm (8- or 9-inch), round, deep cake tin. Choose one with a loose base or with spring-clip sides. Spread cake mixture evenly and cover with the prepared gooseberries.

Using a fork stir the tablespoon of water into the crumble topping. Stir until the mixture clings together in larger lumps. Sprinkle the crumble topping over the gooseberries to cover them. Place the cake in the centre of a moderate oven (180°C, 350°F or Gas No. 4) and bake for 1 hour. Allow the cake to cool before removing from the tin. Sprinkle the surface with icing sugar and serve.

Genoese Sponge with Vanilla Icing

Makes one 18-cm (7-inch) layer cake Time taken 45 minutes
Ice when cold

90 g (3½ oz) plain flour	100 g (4 oz) castor sugar
3 large/standard eggs	40 g (1½ oz) melted butter

For the Icing

225 g (8 oz) icing sugar	2 tablespoons milk
25 g (1 oz) butter	¼ teaspoon vanilla essence

For the Filling

jam or soft fruit	1·5 dl (¼ pint) whipped cream

Sift the flour twice and set aside ready on a square of greaseproof paper. Make sure the butter is melted and warm but not hot. Grease two 18-cm (7-inch) sponge cake tins and line the base of each with a circle of greaseproof paper.

Crack the eggs into a mixing basin and add the sugar. Place the basin over a saucepan half filled with hot water and whisk the mixture until very thick and light. Remove from the heat and whisk for a further few minutes until cool. Sift the flour over the surface and, using a metal spoon, very gently fold into the mixture, taking care not to beat the mixture. When the flour is half folded in, add the warm melted butter. Continue to blend the mixture until all the ingredients are evenly mixed.

Divide the mixture equally between the two prepared cake tins and spread level. Place in the centre of a moderately hot oven (190°C, 375°F or Gas No. 5) and bake for 20 minutes, or until well risen and firm. Remove from the tins and allow to cool before preparing the icing.

Sift the icing sugar into a bowl. Cut the butter in pieces and place in a saucepan along with the milk and vanilla essence. Stir over gentle heat until the butter has melted, but do not overheat. Pour at once into the centre of the icing sugar and mix gently to make a smooth, thick, coating icing. If the mixture is too thick, add an extra teaspoon of boiling water. Sandwich the cake layers with jam or soft fruits and whipped cream, then quickly pour the icing over the top of the cake.

Leave to set before serving.

Dundee Cake

Makes one 20-cm (8-inch) cake Time taken 3 hours

275 g (10 oz) plain flour	225 g (8 oz) soft brown sugar
1½ level teaspoons baking powder	4 large/standard eggs
½ level teaspoon salt	rind of 1 lemon
50 g (2 oz) ground almonds	350 g (12 oz) sultanas
100 g (4 oz) glacé cherries	100 g (4 oz) currants
175 g (6 oz) butter	100 g (4 oz) chopped candied peel
50 g (2 oz) white vegetable fat	18 blanched almond halves

This cake keeps well and improves in flavour after a few days.

Sift together the flour, baking powder and salt. Add the ground almonds and set aside. Rinse the cherries in warm water to remove the sugary coating; cut in half, then pat dry in a clean cloth. Cream together the butter, vegetable fat and sugar until soft and light. Lightly mix the eggs and finely grated lemon rind and gradually beat into the creamed mixture a little at a time. Add a little of the flour along with the last few additions of egg. Using a metal spoon, fold in the remaining flour and then the fruit.

Spoon the mixture into a greased and lined, 20-cm (8-inch), round, deep cake tin. Spread the mixture level and hollow out the centre slightly. Cover with the almond halves arranging them neatly over the surface. Place on the shelf below centre in a very moderate

oven (170°C, 325°F or Gas No. 3) and bake for 1 hour. Lower the
heat to warm (150°C, 300°F or Gas No. 2) and bake for a further
1½ hours. Cool the cake in the tin before turning out.

Frangipane Tarts

Makes 12 Time taken 45 minutes

100 g (¼ lb) rich shortcrust pastry	red jam

For the Filling

50 g (2 oz) butter	3–4 drops vanilla essence
50 g (2 oz) castor sugar	50 g (2 oz) ground almonds
1 egg	1 level teaspoon plain flour

For the Icing

100 g (4 oz) sieved icing sugar	few glacé cherries
hot water to mix	

Roll out the prepared pastry on a lightly floured surface and, using a
6-cm (2½-inch) plain, round cutter, stamp out twelve circles of pastry.
Use these to line twelve tartlet tins. Spoon a tiny blob of jam in the
base of each and set aside while preparing the filling.

Cream the butter and sugar until light. Gradually stir in the lightly
mixed egg and vanilla essence and then stir in the ground almonds and
flour. Place rounded teaspoons of the mixture in each tartlet case and
spread level. Place in the centre of a moderately hot oven (190°C,
375°F or Gas No. 5) and bake for 15–20 minutes. Allow to cool.

Sieve the icing sugar into a basin and stir in sufficient hot water to
make a smooth coating consistency. Spoon a little on to each tart and
decorate with a piece of glacé cherry.

English Madeleines

Makes 8–10 Time taken 1 hour

100 g (4 oz) self-raising flour	2 large/standard eggs
pinch of salt	¼ teaspoon vanilla essence
100 g (4 oz) butter or margarine	1–2 tablespoons milk to mix
100 g (4 oz) castor sugar	

For the Decoration

3 tablespoons seedless raspberry jam	desiccated coconut
or sieved apricot jam	glacé cherries
juice of ½ lemon	

Sift together the flour and salt and set aside. Cream together butter or margarine and sugar until light and fluffy. Lightly mix the eggs and vanilla essence and gradually beat into the creamed mixture, adding a little of the sieved flour if necessary. Fold in half the flour, then the remainder of the flour, with sufficient milk to make a medium soft consistency.

Spoon mixture into 8–10 well-buttered castle or dariole moulds – line the bases with small discs of greaseproof paper. Fill each mould about half full. Arrange the moulds on a baking tray, place in the centre of a moderately hot oven (190°C, 375°F or Gas No. 5) and bake for 15–20 minutes, or until risen and brown. Cool for 5 minutes then loosen the sides and remove the cakes from the tins. Leave to cool.

Cut the tops of the cakes level, so that they will stand upright. Measure the jam and lemon juice into a saucepan. Bring up to the boil, stirring to blend. Boil for ½ minute, then draw off the heat. Spear each cake in turn on a fork and coat the sides and narrow end with the hot raspberry or apricot glaze. As each one is coated, roll in desiccated coconut, then remove from the fork and stand upright, in a paper case. Decorate the top of each one with a piece of glacé cherry.

Chocolate Rum Gâteau

Serves 6 Time taken 1½ hours
Bake a day in advance of serving

150 g (5 oz) plain flour	2 large/standard eggs
25 g (1 oz) cocoa powder	6 tablespoons corn oil
½ level teaspoon salt	6 tablespoons milk
2 level teaspoons baking powder	½ teaspoon vanilla essence
150 g (5 oz) soft brown sugar	

For the Rum Syrup
100 g (4 oz) granulated sugar   2 tablespoons rum
1·5 dl (¼ pint) water

For the Decoration
3 dl (½ pint) double cream   chocolate flakes or curls

Rich enough to serve as a dessert, this cake is a good choice for a dinner party. It is baked, then soaked in a rum syrup and should be made the day before so that it can be left overnight to soak and to allow the rum flavour to develop.

Sift the flour, cocoa powder, salt and baking powder into a large mixing basin. Add the brown sugar and mix well. Crack the egg yolks into a small basin and the whites into a second larger basin. Add the corn oil, milk and vanilla essence to the yolks and mix, using a fork. Pour into the centre of the dry ingredients and, using a wooden spoon, beat well to make a smooth batter. Whisk the egg whites until stiff and fold into the mixture. Pour into a greased and lined, 20-cm (8-inch), deep, round cake tin. Place above centre in a moderate oven (180°C, 350°F or Gas No. 4) and bake for 40–45 minutes. Turn out and cool.

Meanwhile prepare the rum syrup. Measure the sugar and water into a small saucepan and stir over a low heat to dissolve the sugar. Bring up to the boil and simmer for 5 minutes to concentrate the syrup. Draw the pan off the heat and stir in the rum. Stand the cake on a strip of kitchen foil and replace in the original baking tin. The ends of the foil are left over the sides of the tin to help to remove the more fragile soaked cake at a later stage. Prick holes all over the cake top with a skewer, pour the hot rum syrup over it and leave to soak overnight.

When ready to serve, lift the cake gently from the tin using the kitchen foil support. Place on a serving dish. Whisk the cream until thick but not stiff and spoon over the top of the cake. Using a knife, swirl the cream over the top and sides. Decorate with the chocolate flakes or curls, and chill until ready to serve.

Sponge Drops or Fingers

Makes 2 dozen Time taken 30 minutes

50 g (2 oz) plain flour	1 egg white
1 level tablespoon cornflour	50 g (2 oz) castor sugar
2 whole eggs	

Sandwich the sponge drops with jam or lemon curd and lightly whipped cream. Use sponge fingers in desserts, or serve along with fresh fruit compôtes, fruit salad or fruit fool.

Line two or three baking trays with sheets of ungreased grease-proof paper cut to fit. Place them on the trays and fix at the corners with a smear of cooking fat. Sift the flour and cornflour on to a square of greaseproof paper and set aside. Crack the eggs and egg white into a basin and add the sugar. Set the basin over a saucepan half-filled with hot water. Whisk the mixture until thick and light; this should take about 6–8 minutes. The eggs and sugar should be well-beaten so that when a little of the mixture is allowed to fall back off the whisk into the remainder in the basin, it will remain on the surface for a moment before disappearing back into the mixture. Sift the flour over the surface and, using a metal spoon, fold gently but evenly into the mixture.

Spoon the mixture into a cotton or nylon piping bag fitted with a 1-cm (½-inch), plain piping tube. Pipe rounds of the mixture about 3·5 cm (1½ inches) in diameter on to the prepared trays. For sponge fingers, pipe lengths of about 8·5 cm (3½ inches). Sprinkle the sponge drops or fingers with a little castor sugar for a crisp sugary surface. Place in a moderate oven (180°C, 350°F or Gas No. 4) and bake for 10–12 minutes or until crisp and lightly browned. Remove from the heat, draw the sheet of paper with the sponge fingers still attached off the tray and place over a damp cloth. After a few moments the sponge drops will peel off the paper. Cool, then store in an airtight tin.

Pineapple Sponge

Serves 6 Time taken 40 minutes
Fill when cold

75 g (3 oz) plain flour	75 g (3 oz) castor sugar
2 large/standard eggs	

For the Filling

little sherry	1 level teaspoon castor sugar
1 (450 g) (1 lb) tin crushed pineapple	1 slightly rounded teaspoon
6 prunes, soaked overnight	arrowroot

This baked sponge flan ring can also be filled with strawberries or raspberries and glazed for a summer dessert.

Before starting, well-butter a 20-cm (8-inch) sponge flan tin and dust with a mixture of equal quantities flour and castor sugar. Sift the flour on to a square of greaseproof paper and set aside. Crack the eggs into a large basin and add the sugar. Place over a saucepan half-filled with hot water – draw the saucepan off the heat – and whisk the eggs and sugar until thick and light. Remove the bowl from the heat and whisk a further few moments. Then sift the flour evenly over the surface of the mixture and, using a metal spoon, fold in very gently. Pour into the prepared sponge flan tin and spread evenly.

Place in the centre of a moderate oven (180°C, 350°F or Gas No. 4) and bake for 20 minutes. Allow to cool for 5 minutes then loosen the sides, tap the base sharply and turn out. Leave until cold before preparing the filling.

Sprinkle the base of the sponge flan with a little sherry. Drain the pineapple from the tin reserving the juice, and spoon the pineapple over the sponge flan. Simmer the soaked prunes in the liquid they soaked in, until tender, then drain and remove stones. Arrange the prunes around the edge of the sponge flan – the dark colour makes an attractive contrast to the pineapple. Measure the pineapple juice, it should be about 1·5 dl ($\frac{1}{4}$ pint), into a saucepan. Add the sugar and the arrowroot, blended with a little water to make a smooth paste. Stir over low heat until the syrup has come up to the boil and thickened. Spoon over the surface of the sponge flan to glaze the fruit and prunes.

Leave until cold, then cut in wedges and serve with cream.

Note: the non-stick sponge flan tins are ideal for this recipe. The sponges turn out perfectly every time.

Scones

Makes 9–12 Time taken 20 minutes

225 g (8 oz) plain flour	40 g (1½ oz) butter
½ level teaspoon salt	40 g (1½ oz) castor sugar
1 level teaspoon bicarbonate of soda	1 egg made up to 1·5 dl (¼ pint) with
2 level teaspoons cream of tartar	milk

The secret of soft light scones is to dust the tin and the scones with flour before baking.

In a large mixing basin sift together the flour, salt, bicarbonate of soda and cream of tartar (or use 4 level teaspoons baking powder). Rub in the butter and stir in the sugar. Lightly mix the egg and milk. Where possible, measure the egg and milk accurately, but otherwise add approximately 4 tablespoons milk to the egg. Pour the egg and milk into the centre of the dry ingredients.

Using a fork or the blade of a knife, quickly mix to a dough. The mixture should be soft but not sticky. Turn out on to a lightly floured working surface and pat or roll out to a thickness no less than 1 cm (½ inch) – never roll scone dough too thinly. Cut into squares with a floured sharp knife, or stamp out rounds with a 5-cm (2-inch) floured cutter. You should get about 9–12 scones depending on thickness – use up all the trimmings.

Place the scones on a floured baking tray and dust the scones with flour. Place near the top of a hot oven (220°C, 425°F or Gas No. 7) and bake for 10 minutes or until risen and brown.

Serve warm with butter and jam.

Drop Scones

Makes 24 Time taken 20 minutes

100 g (4 oz) plain flour
pinch salt
1 level teaspoon bicarbonate of soda
1½ level teaspoons cream of tartar

25 g (1 oz) castor sugar
1 large/standard egg
1·5 dl (¼ pint) milk

Sieve the flour, salt, bicarbonate of soda, cream of tartar and sugar
into a mixing bowl. Make a hollow in the centre of the flour mixture
and crack in the egg. Using a wooden spoon, gradually mix in the
milk. Stir thoroughly from the centre of the bowl, gradually drawing
in the flour from around the outer edges.

Place a large, heavy, flat-bottomed frying pan over moderate heat to
heat through thoroughly. Rub over the surface with a piece of kitchen
paper dipped in a little salad oil .Place tablespoons of the batter on to
the hot surface – only about 3–4 at a time, spaced apart. When
bubbles have risen to the surface and the underside is brown, loosen
the underside with a spatula and turn them over. Cook for a minute
or so on the second side, then remove from the pan and cool between
folded clean tea cloth. Rub the surface of the hot pan with the oiled
paper again and continue to make the scones until all the batter is
used up.

Serve with butter and jam.

Plain Irish Soda Bread

Makes 1 loaf Time taken 45 minutes

450 g (1 lb) plain flour
1 level teaspoon salt

½ level teaspoon bicarbonate of soda
3 dl (½ pint) sour milk

Quick and easy to make, Irish soda bread is delicious for tea. Serve it
sliced with lots of butter.

Sieve the flour, salt and bicarbonate of soda into a bowl. Make a
well in the centre and pour in all the milk. Using a fork, mix to a
rough dough in the basin, then turn out on to a working surface and
knead lightly about three turns. Turn the dough smooth side up,
flatten with the hand a little and place on a lightly floured baking tray.

Using a floured, sharp knife, cut the dough from one side to the
other in the form of a cross. Cut almost through to the base, dividing
the bread into four portions. Place above centre in a moderate oven
(180°C, 350°F or Gas No. 4) and bake for 25–30 minutes or until

done. To test if cooked, turn and tap the base, a hollow sound indicates that the bread is ready. Place on a wire cooling tray; if a soft crust is preferred, wrap in a clean damp cloth.

Sweet Irish Soda Bread

Makes 1 loaf Time taken 45 minutes

450 g (1 lb) plain flour
1 level teaspoon salt
½ level teaspoon bicarbonate of soda
25 g (1 oz) butter

100 g (4 oz) cleaned currants
1 teaspoon castor sugar
3 dl (½ pint) sour milk

Proceed as above, rubbing in the butter to the dry ingredients, then add the currants, sugar and sour milk. Mix and knead to a dough, then mark and bake as above.

Cranberry Bread

Makes 1 large loaf Time taken 1¼ hours
Bake in advance

225 g (½ lb) fresh cranberries
350 g (12 oz) self-raising flour
rind of 1 orange
2 large/standard eggs
juice of 1 orange

½ level teaspoon salt
175 g (6 oz) castor sugar
50 g (2 oz) melted butter
50 g (2 oz) chopped walnuts

Pick over the cranberries and chop coarsely. Sift together the flour and salt. Add the sugar and finely grated orange rind. Mix thoroughly and make a well in the centre of the ingredients. Add the eggs, orange juice and melted butter. Mix well and then fold in the chopped walnuts and cranberries.

Spoon the mixture into a greased and lined 23 × 13 × 5-cm (9 × 5 × 2-inch) loaf pan, and spread level. Place in the centre of a moderate oven (180°C, 350°F or Gas No. 4) and bake for 1 hour. Remove from the tin and allow to cool.

Allow to stand for 24 hours, then serve, sliced and buttered.

Gingerbread

Cuts into 24 squares   Time taken 1½ hours   Bake in advance

225 g (8 oz) plain flour
½ level teaspoon salt
1 level teaspoon bicarbonate of soda
3 level teaspoons ground ginger
1 level teaspoon ground cinnamon
75 g (3 oz) white cooking fat
100 g (4 oz) soft brown sugar
100 g (4 oz) black treacle

100 g (4 oz) golden syrup
2 large/standard eggs
6 tablespoons milk
50 g (2 oz) sultanas
50 g (2 oz) chopped preserved ginger
25 g (1 oz) chopped candied peel
50 g (2 oz) blanched flaked almonds

Make gingerbread a few days in advance; two or three days in a closed tin or wrapped in foil improves the flavour.

Sift the flour, salt, bicarbonate of soda, ginger and cinnamon into a bowl and set aside. Cut the fat up into a saucepan and add the sugar, treacle and syrup – approximately 2 rounded tablespoons of both treacle and syrup. Warm gently over low heat until the fat has just melted and the ingredients are blended. Draw off the heat and set aside until the hand can be held comfortably against the sides of the pan. Lightly mix the eggs and milk and stir into the contents of the saucepan. Mix together thoroughly.

Pour the egg and syrup mixture into the centre of the flour and mix with a wooden spoon until smooth and glossy. Stir in the sultanas, ginger and candied peel. Pour into a 20-cm (8-inch) square cake tin, which has been greased and lined at the bottom with a greased paper. Sprinkle with the flaked almonds. Place in the centre of a moderately low oven (170°C, 325°F or Gas No. 3) and bake for 1 hour. Do not open the oven for the first 40 minutes or the cake may subside in the middle. Turn on to a rack and cool.

Plum Bread

Makes 2 large loaves   Time taken 2½ hours   Bake in advance

175 g (6 oz) sultanas
100 g (4 oz) glacé cherries
350 g (12 oz) currants
175 g (6 oz) seedless raisins
700 g (1½ lb) self-raising flour
2 level teaspoons salt

1 level teaspoon mixed spice
225 g (½ lb) butter
100 g (4 oz) chopped mixed peel
350 g (12 oz) castor sugar
6 dl (1 pint) warm milk
50 g (2 oz) fresh yeast

Old-fashioned plum bread is fruity and rich. This bread keeps well and is better kept several days before serving.

Grease two large 23 × 13 × 5-cm (9 × 5 × 2-inch) loaf tins and line the base of each with a strip of greased paper. Wash and thoroughly pat dry, the sultanas, cherries, currants and raisins. Cut the glacé cherries in half. Sift the flour, salt and mixed spice into a large mixing basin. Rub in the butter, add the prepared fruit, mixed peel and all but one teaspoon of sugar.

Dissolve the teaspoon of sugar in the warm milk and crumble the fresh yeast over the surface. Stir to mix. Make a well in the centre of the dried ingredients, add the yeast liquid all at once and gradually stir the mixture together to make a fairly stiff dough. Divide the mixture equally between the two prepared tins and spread evenly. Place in the centre of a low oven (150°C, 300°F or Gas No. 2) and bake for 2 hours. Allow the baked loaves to cool in the tins.

Serve sliced and buttered.

Note: this bread is not put to rise; the yeast is added to improve the keeping quality.

Banana Bread

Makes 1 large loaf Time taken 2 hours Bake in advance

225 g (8 oz) self-raising flour	25 g (1 oz) chopped walnuts
½ level teaspoon salt	100 g (4 oz) glacé cherries
100 g (4 oz) butter	2 large/standard eggs
175 g (6 oz) castor sugar	450 g (1 lb) ripe bananas
100 g (4 oz) sultanas or seedless raisins	

Sift the flour and salt into a large mixing basin. Add the butter, cut into pieces, and rub into the dry ingredients, until the mixture is crumbly and the fat evenly distributed. Add the sugar, sultanas or seedless raisins, the walnuts and the glacé cherries, which have been rinsed under warm water to remove the outer sugar coating, then patted dry and cut in half. Mix together and hollow out the centre of the ingredients.

Crack the eggs into the hollow, peel and mash the bananas with a fork and add to the eggs. Using a wooden spoon, beat all the ingredients thoroughly to a soft consistency – no extra liquid will be required.

Line a buttered, 23 × 13 × 5-cm (9 × 5 × 2-inch) loaf tin with a strip of greaseproof paper cut to cover the base and opposite ends. Pour in the mixture and spread evenly. Place in the centre of a moderate oven (180°C, 350°F or Gas No. 4) and bake for 1½ hours. Cool before removing from the tin.

This bread keeps well and is even nicer after a day or so. Serve sliced and buttered.

Macaroons

Makes 24 Time taken 30 minutes

100 g (4 oz) ground almonds	¼ teaspoon almond essence
175 g (6 oz) castor sugar	granulated sugar
2 small egg whites	24 blanched almond halves

Do not stir in too much egg white, the mixture for macaroons should be fairly stiff. A soft mixture runs very flat during baking.

Measure ground almonds and sugar into a mixing basin, beat in the lightly mixed egg whites a little at a time, then add the almond essence. Beat well to make a fairly smooth, stiff mixture.

Rub two baking trays with a little vegetable fat. Dust with flour, then bang the trays to get rid of excess flour. Alternatively, the trays can be lined with rice paper.

Spoon the mixture into a cotton or nylon piping bag fitted with a 1-cm (½-inch) plain piping tube, then pipe on to the prepared baking trays in moulds each the size of a 2p piece. Sprinkle with sugar and decorate each with an almond.

Place in the centre of a moderate oven (180°C, 350°F or Gas No. 4) and bake for 15 minutes or until firm. Cool for a few minutes, loosen the base of each one with a spatula and then lift off the tray.

Brandy Snaps

Makes 24 Time taken 2 hours

50 g (2 oz) plain flour	150 g (5 oz) castor sugar
½ level teaspoon ground ginger	50 g (2 oz) golden syrup
50 g (2 oz) butter	

For the Filling

3 dl (½ pint) double cream	2 tablespoons brandy

Sift the flour and ground ginger on to a plate. Blend the butter and sugar, then beat in the syrup, approximately 1 rounded tablespoon. Stir in the flour and ground ginger. Mix to a rough dough, then turn on to a working surface and knead until smooth and creamy. Cover and allow to rest 1 hour before using.

Round up teaspoons of the mixture and place, four at time, on a baking tray lined with a sheet of silicone paper. Flatten slightly with the palm of the hand. (Silicone paper can be bought in almost any household stationery department and is invaluable in a recipe such as this, since the brandy snaps will not stick to the paper. For this reason also, the sheets of paper may be used over and over again.)

Place just above centre in a hot oven (190°C, 375°F or Gas No. 5) and bake for about 10 minutes or until golden brown and bubbling. Remove from the oven and cool a few moments – this allows the mixture to firm up slightly so that the snaps can be lifted from the paper. Quickly slide a knife under each one, turn over and wrap round the greased handle of a wooden spoon – have at least a couple of wooden spoons handy. These brandy snaps will cool and harden while the next are baking. As soon as the snaps have set firm – this takes only a few minutes – slip them off and have the spoons ready for the next ones.

Leave until quite cold before filling. At this stage they can be kept in an airtight tin. Fill only when ready to use, otherwise they may go soft. Whip the cream with the brandy added and, using a nylon piping bag fitted with a rosette tube, pipe the cream into each one.

Petits Fours

Makes 4 dozen Time taken 1 hour

225 g (½ lb) plain flour	essences and colourings
½ level teaspoon baking powder	
225 g (½ lb) unsalted butter	glacé cherries, angelica and walnuts
65 g (2½ oz) sieved icing sugar	icing sugar

These delicious little biscuits look most attractive. Keep them in a tightly lidded tin so that they remain crisp.

Sift the flour and baking powder on to a square of paper and set aside. Place the butter in a mixing bowl and beat well until soft. Add the sieved icing sugar and beat until the mixture is creamy and pale in colour. Gradually beat in the flour.

Divide the mixture into two portions, or more if you intend to make several variations. To each portion add a few drops of essence and a little colouring. A vanilla-flavoured mixture is best left plain, but along with almond essence you could add a few drops of green colouring, and with lemon a few drops of yellow. Colour any mixture only the most delicate pale shade. Beat the mixture until soft enough to pipe.

Spoon each portion of the mixture in turn, into a large nylon or cotton piping bag fitted with a large star tube. Pipe the mixture out in pretty shapes – small circles, stars or coils – on to greased baking trays. Top each one with some small decoration such as pieces of glacé cherries, angelica or walnut. Place the trays of petits fours in a moderately hot oven (180°C, 375°F or Gas No. 5) and bake for 10–15 minutes, or until just tinged with brown.

Remove from the trays and cool on a wire rack. Dust lightly with icing sugar and store in a tin.

Gingernuts

Makes 18 Time taken 45 minutes

100 g (4 oz) plain flour	1 level teaspoon ground mixed spice
¼ level teaspoon salt	50 g (2 oz) butter or margarine
1 level teaspoon baking powder	50 g (2 oz) castor sugar
1 level teaspoon bicarbonate of soda	1 heaped tablespoon golden syrup
1 level teaspoon ground ginger	

Sift together the flour, salt, baking powder, bicarbonate of soda, ginger and mixed spice. Add the butter or margarine cut in pieces and rub into the mixture. Stir in the sugar.

Measure the syrup into a saucepan and warm over low heat until runny. Add the syrup to the other ingredients and mix, first with a spoon and then with the fingers, to make a soft dough. Turn the dough out on to a clean working surface and shape into a long sausage. Cut into eighteen equal-sized pieces.

Using the palms of the hands, round up each piece of dough and roll in castor sugar. Place well apart on greased baking trays – about six on a tray. These gingernuts spread flat while cooking and are best baked in batches. Flatten each gingernut with the base of a tumbler dipped in castor sugar. Place in the centre of a moderately hot oven (180°C, 350°F or Gas No. 4) and bake for 15 minutes.

Allow to cool on the tray for a few moments until crisp, then remove to a cooling tray. Store in an airtight tin.

Buttercream

Time taken 10 minutes

100 g (4 oz) unsalted butter	flavouring
175 g (6 oz) sieved icing sugar	

The following quantities are suitable for filling or frosting an 18–20-cm (7–8-inch) layer cake. Where a softer filling is required beat in 1 tablespoon cream.

Slice up the butter and beat in a warm basin until softened. Add half the sifted icing sugar and beat until the mixture is light in colour. Gradually beat in remaining sugar. Colour and flavour as required.

Vanilla Beat in ¼ teaspoon vanilla essence and leave uncoloured.

Lemon Beat in ¼ teaspoon lemon essence or 1 tablespoon lemon curd. Add a few drops yellow colouring.

Orange Beat in finely grated zest of 1 orange. Colour with a little orange colouring.

Chocolate Break up 50 g (2 oz) plain chocolate and melt in a basin set over a saucepan half-filled with hot water. Cool slightly before beating in the melted chocolate. Add a few drops of vanilla essence.

Coffee Beat in 2 teaspoons coffee essence or 1 heaped teaspoon instant coffee dissolved in 1 teaspoon hot water.

Glacé Icing

Time taken 45 minutes

200–225 g (7–8 oz) icing sugar   stock syrup (see below)

Sufficient to coat the top and sides of an 18–20-cm (7–8-inch) layer cake. Hot water may be used instead of stock syrup for mixing.

Rub the icing sugar through a sieve into a bowl. Stir in sufficient warm, sugar syrup or hot water to mix the icing to a smooth, thick, coating consistency. Add any colouring or flavouring. Use the icing fairly quickly after preparation so that it sets with a nice even surface.

Pour the icing all at once on to the centre of the cake to be iced and, using the flat edge of a knife blade, spread evenly over the surface.

Stock Syrup

Makes 6 dl (1 pint) Time taken 10 minutes
Prepare in advance of using

3 dl (½ pint) water   450 g (1 lb) granulated sugar

This is used by professional bakers for thinning down fondant icing or for mixing glacé icing. Sugar syrup used for mixing gives a smoother, glossier icing and one that will set quickly.

Bring the water to the boil, then stir in the granulated sugar. Stir until the sugar has dissolved, then bring back to the boil and simmer for 1 minute. Strain through muslin and store in a covered jar or bottle.

18 Baking with Yeast

Few things give a cook more satisfaction than a batch of home-made bread or buns fresh from the oven. Now new and up-to-date methods of using yeast make these quite possible for anyone to bake with every success.

For best results use a strong plain flour. Some plain flours are labelled 'strong', but if your grocer does not stock specially labelled flour, use any good quality plain flour. Fresh yeast is most generally known and used for yeast cookery and may be obtained from a local baker's shop. It should be creamy in colour and in large pieces. Dark-coloured crumbly pieces are stale and should not be used. If fresh yeast is unobtainable, dried yeast gives equally good results, if used properly. To reconstitute dried yeast for use in a recipe, dissolve a little sugar (see recipes) in hand-hot water. Sprinkle dried yeast on top and swirl it round. Leave in a warm place for 10 minutes or until frothy, then add to the dry ingredients. Fresh yeast, if placed in a polythene bag, will keep up to 4–5 days in a cool place or 3–4 weeks in a refrigerator. Dried yeast will keep up to 6 months in a tightly lidded tin in a cool place.

Research has shown that the old-fashioned method of creaming fresh yeast with a little sugar is unnecessary. In fact, this high concentration of sugar with the yeast inactivates many of the yeast cells. It is now recommended that the fresh yeast should simply be blended with the warm liquid in the recipe and then stirred into the dry ingredients. All recipes given here use this method. The temperature of the water used with fresh yeast should be warm – a drop on the wrist should feel cool. Water used to reconstitute dried yeast should be slightly hotter, about 40°C (110°F) or hand-hot – this is very important for good results.

Good kneading strengthens a dough and gives a better finished result to the recipe. Turn the dough on to an unfloured working surface, then fold the dough towards you and push down and away using the palm of the hand. Give dough a quarter turn and repeat kneading. Develop a rhythm and continue until the dough feels smooth, firm and elastic, and no longer sticky.

A good texture is obtained by allowing the dough to prove once, then knocking it back and allowing it to prove again after shaping. There is an alternative quick method for so-called 'quick breads' when the dough is allowed to prove for the first time after it is shaped. In this case the dough must be very well kneaded before shaping. This gives quite satisfactory results, but the resulting texture is a little coarser. Where a dough is richer owing to added sugar, eggs, butter or dried fruit, more yeast will be required. Otherwise 15 g ($\frac{1}{2}$ oz) fresh yeast is sufficient to raise up to 450 g (1 lb) flour, and 25 g (1 oz) up to 1·5 kg (3 lb) flour. Honey in white bread and treacle in brown bread may be used instead of sugar.

Yeast pastries are made from a risen white dough. The butter can be worked into the dough by using either a puff pastry method or a flaky pastry method. At all times the dough must be kept cold and handled quickly – warmth is only required for proving these after shaping the pastry.

For ease and convenience when preparing yeast dough, times for rising may be varied to fit in with your own plans:

45–60 minutes in a warm place
1$\frac{1}{2}$–2 hours at room temperature
8–12 hours in a cold room or refrigerator
12–24 hours in a refrigerator

It's important to remember that only extreme heat kills yeast; cold merely retards the growth. Whatever temperature the dough is risen in, it should be constant and it is advisable to enclose the dough in a greased polythene bag, lightly tied, or in a greased saucepan with a lid. This retains the moisture and stops a skin from forming and preventing the dough from rising properly. The dough is sufficiently risen when it has doubled in size and springs back into shape when pressed lightly with a floured finger.

Quick Wheatmeal Loaves

Makes 2 small wheatmeal loaves Time taken 1½–2 hours

225 g (8 oz) strong plain flour
225 g (8 oz) wholemeal flour
1 level teaspoon castor sugar
15 g (½ oz) fresh yeast
  or

2 level teaspoons dried yeast
8 g (¼ oz) white vegetable fat
2 level teaspoons salt
3 dl (½ pint) warm water
cracked wheat

These loaves have an attractive ridged surface which is achieved by pressing portions of the dough close together in each tin. The cracked wheat used for the topping is obtainable from most health food stores.

Mix the flours and salt in a basin. Add the fat and rub into the mixture then hollow out the centre. Blend the fresh yeast with the warm water. If using dried yeast, dissolve the teaspoon of sugar in the hand-hot water, then sprinkle in the dried yeast. Set aside in a warm place until frothy – takes about 10 minutes.

Add the yeast liquid. Using a wooden spoon, mix to a firm dough that leaves the sides of the basin clean. Turn out on to a clean working surface and knead thoroughly to stretch and develop the dough for about 10 minutes. Divide the dough into two pieces. To shape each loaf divide each piece of dough into four and roll each portion into a round, smooth ball using the palms of the hands. This is best done on an unfloured working surface with a little flour on the palms of the hands. Press down firmly at first then ease up. Place all four balls, pressed close together, in a greased 450 g (1 lb) bread tin. Brush the top of both prepared loaves with salt water and sprinkle with cracked wheat. Place the two loaves in a polythene bag. Tie loosely and leave to prove until the dough rises to the tops of the tins.

Place in the centre of a preheated very hot oven (230°C, 450°F or Gas No. 8) and bake for 30 minutes. Remove from the tins and cool on a wire tray.

Wholemeal Bread

Makes 2 large loaves Time taken 2–3 hours

900 g (2 lb) wholemeal flour
3 level teaspoons salt
25 g (1 oz) white vegetable fat
25 g (1 oz) fresh yeast
  or 1 level tablespoon dried yeast

6 dl (1 pint) warm water
1 teaspoon sugar
1 tablespoon black treacle

Mix the flour and salt in a basin. Add the fat and rub into the mixture then hollow out the centre. Blend the fresh yeast with the warm water. If using dried yeast, stir the teaspoon of sugar into the hand-hot water and sprinkle in the dried yeast. Set aside for 10 minutes or until frothy.

Add the yeast liquid to the dry ingredients all at once, together with the treacle. Knead to a rough dough that leaves the sides of the basin clean. Turn out on to a clean working surface and knead to a smooth dough. Shape into a ball and replace in the basin. Place inside a large polythene bag and set aside in a warm place, until the dough has doubled in size.

Turn the risen dough out on to a working surface and knock back. Knead again lightly and then divide into two equal pieces. Round up the pieces and leave to rest for 10 minutes. Flatten each round out to an oval the same depth as the length of the tin, pull and flap to elongate the pieces. Fold the sides over the middle and turn over so that the seam lies underneath. Smooth over the top and tuck in the ends. Place, best side up, in two greased, large, 900 g (2 lb) loaf tins. Replace in the polythene bag and set aside in a warm place and leave until dough has risen to the tops of the tins.

Dust the tops of the loaves with flour. Place in the centre of a very hot oven (220°C, 425°F or Gas No. 7) and bake a large loaf for 30–40 minutes and a smaller loaf for 30 minutes.

White Tin Loaves

Makes 1 large or 2 small loaves Time taken 2–3 hours

15 g (½ oz) fresh yeast	1 level teaspoon sugar
or	450 g (1 lb) strong plain flour
2 level teaspoons dried yeast	2 level teaspoons salt
3 dl (½ pint) warm water	15 g (½ oz) lard

This quantity of flour makes 800 g (1¾ lb) dough and is sufficient to make one large loaf or two small loaves.

Blend the fresh yeast with the warm water. If using dried yeast, dissolve the teaspoon of sugar in the hand-hot water. Sprinkle in the dried yeast and set aside in a warm place until frothy – takes about 10 minutes.

Mix the flour and salt into a large mixing basin and rub in the lard. Pour the yeast liquid into the centre and, using a wooden spoon, mix to a dough, then knead with the hands until the dough leaves the sides of the basin clean. Turn the dough out on to a clean working surface and knead well until firm and no longer sticky – takes about 10 minutes.

Shape the dough into a round ball and replace in the basin. Place inside a large polythene bag. Allow to rise until it has doubled in size and springs back when pressed lightly with a floured finger.

Turn the risen dough on to a lightly floured board and flatten firmly with the knuckles to knock out the air bubbles, then knead again well. The dough is now ready for shaping.

Divide the dough into the quantity required. Leave the dough whole for a large loaf or divide in half for two small loaves. Stretch the dough to an oblong the same depth as the length of the tin. Fold in three and turn it over so that the seam is underneath. Smooth over the top and tuck in the ends. Place carefully in one large, greased 900 g (2 lb) loaf tin or two small, greased, 450 g (1 lb) loaf tins with the seam still underneath. The loaves are now ready to rise or 'prove'. Put the tins inside a greased polythene bag, and set aside until the dough rises to the top of the tins – takes 30–40 minutes at room temperature.

Brush the tops with salt water and place in the centre of a pre-heated, very hot oven (230°C, 450°F or Gas No. 8) and bake for 30–40 minutes for a large tin and 30 minutes for smaller tins. Baked loaves shrink slightly from the sides of the tins and sound hollow when tapped on the base. Remove from the tin and cool on a wire tray.

Malt Bread

Makes 2 small loaves Time taken 2–3 hours

450 g (1 lb) strong plain flour	25 g (1 oz) fresh yeast
1 level teaspoon salt	or
175 g (6 oz) sultanas	1 level tablespoon dried yeast
100 g (4 oz) (4 tablespoons) malt extract	2 dl (¼ pint plus 3 tablespoons) warm water
1 tablespoon black treacle	1 teaspoon castor sugar
25 g (1 oz) butter	

For the Glaze
2 tablespoons each of: milk, castor sugar and water

Sift the flour and salt into a bowl, add the sultanas and make a well in the centre. Measure the malt extract, treacle and butter into a saucepan. Place over low heat and stir until the butter has melted and the mixture is blended. Remove from the heat and cool until warm, so that the hand can be comfortably held against the sides of the pan.

Dissolve the fresh yeast in the warm water. If using dried yeast dissolve the teaspoon of sugar in the hand-hot water and sprinkle in the dried yeast. Leave in a warm place for 10 minutes, or until the mixture is frothy. Add the yeast mixture and malt mixture to the centre of the flour and work to a soft dough that leaves the sides of the bowl clean. Turn the dough out on to a lightly floured working surface. Knead thoroughly for about 5 minutes, adding extra flour if necessary, until the dough is smooth and elastic. Divide the dough in two, flatten slightly and roll up each piece to make a loaf. Place in two small, greased 450 g (1 lb) loaf tins. Place the tins in a large greased polythene bag and leave in a warm place until the dough rises to the tops of the tins – about 1¼ hours at room temperature.

Place the tins in the centre of a hot oven (200°C, 400°F or Gas No. 6) and bake for 40–45 minutes. Measure the milk, sugar and water into a saucepan for the glaze. Dissolve over low heat then boil for 2 minutes. Draw off the heat and brush the hot loaves with the hot glaze. Cool and keep the malt bread for at least 1 day before cutting. Keep the loaves in a closed polythene bag.

Croissants

Makes 12 Time taken 2–3 hours

450 g (1 lb) strong plain flour	2·5 dl warm water (½ pint,
2 level teaspoons salt	less 4 tablespoons)
25 g (1 oz) white vegetable fat	1 teaspoon castor sugar
25 g (1 oz) fresh yeast	1 egg
or	100–175 g (4–6 oz) butter
1 level tablespoon dried yeast	beaten egg and milk

Sift together the flour and salt into a basin, rub in the fat and hollow out the centre of the ingredients. Dissolve the fresh yeast in the warm water. If using dried yeast, dissolve the sugar in the hand-hot water and sprinkle in the dried yeast. Stir to mix, then leave to stand in a warm place until frothy.

Add the yeast mixture to the flour along with the lightly mixed egg. Mix to a rough dough, then turn out on to a clean working surface and knead for about 10 minutes until the dough feels smooth and is no longer sticky. Roll the dough to a rectangle about 45 by 15 cm (18 by 6 inches), taking care to keep the corners straight.

Beat the butter with a knife until pliable, then spread evenly on a plate and divide into three portions. Mark the pastry into three and place one-third of the butter in small pieces over the top two-thirds of the pastry. Fold the lower, uncovered third of the dough up over the centre, and the top down over both. Seal the edges with a rolling pin and give pastry a half turn. Allow to rest for 10 minutes. Repeat with the remaining butter, then leave the dough to rest in the refrigerator for 1 hour.

Roll the dough out to a large rectangle about 54 cm (21 inches) long and 35 cm (14 inches) wide. Trim the edges neatly with a knife and cut in half lengthwise. Cut each strip into six triangles – the base of each should be about 15 cm (6 inches) long. Brush each triangle with beaten egg and milk, then roll up loosely starting with the wide side, rolling towards the point and finishing with the tip underneath. Shape into crescents and place on ungreased baking trays – allow about six per tray. Brush the croissants with egg and milk and leave at room temperature for about 30 minutes, or until slightly risen and puffy. Brush again with egg and milk, place in the centre of a very hot oven (220°C, 425°F or Gas No. 7) and bake for 20 minutes.

To reheat, place the croissants on a baking tray in a hot oven (200°C, 400°F or Gas No. 6) for 10 minutes. Serve warm.

Fruit Plait

Makes 2 small loaves Time taken 2–3 hours

450 g (1 lb) strong plain flour
50 g (2 oz) castor sugar
25 g (1 oz) fresh yeast
    or
1 level tablespoon dried yeast
2·5 dl (scant ½ pint) warm mixed milk and water
¼ level teaspoon mixed spice

½ level teaspoon ground cinnamon
½ level teaspoon ground nutmeg
1 level teaspoon salt
50 g (2 oz) melted butter
1 large/standard egg
100 g (4 oz) currants
25 g (1 oz) chopped mixed peel

For the Glaze
1 egg
1 tablespoon water

pinch castor sugar
flaked almonds

Sift 100 g (4 oz) of the flour and 1 level teaspoon of the sugar into a bowl. Add the yeast and all the liquid. Stir well and set aside until frothy – takes about 20–30 minutes. Sift the remaining flour and sugar, spices and salt. Add to the yeast batter along with the melted, but not hot, butter, the lightly mixed egg and the fruit. Mix well – it's easiest to do this with your hand; the dough should be soft but not too sticky. Turn out on to an unfloured working surface and knead until smooth and even in texture. Shape into a ball and replace in the basin. Place inside a large polythene bag and set aside in a warm place until the dough has doubled in size and springs back when pressed lightly with a floured finger.

Turn the risen dough on to a lightly floured board and flatten firmly with the knuckles to knock out the air bubbles, then knead well again. Divide the dough into two pieces and then divide each piece into three equal portions. Roll each portion with the hands into ropes 30–35 cm (12–14 inches) long, the ends should be thinner than the middle. Plait the three pieces and pinch the ends to seal them well together. Place each loaf on a greased baking sheet, cover with polythene and put aside to rise again for about 40–50 minutes.

Brush over with a glaze made by mixing together the egg, water and a pinch of sugar. Place in the centre of a preheated hot oven (200°C, 400°F or Gas No. 6) and bake for 20 minutes. Brush again with glaze, sprinkle with the almonds and replace in the oven for a further 20–30 minutes. Cool on a wire tray.

Currant Bread

Makes 1 large loaf Time taken 2–3 hours

450 g (1 lb) strong plain flour	3 dl ($\frac{1}{2}$ pint) warm mixed milk and
1 teaspoon salt	water
25 g (1 oz) castor sugar	1 teaspoon castor sugar
25 g (1 oz) fresh yeast	25 g (1 oz) butter
or	100 g (4 oz) currants
1 level tablespoon dried yeast	

Sift the flour and salt into a mixing basin. Add the sugar and stir to mix. Blend the fresh yeast with the warm mixed milk and water. Alternatively, if using dried yeast, stir the teaspoon of sugar into the hand-hot milk and water and sprinkle in the dried yeast. Leave in a warm place for about 10 minutes or until frothy.

Rub the butter into the dry ingredients, add the currants, mix thoroughly and make a well in the centre. Add the yeast liquid and mix to a dough. Turn out on to a clean, working surface and knead for about 10 minutes, until the dough is smooth and elastic. Flatten the dough out to an oblong the same depth as the length of the tin. Fold in three and turn over so that the seam lies underneath. Place in a large greased 900 g (2 lb) loaf tin. Remove any loose currants from the top of the loaf as they are inclined to burn during baking. Place inside a large, greased, polythene bag and set aside in a warm place until the loaf is well-risen and up to the top of the tin. Sprinkle with flour and place in the centre of a very hot oven (220°C, 425°F or Gas No. 7) and bake for 40–45 minutes. Remove from the tin and cool. Serve sliced and buttered.

To make two small loaves Divide the prepared dough in half. Shape and place each piece of dough in a small, greased 450 g (1 lb) bread tin. Cover and leave until risen, then bake as above for 30 minutes.

Poppyseed Rolls

Makes 12 Time taken 2 hours

450 g (1 lb) strong plain flour	3 dl ($\frac{1}{2}$ pint) warm mixed milk and
2 level teaspoons salt	water
25 g (1 oz) butter	1 teaspoon castor sugar
15 g ($\frac{1}{2}$ oz) fresh yeast	beaten egg
or	poppy seeds
2 level teaspoons dried yeast	

If these rolls are made on the previous day or evening, sprinkle them with water, wrap in foil and reheat for about 10 minutes in a hot oven before serving.

Sift the flour and salt into a mixing basin. Add the butter, cut in pieces, and rub into the flour. Make a well in the centre. Blend the fresh yeast with the warm mixed milk and water. If using dried yeast, stir the teaspoon of sugar into the hand-hot mixed milk and water and sprinkle in the dried yeast. Leave in a warm place for about 10 minutes or until frothy.

Stir the yeast mixture into the centre of the dry ingredients and mix to a dough. Turn out on to a clean working surface and knead well, until the dough is smooth. Shape into a ball and replace in the basin. Place inside a polythene bag and set aside in a warm place until doubled in bulk.

Turn the risen dough out on to a floured working surface. Knead lightly and divide into twelve equal pieces. Roll each piece into a round and allow to rest for 10 minutes. Roll out each piece of dough to a rope about 20 cm (8 inches) in length. Tie loosely in a knot. Place on a well-greased baking tray and brush with lightly beaten egg. Cover and leave to rise for 15–20 minutes or until puffy. Sprinkle lavishly with poppy seeds. Place above centre in a very hot oven (220°C, 425°F or Gas No. 7) and bake for 15–20 minutes.

Serve warm with butter.

Aberdeen Butteries

Makes 1–1½ dozen   Time taken 2–3 hours

450 g (1 lb) strong plain flour
2 level teaspoons salt
175 g (6 oz) lard
175 g (6 oz) butter
25 g (1 oz) fresh yeast
  or

1 level tablespoon dried yeast
3 dl (½ pint) warm water
1 level teaspoon castor sugar

These are the most delicious crisp breakfast rolls and a speciality of Aberdeen in Scotland.

Sift together the flour and salt into a mixing basin. On a plate, beat down the lard and butter, beating well with the blade of a knife or spatula to blend the fats thoroughly, then mark evenly into thirds. Add one-third to the sifted flour mixture and rub in, until the mixture is fine, then make a well in the centre. Blend the fresh yeast in a small basin with the warm water. If using dried yeast, dissolve the teaspoon of sugar in the hand-hot water. Sprinkle in the dried yeast and set aside in a warm place until frothy – takes about 10 minutes.

Add the yeast liquid to the flour, mix to a rough dough, turn out on to an unfloured working surface and knead until smooth. Roll out to an oblong, mark into thirds and over the top two-thirds of pastry place another third of remaining fat. Fold the lower third of pastry over the centre and bring the top down over this, seal the edges with the rolling pin, half turn and rest for 10 minutes in a refrigerator. Roll out again to a rectangle, repeating the procedure with remaining fat. Roll and fold once more and keep chilled until ready to use.

To make the butteries Roll the pastry out to about 1 cm (½ inch) in thickness. Trim the sides and, with a sharp knife, cut into approximately twelve-sixteen squares – professional bakers tear the dough into pieces which gives the butteries their irregular shape, but for the home cook it's easier to cut them with a knife.

Place on a greased baking tray and leave in a warm place to prove until puffy. Bake above centre in a very hot oven (220°C, 425°F or Gas No. 7) for 15–20 minutes. Serve freshly baked with butter and marmalade.

Scotch Baps

Makes 6 Time taken 2 hours

225 g (8 oz) strong plain flour
1 level teaspoon salt
15 g (½ oz) fresh yeast
   or
2 level teaspoons dried yeast

1·5 dl (¼ pint) warm mixed milk and
   water
1 teaspoon sugar
25 g (1 oz) butter
milk

Sift the flour and salt together into a large mixing basin and set in a warm place. In a small basin, blend the fresh yeast with the warm mixed milk and water. If using dried yeast, dissolve the teaspoon of sugar in the hand-hot mixed milk and water. Sprinkle in the yeast and set the mixture aside in a warm place until it is frothy – takes about 10 minutes.

Rub the butter into the flour and stir in the yeast liquid. Mix by hand to a rough dough in the basin, then turn out and knead until smooth. Replace the dough in the basin. Place the basin inside a large polythene bag and leave in a warm place until the dough has risen and is twice the size.

Turn the risen dough out and press with the knuckles to knock out the air. Divide the dough into six portions and roll each one into a ball. Using a rolling pin, flatten each ball of dough out to a round bap. Place on a greased baking tray, brush with milk and dust with flour. Leave, covered, in a warm place until risen and puffy. Just before baking, dust the baps well with flour and press a floured thumb into the centre of each one. Bake in a hot oven (200°C, 400°F or Gas No. 6) for 15–20 minutes.

Serve warm and newly baked, or allow them to cool and reheat in a hot oven for about 5 minutes before serving.

English Muffins

Makes 12 Time taken 2 hours

450 g (1 lb) strong plain flour
1 level teaspoon salt
15 g (½ oz) fresh yeast
   or
2 level teaspoons dried yeast

3 dl (½ pint) warm mixed milk and
   water
1 teaspoon castor sugar
1 egg
25 g (1 oz) melted butter

Sift together the flour and salt into a mixing basin and make a well in the centre. Blend the fresh yeast with the warm milk and water. Alternatively, if using dried yeast, stir the sugar into the hand-hot milk and water and sprinkle in the dried yeast. Leave in a warm place for about 10 minutes, or until frothy.

Pour the yeast mixture into the centre of the flour. Add the lightly mixed egg and the melted, but not hot, butter and mix to a dough. Turn out on to a clean working surface and knead until smooth and elastic – takes about 10 minutes.

Replace the dough in the basin. Place inside a large polythene bag and leave in a warm place until doubled in size – about ½–1 hour.

Turn out the risen dough and knead lightly, then pat or roll out to about 1 cm (½ inch) thick and, using a floured cutter, cut into 6–7.5-cm (2½–3-inch) rounds. Use up all the dough, re-rolling as necessary.

Place on *well-floured* baking trays and dust the muffins with flour. Stand in a warm place to rise for another 30 minutes until the muffins look puffy, then place a few at a time in a large, greased, frying pan, and cook gently over low heat, about 6 minutes each side, until golden brown.

Serve hot with butter. These may be served after one or two days, sliced in half and toasted.

Brioche

Makes 12 brioche Time taken 2–3 hours

225 g (8 oz) strong plain flour
½ level teaspoon salt
1 level tablespoon castor sugar
15 g (½ oz) fresh yeast
   or

2 level teaspoons dried yeast
1½ tablespoons warm water
½ level teaspoon castor sugar
2 eggs
50 g (2 oz) melted butter

For the Glaze
1 egg
1 tablespoon water

pinch castor sugar

Mix the flour and salt into a mixing basin and add the tablespoon of sugar. Blend the fresh yeast with the warm water. If using dried yeast, dissolve the ½ level teaspoon castor sugar in the hand-hot water and sprinkle in the dried yeast. Set aside to stand until frothy.

Add the yeast mixture along with the lightly mixed eggs and the melted, but not hot, butter and mix to a soft dough; then turn out on to an unfloured working surface and knead well for about 5 minutes. Shape the dough into a ball and replace in the basin. Place inside a large polythene bag and allow to rise at room temperature for 1–1½ hours.

Well-grease twelve brioche tins or twelve deep bun tins. Turn the risen dough out on to a lightly floured working surface and flatten firmly with the knuckles to knock out the air. Divide the dough into four equal parts and then each of these pieces into three equal parts. Use about three-quarters of each piece to form a ball, using the palm of the hand. Press down hard at first then ease up. This is best done on an unfloured board with a little flour on the palm of the hand. Place each one in a prepared tin. Firmly press a hole in the centre and place the remaining pieces as a knob in the centre. Place the brioche tins on a baking tray, cover and leave to rise for about 1 hour in a warm place until light and puffy.

Brush the risen brioche with a little egg glaze made by mixing together the egg, water and a pinch of sugar. Place in the centre of a preheated, very hot oven (230°C, 450°F or Gas No. 8) and bake for 10 minutes. Serve warm with butter.

Plaited Orange Bread

Makes 1 large loaf Time taken 2–3 hours

450 g (1 lb) strong plain flour	25 g (1 oz) fresh yeast
2 level teaspoons salt	or
25 g (1 oz) castor sugar	1 level tablespoon dried yeast
100 g (4 oz) mixed dried fruit	1·5 dl (¼ pint) warm water
1 egg	1 teaspoon castor sugar
rind and juice of 1 large orange	beaten egg

For the Icing

50 g (2 oz) sifted icing sugar	1–2 tablespoons orange juice
1 teaspoon grated orange rind	

Sift the flour and salt into a mixing basin. Add the sugar and the mixed dried fruit, and hollow out the centre. Blend the fresh yeast with the warm water. If using dried yeast, stir the 1 teaspoon sugar into the hand-hot water and sprinkle in the yeast. Leave in a warm place for about 10 minutes, or until frothy.

Stir the yeast liquid, the lightly mixed egg, orange juice and finely grated orange rind into the centre of the flour. Mix to a rough dough in the basin. Turn out on to a clean working surface and knead well until the dough is smooth and elastic. Replace the dough in the basin, place inside a polythene bag and set aside in a warm place until double in size.

Turn out the risen dough and knead lightly. Roll out the dough to a

13 × 30-cm (5 × 12-inch) rectangle and cut lengthwise into three even strips. Roll each strip slightly to round the edges. Place the strips on a greased baking tray. Pinch one end to seal the strips together, then plait them into a loaf. Seal both ends well by pressing with the fingers. Brush the loaf over with lightly beaten egg. Cover and leave in a warm place until well risen and puffy.

Brush again with beaten egg, then place in the centre of a very hot oven (220°C, 425°F or Gas No. 7) and bake for 25–30 minutes. Spread with icing while the bread is warm. Blend the icing sugar, grated orange rind and sufficient orange juice to make a thick icing. Drizzle over the bread attractively. Leave until cold, then serve sliced and buttered.

Chelsea Buns

Makes about 12 Time taken 2–3 hours

450 g (1 lb) strong plain flour	1 level tablespoon dried yeast
1 level teaspoon salt	1·5 dl (¼ pint) warm mixed milk and
50 g (2 oz) butter	water
25 g (1 oz) fresh yeast	75 g (3 oz) castor sugar
or	2 large/standard eggs

For the Filling

175 g (6 oz) mixed dried fruit	½ level teaspoon mixed spice
50 g (2 oz) soft brown sugar	25 g (1 oz) melted butter

For the Topping

hot water	2 oz (50 g) sifted icing sugar

Sift the flour and salt into a mixing basin, rub in the butter and hollow out the centre of the ingredients. Blend the fresh yeast with the warm mixed milk and water. If using dried yeast, dissolve the sugar in the hand-hot liquid. Sprinkle in the dried yeast and set aside in a warm place until frothy – takes about 10 minutes.

Pour the yeast liquid into the centre of the dry ingredients and add the sugar and lightly mixed eggs. Mix to a dough by hand then turn out on to an unfloured surface and knead thoroughly for about 5 minutes. Gather into a ball and replace in the basin. Place inside a large polythene bag and leave in a warm place to prove until doubled in size.

Turn the risen dough out on to a lightly floured surface, flatten with the knuckles and roll out to an oblong shape about 1 cm (½ inch) thick. Combine together the dried fruit, sugar and mixed spice for the filling. Brush the surface of the dough with melted, but not hot, butter and sprinkle with the fruit mixture.

Roll up the dough like a Swiss roll, then with a sharp knife cut into 2·5–5-cm (1–2-inch) thick slices. Place neatly in rows, cut side up, in a greased baking tin. Place about ·5 cm (¼ inch) apart so that, as they prove and when baked, they will join together. Cover and set in a warm place until puffy. Place in a hot oven (220°C, 425°F or Gas No. 7) and bake for 20–25 minutes.

While hot, top with a glaze made by stirring sufficient hot water into the icing sugar to make a thick coating consistency. This will soften considerably when brushed on the hot buns. Leave until cold, then pull the buns apart.

Swiss Buns

Makes 16 Time taken 2–3 hours

600 g (1¼ lb) strong plain flour	3 dl (½ pint) warm mixed milk and
1 level teaspoon salt	water
65 g (2½ oz) butter	65 g (2½ oz) castor sugar
25 g (1 oz) fresh yeast	1 egg
or	beaten egg and milk
1 level tablespoon dried yeast	

For the Icing
225 g (8 oz) icing sugar   hot water

Sift the flour and salt into a basin. Add the butter cut in pieces and rub into the mixture. Make a well in the centre. Blend the fresh yeast with the warm mixed milk and water. If using dried yeast, stir 1 teaspoon of the sugar into the hand-hot mixed milk and water. Sprinkle in the dried yeast and set aside in a warm place for about 10 minutes until mixture is frothy.

Add the remaining sugar, the egg and the yeast liquid into the centre of the flour mixture. Mix to a rough dough in the basin, then turn out on to an unfloured working surface and knead for a few minutes until the dough is smooth and elastic. Shape into a ball, replace in the basin. Set inside a polythene bag and leave until the dough has risen and doubled in size.

Turn the risen dough out and knock flat with the knuckles. Divide the dough into sixteen equal parts and, using the palms of the hands, shape each one into a ball. Allow to rest for 5 minutes, then shape each piece into a narrow pear shape. Well-grease two 20–21-cm (8–8½-inch) sponge cake tins and fit eight pieces of dough into each tin. Allow a space between each piece of dough and point the narrow ends to the centre. Set aside in a warm place until the buns have risen and are puffy. Dust with flour and place in the centre of a very hot oven (220°C, 425°F or Gas No. 7) and bake for 15–20 minutes or until well-risen and brown. Remove the buns from the tins, keeping the ring of buns together and allow to cool.

Sift the icing sugar into a small basin, and stir in sufficient hot water to make a smooth, coating icing. Pour the icing over the buns, allow to set, then break the buns apart and serve.

London Buns

Makes 12–14 Time taken 2–3 hours

25 g (1 oz) fresh yeast
  or
1 level tablespoon dried yeast
1·5 dl (¼ pint) warm milk
1·5 dl (¼ pint) warm water, less 4
  tablespoons
1 level teaspoon castor sugar
450 g (1 lb) strong plain flour

½ level teaspoon mixed spice
1 level teaspoon salt
50 g (2 oz) castor sugar
100 g (4 oz) currants
50 g (2 oz) chopped mixed peel
50 g (2 oz) melted butter
1 large/standard egg

For the Glaze
50 g (2 oz) castor sugar

4 tablespoons water

Blend the yeast with the warm milk and water, the sugar and 100 g (4 oz) of the flour. Set aside until frothy, about 20–30 minutes. Mix the remaining flour, mixed spice and salt into a mixing basin. Add the sugar, currants and peel. Add the yeast mixture to the dry ingredients, along with the melted, but not hot, butter and lightly beaten egg. Mix to make a fairly soft dough that leaves the sides of the bowl clean. Turn out on to a clean working surface and knead well, until the dough feels firm and elastic and is no longer sticky, takes about 5 minutes. Shape into a ball and replace in the basin. Place inside a large polythene bag. Leave to rise at room temperature for about 1–1½ hours or until the dough has doubled in size.

Turn the risen dough out on to a lightly floured working surface and flatten firmly with the knuckles to knock out the air bubbles. Divide the dough into twelve–fourteen pieces and shape into buns, using the palm of the hand. Press down hard at first, then ease up.

Do this on an unfloured surface with a little flour on the palm of the hand. Place the buns well apart on a lightly floured baking sheet. Place inside a greased polythene bag, and leave to rise until the buns feel springy to the touch – about 30 minutes. Remove from the bag and place in the centre of a preheated hot oven (220°C, 425°F or Gas No. 7) and bake for 20–30 minutes. When the buns are almost baked, prepare the glaze. Measure the sugar and water into a saucepan, dissolve the sugar over low heat then bring up to the boil. Simmer for two minutes, then, when still hot, brush over the newly baked buns twice. Leave to cool on a wire tray.

Hot Cross Buns

Makes 12 Time taken 2–3 hours

450 g (1 lb) strong plain flour	1 level tablespoon dried yeast
1 level teaspoon salt	2·5 dl (½ pint) warm mixed milk and
½ level teaspoon mixed spice	water
½ level teaspoon ground cinnamon	1 teaspoon castor sugar
½ level teaspoon ground nutmeg	1 egg
50 g (2 oz) castor sugar	50 g (2 oz) melted butter
25 g (1 oz) fresh yeast	100 g (4 oz) currants
or	50 g (2 oz) chopped mixed peel

For the Glaze

2 tablespoons milk	2 tablespoons castor sugar
2 tablespoons water	

Sift the flour, salt, spices and sugar into a warm mixing basin. Stir the fresh yeast into the warm mixed milk and water. If using dried yeast, stir the teaspoon of sugar into the hand-hot mixed milk and water. Sprinkle in the dried yeast and leave for about 10 minutes until frothy.

Stir the yeast liquid, egg, melted butter, currants and peel into the centre of the dry ingredients. Mix the ingredients to a soft dough, turn out on to an unfloured surface and knead well until the dough is smooth. Shape into a round and replace in the basin. Set inside a polythene bag and leave in a warm place, covered with a cloth, until it has risen and doubled in size.

Turn out the risen dough, flatten with the knuckles and knead again, lightly. Divide into twelve equal portions and shape into buns. Place on greased baking trays, cover and leave in a warm place until the buns look puffy.

To make the crosses, either slash the buns with a knife or make professional crosses, using a smooth paste made from flour and water. Spoon into a piping bag and pipe a cross on each bun. Bake in the centre of a very hot oven (220°C, 425°F or Gas No. 7) for 15–20 minutes.

To make the glaze, measure the milk, water and sugar into a saucepan. Dissolve the sugar over low heat, then boil for about 2 minutes. Brush this glaze over the buns while both glaze and buns are hot. Serve warm.

Crumpets

Makes 1 dozen Time taken 1½–2 hours

225 g (8 oz) strong plain flour
½ level teaspoon salt
25 g (1 oz) fresh yeast
  or
1 level tablespoon dried yeast

1·5 dl (¼ pint) milk
2 dl (¼ pint plus 4 tablespoons)
  water
1 teaspoon castor sugar

An old-fashioned girdle should be used for cooking these but a thick heavy frying pan will serve quite well. Crumpet rings are hard to find and the best substitute is inexpensive egg poaching rings.

Sift the flour and salt into a mixing basin and make a well in the centre. Blend the fresh yeast with the warm mixed milk and water. If using dried yeast, dissolve the sugar in the hand-hot liquid. Sprinkle in the dried yeast and set aside in a warm place until frothy – takes about 10 minutes.

Pour the yeast liquid into the centre of the flour. Using a wooden spoon, gradually mix in all the flour and beat the mixture to a smooth thick batter. Leave in the basin, covered with a cloth in a warm place for about 30–40 minutes, until the mixture is light and frothy. Pour into a jug, ready for use.

Grease the girdle or frying pan and the rings. Place the girdle over a moderate heat and warm thoroughly. Crumpets will bake more evenly on a well-heated surface. Place on the rings and then half-fill them with the mixture poured in from the jug. Cook over moderate heat for about 5 minutes, until bubbles begin to appear on the surface. Then reduce the heat and cook until the bubbles have burst and the rings can be loosed easily. Slip off the rings and turn the crumpets over to cook for a few minutes on the other side.

Serve generously spread with butter and in the true Scottish fashion, with a sprinkling of salt, or if you prefer, with jam. If the crumpets cool before serving, toast under a hot grill to heat through.

Rum Babas

Makes 12 Time taken 2–3 hours
Bake in advance

225 g (½ lb) strong plain flour	6 tablespoons warm milk
pinch salt	3 eggs
15 g (½ oz) fresh yeast	1 teaspoon castor sugar
or	50 g (2 oz) currants
2 level teaspoons dried yeast	75 g (3 oz) melted butter

For the Rum Syrup

350 g (¾ lb) granulated sugar	1·5 dl (¼ pint) double cream for
6 dl (1 pint) water	serving
juice of 1 lemon	
4 tablespoons rum	

Rum babas are best made in advance. They should be allowed to stale for one day, then they soak up more of the rum syrup.

Grease and flour twelve dariole or castle moulds. Sieve the flour and salt into a large basin and make a well in the centre. Blend the fresh yeast with the warm milk and stir in the lightly beaten eggs. If using dried yeast, stir the teaspoon of sugar into the hand-hot milk and sprinkle in the yeast. Set aside in a warm place for 10 minutes or until frothy. Stir in the eggs.

Add the yeast mixture all at once to the dry ingredients. Sprinkle a little of the flour over the surface, cover with a cloth and leave in a warm place for 20–30 minutes, until the yeast mixture breaks through the surface of the flour. Beat by hand to a smooth batter. Add the currants and then gradually beat in the melted, but not hot, butter. Mix thoroughly and half-fill the prepared moulds with the batter. Place the moulds on a baking sheet, cover and leave in a warm place until the mixture has risen just to the edges of the moulds. Place in the centre of a hot oven (200°C, 400°F or Gas No. 6) and bake for 20–30 minutes. Remove from the moulds and allow to cool. Where possible store overnight to dry out.

To prepare the syrup, place the sugar and water in a saucepan. Stir over low heat to dissolve the sugar and then bring up to the boil. Simmer for 10 minutes, then draw off the heat and add the strained lemon juice and rum. Prick the babas all over with a fine skewer and soak a few at a time in the hot syrup until well saturated. Drain and place each baba in a paper serving case. Slit lengthwise just to the centre and serve filled with whipped cream.

Sugar and Spice Doughnuts

Makes 10 Time taken 2 hours

225 g (8 oz) strong plain flour	15 g (½ oz) fresh yeast
pinch salt	or
50 g (2 oz) butter or margarine	2 level teaspoons dried yeast
5 good tablespoons warm milk	1 egg
½ teaspoon castor sugar	red jam

For the Sugar Coating

75 g (3 oz) castor sugar	½ level teaspoon ground cinnamon

Sieve the flour and salt into a warm mixing basin and rub in the butter or margarine. Blend the yeast with the warm milk. If using dried yeast, stir the sugar in the hand-hot milk and sprinkle in the yeast. Set aside in a warm place until frothy – takes 10 minutes. Add the egg to the yeast liquid and mix lightly. Pour the mixture into the centre of the dry ingredients and mix to a soft dough. Beat thoroughly by hand for 2–3 minutes, then cover and set aside in a warm place until the dough has risen double in size.

Turn the dough out on to a lightly floured working surface and knead lightly. Divide into ten equal pieces. Shape each into a ball. Flatten a little and place about ½ teaspoon red jam in the centre of each. Gather the edges together over the jam, pinch well to seal and turn over on to a greased and floured baking tray. Leave in a warm place, covered with a cloth until puffy looking.

Fry the doughnuts in hot deep fat until golden brown, turning them in the fat as they fry – takes about 5 minutes. Drain and then roll in the mixed sugar and cinnamon.

Danish Pastries

Makes 16 Time taken 3–4 hours

225 g (8 oz) strong plain flour	2 level teaspoons dried yeast
pinch salt	6 tablespoons cold water
25 g (1 oz) white vegetable fat	1 egg
15 g (½ oz) fresh yeast	1 tablespoon castor sugar
or	150 g (5 oz) butter

Sift the flour and salt into a bowl. Beat down the fat, add to the flour and rub in until fine. Blend the fresh yeast with 5 tablespoons of *cold* water. If using dried yeast, dissolve ½ teaspoon of the sugar in 5 tablespoons of *warm* water and sprinkle the dried yeast on top. Leave in a warm place until frothy – takes about 10 minutes. Mix the egg with the remaining tablespoon of cold water and the sugar.

Add the yeast mixture and the egg mixture to the centre of the flour and mix to a soft dough. Turn out on to a clean working surface and knead lightly until smooth. Cover and rest in a refrigerator for 10 minutes.

Beat the butter until soft and spreadable, then shape into an oblong cake about 1 cm (½ inch) thick. Roll out the rested dough into a square a little larger than the butter. Place the butter in the centre and fold the sides over just to overlap, completely enclosing the butter. Seal the edges and seal the bottom and top. Roll the pastry out to an oblong strip about three times as long as it is wide. Fold evenly in three and turn the pastry so that the open sides face the bottom – as for puff pastry. Cover and rest in the refrigerator for 10 minutes. Repeat the rolling and folding twice more. Finally rest the dough for about 10 minutes in a cool place and prepare the Almond Paste and Custard Fillings given below.

Almond Paste Filling

25 g (1 oz) ground almonds
25 g (1 oz) castor sugar

2 drops almond essence
little egg white

Mix together the ground almonds and castor sugar. Add the almond essence and work to a smooth paste with a little lightly beaten egg white.

Custard Filling

2 egg yolks
25 g (1 oz) castor sugar
15 g (½ oz) flour

1·5 dl (¼ pint) milk
vanilla essence

Whisk together the egg yolks, sugar and flour to make a smooth paste. Bring the milk just up to the boil and stir into the mixture. Blend well and return to the saucepan. Replace over moderate heat and stir briskly until just boiling. Draw off the heat, add a few drops of vanilla essence and allow to cool, stirring occasionally to prevent a skin forming.

To shape the pastries

Half the dough makes 8 pastries

Crescents Roll out *half* the basic dough to a circle 23 cm (9 inches) across and cut into eight sections. Cut a small slit lengthwise near the pointed end. Put a piece of almond paste in the middle and roll up towards the point and curl into a crescent shape. Place on baking sheet about 2·5 cm (1 inch) apart and brush with mixed egg and milk.

Half the dough makes 4 of each

Stars and Envelopes Roll out *half* the basic dough into a rectangle about 15 by 30 cm (6 by 12 inches) and cut into eight 7·5-cm (3-inch) squares.

For Stars, place a small dot of almond paste in the centre. Snip each corner to within 1 cm ($\frac{1}{2}$ inch) of the centre and draw alternate corners to the centre overlapping each other. Brush with mixed egg and milk and place on a baking sheet.

For Envelopes, put a little almond paste or custard filling in the centre. Fold the four corners to the centre and press down well. Brush with mixed egg and milk and place on a baking sheet.

To bake the pastries

Leave all these pastries to prove in a slightly warm place until puffy (about 15–20 minutes). Do not prove in as much warmth as is usual with most yeast doughs or the fat will run out and spoil the pastry. Bake above centre in a hot oven (200–225°C, 400–425°F or Gas Nos. 6–7) for about 12–15 minutes. Ice and finish while still hot. Brush the crescents with a little glacé icing and sprinkle with flaked almonds. Put a little custard in the centre of each star and top with a spot of red jelly or bits of glacé cherry. Fill the slits at corners of the envelopes with custard and replace in oven for 1 minute to set. Decorate with glacé icing and chopped nuts.

Arrange the pastries attractively and serve.

Devonshire Splits

Makes 8 Time taken 2 hours

225 g (8 oz) strong plain flour
$\frac{1}{2}$ level teaspoon salt
25 g (1 oz) lard or butter
15 g ($\frac{1}{2}$ oz) fresh yeast
  or

2 level teaspoons dried yeast
1·5 dl ($\frac{1}{4}$ pint) warm mixed milk and
  water
1 teaspoon castor sugar

For the Filling

strawberry jam   1·5 dl (¼ pint) clotted cream

Sift the flour and salt into a bowl. Add the lard or butter cut in pieces, and rub into the mixture. Blend the fresh yeast, with the warm milk and water. If using dried yeast, stir the sugar into the hand-hot milk and water. Sprinkle in the yeast and set aside in a warm place for 10 minutes, or until frothy.

Stir the yeast liquid into the centre of the flour and mix together to make a rough dough in the basin. Turn out on to an unfloured working surface and knead thoroughly to make a smooth dough that is not sticky. Shape into a round and replace in the basin. Place inside a polythene bag and set aside to prove until double in size.

Turn the risen dough out and knock flat with the knuckles. Divide the dough into eight equal-sized portions and round up each one neatly. Place the rounds of dough on greased baking trays and leave in a warm place until well-risen and puffy looking. Dust with flour and bake in the centre of a hot oven (220°C, 425°F or Gas No. 7) for 15 minutes.

When baked, leave to cool. Before serving split and fill with strawberry jam and clotted cream.

Apricot and Walnut Bread

Makes 2 small loaves Time taken 2–3 hours

350 g (12 oz) strong plain flour	3 dl (½ pint) mixed milk and water
100 g (4 oz) wholemeal flour	1 teaspoon castor sugar
2 level teaspoons salt	175–225 g (6–8 oz) chopped dried
25g (1 oz) castor sugar	apricots
25 g (1 oz) fresh yeast	50 g (2 oz) chopped walnuts
or	
1 level tablespoon dried yeast	

An unusual fruit bread for tea, with chopped apricots and walnuts throughout.

Mix the flours and salt into a basin. Add the sugar and make a hollow in the centre. Blend the fresh yeast with the warm milk and water. If using dried yeast, stir the teaspoon of sugar into the hand-hot milk and water and sprinkle in the yeast. Leave in a warm place for about 10 minutes, or until frothy.

Stir the yeast liquid into the dry ingredients and mix to a dough. Turn out on to a clean working surface and knead well until the dough is smooth. Replace in the basin, place inside a polythene bag and set aside in a warm place until double in size.

Turn out the risen dough and knock flat with the knuckles. Add the chopped apricots and walnuts and knead thoroughly into the dough. Flatten the dough out to an oblong the same depth as the length of the baking tin. Fold in three and turn over so that the seam is underneath. Place in a large, greased, 900 g (2 lb) loaf tin. Place in a greased polythene bag and leave in a warm place until the loaf is well-risen and up to the top of the tin. Place in the centre of a very hot oven (220°C, 425°F or Gas No. 7) and bake for 40–45 minutes. Allow to cool before serving.

Serve sliced and buttered.

Savarin

Makes one savarin – serves 6–8 Time taken 2–3 hours
Bake a day in advance

25 g (1 oz) fresh yeast	½ level teaspoon salt
or	25 g (1 oz) castor sugar
1 level tablespoon dried yeast	4 large/standard eggs
6 tablespoons milk	100 g (4 oz) soft butter
225 g (8 oz) strong plain flour	

For the Syrup
4 tablespoons honey	rum to taste
4 tablespoons water	

For the Glaze
4 tablespoons apricot jam	2 tablespoons water

A savarin is a rich yeast mixture baked in a ring mould, then soaked in a rum-flavoured syrup and glazed. It is usually served as a whole, often with fresh fruit or cream in the centre.

Mix together the yeast, milk and 50 g (2 oz) of the flour until smooth. Set aside in a warm place until frothy – about 20 minutes for fresh yeast. If using dried yeast, set aside for 30 minutes. Add the remaining flour and all other ingredients and beat thoroughly, using a wooden spoon, for about 3–4 minutes.

Grease a 20-cm (8-inch) ring mould and half-fill it with the mixture. Place inside a polythene bag and allow to rise until two-thirds full. Place in the centre of a preheated hot oven (220°C, 400°F or Gas No. 6) and bake for 20 minutes. Turn out; if preferred allow the savarin to 'stale' for 24 hours. This allows for greater penetration of syrup. Place on a wire rack and set over a large plate.

Prick the savarin all over with a skewer – this helps the syrup to soak in. Prepare the syrup by warming together the honey, water and rum to taste. Spoon the warm syrup over the savarin; any that runs into the plate below should be spooned over again, until the savarin has absorbed all the syrup. Lift on to a serving plate.

Sieve the apricot jam into a saucepan to remove any pieces of fruit. Add the water and bring up to the boil slowly. Draw off the heat and brush over the savarin to glaze it. Leave to cool. Serve the savarin with sweetened whipped cream, or diced fresh fruit, in the centre.

Cinnamon Rolls

Makes 12 rolls Time taken 2–3 hours

450 g (1 lb) strong plain flour	2 level teaspoons salt
25 g (1 oz) fresh yeast	25 g (1 oz) castor sugar
or	1 teaspoon castor sugar
1 level tablespoon dried yeast	50 g (2 oz) soft brown sugar
3 dl (½ pint) warm mixed milk and water	1 level teaspoon cinnamon

For the Icing
50 g (2 oz) icing sugar   hot water to mix

Sift the flour and salt into a mixing basin. Add the sugar and hollow out the centre. Blend the fresh yeast with the warm mixed milk and water. If using dried yeast, stir the teaspoon of castor sugar into the hand-hot milk and water and sprinkle in the yeast. Leave in a warm place for about 10 minutes, or until frothy.

Stir the yeast liquid into the centre of the flour and mix to a rough dough in the basin. Turn out on to a clean working surface and knead thoroughly until the dough is smooth. Replace in the basin, set inside a polythene bag and set in a warm place until double in size.

Turn out the risen dough, knead lightly. On a lightly floured surface roll the dough out to a rectangle about 30 × 23 cm (12 × 9 inches). Mix the sugar and cinnamon and sprinkle over the dough. Roll up, beginning at the long side. Cut the roll into twelve slices about 2·5 cm (1 inch) thick. Place slightly apart in a greased 28 × 18-cm (11 × 7-inch) shallow baking tin. Place inside a large polythene bag or cover with a damp cloth and set aside until the rolls are well risen and puffy. Place in the centre of a very hot oven (220°C, 425°F or Gas No. 7) and bake for 25–30 minutes.

Mix the icing sugar and water to make a smooth thick icing. While the rolls are still warm, spread the icing over the surface. Leave until cold before serving.

19 Sweets & Confectionery

Recipes for homemade sweets require simple everyday ingredients but demand careful attention during cooking. Their preparation can provide hours of amusement and an attractive arrangement of the finished product makes a thoughtful gift for a friend or relation.

In all cases where a recipe begins with a syrup made using sugar and water, care must be taken to ensure that the grains of sugar are completely dissolved in the water over low heat before bringing the mixture up to the boil. Some sugar grains may adhere to the sides of the pan and these can be removed by brushing the sides of the pan down with a pastry brush dipped in water. Alternatively the prepared sugar syrup can be strained through muslin into a second pan. This makes certain that any grains of sugar remaining are removed. Golden syrup, liquid glucose or cream of tartar are often added to retard or check crystallization.

For accurate results every time it is advisable to use a sugar thermometer. An alternative method is to spoon a little of the mixture into a saucer of cold water and test the consistency. The six stages in the process are:

100°C, 212°F	temperature of boiling water. Keep the sugar thermometer handy in a pan of simmering water ready to use. Check the reading on the thermometer for accuracy.
102–103°C, 216–218°F	'thread' Wet fingers in cold water and take a little of the syrup between thumb and index finger. Stretch them apart and a fine thread should cling between the two.
114–116°C, 238–240°F	'soft ball' A little of the mixture spooned into a saucer of cold water should form a 'soft ball' when rolled between finger and thumb.
118–121°C, 245–250°F	'hard ball' As above but this time the mixture forms a hard ball or firmer ball.
138°C, 280°F	'crack' A little of the mixture spooned into a saucer of cold water should form a brittle thin film, and crack or snap easily.
154–156°C, 310–312°F	'hard crack' or 'caramel' After about 138°C (280°F) the syrup contains very little water. Already a pale straw colour, it now rapidly becomes a darker golden yellow and when golden brown has become caramel.

Packing of Prepared Sweets

Choose attractive oblong, square or round boxes for arranging sweets. Those with cellophane coverings or lids are the best for showing off the contents. Arrange the sweets in coloured paper cases. With a round box, pack them in from the outside to the centre. Arrange them in neat rows in a square or oblong box. In all cases pack the sweets tightly, and any with a strong peppermint flavour should be packed separately.

Chocolate Fudge

Makes about 700 g (1½ lb) Time taken 1½ hours

450 g (1 lb) granulated sugar
1·5 dl (¼ pint) water
1 rounded tablespoon golden syrup
1 small tin evaporated milk

25 g (1 oz) butter
100 g (4 oz) plain chocolate
1 teaspoon vanilla essence
50 g (2 oz) chopped walnuts

Make a point of selecting a large saucepan to make chocolate fudge in. The mixture froths and boils up in the pan, after the evaporated milk is added, and can easily boil over.

Measure the sugar and water into a large saucepan. Stir over low heat until the sugar has dissolved. Stir in the syrup, and the evaporated milk. Bring up to the boil and cook rapidly until the temperature on a sugar thermometer reads 116°C (240°F) or until a little spooned into a saucer of cold water forms a soft ball. Stir fairly constantly towards the end of the boiling time to prevent the mixture catching. Draw the pan off the heat and add the butter. Do not stir in, allow the butter to melt on the surface and leave the fudge to cool in the pan until the thermometer shows a temperature of 82°C (180°F) or until the hand can be held against the sides of the pan.

Meanwhile break the chocolate into a basin set over a pan of hot water; allow to melt and stir until smooth. Add the vanilla essence and the chocolate to the fudge and beat with a wooden spoon, until the mixture becomes creamy. Immediately stir in the walnuts and pour the mixture into a buttered, shallow, 18-cm (7-inch) square pan. Mark into squares while warm, then leave until quite cold. Break into pieces and store in a tin.

Butterscotch

Makes 600 g (1¼ lb) Time taken 45 minutes

450 g (1 lb) Demerara sugar   1·5 dl (¼ pint) water
2 heaped tablespoons golden syrup   75 g (3 oz) unsalted butter

Measure the sugar, golden syrup and water into a saucepan. Stir to dissolve the sugar over low heat. Brush down the sides of the pan frequently with a pastry brush dipped in water. When the sugar grains have all dissolved bring up to the boil. Boil rapidly without stirring, or until the temperature on a sugar thermometer reads 116°C (240°F), or a little dropped into a saucer of cold water forms a soft ball. Keeping the pan over the heat, add the butter in small pieces and continue boiling until the reading on the sugar thermometer shows 138°C (280°F), or a little dropped into a saucer of cold water forms a hard ball.

Draw the pan off the heat and allow the bubbles to subside. Pour the mixture into a buttered, shallow baking or roasting tin. The butterscotch should be about ·5 cm (¼ inch) in depth. Allow to cool until beginning to firm up, then mark deeply into squares with the blade of an oiled knife. Leave until quite cold, then break into pieces.

Vanilla Fudge

Makes 1 kg 150 g (2½ lb) Time taken 1¼ hours

900 g (2 lb) granulated sugar
3 dl (½ pint) water
1 large tin sweetened condensed milk

50 g (2 oz) butter
1 teaspoon vanilla essence

Measure the sugar and water into a large saucepan. Stir over low heat until the sugar has dissolved. Add the condensed milk and the butter. Bring the mixture up to the boil. Simmer gently, stirring occasionally, until a little dropped into a saucer of cold water forms a soft ball, or the temperature on a sugar thermometer reads 116°C (240°F). It takes about 40 minutes and by this time the mixture should have turned to a golden brown.

Draw the pan off the heat, cool for a moment, then stir in the vanilla essence. Beat with a wooden spoon, until the mixture cools and begins to thicken. This grains the mixture and gives a smooth texture but take care that the fudge does not set in the saucepan. Pour into a buttered, shallow, baking or small roasting tin and set in a cool place to harden. Once the surface has set, mark the fudge into squares. Leave to set firm, then turn out and break into squares.

Crème de Menthe Jellies

Makes 700 g (1½ lb) Time taken 1 hour
Leave overnight

4 tablespoons cold water
2 level tablespoons powdered
   gelatine
450 g (1 lb) granulated sugar

1·5 dl (¼ pint) water
6 drops oil of peppermint
few drops green colouring

For the Dusting Mixture
25 g (1 oz) cornflour

50 g (2 oz) icing sugar

All peppermint sweets have a very strong flavour. Keep them separate from other varieties.

Measure the 4 tablespoons of water into a teacup and sprinkle in the gelatine. Set aside to soak.

Measure the sugar and the 1·5 dl (¼ pint) water into a saucepan. Stir over low heat to dissolve the sugar. Strain through muslin into a clean saucepan. Bring back to the boil and boil briskly without stirring until the temperature on a sugar thermometer reads 116°C (240°F), or until a little spooned into a saucer of cold water forms a soft ball.

Draw the pan off the heat. Add the soaked gelatine. Return the pan to very low heat and stir very gently for 1 minute only, to dissolve and blend the gelatine. Draw the pan off the heat and stir in the oil of peppermint and a few drops of colouring. Pour the syrup into a buttered, 18-cm (7-inch) square cake tin and leave overnight until firm.

Sift the cornflour and sugar together on to a square of greaseproof paper. Loosen one corner of the jelly mixture and pull out of the tin on to the bed of sugar. Cut into 2·5-cm (1-inch) strips and then into 2·5-cm (1-inch) squares. Dip the cut edges into the sugar mixture to prevent them sticking together. Store in a covered tin.

Praline

Makes 225 g (8 oz) Time taken 20–30 minutes

100 g (4 oz) whole, unblanched almonds	100 g (4 oz) granulated sugar

Praline adds the most delicious flavour to many desserts and ice creams. Once prepared it can be kept for a limited time in a screw-topped jar.

Put the almonds and sugar in a large heavy pan. Set over low heat and stir occasionally until the sugar has melted and is beginning to caramelize. Continue to cook until the mixture is an even, dark-golden brown and the nuts are glazed. Draw off the heat and pour at once on to an oiled, marble surface or an oiled baking tray. Leave until quite cold and firm.

Place the praline on a wooden board and, using a rolling pin, crush to a fine powder. Use as required.

Oranges and Grapes Glacé

Makes 2–2½ dozen Time taken 30 minutes

2 large oranges	1·5 dl (¼ pint) water
225 g (½ lb) black grapes	1 tablespoon golden syrup
450 g (1 lb) granulated sugar	

These petits fours quickly lose their crispness and should be eaten the day they are made.

Mark the oranges in quarters and remove the peel, taking away as much white pith as possible. Separate each orange into segments taking care not to break the thin, covering skin. Place the segments of orange on a piece of absorbent paper or a clean cloth, and turn the pieces to make sure they are quite dry. Snip pairs of grapes leaving short stalks adhering.

Measure the sugar and water into a saucepan. Stir over low heat to dissolve the sugar. Brush down the sides of the pan with a pastry brush dipped in cold water to remove any sugar grains. Add the golden syrup and bring up to the boil. Boil fairly briskly until the syrup shows a temperature of 143–149°C (290–300°F) on a sugar thermometer, or until a little dropped into a saucer of cold water immediately forms a very crisp brittle piece. Draw off the heat at once. At this stage the mixture is at a very high temperature and will be a pale straw colour.

Working as quickly as possible, dip the fruits one at a time into the syrup to coat the fruit completely. The stalks may be used for holding the grapes, it is advisable to use the prongs of a fork to hold them. Orange segments can be dropped into the syrup, turned over and lifted out with a fork. On no account should the fruit be pierced or the juices will flow out and spoil the syrup coating. As each piece of fruit is dipped, drain for a few seconds over the pan and then place on an oiled baking tray and leave to set. Put in small paper cases and serve.

Marzipan Sweets

Makes 3 dozen Time taken 30–40 minutes

50 g (2 oz) icing sugar	2 tablespoons lightly beaten egg
100 g (4 oz) ground almonds	few drops almond essence
50 g (2 oz) castor sugar	colouring as required

Sieve the icing sugar into a mixing bowl. Add the ground almonds and sugar. Mix the egg with a few drops of almond essence. Stir in sufficient of the lightly mixed egg to mix the ingredients to a smooth, firm dough. Turn the mixture on to a working surface lightly sprinkled with castor sugar, and divide the mixture into portions. Add different colours to each, leaving one plain.

Make into Walnut Rounds or Marzipan Logs as shown below. Remember to work and roll the marzipan out on a working surface lightly dusted with castor sugar, so that the marzipan does not stick.

Walnut Rounds

Using plain marzipan roll the piece out to a thick rope. Cut into equal sections and roll each one into a small ball. Press a nice walnut-half into each and sprinkle with castor sugar. Alternatively top with a glacé cherry-half.

Marzipan Logs

Select two portions of marzipan of different colours and roll each out to a rope about 1 cm ($\frac{1}{2}$ inch) thick and the same length. Leaving one as it is, flatten the second with a rolling pin, wide enough to enclose the first completely. Trim the edges evenly and brush the surface with a little warmed apricot jam.

Place the rope of marzipan down one edge and enclose completely to make a double-coloured roll. Leave to harden 2–3 hours, then cut in 1-cm ($\frac{1}{2}$-inch) slices.

Crystallized Primroses

Time taken 2–3 days

1 saltspoon gum tragacanth	small bunch fresh primroses
2 tablespoons triple-strength rose water	castor sugar for coating

Crystallized primroses can be used to decorate iced cakes; they look particularly pretty on a chocolate cake.

Put the gum tragacanth in a small screw-topped jar and add the rose water. Leave in a warm place for 24 hours. Give the jar an occasional shake until thoroughly dissolved. If the mixture is a little too thick, add extra rose water.

Choose fresh primroses and shorten the stem on each to 2·5 cm (1 inch). Hold the flower by the stem and, using a fine brush, paint both sides of each petal thinly with the liquid. When the whole flower is painted, sprinkle or dip lightly in castor sugar. Place, flower downwards, on a wire tray – it is best to use a wire cooling tray for cakes. Allow to dry overnight, then snip off the stems and store the flowers in an airtight tin or jar. These keep indefinitely.

Candied Orange Peel

Makes 8 candied orange halves Time taken 2–3 days

4 oranges
8 g (¼ oz) bicarbonate of soda
generous 1 litre (2 pints) water

500 g (1 lb 2 oz) granulated sugar
3 dl (½ pint) water

Wash the oranges and cut them in half. Remove the peel and the pith by inserting the handle of a teaspoon between the pith and the skin all the way round the fruit, before removing the flesh of the fruit with the fingers.

Mix the bicarbonate of soda and the water in a bowl. Add the orange peel and allow to soak for 20 minutes. Drain the peel and rinse in cold water. Simmer gently in fresh water until the peel is tender. Dissolve 350 g (12 oz) of the granulated sugar in the 3 dl (½ pint) of water. Bring to a brisk boil and drop in the peel. Remove from the heat and turn into a deep basin. Cover with a plate to keep orange peel submerged and allow to stand for 48 hours.

Drain the syrup from the peel into a small saucepan, add the remaining 175 g (6 oz) of sugar. Stir over low heat to dissolve the sugar. Bring this to the boil and add the peel. Lower the heat and simmer very gently for about 2 hours until the peel becomes transparent.

Carefully remove the peel from the pan to a wire rack and drain. Boil up the syrup, then draw off the heat and stir with a wooden spoon until the syrup becomes cloudy. Quickly dip each piece of peel into it. Drain and leave on a wire rack to dry in a cool place for 2 days. Store in an airtight container.

Sugared Walnuts

Time taken 45 minutes

100 g (¼ lb) walnut halves

For the Orange Coating
225 g (8 oz) granulated sugar
rind and juice of 1 orange

little orange colouring

Select unbroken walnut halves and, when ready to begin the recipe, place these on a baking tray or tin in the centre of a moderate oven (180°C, 350°F or Gas No. 4). Leave to become crisp and hot – takes about 15 minutes.

Meanwhile, measure the sugar into a saucepan and add the strained orange juice, which has been made up to 1·5 dl (¼ pint) with water. Dissolve the sugar in the water over low heat. Bring to the boil and cook rapidly, without stirring, until the temperature on a sugar thermometer shows 116°C (240°F), or when a little of the mixture spooned into a saucer of cold water makes a soft ball.

Draw the pan off the heat and add the finely grated orange rind and the hot walnuts. Stir until the walnuts are well-coated and the mixture becomes creamy. Quickly turn out on to a large buttered plate or tin and separate the walnuts with a fork. When cold, store in an airtight container.

Candied Grapefruit Peel

Makes 225 g (½ lb) Time taken 1½ hours
Leave for 2 days

peel of 2 grapefruit   3 dl (½ pint) water
225 g (8 oz) granulated sugar
1 rounded tablespoon golden syrup   castor sugar

Remove the peel from the grapefruit in quarters. Place in a saucepan and cover with cold water. Bring to the boil and simmer for 10 minutes, then drain. Re-cover with cold water and repeat the process three times in all. Drain the peel and cut into thin strips.

Measure the sugar, golden syrup and water into a saucepan. Stir over low heat to dissolve the sugar. Add the peel and bring up to the boil. Boil gently uncovered for about 40 minutes, or until most of the syrup is absorbed. Drain in a coarse strainer and then roll the peel in castor sugar. Arrange in a single layer on waxed paper and allow to dry for two days.

Sherry Sugar Balls

Makes 2 dozen Time taken 2–3 hours
Make in advance

100 g (4 oz) plain chocolate   2 tablespoons sweet sherry
3 tablespoons single cream
50 g (2 oz) castor sugar   castor sugar for coating
1 box of 16 sponge-finger biscuits

Brandy or rum may be used in place of sherry. These sugar balls improve considerably in flavour on keeping.

Break the chocolate in pieces, place in a basin and set over a pan half-filled with hot water. Stir occasionally until the chocolate has melted. Remove the basin from the heat and stir in the cream and sugar. Finely crush the sponge-finger biscuits and add to the chocolate mixture with the sherry. Blend well and leave the mixture in a cool place for several hours to stiffen up.

Shape heaped teaspoons of the mixture into balls and roll in castor sugar. Store in a screw-topped jar or tin. Allow to mature for at least 24 hours.

Peanut Brittle

Makes 600 g (1¼ lb) Time taken 45 minutes

100 g (4 oz) salted peanuts   1·5 dl (¼ pint) water
450 g (1 lb) granulated sugar   25 g (1 oz) butter

Preheat the oven to moderately slow (170°C, 325°F or Gas No. 3). Spread the peanuts on a baking tray or roasting tin ready to heat through.

Measure the sugar and water into a saucepan. Place over low heat and stir to dissolve the sugar. Brush down the sides of the pan with a pastry brush dipped in cold water. When all the grains of sugar are dissolved, bring the syrup up to the boil. Boil, without stirring, until the mixture turns to a golden brown caramel in the saucepan – takes about 15 minutes. During this time put the peanuts in the oven to heat through.

Draw the pan off the heat before the mixture becomes too dark in colour. Add the butter cut in pieces and the hot peanuts. Stir quickly and thoroughly to blend, then pour immediately into a large buttered roasting tin or shallow baking tin. The brittle should be allowed to run fairly thin. Spread the nuts evenly through the mixture and then leave until cold and set firm. Break into pieces and store in an air-tight container.

Toffee Apples

Makes 8 Time taken 45 minutes

8 eating apples   1·5 dl (¼ pint) water
450 g (1 lb) granulated sugar
3 heaped tablespoons golden syrup   8 wooden skewers

Any surplus toffee can be poured into a buttered shallow tin and left to set. Break into pieces when hard.

Select good, sound apples and wash, then wipe each one dry. Insert a fine wooden skewer into the stalk end of each one. For this buy ·5-cm (¼-inch) dowel rod from an ironmonger, cut into 13-cm (5-inch) lengths and sharpen at one end. Push each skewer about half-way into the apple. Have all the apples ready before starting.

Measure the sugar, golden syrup and water into a large saucepan and stir over low heat, until the sugar has dissolved. Increase the heat and bring the mixture to the boil. Cook rapidly, without stirring, until a temperature of 154°C (310°F) is reached on a sugar thermometer, or until the mixture is beginning to caramelize. Draw the pan off the heat and immediately begin to dip the apples. Tilt the pan sideways so that each apple can be coated with syrup. Drain from the pan and stand the dipped apples on a buttered baking tray or buttered plate to harden. When cold, wrap each one in a square of waxed paper and fix with an elastic band. Keep in a dry place; they should store well for several days.

Chocolate Truffles

Makes 2 dozen · Time taken 30 minutes
Leave overnight

100 g (4 oz) plain chocolate	225–275 g (8–10 oz) icing sugar
2 tablespoons double cream	
1 tablespoon brandy or rum	chocolate vermicelli

Break the chocolate into pieces, place in a mixing basin and set over a pan of hot, not boiling, water. Stir occasionally until the chocolate has melted, then lift the basin away from the heat.

Stir in the cream and brandy, or rum, and blend until smooth. Gradually stir in the sieved icing sugar: the amount the mixture will take may vary, but sufficient should be added to make a smooth, fairly stiff, consistency.

Roll teaspoons of the mixture into small balls and then roll in chocolate vermicelli. Set in small, paper sweet-cases and leave in a cool place until set firm.

Marrons Glacé

Time taken 1 week

1–1·5 kg (2–3 lb) chestnuts	1 litre (1¾ pints) water
725 g (1 lb 10 oz) granulated sugar	

Marrons glacé are expensive to buy. They can be made at home, but the process is rather a long one. The chestnuts are first cooked and then soaked in a hot sugar syrup, which is slowly increased in strength as it penetrates the chestnuts.

Select best quality Spanish or French chestnuts, these are larger than English chestnuts. Make a small slit in the skin on the flat side of each chestnut and place them on a baking sheet. Place in a hot oven for 8–10 minutes. Remove from the oven and peel off the outer and inner skin. Take care to keep the chestnuts whole. Cover the chestnuts with water, bring up to the boil and simmer gently for 30 minutes or until tender. Drain and place in a deep heat-proof bowl.

To prepare the syrup, dissolve 450 g (1 lb) of the granulated sugar in the 1 litre (1¾ pints) water, over low heat, stirring occasionally. Bring to the boil and pour over the chestnuts. Leave overnight covered with a clean cloth.

On the second day drain off the syrup into a saucepan, add 50 g (2 oz) granulated sugar, dissolve and bring to the boil. Pour over the chestnuts. Repeat this once a day for 4 more days.

On the fifth day drain the chestnuts from the syrup. Separate the whole ones from any broken pieces. Rub all the broken pieces through a sieve and mix with a little of the syrup to make a purée. This purée can be used in recipes or desserts. Pour the remaining syrup into a saucepan and bring up to the boil. Stir with a wooden spoon until the syrup becomes a little cloudy, then draw the pan off the heat. Using a fork, dip each of the chestnuts into the syrup to coat, then drain and place on a wire cooling tray. Slip a plate underneath to catch the drips and place in the lower half of a very cool oven (130°C, 250°F or Gas No. ½). Leave with the oven door slightly open for 2–3 hours, or until surface of the chestnuts are no longer sticky. Place the chestnuts in an airtight box, lined with wax paper.

Coconut Ice

Makes 700 g (1½ lb) Time taken 45 minutes

450 g (1 lb) granulated sugar
1·5 dl (¼ pint) water
1 teaspoon vanilla essence

100 g (4 oz) desiccated coconut
1 tablespoon single cream
little pink colouring

Measure the sugar and water into a saucepan. Dissolve the sugar over low heat, then bring up to the boil. Cook rapidly until the temperature on a sugar thermometer reads 116°C (240°F), or until a little of the boiling syrup spooned into a saucer of cold water forms a soft ball.

Draw the pan off the heat and allow bubbles to subside. Stir in the vanilla essence, coconut and cream. Stir gently until the mixture thickens and goes a little cloudy. Then pour half the mixture into a buttered, shallow, 18-cm (7-inch) square tin or a loaf tin. Very quickly colour the remainder in the saucepan with a drop of pink colouring and pour on top. Leave until quite cold and set firm. Then turn out and cut the coconut ice first into bars and then into pieces.

Orange Fondants

Makes 2–3 dozen Time taken 45 minutes

450 g (1 lb) granulated sugar
1·5 dl (¼ pint) water
1 tablespoon single cream or
    evaporated milk
1 teaspoon orange flower-water

few drops orange colouring
1 tablespoon finely chopped candied
    peel
1 tablespoon finely chopped walnuts

Measure the sugar and water into a saucepan. Stir over low heat until the sugar has dissolved. Bring up to the boil and cook rapidly until the temperature on a sugar thermometer reads 116°C (240°F), or until a little spooned into a saucer of cold water forms a soft ball. Draw the pan off the heat and allow to cool until the thermometer shows a temperature of 82°C (180°F), or until the hand can be held against the sides of the pan.

Add the cream or evaporated milk, orange flower-water and a few drops of colouring. Stir until the mixture turns creamy, then quickly stir in the chopped candied peel and walnuts. Spoon out in rounded teaspoons on to a buttered or oiled baking tray or plate. Leave until quite cold.

Sugar Plums

Makes about 2 dozen Time taken 45 minutes
Leave overnight

225 g (½ lb) tenderized prunes   castor sugar

Place the prunes in a basin and cover with boiling water. Allow to stand for 5 minutes, then drain and re-cover with fresh boiling water. Allow to stand for a further 5 minutes, then drain and continue with the recipe.

Weigh the prunes and place in a saucepan with an equal quantity of castor sugar – about 225 g (8 oz) in this case. Just cover with cold water and bring slowly up to the boil. Simmer gently, stirring occasionally, until the prunes are tender and the syrup thickens. It takes about 5–10 minutes. Using the prongs of a fork, drain the prunes one at a time from the hot syrup. Roll in castor sugar. Leave overnight in a warm place to dry, then store in a screw-topped jar.

Crystallized Pineapple

Makes 8 rings of pineapple Time taken 14 days

1 (750 g) (1 lb 11 oz) tin pineapple rings
3 dl ($\frac{1}{2}$ pint) fruit juice
550 g (1 lb 4 oz) granulated sugar

Use fruits which have a pronounced flavour for crystallizing; sugar overcomes the flavour of the more delicate ones. Good results come from using good quality tinned pineapple.

Drain off the pineapple syrup from the tin and put the fruit in a large bowl. Measure the syrup and make up to 3 dl ($\frac{1}{2}$ pint) with water if necessary. Place in a saucepan with 225 g (8 oz) of the sugar and heat gently until dissolved. Then bring to the boil and pour over the fruit. Place a saucer on top to keep the fruit submerged and leave for 24 hours.

Pour off the syrup and reboil with an extra 50 g (2 oz) of the sugar as above. Pour over the fruit and leave for a further 24 hours. Repeat this process twice more with an extra 50 g (2 oz) of sugar each time.

Strain the syrup into a saucepan, add 75 g (3 oz) of the sugar and stir until dissolved. Add the fruit, bring to the boil and leave for 48 hours. Repeat this once again adding the last 75 g (3 oz) of sugar. Simmer the fruit in the syrup for about 5 minutes until the syrup has thickened like honey. Pour into the bowl and leave for 3–4 days.

Drain the pineapple from the syrup and place on a wire tray. Slip a plate underneath to catch any syrup that may drip from them. Place in a cool oven (130°C, 250°F or Gas No. $\frac{1}{2}$) and leave for several hours until the surfaces are dry and no longer sticky – turn occasionally so that they dry out evenly. Store in cardboard boxes or jars lined with waxed paper, do not seal airtight.

Peppermint Creams

Makes 3 dozen Time taken 30 minutes
Leave overnight to dry

1 large egg white
350 g (12 oz) icing sugar
few drops oil of peppermint
few drops green colouring

Use oil of peppermint for these; it is obtainable from a chemist and gives the best flavour.

Crack the egg white into a large mixing basin and beat with a fork until frothy. Sieve the icing sugar and add about half to the egg white. Beat well with a wooden spoon. Add a few drops of oil of peppermint, but too little rather than too much at this stage. Gradually beat in more of the icing sugar, until the mixture is fairly stiff.

Sift the remaining icing sugar on to a working surface. Turn out the peppermint mixture and knead in as much of the remaining icing sugar as possible. The amount of sugar required is determined by the size of the egg white used. Either leave the mixture plain, or colour with a few drops of green colouring. Check the flavouring, kneading in a few extra drops of peppermint if necessary. Keeping the surface of the table well-dusted with icing sugar, roll the mixture out about ·5 cm (¼ inch) thick. Using a small, 2·5-cm (1-inch) round cutter stamp out circles of the mixture. Place on a tray lined with grease-proof paper. Knead the trimmings and re-roll to get as many peppermint creams as possible. Place in a warm place – an airing cupboard is ideal – for 24 hours so that the peppermints dry out. Loosen from the paper and store in an airtight container.

Honey Raisin Clusters

Makes 1½ dozen Time taken 30 minutes

100 g (4 oz) plain chocolate
2 rounded tablespoons clear honey
175 g (6 oz) seedless raisins

small pieces of glacé cherry or angelica

Break the chocolate into pieces and place with the honey in a small mixing basin. Set over a saucepan of hot, but not boiling, water and stir occasionally until the chocolate is melted and the mixture smooth. Stir in the raisins and blend well.

Drop teaspoons of the mixture on to a buttered or foil-lined baking tray. Decorate with pieces of glacé cherry or angelica and chill until set firm.

Quick French Mints

Makes 2–3 dozen Time taken 45 minutes

450 g (1 lb) granulated sugar
1·5 dl (¼ pint) water

6 drops oil of peppermint
few drops green colouring

Measure the sugar and water into a saucepan. Stir over low heat to dissolve the sugar. Bring up to the boil and cook rapidly until the temperature on a sugar thermometer reads 116°C (240°F), or until a little spooned into a saucer of cold water forms a soft ball.

Remove the pan from the heat. Allow the mixture to cool until the thermometer reads 82°C (180°F), or until the hand can be held against the sides of the pan. Add the oil of peppermint and a few drops of green colouring. Stir gently until the mixture goes creamy. Spoon quickly on to waxed paper using two teaspoons. If the mixture becomes too firm, warm gently until softened. Continue until the mixture is used up. When set firm, lift from the paper and store in an airtight container.

Prunes in Brandy

Time taken 30 minutes
Leave a week before using

450 g (1 lb) tenderized, pitted (stoned) prunes	100 g (4 oz) soft brown sugar 1·5 dl (¼ pint) inexpensive brandy

Use an attractive glass storage jar with a tight fitting glass top. Make sure the jar is large enough – the prunes and syrup should not more than three-quarters fill the jar. Prunes plump out and absorb the liquid during storage.

Cover the prunes with cold water, bring up to the boil and simmer for 3 minutes. Draw off the heat, strain and reserve about 1·5 dl (¼ pint) of the liquid. Pack the prunes into the storage jar.

Return the reserved syrup to the pan. Add the sugar and stir over low heat until dissolved. Bring up to the boil and simmer for 2 minutes. Remove from the heat and allow to cool for a few minutes. Pour over the fruit and then add the brandy. The prunes should be well covered with liquid.

Cover and store. Shake the jar during the first week to blend the ingredients. Store in a cool dark place. These prunes will keep for several months.

20 Preserves

Homemade preserves are extra special. All year round there are fruits and vegetables with which to make jams, jellies, marmalade, pickles and chutneys. Store them in a cool, dark and dry cupboard and supplies will keep from one season through to the next.

General Notes on Jam and Jelly Making

1 Choose sound, slightly under-ripe fruit; never use any soft, damaged or mouldy fruit. Pick over carefully, and remove stalks and hulls. Wipe or wash to clean the fruit.

2 It is always advisable to use a large preserving pan, household saucepans are rarely big enough. To get a good set, jam must be boiled fast and at this stage the jam will boil up to three or four times its original bulk.

3 All fruit needs softening before the sugar is added. Soft fruits require no additional water. It is only necessary to crush a few of the berries in the pan. Add the remaining berries and heat gently for a few minutes to draw out sufficient juice to dissolve the sugar. Tough-skinned fruits such as gooseberries, blackcurrants and damsons must be stewed in water until quite tender before adding any sugar. Sugar added too soon causes toughening of skins and fruit. Once sugar is added it must be completely dissolved before the jam is allowed to boil. Failure to do this often causes the sugar to re-crystallize in the finished preserve.

4 *To test for a set*   Remove the pan of boiling jam or jelly from the heat. Spoon a few drops on to a cold plate. Cool quickly by placing in the refrigerator or a cool corner for a few moments. Test by pushing with the little finger. If a wrinkled skin forms on the surface, the jam or jelly will set. If no wrinkled skin appears, return to the heat and boil briskly for another 5 minutes, then test again.

5 Most jams and all jellies are potted within 2–3 minutes of reaching setting point. However, any jam with large berries such as strawberries, or cherry jam should be allowed to cool for about 30 minutes first. This helps to prevent the fruit from floating to the tops of the jars and keeps it evenly suspended.

6 Stand the jars for filling on a wooden surface – a table-top or large pastry board will do – or on folded newspaper. Ladle or pour the jam using a small jug into the jars, filling each one up to the neck. Wipe any drips from the sides of the jars with a hot damp cloth while they are still warm. While still hot, cover the jam surface with waxed paper circles, then moisten one side of the cellophane cover with a damp cloth and place it over the jar, *damp side upwards*, and fix in position with an elastic band or thin string. When cold, label the jars and then store in a cool, dry, dark cupboard.

SPRING AND SUMMER PRESERVES

Gooseberry and Orange Jam

Makes 2 kg 700 g (6 lb) Time taken 1 hour

1 kg 350 g (3 lb) green gooseberries
4·5 dl (¾ pint) water
rind and juice of 2 oranges

1 kg 600 g (3½ lb) granulated or
preserving sugar

Rinse the gooseberries, and top and tail them. Place in a large saucepan or preserving pan, and add the water, finely grated orange rind and juice. Bring slowly to boiling point and simmer gently, squashing the fruit occasionally with a wooden spoon. When the fruit is quite tender – takes about 30 minutes – add the sugar. Stir over low heat until the sugar has dissolved. Bring up to the boil and boil briskly for a set – takes about 10 minutes. Draw off the heat, skim and then spoon into six clean warm jars. Cover and seal while hot. Label when cold.

Rhubarb and Ginger Jam

Makes 3 kg 650 g (8 lb) Time taken 1 hour
Leave prepared fruit overnight

2 kg 700 g (6 lb) prepared rhubarb
2 kg 700 g (6 lb) granulated or
  preserving sugar
2 large lemons

50 g (2 oz) root ginger
100 g (4 oz) preserved ginger or
  crystallized ginger

Wipe the rhubarb, trim the ends and cut the stalks into 2·5-cm (1-inch) lengths. Weigh the quantity required and place in a large basin in layers with the sugar. Finely pare the lemon rind and tie in a muslin bag with the bruised root ginger. Add to the fruit. Drain the preserved ginger from the syrup or wash off any sugar coating from the crystallized ginger. Chop finely and add. Cover the basin and leave overnight.

Next day, pour the contents of the basin – both juices and rhubarb – into a large saucepan or preserving pan. Add the lemon juice and bring up to the boil slowly, stirring occasionally to make sure that all the sugar has dissolved. Boil rapidly for a set – takes about 10–15 minutes. When setting point is reached, draw the pan off the heat. Remove the bag of flavourings at the last minute, or when the jam is sufficiently flavoured to taste. Pour into clean, warm jars. Cover and seal while hot. Label when cold.

Blackcurrant Jelly

Makes 2 kg 700 g (6 lb) Time taken 2 hours

1 kg 800 g (4 lb) blackcurrants
1·5 litres (3 pints) water
350 g (¾ lb) granulated or

preserving sugar for each
generous ·5 litre (1 pint) of fruit
juice

Wash the fruit and remove any leaves; there is no need to strip the berries from the stem. Place the fruit in a large saucepan and just cover with about 1 litre (2 pints) of the cold water. Bring to the boil and simmer gently for about 30 minutes or until the fruit is tender. Mash the fruit well and draw off the heat. Ladle the fruit and juice into a scalded jelly bag. Leave to strain for about 15 minutes. Remove the pulp from the jelly bag and replace in the pan with the remaining ·5 litre (1 pint) water. Bring to the boil, simmer for 30 minutes and then strain through the jelly bag again. This second boiling makes the preserve more economical.

Measure the fruit juice back into a saucepan and, for every ·5 litre (1 pint) of juice, add 350 g (¾ lb) sugar. Stir over low heat until all the sugar has dissolved, then bring up to the boil and simmer rapidly for a set – takes about 10 minutes.

When setting point is reached, draw the pan off the heat and ladle the jelly into clean, warm jars. Cover and seal while hot. Label when cold.

Mixed Fruit Jam

Makes about 2 kg 700 g (6 lb) Time taken 1 hour

900 g (2 lb) green gooseberries
450 g (1 lb) strawberries
450 g (1 lb) raspberries

3 dl (½ pint) water
1 kg 800 g (4 lb) granulated or
  preserving sugar

Top and tail the gooseberries and place in a saucepan along with the hulled strawberries and raspberries. Add the water and bring to boil. Simmer gently until the fruit, especially the gooseberries, are quite soft – takes about 30 minutes.

Add the sugar and stir over low heat until the sugar has dissolved. Bring to the boil and cook rapidly until setting point has been reached – takes about 10–15 minutes. Draw the pan off the heat, skim and pour into clean, warm jars. Cover and seal while hot. Label when cold.

Lemon Curd

Makes 700–900 g (1½–2 lb) Time taken 30 minutes

100 g (4 oz) butter
350 g (12 oz) granulated sugar

rind and juice of 3 lemons
8 egg yolks or 4 whole eggs

Home-made lemon curd has an excellent flavour but a limited keeping time, and it is better to make small quantities at a time.

Place the butter, sugar, finely grated lemon rind and the strained lemon juice in a basin and place over a saucepan half-filled with simmering water. Stir occasionally until the butter has melted and the sugar dissolved. Stir in the lightly mixed egg yolks or strain in the lightly mixed whole eggs, whichever is being used. Continue to stir over the simmering water until the curd thickens. Remove from the heat and pour into clean, warm jars. Cover and seal while hot. Label when cold.

Strawberry Jam

Makes 2 kg 250 g–2 kg 700 g (5–6 lb) Time taken 1½ hours

1 kg 800 g (4 lb) strawberries
1 kg 600 g (3½ lb) granulated or
  preserving sugar

juice of 2 lemons

Wipe the strawberries clean and remove the hulls. Place in a large, heavy saucepan, crushing a few of the berries near the base of the pan. Stew gently over very low heat for 15 minutes, until the fruit is soft and the juices run.

Add the sugar and stir over low heat until dissolved. Add the lemon juice and bring up to the boil, cook rapidly for 15–20 minutes until setting point is reached.

During this time, stir only to prevent sticking, and remove any scum as it rises. Once setting point is reached, draw the pan off the heat, and allow the jam to cool for at least 30 minutes, or until the jam is half cold. This distributes the berries evenly throughout the finished jam. Stir gently and pour the jam into clean warm jars. Cover and seal while hot. Label when cold.

Fresh Apricot Jam

Makes 2 kg 700 g–3 kg 200 g (6–7 lb) Time taken 1 hour

1 kg 800 g (4 lb) apricots
4·5 dl (¾ pint) water

1 kg 800 g (4 lb) granulated or
  preserving sugar

The added kernels from the apricot stones give a delicate, almond-like flavour to this preserve.

Choose fruit that is slightly under-ripe. Wipe and remove any stalks and damaged fruit. Slit the fruit right through to the stone all round, following the line of the skin. Twist the two halves in opposite directions to separate but avoid pulling them apart. Remove the stones. Place the fruit and water in a large saucepan or preserving pan and simmer gently for 10–20 minutes, or until the fruit is tender.

Meanwhile crack about a dozen stones and remove the kernels. Blanch these by dipping into boiling water for a minute, then drain. Reserve the kernels for adding to the jam.

Add the sugar and stir over low heat until the sugar is dissolved. Bring to a brisk boil and boil rapidly for a set – about 15–20 minutes. Test after 15 minutes. When ready draw off the heat and add the reserved kernels. Skim and pour into clean, warm jars. Cover and seal while hot. Label when cold.

Gooseberry Mint Jelly

Makes 8 (225 g) (½ lb) jars of jelly Time taken 2–3 hours

1 kg 800 g (4 lb) green gooseberries
generous 1 litre (2 pints) cold water
1 large bunch fresh mint

3 dl (½ pint) distilled malt vinegar
granulated or preserving sugar
green food colouring

Although apples usually form the basis for mint jelly, gooseberries can also be used. The addition of a little vinegar gives the jelly a pleasant, piquant flavour.

Wash the gooseberries (no need to top and tail them) and place in a large preserving pan. Add the water and bring up to the boil. Add about half of the washed mint tied in a bunch. Reduce the heat and simmer the gooseberries gently until they are tender – takes about 30 minutes. Crush the fruit occasionally with the back of the spoon while they are cooking. When the berries are tender, add the vinegar and simmer for a further 5 minutes.

Draw the pan off the heat and strain through a scalded jelly bag for several hours until all the juice has dripped through. Measure the juice back into the rinsed preserving pan. Add the sugar allowing 450 g (1 lb) for every 6 dl (1 pint) of juice. Stir over gentle heat until the sugar has dissolved, then bring up to the boil and cook rapidly without stirring until setting point is reached – takes about 10 minutes.

When setting point is reached, draw the pan off the heat, skim and stir in the remaining chopped mint and a few drops of green colouring. Cool in the pan until a thin skin forms on the surface. Stir, then pot at once. Pour into clean, warm, 225 g (½ lb) jars. Cover and seal while hot. Label when cold.

AUTUMN AND WINTER PRESERVES

Victoria Plum Jam

Makes 3 kg 200 g (7 lb) Time taken 1 hour

1 kg 800 g (4 lb) Victoria plums
4·5 dl (¾ pint) water

1 kg 800 g (4 lb) granulated or
preserving sugar

Choose slightly under-ripe fruit. Pick over, and remove any stalks and damaged fruit. Slit the fruit through to the stone all round, following the line of the skin. Twist the two halves in opposite directions to separate them.

Remove the stones. If the stones are difficult to remove, cook the plums whole. Remove as many of the stones as possible with a perforated spoon, as they rise to the surface. Place the fruit and water in a preserving pan and simmer gently for 10–20 minutes, or until the fruit is tender.

Meanwhile crack about a dozen of the stones and remove the kernels. Blanch these by dipping into boiling water for 1 minute, then drain. Reserve the kernels for adding to the jam.

Add the sugar and stir over low heat until the sugar is dissolved. Bring up to a brisk boil and cook rapidly for a set, about 15–20 minutes. Test after about 15 minutes and, when ready, draw off the heat. Add the reserved kernels. Skim and pour into clean, warm jars. Cover and seal while hot. Label when cold.

Apple and Plum Jam

Makes 4 kg 500 g (10 lb) Time taken 1½ hours

1 kg 350 g (3 lb) cooking apples	2 kg 700 g (6 lb) granulated or
1 kg 350 g (3 lb) red plums	preserving sugar
1·25 litres (2½ pints) water	

Peel, core and slice the apples. Halve and remove the stones from the plums and put the fruit, together with the water, into a large saucepan. Bring to the boil, reduce the heat and then simmer gently, stirring frequently, until the fruit is thoroughly pulped and the contents reduced by about one-third – takes about 40–45 minutes.

Add the sugar and stir over low heat to dissolve. Bring to a brisk boil and cook rapidly for a set – takes about 15 minutes. When ready, draw the pan off the heat. Skim and pour into clean, warm jars. Cover and seal while hot. Label when cold.

Blackberry and Apple Jam

Makes 4 kg 500 g (10 lb) Time taken 1 hour

1 kg 800 g (4 lb) blackberries	2 kg 700 g (6 lb) granulated or
3 dl (½ pint) water	preserving sugar
700 g (1½ lb) cooking apples	

Put the washed blackberries in a preserving pan with half the water and stew until tender. Peel, core and slice the apples. Place in another pan, add the remaining water and cook until the fruit is quite soft. Stir the pulps together. (If seedless jam is required, sieve the blackberry pulp first.)

Add the sugar and stir over low heat until dissolved. Bring up to the boil and cook rapidly until setting point is reached – takes about 15 minutes. When ready, draw the pan off the heat. Skim and pour into warm, dry jars. Cover and seal while hot. Label when cold.

Pumpkin Cream

Makes 2 kg 700 g (6 lb) Time taken 1 hour

1 kg 800 g (4 lb) fresh pumpkin
cold water
1 kg 800 g (4 lb) granulated or
   preserving sugar

225 g ($\frac{1}{2}$ lb) butter
juice and rind of 4 lemons

Pumpkin has an unusual, sweet flavour and this recipe is sometimes called mock lemon curd as it has a remarkable resemblance to lemon curd in both flavour and appearance.

Any greengrocer will cut a piece of the desired weight off a large pumpkin. Remove centre seeds from the pumpkin piece and cut away the peel. Chop the flesh and place in a large saucepan, cover with cold water and bring to the boil. Simmer gently until tender – about 15 minutes – then draw the pan off the heat and strain.

Purée the pumpkin flesh either in an electric blender or by rubbing mixture through a sieve. Return the pumpkin purée to a saucepan, add the sugar, butter, finely grated lemon rind and strained lemon juice. Stir over low heat until the sugar has dissolved, then bring to the boil and simmer for 5 minutes. Remove the pan from the heat, cool slightly and pour into clean, warm jars. The mixture looks very thin while hot, but thickens up on cooling. Cover and seal when cold.

Cranberry Orange Jelly

Makes 4 (225 g) ($\frac{1}{2}$ lb) jars jelly Time taken 20 minutes

450 g (1 lb) fresh cranberries
rind of 1 orange

3 dl ($\frac{1}{2}$ pint) water
450 g (1 lb) granulated sugar

This is a quick, very easy recipe to make, and one that has a delicious flavour. Pick over the cranberries and discard any bruised or soft berries. Place in a saucepan and add the finely grated orange rind and the water. Bring up to the boil over moderate heat and simmer for 10 minutes. Stir occasionally with a wooden spoon. The cranberries will pop and the mixture will become a thick pulp. Draw the pan off the heat. Press berries and liquid through a sieve to make a purée.

Return the purée to the saucepan and add the sugar. Stir over low heat until the sugar has dissolved and then bring just to the boil. As soon as the first small bubbles appear around the edge of the pan, draw off the heat. Pour into clean, warm jars and leave to set. Cover and seal when cold.

Serve with hot or cold roast turkey.

Crab Apple Jelly

Makes about 2 kg 250 g (5 lb) Time taken 2–3 hours

1 kg 800 g (4 lb) crab apples	4 cloves
generous 1 litre (2 pints) water	granulated or preserving sugar

Wash and pick over the fruit. Cut away any bad or bruised parts and cut any large crab apples into quarters. Smaller crab apples can remain whole. Put the fruit in a pan, add the water and cloves. Cover and simmer gently until soft and pulpy. Strain for several hours through a scalded jelly bag or strong linen cloth. Do not squeeze the bag or the resulting jelly will be cloudy and unappetizing.

Measure the juice back into a saucepan. For every 6 dl (1 pint) of juice add 450 g (1 lb) sugar. Stir over low heat to dissolve the sugar, then bring up to a brisk boil. Boil steadily for a set – takes about 10–15 minutes. When ready draw off the heat and skim very thoroughly for a clear sparkling preserve.

Pour into clean, warm jars. Cover and seal while hot. Label when cold.

Quince Jelly

Makes 2 kg 700 g (6 lb) Time taken 2–3 hours

1 kg 800 g (4 lb) quinces	1 kg 350 g (3 lb) granulated or
3·5 litres (6 pints) water	preserving sugar

Wash the quinces and cut up coarsely. Place in a saucepan along with 2·25 litres (4 pints) of the water and simmer gently, covered with a lid, until tender – takes about 1–1½ hours. When soft, squash the pulp with a potato masher.

Draw the pan off the heat and ladle the fruit and liquid into a scalded jelly bag. Allow to drip for 30 minutes, then remove the pulp from the bag back into the saucepan and add the remaining water. Simmer for a further 30 minutes. A second boiling increases the amount of jelly and makes a more economical recipe. Ladle the fruit and juice into the jelly bag again and leave to drip for several hours.

Measure all the juice back into the saucepan – should make about 1·5 litres (3 pints). Bring up to the boil, and for every 6 dl (1 pint) of juice add 450 g (1 lb) granulated or preserving sugar. Stir over low heat to dissolve the sugar, then bring up to the boil. Skim and cook rapidly until setting point is reached – about 10 minutes. Draw the pan off the heat, skim again and pot quickly in clean warm jars. Cover and seal while hot. Label when cold.

Serve with all cold meats, roast game, pork or lamb.

Damson Cheese

Makes ·5–·75 litre (1–1½ pints) Time taken 2 hours

1 kg 350 g (3 lb) ripe damsons	·5–·75 litre (1–1½ pints) water
3 cloves	granulated or preserving sugar

Fruit cheeses are turned out of small moulds on to a plate and they are then cut with a knife or spoon for serving. They may be eaten as a preserve or used as a sweet accompaniment to hot or cold duck, pork or ham.

Rinse the damsons and remove the stalks. Place the fruit in a pan with the cloves and add the water. The water should almost cover the fruit. Bring to the boil and simmer gently until the fruit is very soft. Draw the pan off the heat and rub the fruit through a nylon sieve to get a smooth pulp. Discard all skins and stones.

Measure the pulp back into the saucepan and for each 6 dl (1 pint) of pulp add 350–450 g (¾–1 lb) sugar, according to the sweetness required. Return the pan to the heat, where possible place over an asbestos mat. Simmer the pulp stirring frequently until it thickens. The whole process should be carried out very gently and the pulp should not be allowed to boil. When the pulp is ready, a wooden spoon drawn across the bottom of the pan will show a clean line for a few seconds. Draw off the heat. Pot the damson cheese in small hot moulds or basins – easier for turning out. Cover with waxed paper and, when cold, cover and label.

Quick Apple Jelly

Makes 1 kg 350 g–1 kg 800 g (3–4 lb) Time taken 1½–2 hours

cooking apples	juice of 1 large lemon
3 dl (½ pint) water	granulated or preserving sugar

Undoubtedly one of the quickest and most useful methods of making apple jelly is that using the pressure cooker. Quantities are small but the method is really quick and several batches can be made on different days, when there are lots of apples around.

Wash and cut up sufficient cooking apples to half-fill the pressure cooker. Add the water and strained lemon juice. Cover, bring up to 4 kg 500 g (10 lb) pressure, and cook for 7 minutes. Draw off the heat and allow the pressure to reduce slowly. Open the cooker and mash the fruit very thoroughly. Strain through a scalded jelly bag or strong linen cloth.

Measure the juice back into the cooker base or a large saucepan. For every 6 dl (1 pint) of juice add 450 g (1 lb) sugar. Stir over low heat in the open cooker until the sugar has dissolved, then boil rapidly for a set – takes about 10 minutes. Pour into clean, warm jars. Cover and seal while hot. Label when cold.

To make one batch a mint jelly, add a few drops of green colouring and 3–4 tablespoons finely chopped fresh mint.

HOMEMADE MARMALADE

The principles of marmalade making are the same as for jam: the fruit must be tender before the sugar is added and boiled for a set. Citrus fruit peel is tougher than fruit and requires longer to cook, so more water is used. It is important to remember that the pectin which sets marmalade is contained in the pips, pulp and white pith of the fruit, and must be included when simmering the fruit, in order to extract the pectin.

Five Points for Success
1 Long slow simmering until the peel is quite tender is essential. A piece squeezed between finger and thumb should feel quite soft before the sugar is added.
2 Once the sugar is added, stir until every grain is dissolved before boiling for a set. Any sugar crystals remaining will cause the marmalade to go sugary when stored.
3 Once the marmalade has come up to the boil, boil fast for 15 minutes. It is essential to have a large preserving pan for fast boiling. *Draw the pan off the heat* and test for a set. Marmalade should reach setting point within 15–20 minutes' boiling time, provided the marmalade has been boiled quickly in a large pan.
4 Have one or more cold saucers ready in the refrigerator. Spoon

a little of the marmalade on to one and leave to cool for a few minutes. The surface should set and crinkle when pushed with the little finger. An alternative method of testing is to use a sugar thermometer. When it reads 104°C (220°F) then the marmalade is ready.

5 Allow marmalade to cool for 10–15 minutes before potting. This helps to distribute the peel evenly.

Seville Orange Marmalade

Makes 3 kg 650 g–4 kg 500 g (8–10 lb) Time taken 3 hours

1 kg 350 g (3 lb) Seville oranges
juice of 2 large lemons
3·5 litres (6 pints) water

2 kg 700 g (6 lb) granulated or
preserving sugar

Scrub the oranges well and pick off the small disc at the stalk end. Cut the fruit in half and squeeze out the juice and pips. Quarter the peel and cut away any thick white pith. Shred the peels finely. Cut up the white pith coarsely and tie loosely in a large square of muslin along with the pips. The bag should be loose so that the water will circulate through the pith and pips, and extract the pectin.

Place the peel, strained orange and lemon juice, the muslin bag of pith and pips, and the water in a preserving pan. Bring to the boil and simmer gently for 1½–2 hours, or until the peel is quite tender. (At this stage it can be left until the next day.)

Remove the bag of pith and pips and squeeze it well, by pressing between two dinner plates. Add the sugar and stir over low heat to dissolve. Bring to the boil and boil rapidly for a set – about 15–20 minutes. Draw the pan off the heat. Skim and cool for about 15 minutes. Pour into clean, warm jars. Cover and seal while hot. Label when cold.

Coarse Cut Marmalade

Makes 3 kg 650 g (8 lb) Time taken 2 hours

1 kg 350 g (3 lb) Seville oranges
2·5 litres (4½ pints) water
about 2 kg (4–5 lb) granulated or
preserving sugar

juice of 2 lemons
2 tablespoons dark treacle

Scrub the oranges, place in a large saucepan and cover with 2·25 litres (4 pints) of the water. It may be necessary to use two saucepans with a generous 1 litre (2 pints) water in each. Cover with a lid and simmer for about 1 hour, or until the oranges are quite soft. Lift out the softened oranges, reserving the water they were cooked in. Cut each orange in half and scoop out the pith and pips from the centre of each into a smaller saucepan. Add the remaining ·25 litre ($\frac{1}{2}$ pint) of water, bring to the boil and simmer for 10 minutes.

Coarsely chop or mince the soft peel and return to the original saucepan containing the water. Measure the peel and juice and, for every 6 dl (1 pint), add 450 g (1 lb) of sugar. Add the treacle, lemon juice and the strained water from the pith and pips. Stir over low heat until all the sugar has dissolved, then bring up to the boil and cook rapidly until setting point is reached – about 15 minutes. Draw the pan off the heat, either stir in a nut of butter, or skim and allow to stand for 10 minutes. Ladle into clean, warm jars. Cover and seal while hot. Label when cold.

Mixed Fruit Marmalade

Makes 3 kg 650 g–4 kg 500 g (8–10 lb) Time taken 2–3 hours

450 g (1 lb) Seville oranges	3·5 litres (6 pints) water
450 g (1 lb) sweet oranges	2 kg 700 g (about 6 lb) granulated
2 large lemons	or preserving sugar
1 grapefruit	

Scrub all the fruit and pick off the discs at the stalk end. Halve the fruit and squeeze out the juice. Quarter the peels and remove excess pith. Slice the peels evenly and thinly – a vegetable slicer is invaluable for this. Tie the pips and chopped white pith loosely in a muslin bag. Put the sliced peel, the fruit juices and muslin bag of pith and pips all together in a preserving pan. Add the water. Bring up to the boil, cover the pan and simmer gently for 1$\frac{1}{2}$–2 hours, or until peel is tender.

Draw the pan off the heat. Remove the bag of pith and pips, squeeze out all the juice by pressing between two dinner plates and discard the bag. Measure the fruit and juice, and for every 6 dl (1 pint) add 450 g (1 lb) of sugar. Stir over low heat to dissolve the sugar. Bring up to the boil and boil rapidly for a set – about 15–20 minutes. Draw the pan off the heat. Skim and cool for 15 minutes so that the peel is evenly distributed. Pour into clean, warm jars. Cover and seal while hot. Label when cold.

FRUIT BOTTLING

Bottling is a means of preserving fruit achieved by first sterilizing it in bottles and then making the bottles airtight. There are two main methods: the water-bath method and the oven method.

The water-bath method gives the best flavour, it is the more accurate and is suitable for bottling all types of fruits. The oven method is best for small quantities.

There are two widely used types of preserving jars, the screw-band type and the clip type. If you use jam jars make sure they are standard shape 450 g (1 lb) or 900 g (2 lb) jars, and buy the special metal clips, rubber bands and tops. Follow the maker's directions for fitting. The screw-band type can be purchased, both the special jars and the tops together. They come in 225 g ($\frac{1}{2}$ lb), 450 g (1 lb) and 900 g (2 lb) sizes. Examine the bottles and jars carefully before using them and never use any which are cracked or chipped; any metal tops or rubber bands should be renewed each time the jars are used.

Wash, rinse thoroughly and leave upside down to drain. It's not necessary to dry them, as fruit slips more easily into place on a wet surface. Place any rubber bands to steep in a basin of warm water until required.

General Instructions for Bottling Fruit

Select fruit in prime condition, it should be just ripe and without blemishes, and always bottle as fresh as possible. Grade the fruit for size and ripeness, so that all the fruit in one bottle will be approximately the same and will cook evenly.

Prepare according to kinds, removing stalks or leaves. Special points to note are:

Fruits Best for Bottling in Autumn

Pears Use ripe dessert pears or, if using cooking pears, stew first in syrup until tender. Peel and halve the pears and scoop out the cores with a teaspoon. Immerse at once in a large bowl of cold salted water – allow 1 tablespoon of salt to 2·25 litres (4 pints) of water. This helps to keep the pears a white colour. Place a plate over the pears to keep them pressed well down in the salt water. Pears are usually bottled in halves and should be rinsed well before placing them in the bottles.

Plums Victoria plums are a good type to bottle; greengages and damsons also come under this heading. Plums can be halved and

stoned and packed cut-side down – this is the more economical way
of packing them – or they can be left whole.

Fruit salad Prepare and bottle a selection of fruit including Victoria
plums, sliced peaches, pears and green grapes, halved and deseeded.
Take care not to use fruit with dark skins as these tend to colour all
the other fruit.

Peaches and apricots These are usually halved and, in addition,
peaches are often sliced. To remove the skins, plunge into boiling
water for 1 minute.

Apple pulp This useful preserve can be served as stewed fruit or
used as a ready-to-serve apple sauce. Wash, peel and core the apples,
then stew in a very little water with just sufficient sugar to sweeten
slightly, until the pulp is formed. Add a little green colouring if liked,
and spoon into the bottles.

Tomatoes These are useful for adding to soups, stews or casseroles.
Use firm ripe tomatoes, and remove the skins by plunging in boiling
water for 1 minute before peeling. Cut in halves or quarters and pack
into jars cut-side down, sprinkling each layer with a mixture of 1
rounded teaspoon each of salt and sugar for every 900 g (2 lb)
tomatoes. Tomatoes are best bottled without any liquid added.

Blackberries Choose fresh blackberries and hull and wash them. One
of the nicest ways to bottle blackberries is to fill the jars with alternate
layers of blackberries and sliced apples.

Fruits Best for Bottling in Early Summer

Blackcurrants Remove the stems but leave on the brown heads.

Gooseberries Bottle firm green gooseberries. Top and tail close to the
berry so that there is a small cut surface which allows the fruit syrup
to penetrate.

Raspberries Bottle as quickly as possible after purchasing. A mixture
of raspberries and redcurrants is very nice.

Rhubarb Bottle young tender rhubarb, cut into 5-cm (2-inch) lengths
for easier packing.

Preparing the Syrup

With the exception of tomatoes, all fruits have a better colour and
flavour if preserved in syrup, but water may be used if liked. Proportions of 100–225 g (4–8 oz) sugar to 1·5 dl (1 pint) water is the
usual strength of syrup. A heavier syrup is pleasant with fruits such
as raspberries, peaches and pears and blackcurrants; allow 350 g
(12 oz) sugar to 6 dl (1 pint).

Measure the sugar to be used into a saucepan with the water. Stir over low heat to dissolve the sugar and then bring to the boil. Simmer for 1 minute, then draw the pan off the heat. Use while boiling hot or allow to cool according to the method used.

Sterilizing by the Water-bath Method

Prepare the fruit and pack into the jars. Stand the jars in turn on a plate and fill to overflowing with the cool syrup or water. Give the jars a quick twist round to remove any air bubbles, cover with the rubber band, lid and clip or screw-band. If a screw-band is used, screw up tightly and then unscrew half a turn to allow for expansion—the clip acts as a spring and allows for expansion automatically.

Half-fill a large pan or preserving pan with cold water and fit a rack or false bottom in the pan. Place the jars on the false bottom, taking care that the jars do not touch each other, and fill the pan with cold water to *cover the jars completely*. Cover with a lid and turn on the heat underneath very low.

Allow about 1½ hours for the water to come just to simmering point. The water should bubble very slightly and be held at this temperature for 10–15 minutes according to the fruit. (See table below.)

When the sterilizing time is completed, turn off the heat. Either lift out the jars with tongs, or ladle out enough water to expose the jars half-way down, and lift out with a cloth. Be careful never to stand the jars on a cold surface or they will crack immediately. Put them on a board, folded cloth or newspapers. Screw any metal bands up tightly immediately, and leave to cool without disturbing for 12 hours.

Fruit	Time		Temperature at 1½ Hours
Apples	10 minutes		
Apricots and peaches	15	,,	
Black- and redcurrants	10	,,	
Damsons	15	,,	
Gooseberries	10	,,	74°C, 165°F
Plums	10	,,	
Raspberries and soft fruits	10	,,	
Blackberries	10	,,	
Rhubarb	10	,,	
Pears	20	,,	88°C, 190°F
Tomatoes	25	,,	

When quite cold remove the clips or screw-bands; test the seals by lifting the jars by the lid, the vacuum inside should be strong enough to keep the lid in position. Label and store in a cool dark place. Should any bottles be found to be imperfectly sealed, they can be re-sterilized at once, or the fruit eaten.

Preserving by the Oven Method

Prepare and pack the fruit as above. Cover with boiling syrup to within 1 cm ($\frac{1}{2}$ inch) of the brim of the jars. Put on the rubber rings and covers but do not fix down. Stand the bottles on a baking tray so that they don't touch each other, and cover the tray with newspapers to catch any syrup that overflows. Place in the oven centre and heat very gradually in a pre-heated slow oven (150°C, 300°F or Gas No. 2). Leave for 1$\frac{1}{2}$ hours or longer. The time will vary according to the fruit and the number of jars in the oven. Never put in more than 4 kg 500 g (10 lb) at one time.

When tiny pin-head bubbles appear on the fruit, or a slight space is noticeable at the bottom of the bottles, the fruit is ready for sealing. Remove the bottles from the oven, one at a time. Seal immediately by screwing down or clipping on the tops. Cool, then test the seal. *Note:* a large number of jars in the oven may lengthen the time needed to 2 hours. Pears, apples and tomatoes, in any case, are best heated for 3 hours.

To Use Bottled Fruit

During the winter months a store-cupboard of bottled and preserved fruit is a wonderful standby. In most cases the bottled fruit will need sweetening before serving. *For simple stewed fruit* empty the bottled fruit into a saucepan, add 25–50 g (1–2 oz) castor sugar according to taste, and heat slowly to dissolve the sugar. Serve warm with custard sauce.

Bottled plums, damsons, rhubarb or apple purée make an excellent base for a cake pudding or a fruit cobbler, but take care not to add too much of the juice from the bottles. Spoon the fruit into the base of a 1-litre (1$\frac{1}{2}$–2-pint) baking or pie dish, along with a little sugar and about 2 tablespoons of the fruit juice. Then top with a plain Victoria sponge cake mixture (your own recipe) and bake in the centre of a moderate oven (180°C, 350°F or Gas No. 4) for 35–40 minutes. Alternatively the fruit can be topped with scone dough. Stamp out circles with a 5-cm (2-inch) cutter and arrange them to overlap. Sprinkle with sugar and bake just above centre in a hot oven (200°C,

400°F or Gas No. 6) for 15–20 minutes. Either of these hot puddings are delicious served with cream or top of milk.

Other ideas are to spoon bottled fruit into the base of a trifle along with sponge cake pieces, or into the base of a pie dish along with Swiss roll, top with an egg custard mixture and bake. Or you can place a little fruit in the base of a steamed pudding mould before adding the pudding mixture, then serve baked pudding with the remaining fruit. Bottled fruit goes marvellously with pastry. It can be used as a fruit pie filling, or topped with shortcrust or flaky pastry in fruit turnovers, fruit crumble or even fruit tartlets – the juice in this is thickened with cornflour and used as a glaze.

Mothers with young babies or children will find that bottling fruit purée, such as apple, rhubarb or raspberry, is particularly useful for infant feeding and brightening up children's desserts.

CHUTNEYS AND PICKLES

Both chutneys and pickles are an excellent way of using up surplus garden vegetables. Whereas the best fruit and vegetables should be used for jam making, bottling or freezing, the bruised or second best may be used for chutneys and pickles. The spicy pungent relishes that result can turn the plainest cold meat into an appetizing meal. Individual tastes do vary enormously where chutneys and pickles are concerned. It is always advisable to make small quantities of any new recipe the first time and, if this is too hot, or too mild even, the spices or quantities can be altered the next time.

There are a few general rules that should be remembered in each case. Either square-shaped or round jam jars may be used, and it's important to have the correct tops. Greaseproof or cellophane jam covers are not suitable, they allow the pickles and chutneys, both of which contain a high proportion of vinegar, to evaporate. Use either metal caps lined with the vinegar-proof paper called Cerasin, or a synthetic skin such as Porosan, or the more old-fashioned method of double thickness squares of muslin dipped in melted paraffin wax. The choice of sugar and vinegar is also important. Castor sugar and distilled malt vinegar give a good light colour which may be important, especially in some fruit and tomato chutneys. Brown sugar and darker malt vinegar give a deeper colour, and in some cases a better flavour. Whole spices that are not to be left in the finished relish should be tied in a small muslin bag so that they can be easily removed when the recipe is finished. For this, buy a 7·5-cm (3-inch) wide plain bandage and then cut into lengths. Tie the bag with fine string and attach the end to the pan handle, this avoids searching for it afterwards.

All chutneys and pickles improve in flavour on keeping – flavours develop and harshness mellows. If chutneys are too spicy at first, give them a chance to keep before changing the recipe.

Ripe Tomato Chutney

Makes 1 kg 800 g (4 lb) Time taken 2–3 hours

2 kg 700 g (6 lb) ripe tomatoes	pinch cayenne pepper
225 g (½ lb) onions	1 level tablespoon salt
3 dl (½ pint) distilled malt vinegar	1½ level teaspoons paprika pepper
pinch mixed spice	350 g (12 oz) granulated sugar

Dip the tomatoes, a few at a time, into a saucepan of boiling water. Leave for ½–1 minute, then lift out with a perforated spoon and place in a bowl of cold water. Peel away the skins, cut up the tomato flesh and place in a preserving pan – do not use a brass, copper or iron pan. Chop the onions, place in a small saucepan and just cover with cold water. Bring to the boil, simmer for 5 minutes, then drain and add the onions to the tomatoes. Cook the onions and tomatoes over moderate heat until a thick pulp is obtained. Tomatoes contain a high percentage of water and must be well reduced, otherwise there is a danger that the added vinegar, which is in fact the preservative, will be diluted and the finished chutney will not keep well.

Add half the vinegar and the spices, and simmer again until thick. Add the sugar, dissolved in the remaining vinegar, and cook until the chutney is of a fairly thick consistency and no free vinegar remains in the pan. Pour into clean, warm jars and cover with plastic tops.

Apple Chutney

Makes 1 kg 800 g (4 lb) Time taken 2–3 hours

1 kg 350 g (3 lb) cooking apples	175 g (6 oz) sultanas
generous 1 litre (2 pints) malt vinegar	25 g (1 oz) ground ginger
450 g (1 lb) onions	25 g (1 oz) salt
700 g (1½ lb) soft brown sugar	½ level teaspoon cayenne pepper

Wash, peel, core and chop up the apples. Place in a large saucepan and add the vinegar. Peel and finely chop the onions. Simmer the

onions for 5 minutes in boiling water. Then drain and add to the pan.
Vinegar has a hardening effect on onions and so it is better to cook the
onions a little first, before adding to the remaining ingredients. Add
the onions to the pan along with the sugar, sultanas, ground ginger,
salt and cayenne pepper.

Heat slowly until the sugar has dissolved, then bring to the boil and
simmer gently, stirring occasionally until the chutney is thick and
smooth. Chutney should have a long slow cooking and anything from
1½-2 hours is usually necessary. Continue simmering until no free
liquid shows in the base of the pan when a spoon is drawn across the
mixture. Draw off the heat and, using a jug, pour the mixture into
clean, dry, warm jars and cover with plastic snap-on covers or with a
square of muslin dipped in melted paraffin wax. Store for 1 or 2
months before using.

Sweet Cucumber Pickle

Makes 1 kg 800 g (4 lb) Time taken 4 hours
Leave until cold before potting

900 g (2 lb) cucumber	1 large green pepper
2 large onions	50 g (2 oz) salt

For the Syrup

4·5 dl (¾ pint) cider or wine vinegar	¼ level teaspoon ground cloves
350 g (12 oz) soft brown sugar	1 level dessertspoon mustard seed
½ level teaspoon ground turmeric	½ level teaspoon celery seed

Sweet cucumber pickle is often called 'Bread and Butter Pickle'
simply because this particular recipe is delicious eaten on sliced fresh
bread and butter.

Wash the cucumbers, but do not peel them, and slice thinly. Peel
and slice the onions. Halve, deseed and shred the green pepper.
Place the sliced cucumber in a large mixing basin along with the
onion, shredded green pepper and the salt. Mix well, then cover with
a plate and stand for 3 hours. Rinse the vegetables very thoroughly in
a colander under cold running water, drain well and place in a large
saucepan. Add the vinegar, bring to the boil and simmer gently until
the vegetables are soft – takes about 20 minutes.

Add the sugar and spices to the pan, stir over a low heat to dissolve
the sugar, bring up to the boil and draw the pan off the heat. Turn
into a large mixing basin and set aside until cold. Pour into jars and
cover with screw tops.

Serve with all cold meats, raised pies, or cheese and biscuits.

Sweet Pickled Damsons

Makes approximately 6 jars Time taken 2 days

1 kg 350 g (3 lb) damsons
1 kg 350 g (3 lb) granulated sugar
6 dl (1 pint) distilled malt vinegar

50 g (2 oz) mixed pickling spices
2·5 cm (1 inch) of cinnamon stick

Rinse and pick over the damsons, removing the stalks. Prick with a stainless steel fork or skewer and put into an earthenware bowl. Dissolve the sugar in the vinegar over low heat. Add pickling spices and the cinnamon tied up in a muslin bag. Bring to the boil and simmer for 5 minutes. Pour over the damsons and leave to soak for 24 hours.

Strain off the vinegar into a saucepan, add the spice bag, and bring back to the boil. Pour over the damsons again and leave for a further 24 hours. Repeat this once more.

Next day remove the spice bag, discard it and strain off the vinegar. Pack the damsons into clean, dry jars not quite up to the shoulder. Stand the jars on a thick pad of folded newspaper and heat in a very slow oven (150°C, 300°F or Gas No. 2) until the jars are hot to touch. Meanwhile simmer the vingar until it is reduced by about one-third and is slightly syrupy in consistency. Pour over the damsons. Cool, then cover with plastic covers and label when cold. Leave 3–4 weeks to mature.

Serve with cold pork or ham, brawn or raised pies.

Pickled Onions

Makes 1 kg 800 g (4 lb) Time taken 3 days

1 kg 800 g (4 lb) small onions

brine solution

For the Spiced Vinegar
generous 1 litre (2 pints) malt
   vinegar
1 small piece stick cinnamon
6 cloves

5 pieces of mace
3 bay leaves
1 dessertspoon whole allspice

Using a stainless steel knife trim away both ends of each onion. Peel and then place the onions in a brine, made using 225 g (¼ lb) kitchen salt to 2·25 litres (4 pints) of cold water. Leave the onions to soak for 36 hours making sure that they remain below the surface of the brine.

Meanwhile prepare the spiced vinegar. Place the vinegar and spices in a basin and cover with a plate. Set the basin over a saucepan of cold water and bring the water slowly to the boil. Remove the basin from the heat and leave to stand for 3 hours, then strain. This spiced vinegar can be prepared in advance ready for use.

Drain the onions from the brine, rinse in cold water and drain very thoroughly. Pack the onions tightly into one or more jars leaving the neck of the jar free. If any water settles at the bottom of the jars during packing, this should be poured away before adding the spiced vinegar. Cover the onions with the cold spiced vinegar which should come at least 1 cm ($\frac{1}{2}$ inch) above the onions to allow for evaporation. Cover the jar with synthetic skin, or use screw tops with a Cerasin or plastic lining on the inside. Keep for 3–4 months before using.

Piccalilli

Makes 2 kg 250 g–2 kg 700 g (5–6 lb) Time taken 1 hour
Leave vegetables in brine for 24 hours

450 g (1 lb) pickling onions
450 g (1 lb) marrow
1 small cauliflower

1 cucumber
225 g ($\frac{1}{2}$ lb) runner beans
brine solution

For the Sauce
75 g (3 oz) plain flour
100 g (4 oz) castor sugar
50 g (2 oz) dry mustard

15 g ($\frac{1}{2}$ oz) turmeric powder
generous 1 litre (2 pints) malt
vinegar

Clean, prepare and cut the vegetables into pieces of a suitable size for eating, leaving the onions whole and breaking the cauliflower into sprigs. Cover with a brine solution of 100 g ($\frac{1}{4}$ lb) kitchen salt dissolved in 1·25 litres (2$\frac{1}{2}$ pints) of water. Leave for 24 hours, then drain.

To prepare the sauce, measure the flour, sugar, mustard powder and turmeric into a saucepan. Add a little vinegar and blend to a paste, then stir in the rest of the vinegar. Stir over gentle heat until boiling and thickened. Add the drained vegetables and cook for 5 minutes. Pack the vegetables into clean, hot jars distributing the different varieties evenly. Pour over sufficient piccalilli sauce to cover. Seal and store a few weeks before using.

Note: this makes a fairly crisp pickle; the vegetables may be cooked for up to 10 minutes, but take care not to overcook otherwise they go soft and the pickle is spoilt.

Index

Katie Stewart
The Times Calendar Cookbook £1.50

A superb yearbook for the kitchen, containing a wide variety of recipes from winter soups, stews and casseroles to summer salads and picnic spreads. A complete guide to the most delicious and practical use of fruits, vegetables, fish, meat and game in season through the year.

'A truly superb cookery book' LEICESTER GRAPHIC

'A mouth-watering collection of recipes' HOUSE & GARDEN

Marika Hanbury Tenison
Deep-Freeze Cookery 80p

A truly comprehensive guide, which happily combines the general subject of domestic deep-freezing with a host of delicious recipes, all home tried and tested. There is advice on buying and choosing a deep-freeze and clear instructions on its maintenance. The author suggests how the freezer can be used as a budget saver, but also warns on what *not* to freeze.

Deep-Freeze Sense 75p

The definitive guide to the sensible and economical use of your deep-freeze. Marika Hanbury Tenison, herself a deep-freeze user for over sixteen years, tells you everything about the practicalities, advantages and pitfalls involved.

There is much useful advice on such aspects as preparation and packaging, costs and economy, buying in bulk and length of freezer life of various foodstuffs. In addition to the delicious recipes in the book, there is a seasonal guide to fresh products.

Kathleen Broughton
Pressure Cooking Day By Day 95p

In this authoritative and comprehensive guide Kathleen Broughton explains how to look after your pressure cooker and shows how to save time, fuel and money by using it effectively.

The preparation of baby foods, invalid and vegetarian dishes are included in a wealth of recipes, all specially adapted to pressure cooking.

Enrica and Vernon Jarratt
The Complete Book of Pasta £1.25

Heaped with authentic Italian sauces, or delicious simply with parmesan and butter melting over it, the enormous range of pasta has long been a staple ingredient of Italian kitchencraft. The Jarratts, Rome's most famous restaurateurs, guide you through the ways to make your own pasta and prepare the traditional and mouthwatering sauces to complete the dish in real Italian style.

'A boon to British cooks' TIMES LITERARY SUPPLEMENT

Antony & Araminta Hippisley Coxe
The Book of the Sausage 70p

The incredible history of the sausage – from Ancient Rome to the succulent Seventies . . . the A to Z of the Sausage – from Alpenkluber to Zampone . . . the Gastronome's geography of the Sausage . . . the arts of complete do-it-yourself sausage-making . . . how to serve and enjoy the banger plus a guide to drinking with Sausages . . .

Marguerite Patten
Learning to Cook 70p

A book which tells you how to cook easily and economically, serve simple, appetizing meals, and know which foods should be at their best in each month of the year. The author gives advice on choosing kitchen equipment, filling the store cupboard, and what to do if things go wrong. There are suggestions for using up leftovers and ideas for parties, picnics and Christmas. Keep this book handy – and your family contented!

Lousene Rousseau Brunner
New Casserole Treasury £1.00

This collection of over four hundred delicious casserole recipes comes from many countries, from great chefs and country kitchens. And the ingredients range from truffles and paté to cabbage and beer.

Although so varied, these recipes all share one great advantage of casserole cookery: much of the preparation can be done in advance. And Mrs Brunner has added to the simplicity of her recipes by the sensible use of convenience foods.

Her clear, detailed and precise instructions make these dishes a joy for even the most inexperienced cook to create.

Gail Duff
Fresh All The Year 95p

A cook's calendar which contains a wealth of original and practical recipes. Month by month Gail Duff lists the fruit, vegetables and herbs that are in season, plentiful and cheap and shows how they can form the basis of a healthy and varied diet all the year round.

Kenneth Lo
Cheap Chow 80p

Chinese Cooking on next to nothing. Kenneth Lo is Britain's leading Chinese gourmet and cookery writer and he admits that some of the best Chinese eating he's known has been in bedsitters where funds are short. His healthy diet is easy and economical.

'For adventurous cooks . . . a must' HOUSE & GARDEN

Savitri Chowdhary
Indian Cookery 60p

In this mouth-watering collection of Indian recipes, Savitri Chowdhary explodes the two great myths about Indian food: that the ingredients are unobtainable; and that it is always 'hot'.

Using ingredients that you can easily obtain at your local grocer's or store, she displays the magnificent variety of the Indian cuisine – from sweets and savouries to curd preparation and vegetable dishes – and shows that spicing is a matter of taste: curries can be as mild or 'hot' as you like.

Clear, practical and comprehensive, Mrs Chowdhary's book is a treasury for anyone who likes something different.